THE
PIONEER
YEARS
1895~1914

THE PIONEER YEARS 1895~1914

Memories of
Settlers Who Opened
the West

BARRY BROADFOOT

A
PaperJacks
Special

PaperJacks

A division of General Publishing Co. Limited
Don Mills, Ontario

A CANADIAN

PaperJacks LTD.

One of a series of Canadian books
by PaperJacks Ltd.

THE PIONEER YEARS
PaperJacks edition published February 1978

ISBN 0-7701-0060-0

This PaperJacks edition is published by arrangement
with Doubleday Canada Limited.

Preface

The Pioneer Years *is the story of the opening up of the Canadian West by settlers during those historic years between the turn of the century and 1914.*

True, there were infiltrations into those tens of millions of acres before 1900 and there would be movements later, but in terms of significance to the economic, social, cultural, and philosophical life of the West, the 1895-1914 period was most important. That was when the West was molded. That was when that gap between Ontario and British Columbia was solidly bridged, making Canada one nation from sea to sea.

The Pioneer Years *is a collection of stories told by those settlers. It tells how three million and more people rushed into the West from all parts of the globe, traveling on luxurious passenger trains, in cattle-like colonist cars, by horse- or ox-drawn wagons, even by auto, truly a rare and wondrous thing in those early years.*

The vast majority came because they could take up 160 acres for a 10-dollar filing fee and call themselves homesteaders. Others rejected the free land or found none available and bought cheaply off the railroads, which had received huge land grants as part of their construction payment. Still others bought from promotion-minded colonization companies at higher prices, but they could usually dicker for the deal they wanted. Those who found they were not suited for farm life helped start villages, settled in towns already established, or went to the small cities that were located in strategic spots across the West.

The settlement of the Canadian West was unlike that of the American West as depicted in story, song, and Wild West movie—and if you say it was to any pioneer he will laugh in your face. Everything proceeded at a measured pace, everything happened in its own good time. What had to be done was done, with intelligence, reason, and diligence.

It is an exciting story in its own way because it was one of the great migrations in history—and the last great migration to a new frontier, peaking with the arrival of over 375,000 persons in 1913, the year before the First World War erupted.

Nowhere in the world was arable land so cheap and so accessible, and nowhere was it so good. In an ever-increasing industrial society the world demanded more wheat and the Canadian West could produce bountiful crops—the best milling wheat in the world—at a time of rising prices.

But there also was another reason why people came. Many were fleeing oppression, the rider in the night, the lash and goad of czar, king, emperor, landowner, or factory overseer. To these people Canada meant freedom.

To survive they had to work. The land would not tolerate slackers. Whether a man took up land on the prairies or the parklands or went into the bush with an axe, he worked, and worked hard. His wife worked equally hard at her tasks and when the children came along they worked too. Everyone had that one goal: to make their homestead a farm and to make that farm prosperous.

In the villages and towns it was the same. The work may not have been as physically hard but the hours were long, and whether a man was a stonemason, accountant, clerk, grocer, or blacksmith he worked and the goal was the same, to make the village prosperous, to provide a good home, to have a good life.

To obtain the stories I used the same techniques I used for assembling my first two books, Ten Lost Years and Six War Years. I traveled across the West several times—about 10,000 miles, I should say—and I found the people. I interviewed them with tape recorder and notebook and I edited their stories into their present form. I did not meet one person who refused to talk to me. They were eager to talk. They felt their story had never been told before.

They told me of the wrench of leaving home, the long trip across ocean and continent and, often, the arrival at a railway shack with no one to meet them and no idea of where to go. Most of them trekked by wagon to their piece of land and built their first home—a cabin, a soddy, or an ugly little poplar-pole shack. They recalled the cruelty of the prairie winter and the hammering heat of July when the green shoots of their first crop came up through the black earth and then withered and died. They described the trips to town with their crops and the schoolteacher and the small school they built her and the dances and weddings and prayer meetings they held in it, opportunities for members of a new community to get together and meet one another. They had good words for the mounted police and harsh words for bad neighbors. They remember, too, the Canadian Pacific Railway and the freight rates they felt were too high, forgetting that if it had not been for the railroads they would not have been in the West.

There is something unforgettable about sitting in the tiny living room of a house in a modern town and hearing an old woman talk, sometimes hesitantly, as if she had never said it before, of the decision to come west, to seek a new horizon, to walk over their new land, and to make bread from flour ground from Marquis wheat on the first acres broken.

Or perhaps she just looked out the window, beyond the green hedge, and said, "And then Harold took that grain to the miller and he brought the money to me and I took it and I . . ." and her thoughts soared beyond me and it was 70 years ago in that little room.

I am not an historian. I am a person who travels across the country and listens to people talk about themselves. I call myself a chronicler, a gatherer of stories, a collector of reminiscences— before it is too late. So, in this book you will not find much about the economic forces that shaped the West. No discussion of Sir John A. Macdonald's National Policy and how it was applied by subsequent prime ministers. No details of national conferences and western alliances and politics, and very little about Ottawa's immigration policies and the arrogance of the East toward the West. No diagrams, no progress charts and graphs, no statistics on rates of growth. For these you must look elsewhere.

The fact is, there is nothing here but the people.

And let me close with a few words about the people. They were wonderful. Sharp and zippy, scrappy and zestful, sincere, *sentimental. They had verve and style. Sly humor, robust humor. They had prejudices, some deep-seated, but isn't that natural? They were amazingly well informed of the events of the day while looking back on the past with affection. As for the future, they are running toward life.*

There was not one person I met whom I did not like. I am proud to have met them and I salute them.

In The Pioneer Years *I hope you will learn what our history books do not tell us about the pioneers and about a vital period in our nation's history.*

Barry Broadfoot
Vancouver, B.C.
June, 1976

Contents

THE
PIONEER
YEARS
1895~1914

1

The Way It Was

No Hope for Me in England . . . We Sailed to Canada . . . Strangers in a Strange New Land . . . No More Farming for Us . . . The Greatest Country in the World . . . The Little Soddy on the Prairie . . . The Mail, Frontier Style . . . The Hired Hand . . . I Built the Schoolhouse . . . That Plump Little Midwife . . . Hacking It on the Grub Line . . . There Isn't Much Left for Old-Timers Now

In the beginning was the land, vast and ageless. Eventually came Indian tribes, each with its territory and rights. Then there were the explorers and fur traders who paved the way for the European settlers. They came, slowly at first, and by the mid-19th century the prairie was dotted with settlements, like tiny stars tossed here and there on the vast field of night.

Then the pace quickened. Steamboats began coming up the Red River to Winnipeg from the United States. A railroad arrived from the south. From Winnipeg, gateway to the West, wagon trails snaked in every direction, and from other points along the line as far west as Montana other trails pushed north. And finally that great step in Prime Minister Sir John A. Macdonald's National Policy was taken: a railroad, the Canadian Pacific, two gleaming rails from Ontario, through Winnipeg, crossed the prairies into Fort Calgary and on into the Rockies to meet with other rails from Vancouver. Canada was joined. The West was opened.

And over the next few decades, until the First World War in 1914 ended the surge, they came by the hundreds of thousands,

1

from the United States, Great Britain, Scandinavia, Russia,
Poland, the Ukraine, all the predictable places, and from un-
predictable lands too—Argentina and South Africa—and from
improbable places like Iceland and the Falkland Islands and
Tasmania.

A good majority of the newcomers knew how to farm but, of
course, tens of thousands didn't. They had never harnessed a
team of horses or oxen, never hoed a plot of potatoes. Some
thought bullocks gave milk.

Most had never imagined that prairie summers could be so
hot or the winters so harsh, but most survived, hanging on and
building up good farms. Others fled to the new towns and cities.
But all who stayed at one time or another knew the meaning of
hardship and despair.

This chapter is a preview of what is to come. It describes the
way it was during those prairie years—the way it was.

No Hope for Me in England

Oh, it was bad times in England. No work. You'd see an advert
in the evening paper, and next morning: up at four in the
morning and put on your best suit and your bowler and hike
over there to be first in line for an office boy's job. Standing in the
street would be 40 or 50 men and boys, all wanting an interview.

I was 20. Too old to be treated as a child and too young to be
treated as a man. It was hard. I walked the streets of London
day after day knocking on doors. Doors and more doors.

I would come home weary at night and my father would be
sitting in the parlor. He was a master plasterer, a foreman and
even he couldn't find his own son a spot. He'd say, "Well?"
"Nothing." He'd grunt. Next day, "Well?" I'd say I'd been over
to Trafalgar Square to try the Navy, but they told me there that
they weren't taking recruits. England had been in the Boer War
and people were tired of war. They still needed Army recruits

but the Army Sergeant wouldn't take me because of this bad eye of mine.

Finally there was no way out. I said to my dad I'd like to go to Canada and settle. That was fine with him. He didn't want me around. I got money from him and the rest from my sister's aunt and I went to the Salvation Army and they got me on this here ship. The *Laurentic*. The Salvation Army did that. They got a lot of people together in those days and they made a cut-off with the shipping company and everybody cut a cheaper rate. A lot of people were sick on the way over but not me, and I landed at Quebec July 1, with my five pounds, which is what the Canadian government said you had to have to land in their country. My ticket said Humboldt, Saskatchewan.

I came out on those little colonist cars, filled with squalling brats and people cooking their food on the little stove at the end of the car, and every place where the train stopped we'd all run out and buy buns and bread and things like that.

I was going to see a chap who had been engaged to my sister at one time.

Anyway, I got off at Humboldt and everything was new and startling to me, and I knew absolutely nothing about Canada—there had been no studying up on it—so I walked into the ticket office and I asked how to get to Lac Vert. That's Green Lake in English. That's where this chap was supposed to be living. He said, "Why, you should have got off two stations down the line. At Watson. Two stations back. There's a train goes through here this afternoon and get off at Watson."

So I did and I went into the hotel on the main drag and I asked what time the bus left to go to Lac Vert. The fellow said, "Ain't no bus." I asked him then what time the tram left. "No tram either," he said. This is how dumb I was. All you could see for miles around was prairie, bald prairie, and here is this Englishman asking about buses and trams, just as if he was in the middle of London. My, when I even think of it now. Buses and trams.

So I asked the fellow how did I get there. He said, "You got two legs?" I said yes and he said, "Use 'em." I asked how far it was and he didn't know. He said just to take the trail north out of town. A suitcase in one hand and a big kit bag in the other.

So I took the trail north and I walked and I thought my legs would fall off and my arms come out of my sockets, and I was chased by a bull although he was inside a fence, and an old German let me sleep on some straw in his barn that first night and he fed me in the morning. Then I came to a house way out on the prairie. It had a blue roof, painted blue, I mean, and a Norwegian lady gave me six eggs and a big piece of ham, and to be polite I managed to stuff them down. She said the town of Spalding was up the road. I got too tired to walk, hot, and an Irishman named Cardiff gave me a ride in his wagon and charged me a dollar, which was a lot of money in those days. After the German and the Norwegian family, I thought all new people to the country were treated free but I found out different from that Irishman.

At Spalding I was still so dumb I asked if there was a bus or a tram going north and got the horse laugh in the store there. So I started out walking again and finally I came to a house, and three big dogs ran at me. A man came out and called them off and his name was C. Wallace Stewart. He said, "Come on in, how are you and who are you?" I said I was looking for Charlie Sandwell and he said Charlie worked for him, and he gave me a big meal and we waited for Charlie to get back.

That ended my second day on the prairies. A dumb English kid.

We Sailed to Canada

Saint John, that's where we landed. Eleven days, 1,967 people on board. We called it 2,000. Oh ho ho, the finest people that ever lived. You see, they were romantic. We had rich people, trades-people, engineers, fine workmen, all from England and all ad-venturous. We were supposed to have 500,000 dollars on that ship of immigrants to start spending once we got to Saskatoon.

Saskatoon, mind you. Can you picture it? A village on the prairie with 110 people in it, and 2,000 colonists landing in on them. Just imagine it. They came from all over Canada and the United States to take us.

But before that, the boat. The crossing. As soon as we got on the boat at Liverpool and saw the conditions—sordid conditions—a lot of our enthusiasm was deflated right away. The boat was old, making its last trip, and it was a transport. It had taken soldiers and mules and horses to the South African War. But it wasn't its last voyage. It kept going and it is the only boat of that shipping line I know wasn't sunk in the First World War.

It was 8,500 tons with 2,000 people on, the same number of passengers in later years as the *Queen Mary* and the *Elizabeth*, 65,000 tons. Packed like that. Sardines. I was among 300 people in one small space. All the men, the bachelors, were put in the hold where the horses and mules had been, below the water-line. It was in the bow and when the ship did this, up and down, we all got seasick. It had collapsible tables down the center between the tiers of bunks, and the men from the pantry they daren't come in. We'd have killed them. They stood at the door with a great big tin pan of meat cut up in chunks and they threw it to us. They daren't go in; it was a riot. Half the men were in the bunks puking and the other half didn't get seasick and they wanted to kill somebody for the poor food. And potatoes. Not peeled, just in their skins. Just like a baseball game. Good catchers got the most grub.

That's how we were fed. Like animals.

And there were 300 more men in the stern. Six hundred men, like animals.

Women upstairs, of course.

But down below, hundreds of men in such a small space and everybody yelling or sick and everybody was armed, being Englishmen, you know. Everybody carried a Bowie knife for the Wild West, or one of those multi-bladed fishing knives. And swords. Myself, I had a 12-gauge shotgun. Ha ha ha ha. I didn't use it on the ship, but it kept us fed on the homestead. Bought it in Nottingham, three guineas. Ha ha.

The sanitation? It was like this. I went into the toilet and the last time was three days out and I said, "Never again." I'd do my business at night on the deck on a piece of paper.

We had riots on board. We put our heads together and got a delegation and went and saw the captain, you know; so he improved the grub because we said we were going to take over the ship and take it back to Liverpool. What the captain did was this. He knew the ship was terribly overloaded so he gave about 50 men free passage, gave them their money back to help the crew feed us and prepare the meals decently and clean out the toilets and anything that wanted doing. I wasn't one.

I did what I have done all my life. I observed and I remembered and I have never forgotten it. The conditions on that ship were unbelievable.

The only good thing was that it was not a stormy crossing. If we'd had one of those North Atlantic gales it would have been something terrific. The ship and all who sailed her would not have survived. The old bird couldn't do more than 250 miles a day, took 11 days, and she would not have made it.

But we made it—but we were a sorry lot at Saint John, let me tell you.

Strangers in a Strange New Land

When we got to Elbow the Stevensons were supposed to meet us, but we found out later that even though our letter had been sent a month before we left England it didn't arrive in Saskatchewan until three weeks after we got there.

My husband had about 20 boxes and bags and they were all piled up on the platform and the station agent came over and he said, "Whereya from?" That's the first thing anybody asked anybody else in the new land. We said Maidstone and he knew the place well so he was friendly. He said he'd get Jenks and he hiked off up the street of this tiny, wee village, leaving us there on the platform, husband, wife, two children, strange and very unsure of ourselves in a strange new land. In about 15 minutes he came back and said, "Jenks is coming. He's the drayman and he'll take you to where it's open and you can look around, choose some land, and then go and file on it." He meant for the homestead.

He said, "Don't look for beautiful forests and running brooks full of fish. There'll be poplars and Balm of Gilead, some, and I'd advise you to file with a slough on your place." We didn't even know what a slough was then. This man Jenks came and with his wagon full of our goods there was hardly room for us, but we made it and away we went. He said, "South, north, east, or west?" and my husband asked what difference it made. He said, "It's gonna be your home and I wouldn't want you to be blaming me for years if it doesn't work out." Dad said north. So north we went, off down a trail into the new land.

We found a place, after asking Mr. Jenks what a slough was and he told us it was a depression, a place where there usually was water the year round, and that certainly made sense. After all, we'd be having horses and a cow and chickens. Mr. Jenks when we got about three miles out, he just swept his arm around and said, "Take your pick. The choice is yours." There wasn't too much choosing involved. We chose a quarter which had a slough in one corner of it and it was flat except for a little knoll. Mr. Jenks nodded his head, nodded it wisely, and said, "Same place I'da picked." Father and I felt very good about that. After all, this rough man had been in the country for many years.

When we unloaded he told my husband it was best he go right back and catch the train to Regina and file and get everything cleaned up and buy a pair of horses, a wagon and a plow and harrows and some potato seed. He was real helpful. He warned him that he wasn't to buy any mustangs that the ranchers were bringing up from Montana and over in Saskatchewan, but he was to buy draft horses. Make sure they come from Ontario, he said, or you'd have nothing but trouble because the mustangs, the bronco horses, were too wild.

Then he asked what he knew about plowing. Well, of course he knew nothing. I knew more about plowing than he

did. At least I had been born on a farm. His father ran a stationery store. Mr. Jenks said that the first thing to do when he got
back was to plow out a fireguard. Make it 15 or 20 furrows.
Take the furrows, the sod, and pile it up carefully and Dad said
why. Why do that? "Because that's going to be your house for
the winter and you're gonna be mighty glad you have it," he
said. "When you get back you spread the word and I'll get a few
of the lads out here and we'll help you. Do it right and you won't
be doing it over in February." This was kind of crazy, I admit
now. Here, all the way out I had been getting the impression
that Mr. Jenks was an uncouth sort of person. Well, a rascal if
you want to put it that way. And now here he was offering to
bring out some people from the town to help us build our house.

Well, let me tell you, I quickly got my manners back, right
there and then, and I asked him if he'd like some tea. I know
now that he'd rather had a good big snort of whisky but he said
thank you, that would be nice. So we got out the little stove,
right there on the bald-headed prairie, and put it behind a box
for a windbreak and in about 15 minutes we had a little tea
party going. Tea, biscuits, butter, and strawberry jam.

I remember him saying, "It is a hard life, ma'am. There will
be times when you will long for England, but next spring when
you hear the first meadowlark"—and he whistled, imitating it—
"you'll know you'll never want to leave this country again."
Oh, it didn't quite work out that way. There was a hundred
times, spring, fall, and winter, when I wanted to leave, when I
would have left at the drop of a hat. Winters so cold you
wouldn't believe and mosquitoes so fierce they made life sheer
misery. Then I would have gone. Gladly. Happily. My children
with me and left him to work his heart out. But, I am glad to
say, I never did.

When tea was over Mr. Jenks helped my husband put up our
big white bell tent and moved some of our goods inside. We
were to be alone for a few days. My husband gave me his rifle
and his shotgun and he said I was only to use them only when I
had to and Mr. Jenks said, "Only on mighty fierce jackrabbits,
ma'am."

Before they left he wandered out and he came back with an

armload of brown things. Dried things and shrunken, and he dropped them in front of the tent. "What on earth . . . ?" I asked.

"Buffalo chips, ma'am," he said. I said what? "Buffalo dung. You burn it. It makes a good fire and no sense using your fuel in that little stove. Chips are good."

Then my husband kissed me and hugged the children and he climbed into the wagon and away they went down the trail. There I was, with my two children, Peg and James, hand in hand, looking rather forlorn, I must say. I had forgotten to ask Mr. Jenks if we had any neighbors, and I thought to myself there probably were a hundred things other I should have asked him but it was too late. They were gone, hidden by a dip in the land, and there I was with my two children alone in a new land. Me and my children, my tent and my English biscuits and surrounded by buffalo chips.

No More Farming for Us

Our first was a shack. This was a comedown for Mother, who had given up a good home in England. After doing what Dad said and packing up and leaving her fine cottage of about 11 rooms, to land on the bald prairie south of Battleford. This was about 1907.

Mind you, she never said a word and she could have said plenty. I was 12, my brother was nine, and my sister Mary just sat on the grass and ate bugs and anything else that came along. She was two. The only word of complaining I heard my mother say all the time that first year was when she looked at Mary. On the grass eating bugs and dirt and said to my father: "We should have brought Annie." Annie was the maid that had looked after all of us. My father said, "Annie, be damned, just one more mouth to feed." Mother kept quiet after that.

Mary did well on her diet of bugs and dirt because soon she was walking, staggering all over the place, and getting in the way. Pretty soon she was picking up the nails that we dropped when we were building that shack: Totter over to the sack and drop them in and go back for more. Mother said she was getting to be a great little worker.

Our house was 14 by 20 feet, and it took about three wagonloads of lumber that Dad brought all the way from South Battleford. It had a big kitchen and two bedrooms, and was one-ply lumber for the wall, a layer of tarpaper on the roof, and then two-ply lumber on top of that. And we had never built a house before. The last thing on Dad's mind when he packed us up was that he was going to have to work with his hands. He told us later when we were growing up that he was going to homestead and buy more land from the government. You could do that because the free homestead land and the land that the government had for sale was side by side. If you imagine a checkerboard, then one and three and five was free land and two and four and six was land you could buy for about a few dollars an acre. That was Dad's plan.

We all worked on that house because we needed that roof over our heads before winter. When Dad was at the Battlefords getting lumber and supplies my mother and I were building that house. When I think of it, how foolish the whole thing was. Mother had never done anything more strenuous than drive a pony cart or do embroidery or pick flowers, and here she was, up on the roof with rope tied around her skirt on each side so the legs wouldn't show just in case a neighbor came along. Neighbors did come along and they said the house was too big: "What do you want such a big shack for? It will be too hard to heat." Mother would only say we'd manage.

When it was all done we all went back about 100 yards and had a picnic on the prairie and admired our house. It was ugly and looked half finished, but my parents were happy with it.

So we were having our picnic and all of a sudden we saw smoke coming out of it. Then a lot more came out and then soon it was blazing out the roof, and, well, you can see the fix we were in because there was no water except in the coulee and nothing to haul it in. The house was done for. Dad and Mother managed to get some barrels of china and goods out of the door.

They also got out a couple of trunks of clothes. That was it.

It was Dad's pipe that started it. In the mess we found it by the bench where he'd been shaving wood. He'd laid it down, I guess, and it had fallen down.

Mother said, "What are we going to do?" and Dad said he'd . . . we'd all go to town, take everything we had and sell what we didn't need and he'd find a job. That's what we did. No more farming for us. Shouldn't say no more. We hadn't done any yet. We kept the cow for town.

The Greatest Country in the World

I got to Lashburn and located my quarter section. My boy and I lined up stakes along the edge of the quarter and I hitched up a horse I had that was about 1,400 pounds and a mare about 1,000 pounds. I sunk the blade of my hand plow in and I got them going up that stake line and I went a half mile without a quiver. Then I stopped and looked back and there was my furrow, stretching away for half a mile, straight as a gun barrel. The land was black and rich and beautiful and I knew I was in the greatest country in the world.

The Little Soddy on the Prairie

The thing you never hear much about is the soddy. I think that's an American term, the soddy, but hundreds, no, tens of hundreds of sod houses were built in Canada, on the western plains.

I wonder if there is one left. I doubt it.

The first thing you'd do was figure out where you were going to put your sod house. Then you'd plow out that. Maybe 16 by

24. That is feet. You could make it any size. You see, what you were working with was the native soil and it was tough. It had been there since the beginning of the world after the Ice Age went away, and it was like board in a way in that it had millions of tiny roots in it and it was tough.

So you went into the hills or wherever you could find wood, poplar to all occasions I should say, and you put up a skeleton frame. It just sort of guided you and then you plowed out these big pieces of sod, which actually were your bricks. And then, because you had to plow out a fire guard anyway, the more you plowed out, then the better protected you were from prairie fires, which could come at you at any time. I mean, I have seen terrific prairie fires in July, but I have also seen them in February in a winter when there was no snow, no snow at all. It happened. Does it happen now? I don't seem to notice anymore. But a fire could just be in the grass or it could be 15 feet high and throwing sparks, brands, half a mile. A woman once said a fire with its own windstorm threw brands four miles ahead. But anyway . . .

You had your frame of poles of poplar and it was a skeleton thing and you built your sod house against it. More for guidance, I would say, to make sure you were going right, than anything else. Until you got to the roof. A house, say 16 by 24, might have 4,000 sods. Like bricks. Each would be about two inches thick, one and a half inches. Probably one and a half inches. Twelve inches wide, two feet long. And you piled them up and up with just a tiny slant inward, the weight to bear down to keep everything firm and then layer by layer you built everything up. I seem to remember that when my father was plowing to plant oats it was my mother and my sister and myself who built the house. Up and up it went. I was 12.

Then the roof. No, first the door and windows. Two windows. And the door. It was sort of like making a house of your own out of those children's blocks, and with sod you could put anything where you wanted it. I remember our door was low and tiny and Dad had to stoop down and low to get in, and the windows were tiny but they were windows. That was something. The Gillies [Galicians] had no windows, no glass, just a dark earth hole above ground.

But then the inside. That was boards and blankets laid out along them so to make little rooms. One for my mother and father. One for us. A kitchen. I think we had a toilet, which just meant digging another hole in the ground every month.

The roof was different. Government shingles. That's what we called the sod we used. Poles, close together. Hay. Sod. Hay. Dirt. Like one of those sandwiches. It leaked but we didn't mind. Government shingles. Haven't used that expression for 50 years. I wonder how it came back to me.

Back in the house, it was quite nice. You put up what was called felt cloth. You could buy it at the Bay or stores in the town. It was pinned in to the sod with wooden pegs. I'm not sure what the purpose was for except, I guess, to make you think you weren't living in a sod house. But everybody did.

I think the last sod house I saw was about '16. I was coming back home on leave before going to France and I got a horse and rode across the prairie. You could still do it in that part of the country those days. South and west, deep south of Edmonton. I rode into this big slough country and there was a soddy sitting in on the earth, looking comfortable as hell as though it belonged to the land. It just fitted.

The man who had it was old. Today you'd call him a character. He was a muskrat hunter and he sold the skins and ate the meat. He kept saying that he liked young girls and we talked for an hour and I ate muskrat for the first time and last time in my life. I remember as I rode off he yelled, "Now you hear me, boy. Send me a young girl."

There must have been 10,000 sod houses built in Manitoba, Saskatchewan, and Alberta but I don't think there is one left. I don't know if you could build one. Takes that right kind of turf. Tough. It's all been ripped up. Gone.

I never regretted living in a soddy. Warm in winter. Cool in summer. They had a feeling about them.

The Mail, Frontier Style

You could get a letter from England in less than three weeks—from London by ship and then by train. The mail service would come out from town Tuesday and Friday to Sutton's Place, and Mr. Sutton would take the bags to a granary near the house and dump everything. Then he'd take every letter and every magazine and box and put it so the address would be showing. The neighbors used to come and find their own mail. That was Mr. Sutton's way of being a postmaster. If you had letters to mail, you just left them with stamps or money in a big box and the mailman picked them up next trip around. Mrs. Sutton was no help. She was one of those ignorant Lancashire women who couldn't read or write and wouldn't try.

If we'd go, we'd find our own mail and then pick up mail for people along the way and people on past us. We had a box at the corner of our quarter, so people would come down our way and get their mail. Or if somebody going further north was going by, they'd take their neighbors' mail. It was kind of like a pony express. It worked, but not as well as I've said it. Sometimes people would forget the relay system, or we wouldn't get to town, or a blizzard would hit, or a lot of things, but it worked better than no system at all. We did that for three years until they did get a man on the route once a week, and by that time things were working out pretty well.

The Hired Hand

The first time I hired out, I was about 12, just a little fellow. I was strong enough but I was just a kid, and these two brothers, these farmers, were looking for a fellow and I got the job. I guess I was the only one around.

They wanted some disking done and they give me four great

big horses, the biggest horses in the country, and I couldn't even put the harness on the blamed things. I had to climb up on the mangers to put the collars on, and I heard one of the brothers say what good was having a hired man if he couldn't even harness his horses. But he meant it good-naturedly and I finally got them four big buggers harnessed. But it was a job, I'll tell you.

I was there three days and a half and I worked hard and I did a good job for them two fellows, and when I was through, one says to the other: "What do we pay this fellow?" The other says, "Pay him the going rate. He did a man's work, didn't he? Pay him wages." And here I was, a little fellow of 12. So he ups and pays me a 10 and, well, you'd have thought I had half the money in the country.

I had half a mile to go home and I just had to show my folks the money. I crumpled that 10-dollar bill in my hand and I ran as hard as I could go, and when I got home the bill was absolutely wet. The sweat of my hand had just absolutely mushed it.

Mother said she didn't know what we were going to do with the bill, but she straightened it out and ironed it and then everybody just sat around and looked at it lying on the table. Because, see, that much money all at once was a pretty rare sight in our house. You didn't get farm people much poorer than we were, and to have 10 dollars—well, that bought one awful lot of groceries and store groceries was something we didn't see too much in our house.

I Built the Schoolhouse

When Regina was still in the Northwest Territories, Dad sent a letter to the government there with the object of organizing a school district for our area. They said yes, so notices were posted. I went around putting them up.

The meeting voted unanimously to organize a school district

and they voted to call it Little Flower School District. This was in February of 1904. Mr. Stenerson was elected chairman.

The first resolution, as I guess it had to be, was that there had to be a school, so in June of 1904, I went around putting up notices saying they were going to bond the district for 600 dollars over 10 years and that was to pay for a school and equipment like desks.

Then they called for tenders and on June 21 they opened them and they accepted the lowest tender, 135 dollars, for hauling the lumber from town and putting up the school building 18 feet wide, 26 feet long, and 10 feet high and two outhouses, four by four by six. Guess who got the winning bid? Me. H. H. Hanson.

So that summer I built the schoolhouse and I did it for the price of 135 dollars, which was what I said I'd do it for. I posted the notices about the school district and then about the tenders, and then I submitted my bid and won it and built the school, and then they hired Miss Delougheri as teacher. I was 20 but still didn't have much of an education, it being on the prairies in those days, so that fall I went to school. At the age of 20, I took my lessons in the school that I'd built.

That Plump Little Midwife

It soon became apparent to me that my mother was expecting a baby.

Then, late in August, my father asked me if I would like to go for a drive in the democrat. We drove north over the rough prairie, new country to me. After several miles of empty prairie we came to a trail of sorts that led us over a slight rise. There below us, about half a mile away, were some buildings which seemed to merge into the land. A sod house and a barn. The sun reflected on the small windows of the house which had white curtains. In one window by the door there was a red geranium blooming.

A plump little woman with gray hair came to the door and she said we were very welcome callers. It was a lonely life for a woman out there on the prairie. We stayed for lunch and she and my father talked, and on the way home he told me that Mrs. Sales was the woman's name and she would be coming to help my mother when the new baby was to be born.

It was dry for the rest of the summer and my father had to haul water twice a week in barrels from four miles away. September passed and snow came early that year. In October—the middle of October—it was then that Mrs. Sales came to stay. We had only two rooms but the kitchen was large and easily heated by the big range with a small heater in the bedroom. We all got by.

Well, the days grew short and the evenings long and the weather kept getting colder. Mrs. Sales with her motherly ways became a member of our family, and in the evenings we'd play cards and croquinole or play records. It was a Victor with a big horn and you had to wind it up for every record. Mother or Mrs. Sales sometimes made candy or popped corn for us.

One evening my mother popped corn and then suggested that we get into our heavy clothes and go to our grandmother's home for the night. We didn't want to go, but my father insisted, so me and my brothers got into our coats and went across, which wasn't very far away. By this time I knew what was happening. Our mother was having a baby. We lay in bed at grandmother's and talked about the new baby that was coming. Long before, I said I wanted a sister because of my two brothers, and I had named the baby Jessie.

Next morning we had forgotten all about our talks and we each had a big plate of pancakes and then we walked back to our house, although I helped with the dishes before I did that. When we walked in the door Mrs. Sales was alone in the kitchen. Dad was out doing the chores. I asked where my mother was. Mrs. Sales smiled and said, "In the bedroom. I think she wants to see you." I went in and it was unusual to see my mother in bed. She was always up before us in the morning and went to bed after us at night, but she smiled and pulled back the cover and there was a small head at her side.

I yelled and she said, "Ssshhhh." Then she said, "Yes, it is

Jessie." I was overcome with joy and Mom looked pale but happy and then Mrs. Sales came in with a cup of hot tea for Mom. She let me hold the baby while she sat up and drank the tea.

And so that is how the first baby came to that new Saskatchewan farming district.

Hacking It on the Grub Line

They talk about the hospitality of the range, the romance and the friendliness of it all, but I'm afraid I never saw it. Anything you've ever heard of it you must have got out of a novel.

The difference between the big house and the bunkhouse was as far apart as you could get. The owner in the big house, he thought of cowboys as shit, just as low as you can get. He treated them as low as you can get and he paid them as low as he could get.

He usually had a superintendent who thought the same way, or a foreman or manager. I'm talking about the big ranches in Alberta. Not the small ones with 100 or 200 cows but the big ones. On the big ones they'd keep a few cowboys over the winter —just as few as they could get away with—and in the spring they'd hire a batch and work them like the very devil all through summer and then through fall and then let them go. And where would those .poor devils go? Well, they'd hit the grub line. That's what. They'd drift around all winter, stopping at this ranch for a couple of days, and the boys would sneak food out to them in the bunkhouse while they stayed hid and then they'd move along. Sometimes they could catch on at a big ranch and at you know what wages? Nothing wages. They worked hard for their grub and feed for their pony and that's all. No money.

Or they'd go to town. Calgary, High River, Macleod, Lethbridge, all over that country. All sorts of livery barns, feed barns, everywhere. Every block had one of them. These fellows

would work for free for these owners, cleaning out, forking
down hay, doing a hundred-and-one things for the privilege of
putting their horse in the stall while they slept in the loft in their
saddle blanket. They got no pay for that either. If some traveling salesman, some businessman, came in and they'd curried
his horse for him or done some job he flipped this cowboy a
quarter, they hustled over to the Chinaman's place and bought a
meal. That's how they lived. On the grub line or in livery barns.

Oh sometimes one of them would move in with a homesteader
in his shack somewhere, but he still had to do the woodcutting
and keeping the waterhole open and such—and the Mounties
were always coming along rousting them. When it came to the
rancher and the cowboy, you always knew what side the
Mountie was on. The Mounties were all for law and order, law
and order whatever. In their eyes the fact a man was unable to
earn his living practically made him an outlaw.

You didn't see many old cowboys. By old, I mean 40 or so.
Oh, maybe the cook on the chuckwagon or the night wrangler
or something like that, or somebody doing handy jobs around
the big house like clipping the lady's hedge or polishing up the
buggy. But all the cowboys were young. Young and tough.
Young, tough, and underpaid. For what they had to do they
should have been paid double, triple. Why, those ranchers in
good years were making fortunes. Fortunes. But they paid in
pennies.

You ask a fellow if he'd ever been a cowboy and likely he'll
say yes, but you'll notice he's not a cowboy now, nor has been for
a long time. Too many broken legs. Horses rolling on you.
Busted shoulders. Kicks. Even a good horse will let fly at you
with a kick some time or another. Fingers broken, torn off.
Caught in the bight of the rope. When the dally didn't hold and
it ripped you. I never saw a cowboy over 30 who didn't limp and
do an awful lot of groaning every morning just trying to get out
of bed, even in a warm bunkhouse.

There has been more bullshit written about the cowboy than
any other person in the world. I'll say that to anybody.

You know, the cowboy could never hope to own his own
ranch. I'd say all that was finished by 1900. All he could do was

work for somebody else and the hardest work in the world. When you really get down to it, the cowboy as he was, well, he was a simpleton.

Had to be. Stands to reason, to work the way he did.

They'd read, you know. In those days they had these Wild West books and magazines. There's nothing new about them at all. They'd read these stories and how the honest, tough cowboy would get the rancher's daughter Sally. But they never, I'm sure, ever put two and two together and said, "Hell, that's me this guy's writing about." No, their life was just too far away from that, too rough and too mean. They thought these things happened in some faraway, never-never land—New Mexico, Texas, Colorado. They never thought of themselves as that kind of cowboys, although they liked the stories.

But anybody says that there was a real friendship between the big house and the bunkhouse, like "Let's sit around this fire and sing songs, fellows," there was none of that. I'd say the big owners, the big brands, they didn't think any more of the cowboy than of a slave. Maybe he'd think more of a slave because a slave was worth so many dollars. He'd bought that black boy for so many dollars and he could sell him for so many dollars. But a cowboy, hell. Come fall, the foreman would just have to say, "Jake, when you're finished with that bit of fencing come on up to the office and get your time." That was it. Back on the grub line.

There Isn't Much Left for Old-Timers Now

It is quite a feeling to look back, when it was prairie land, bush land, over the years, to look back and think that you came into this country in 1902 or '06 or '08 and there was nobody in it, just a bachelor's sod shack here, one there, and no towns and not even any Indians. And to look at it today, paved roads and every bit of land being cultivated and school buses taking all the children into the town school and all the old-timers sitting in their bungalows watching TV. You wonder what they are thinking.

I wake up at nights sometimes after I've dreamed of things that happened in those early days. Just the other day I dreamed of when I was taking a load of lumber home from the mill to add to the house and the current at this ford took the outfit away. From the time I'd passed over, loaded up at the mill, and come back I didn't realize the creek had got so high. Daydreaming, I guess. There must have been a bad storm in the hills. I lost both horses, but I grabbed on to a beam and got carried down okay. I went back next day and got the harness off the horses but there was nothing left of the wagon. When I woke up the other night after dreaming of that, I was as scared as when I was going down that creek holding on for dear life to that beam.

I wonder how many old-timers like myself think of the old days? Some do, I know. A lady over in town said to me not too long ago that she thought a lot of the old days now. All the time. I guess that's the way with me.

There isn't much left for old-timers now. Nobody thinks of us. I guess we don't even think of ourselves. Last week everybody was excited because they had chartered a bus and were taking all the senior citizens into Calgary for the day, to see the zoo, the park, have lunch, and visit some other project they've got going there. There's nothing in that. It's just kind of kid stuff, to keep us busy so we won't raise any fuss. As if we could.

2 *The Lure of the Land*

Best Propaganda: Letters Home . . . The Apple Orchard Joke . . . A Fortune in a Short Time . . . C.P.R. Land—a Good Deal . . . Just About Anybody Could Sell Land . . . Locating Your Quarter Section . . . No Regrets. Happy I Came . . . People Were on the Move

The land in the West wasn't free—but one could say it was the cheapest and also some of the best land in the world. You paid a 10-dollar filing fee for 160 acres of government land. Or you could buy land from the C.P.R. And then there were the land companies, which bought vast tracts from the government and the railways for two or three dollars an acre and sold it to settlers for double or triple that.

All three groups staged massive land promotional campaigns, playing up the attractive features of the West and ignoring the bad ones. There were settlers who complained that they had been deceived, but most figured it was a chance to make a new start. And there was no law against your getting more land and expanding. If you knew farming. If you were successful—or lucky with the weather. If you had a strong back and strong sons. Plenty of "ifs." But the lure of the land was strong, and the people came, and the West filled up.

Best Propaganda: Letters Home

It was so often letters. What people today call word-of-mouth. Frau Schmidt in Upper Silesia would be boasting that her Herman had 320 acres of wheat land in Saskatchewan and the word would get around. Big stuff. That dumb cluck. Left four years ago with nothing but his clothes and a packsack, and now he's got 320 acres of land. You know what I mean. Land to the European was sacred. That's what nine out of 10 of their wars was about. Canada there, all that land. My God!

So if it was Germany or Russia or England you came from, you'd send letters to your home town and the letters would get passed around. Talked about. Soon another family would pack up, sell what they couldn't carry, and be off to Canada.

If people couldn't read—say in Poland or Russia where the peasants couldn't read—then the village priest would read it, I guess, and they'd hear about Canada. Probably didn't even know where the damn place was. The land was the thing. Free land. Cheap land. No cossack riding you down, no landlord, no lord, no boss. No man was a peasant or a serf in Canada. Every man was free. The letters told it all. The best advertisement for a new car, they say, is the man who has one and is happy with it. Same with Canada and the land. I think Sifton [Canada's Minister of the Interior, 1896-1905] realized this. That's why they were so eager to get settlers on the land and make them happy. Everybody wants a good thing going, and when they got it they wanted to boast. Like Herman Schmidt.

You know, I haven't found people much different today than they were 60 or 70 years ago. My father would be rolling in his grave if he knew what was going on on television these days. All that shooting. But still, my grandson with his long hair and beard, he wants what my father wanted for us. Land, a home, security. A good life. It's what everyone wanted, whether you were from Russia or the finest home in London town. It's human nature. The fellow with the spear in Australia hunting up lizards to eat, he's no different, really, from you or me.

I know my father sent letters back. Lots of them. I can see

them now. He always started the same way and he would say: "It is with a great deal of pleasure that I take pen in hand to tell you that all is going well with your brother and his own and hope that the same good fortunes are your lot." That's pretty close to it. Very formal, and then he'd tell them about the new land broken, the new bull, this done or that done. They'd get the idea that things were going well.

Things might not be going so well. I remember years when we got no more than five bushels to the acre—or none—and winters that would snap the barbed wire on the fence posts. But usually it was a pretty rosy picture my father painted. And they were doing it all over the West, and people in Europe were reading those letters and passing them on to their friends, and you could almost hear the wheels turning. Should we go? Should we stay? Why not go? We can always come back. The thing is, very few ever went back. They would move around a lot. The West was like an old ant pile, in constant motion. But once they came to the West they were more than likely to stay, tough as it was.

And it *was* tough. No doubt about it.

But they came and they stayed and they in their turn sent back letters and more letters, and that's the way it was done. It was like going to a carnival. I've never seen a person yet who would walk through the gates and then turn right around and walk out again. They always have to go through it. Same with the immigrant. He might start on a farm and find he was a lousy farmer, didn't like it and become a baker in town. Or go to a town and then wind up on a farm or a big garden patch. Same with the city. A big anthill. In and out, back and forth. Be a shoemaker. Be a carpenter. Run a café. A man could do anything. Everybody always wound up doing the thing that usually turned out right for him.

But in the beginning it was those letters, that letter from Herman Schmidt to Mamma saying he now had 320 acres in Saskatchewan. Free land.

The Apple Orchard Joke

A family joke. If a few of us got together, sooner or later somebody would say, "Is the apple orchard blooming yet?" or "Joe, go out and pick us some peaches for dinner." Things like that, and then we'd all roar with laughter. I still get a chuckle out of telling it.

This was some of the junk they had on the pamphlets that were going around England—our home, Leeds. At that time they were trying to get people to go to Canada. It was right after the Boer War, about 1903. There was a Depression in England and a lot of people were looking around and wondering if the homeland was such a great place after all. A war over, a war we should have won easily, but it took three or four years, and then a Depression and it was a bad one. Factories closing. Men coming to the door and begging and you don't see that, not in proud England as they say.

The pamphlets, the ones they handed out, they said that everybody could have land. Those pamphlets were like those you get from fishing lodges in this country. You know: Come to Lost Lake and the fish jump into your boat. That kind of thing. These pamphlets said that in Saskatchewan in three years you'd have your own apple orchards and peach orchards and fields of waving grain where the yield was highest in the world. That kind of thing. Imagine. Them saying peach orchards in Saskatchewan. Peach orchards in B.C., yes. But in Saskatchewan, where you could open the door on a winter's morning and see the thermometer hanging there and it would be 30 below, 35 below, even 40 below. So much for peach orchards. Tell me, have you ever seen so much as a single apple tree around Regina? Not a crabapple. Not those winky, sour-faced little things but a decent-sized apple. No, you bet you. Or bubbling streams around Regina? The only bubbling streams I ever saw in that part of the world was in spring when the run-off would bubble away cutbanks, make new channels, and carry away your house and barn sometimes. But right there in the pamphlet, peach orchards and bubbling streams. They had other lovely things to say about Saskatchewan, which is, as you know, the land God gave to Cain.

But there we were, the Locke family, sitting around the big table in our English cottage and Dad working in a pump factory not knowing when the rap was going to hit him and he'd be on the dole. So peach orchards and land at practically nothing an acre looked pretty good. Did we know anything about Canada? Certainly not. Everybody read about it in those days because there was a lot in the papers—letters to the editor and such— but it never meant much to us. They were talking about other parts of Canada anyway. My dad's brother Mylwyn would walk up from his digs down the hill, and he'd tell us what he knew of Canada and that was Buffalo Bill and the Ned Buntline books, which everybody read. Indians, shooting buffalo, the Wild West. Rip-roaring days. Those days, as you know, never existed except in some people's imaginations and, besides, that was America and not Canada.

So, after a while even though Dad hadn't been chucked, nothing but we'd go to Canada. And to Canada we went, the whole fam damily. Everybody wanted to get his share before it was all gone, so Dad sold his equity in his house, the furniture, all our shares in the death society at half or quarter price, and away we went, away on the big boat from Liverpool, down the Mersey tide with about a thousand other fools, and there we were. Peach orchards, apple orchards, bubbling streams.

Oh, as they say, the first 10 years were the worst. About two years later Uncle Mylwyn came over and helped Mother put some steel in Dad's spine because it was getting pretty limber and things went better after that. He gave us some confidence we needed. He showed us what we had if we wanted to work for it. So things went on. We got out of the shack and Dad started to build up a little milk herd and the government helped with things, advice. Seems there always was a government man running around in a democrat telling you to plant this or that. In a few years we started to see daylight, but as I live and breathe and I lived there for 50 years, I never saw a peach orchard in Saskatchewan and I never heard of one either.

A Fortune in a Short Time

The promotion about the West in the Old Country? By the Canadian Pacific Railway? It was in booklets and pamphlets. About Manitoba—we pronounced it ManitoBAH in Glasgow— and Saskatchewan and Alberta. The railroad wanted settlers to buy land in the West, and you couldn't walk down the street in Glasgow without somebody handing you a phamplet or a book- let about the glorious West. I imagine it was the same in every big city in Britain, although you'd think they'd mail them out to the farmers. They were the ones who knew how to farm. What did people in Glasgow know about farming?

These pamphlets described the great opportunities there were and how you could get land so easily and how you could make a fortune in a short time. And so on.

Then they had movies. Not movies as we know them today, but in places where you could buy tickets to Canada and in other shops, they had just an ordinary kind of magic lantern that would flip over the slides and you'd see the train rushing through the West and the great fields of grain and so forth.

It was quite strong propaganda, you might say, but I can't say it was unfair. I mean, the railroad wasn't rooking people. The land *was* there and it *was* cheap, and a fortune could be made if you knew how to go about it. The thing was, how many people knew how to go about it? To farm?

But to be fair to the railroad, I don't think they oversold the thing that much. I think the people got the idea in their own minds and they oversold it to themselves. Canada—that was all anybody could talk about. The C.P.R., all said and done, their propaganda was heavy but I think it was fair.

You know, a lot of people were desperate in those times. Depression. Many men without jobs and England and Scotland seemed like a dead end. It wasn't going anywhere and Canada was there, cheap transportation, and it was thought to be a colony of England's which, if you wanted to follow that through, that's what it actually was despite Confederation. People could see a way out of their troubles. Most of them or a lot had relatives in Canada, in the Maritimes and Ontario. Those two places they thought were right next to the West. Even if they looked at a map they'd have thought the same. So they said, "Well, the game's played out here. We'll try Canada," and so they did. Some made it fine and some didn't and suffered terrible hardship, but it's the same in any venture.

I don't think the C.P.R. can really be blamed for all that much. They were a commercial company selling a commercial product, which was land. One thing you've got to remember, too, is that when so many of those people did come out here, they didn't buy railroad land. They homesteaded, so much of the C.P.R.'s effort, and the other railroads' efforts, probably went in vain.

C.P.R. Land—a Good Deal

Actually an awful lot of people found out it was cheaper to buy C.P.R. land at five dollars an acre than it was to do the whole homesteading business.

You know, in the beginning, people would curse the C.P.R. because they had every other section. This meant that in a new district the new people would make a rush for the government land and that meant one section would have four homesteads on it and then the next would be C.P.R. land and vacant and so on, through township after township. It made the development of a district higgledy-piggledy, like you had a checkerboard as a land development and you settled on only the black squares. Oh, you could graze on the C.P.R. land, the school district land, and the Hudson Bay land, but it made for a rather disjointed way of building up a community.

But people would say, you know, "Why buy C.P.R. land when you can get it free?" That made good sense, I guess, except not everybody could carry through on the government regulations, do their duties. The 10-dollar filing fee was attractive, 160 acres for 10 dollars; but you had to clear 10 acres a year for three years, and you had to live on your holding for six months a year—and those two things were a hardship. Some people just did not have the money for horses, oxen, plows, harrows, seed oats, things like this, and they had to fight like the very devil to find work just to keep their families alive.

A lot lost their homesteads. Maybe they just walked away and went back to the city. Or maybe they didn't file on them within the five years they were supposed to and the land titles man, the government man, was tough about it and ordered them off. I often wondered about some of those government men, whether they weren't just feathering their own nest in a lot of ways.

But if you had the money, most people finally decided it was best to buy from the railroad. You at least got the land free and clear. It was your land right off the bat, and nobody could take it away from you or try and jump your claim. You could go to the bank and take a mortgage on it and you couldn't do that when you were homesteading, proving up your land.

A lot of people came out to Saskatchewan and Alberta with not 30 dollars in their pocket, but a lot came with plenty of money. A lot of these people were from the British Isles and Germany and Sweden and from the States and they had good money in their pocket, and when they went homesteading they frittered a lot of good money away.

But with the railway you could pay cash or a down payment and so much a year. I think it was five years. Six percent. That was the going rate then. You had your land and you didn't have a lot of government regulations and a lot of people fussing around you and it was a straight transaction. After all, the railroad was in the business of selling all this land. There wasn't much nonsense about them. A deal was a deal. With the government there always seemed to be some fussing around and you'd prove up and you wouldn't get your title for three, four, five years and things like that.

I know more than one person, and in fact I know a lot more than one, who did homestead, did take up land but then after a couple of years when they had a bit of money together and they knew they were going to stay, they went and bought C.P.R. land. It wasn't any better land, mind you, but there was still a lot of it left and they had like a second choice and they found it worked out all right for them.

With C.P.R. land somewheres between two and half and five dollars an acre, say three dollars or three and a half, that was a pretty good deal for just about anybody if they had cash in their pockets. It made everything neat and even. A business deal you could understand.

Just About Anybody Could Sell Land

Well, yes, they did have land companies, although I think they were best described as colonization companies. There were lots of them. Some were good, but if memory serves me correctly a lot of them were bad, or perhaps I should say badly managed. There were always a lot of people who would do you for every cent they could get. Some of these land companies were like that.

Anybody, really, could set up a company. The railway wanted to get rid of its land as fast as it could, all those 24 million acres, although less than half of that land was any good. The Canadian government wanted to fill up the West. In fact, they had agents all through Britain and Europe, Argentina and the United States. Pretty brochures. Pictures. Sweet talk and so on.

Many came from the United States—Minnesota, Wisconsin, the Dakotas—although why anybody would want to leave that lovely land I don't know. I'm not saying a lot didn't come from Europe. Good heavens, man, they came by the thousands. Somewhere I read that more than 70,000 families came from Europe before the First World War. From Rumania, Galicia, Russia, Ukraine, Hungary, and, of course, lots of Polanders. But a lot of these came under some sort of arrangement with the Canadian government and I think they got special grants. After all, they had nothing. They had nothing in Europe except a hut and a cow and a pig and some chickens, so how could you expect them to have much when they got here? No. I'm quite sure the government helped them in some ways and maybe the railroad too. Like a fare to Winnipeg from Poland might be 20 dollars.

Of course there were the Germans and the Scandinavians, but they were different. They had money. They were smart. A lot of these settled in Alberta. Alberta was the promised land. It was mostly open. Miles and miles and miles of just prairie, plain, river valleys, and nobody on it. Why, you could go beyond Athabaska and up into the Peace River Country in 1913, 1914, and go for miles and miles and never see a farm. That was still fur country. In 1913. All that came after the big war.

So there was the land, in Saskatchewan and Alberta. I remember along the South Branch there in 1908 or so, that's where the big ranches were. There was, I think, better grass and water along the foothills line, but the big ranches were in Saskatchewan. That's where the Matador was. A big one. American. Some were financed by English and Scottish money. I heard one fellow, years later, saying that if he didn't get 35 to 40 percent of his return on capital investment in a good year he was disappointed. In 1906 and 1907, I remember, that was the bad winter and it never stopped being bad and the chinooks just seemed to stop coming, and those ranchers took a licking. My brother worked for one rancher that year and he lost one ear and toes on his left foot from freezing. And the man he rode for, he had 800 cows and in the spring he found less than 500. That's a story.

About those land companies. From the States. They'd buy up huge stretches of country. All along that Soo Line country, south of Regina, and up in the Tramping Lake district and west of Elbow. Around Stettler. They'd buy hundreds of thousands of acres, maybe for between one and two dollars off the railroad. That suited the C.P.R. fine. If somebody wanted to buy it, then they didn't have to go to all that darned trouble of promoting it, pushing it, selling it, the legal work, the advertisements, all the trouble you get with people.

There was one hitch. The railway, all the railways, wanted to sell in huge blocks, but you've got to remember, it was one for you, one for me, and so on. One section for the C.P.R. and then one government land, free and open to homesteaders. That put a bit of crimp in their style. But I guess there was times people wondered who was running the government down in Ottawa, the government or the C.P.R., and they did get some pretty big solid blocks.

These promoters worked among the farmers in the American Midwest—Nebraska, Kansas, Illinois. Well, I've head it said that a lot of that American land was just grabbed off the Indians and people in Washington were raising a stink and there might be an adjustment, so some people were glad to move on. I don't think the International Border meant anything. Not in those days.

Another thing, those farmers down there were established. But more and more people were coming west and they could sell their farms at good prices, and then come up to Canada and buy good land, damn good land, at five or seven dollars an acre —in there somewhere—and they got good terms. Low down, low interest, long payment—just what a dry land farmer needs. So they couldn't help but win. Contract for five years and five payments and the land was theirs forever.

I can think of half a dozen companies, but I think the biggest was the Luse Land Company. St. Paul, Minnesota. I've seen it spelled Luce, but it really is Luse. I guess that was the man's name. There's a little town over toward the Alberta border called Luseland. A little place. Kind of a poky place. I'd call it a typical prairie town. These people were big. Nothing by halves, no sir. Before they started they chartered a special train that came up through Winnipeg, and they took 200 newspaper editors and writers on a tour of the prairies where they were going to operate and, well, all I can say is that to get the good word around, give a newspaperman a good time. Then they did the same thing with bankers. About 150 of them. High style. Nothing but the best. Now these men, a banker was the most influential man in any town and if they said Canada was good, people believed it.

Then they advertised. There must have been a lot of money behind that company, but they'd bring farmers and other people to Saskatchewan and Alberta on special trains and give them the works. I said farmers but they also brought merchants and blacksmiths and bakers and printers and doctors and others because, you see, they weren't only trying to sell off these areas of hundreds of thousands of acres. They knew that there had to be towns and businesses for the farmers. No Minnesota farmer is going to come up if he has to hump it in a democrat 40 miles to the nearest town to get a new harness strap.

They used to come into town, these trains, and I've seen 'em because I was up around Scott when Luse Land was going full blast. They'd hire every democrat and surrey and jumper in town and then go out and get the farmers to come in, and they'd load these farmers in and away they'd go. You know what they liked? The promoters, I mean. They liked a lovely, sunshiny day, one of those prairie mornings. They liked a nice new farm in the district and on the fields for 100 acres or more they'd like a sea of golden wheat waving softly in the light breeze. That sight was more than all the words that any promoter could ever utter. Far more. "Right before your eyes, gents, right there is a 30-bushel crop and only a five-mile haul to the elevator." That's what that field of wheat was saying.

They'd go around the whole district, at least a full day and sometimes two, and the Yankees would talk to the farmer and for all anybody knows, maybe those farmers were paid by the land company to tell a pretty good yarn. I'm not putting it past human nature for one little second. Do it myself.

Then they'd go back to town and there would be three or four real nice fellows, all so friendly and eager to help, and these were the fellows that signed you on the dotted line. Some wouldn't buy, of course. Wanted to go back and talk it over with the wife. Didn't like English royalty. Heard the country was too cold—and it was too, if you was from Illinois, so I've heard, but not from Minnesota. But an awful lot of them signed on the dotted line, a fifth down, or you could have a fourth down but then you paid higher interest. I think it was seven percent. No, even in those days interest on land was pretty high. People were pretty close with their money too, so they watched that interest pretty closely, I'd say.

They did play one kind of a dirty trick, though. There was this livery stable fellow and they'd been using him for two or three summers and they told him next summer would be bigger than ever. They suggested he buy a bunch more buggies and horses and he'd easily pay them off the next summer taking people around. Then next spring when they got going, they showed up with a bunch of Reo automobiles. You can imagine. The poor fellow was left with a bunch of buggies and driving horses he couldn't use.

The Luse people sold more than three million acres in Alberta and Saskatchewan. I don't know if they did much in Manitoba. Three million acres. But look, a farmer is a farmer. Let's say he is a good one. His business, just like yours is writing, is to convert his toil and good seed into big crops into cash. Yours is words to books to cash. Right? So when these good farmers came along, they weren't going to be raked in by what some newspaper editor wrote or what some banker said or by some pretty picture in a pamphlet somebody handed him. No, he's going to go out and walk that land and stick his hand in it and then he makes up his own mind, and I think, really think, that in most cases when those fellows did come up they saw some of the finest grain-growing land in the whole wide world. They may have come up after planting down there, mostly maybe as a free vacation for four or five days, but I think that when they got up here all that went from their minds. They became deadly earnest.

So these fellows would go back home, clean up their winter wheat, and get things ready and come up. By train, of course. I remember watching them unloading day after day and this was about 1909. Just a kid, but I could pick up a dollar easily helping a man unload and get the stock tied up to the fence posts along the track and bring them, the animals, a bucket or two of water. I noticed that all the pigs were black. Well, I hadn't seen all that many pigs, but the ones I'd seen were white or roan. So I asked this one fellow why all the Yankee pigs were black when pigs should be white, and he looked at me for a moment and then he said, "You must be one of those crazy Canadians we've been told about." That's all he said.

But they were all nice people. They got along pretty well and were always wanting to start things like the Masonic Lodge and sports meets and tally-ho parties and things we'd never thought of. They were what I recognize now as go-getters. They were good farmers too. Every one of them.

Locating Your Quarter Section

When you got off the train at your station, nothing to the north of you and nothing to the south but land. And there was no roads but trails and you were looking at hundreds of thousands of acres right to each horizon and in there somewhere you had to find your homestead.

That is, if you'd filed on a homestead and you got a legal description of your land, which would be something like a series of numbers. This told you exactly where your land was. If it were today and you had a helicopter and the big map and your legal description, as long as you had the code you could land that plane right on your own quarter section.

In those days it was a far different matter. Each section had an iron stake, and then there were the wooden stakes marking off the quarter sections. So far so good. Except somebody might pull up the iron stake and throw it in their wagon to use as a picket stake later on. Grass fires might burn off the wooden stakes, or the Indians sometimes used to pull them up just for hellery.

But everything was marked off from the First Meridian, which was set about 10 miles west of Winnipeg. Then the meridians went west at intervals and if your description said west of the Fifth Meridian and you had the map, there was no sense in getting off the train at Regina or Saskatoon. You'd get off at Calgary or Edmonton where the Fifth Meridian was near. And so it went.

Then, after the meridians, the land was marked off in ranges, and you could find the ranges from the map; and the ranges were broken down into townships, and you could find them from other maps you could look at in the land titles office. Of course, you know all about townships. Townships were what you were looking for—X Township or Y Township or Z Township. You were getting close. Then sections, which are a mile square. Each township has 36 sections and the sections are really what you are concerned with. Because in each section there are four quarters. Each township had its sections numbered off from bottom right to left, one, two, three, four, five, six, and then up one step above six and that was seven and so on until you got to section 36.

In there, well, there was some tricks. Like section one would be railway grant, which the government gave to the railways for putting tracks through to bring in the settlers. Section two would be homestead land, free, and that's what you were after, although thousands did buy land from the railroads, too, because after all the railroads were in the land business as much as the government although they were selling it, so much an acre. Railroad, free, railroad, free, across and up and across and up and back across except for two sections, always eight and three quarters of 26 which the Hudson's Bay Company got because they once owned the land and sold it off. Then section 11 was always reserved for school purposes. So that's the way it was lined up.

It sounds complicated but it was really simple. The whole West was laid out that way. The meridian told you in what large area you were, and the range put you in closer to your mark and generally told you where to get off the train because the stations were marked on the maps. Then it was a case of locating the section and then going and putting your heel down into the dirt of your quarter and saying, "Goddamn it, now this is my land."

Sometimes it didn't work out that way. If you filed, say, in Edmonton and then went south from there, you might find that your land was half taken up with a big gully running smack through it and running into the Red Deer River. Or it might be full of big rocks. The ground on the prairies changes almost as fast as you can blink. It was tricky. Then you'd hike back to Edmonton and look for another piece, or you'd hunt around there until you found a piece and got an idea which piece it was and then go back to Edmonton. You'd file again. Drop the first claim, wait, and file on a second.

Finding the right place, of course, was tricky, but there were fellows called locators who would help you. Every town had at least one, and when the settlers were coming in thick and fast there might be more. The railway would help you find your place too. They knew the country, they'd walked and rode over it, and they could measure off distances pretty well by the buggy-wheel method. That? You tie a something to the buggy wheel and you know the roundness of the wheel so every time the white tag tied to the wheel comes up, you count off another . . . 30, 31, 32, and if the wheel was 15 feet around then you knew you'd traveled 32 times 15 feet across the prairie. What's that work out to? Doesn't matter. But those fellows came pretty close and they could usually find the stake the first time around.

They charged you what they figured they could make out of you. If you were in rags, it would be less. Dress like an English lord and it would be more. The least I guess would be five dollars and maybe they'd skin somebody else for 25 dollars. Whatever they charged, it was worth it though. Finding where the section was was not too hard, but finding that exact plug in the ground for your quarter section, now let me tell you, *that* was a bearcat and two hound dogs fighting it out in a sack. You had to be right, you see. If you were wrong and did some work or a lot of work and somebody came along and said you were working his homestead, then, mister, you were just out of luck. All that work for nothing. It didn't matter if he were a nice guy or a bastard, he had his rights because that was his filed land. And because you'd said, "Oh, I don't need a locator," and gone and done it yourself, you had only yourself to blame. A locator was usually a pretty damn good investment, and most of them knew their stuff and was honest. They had to be. They usually were men who were homesteading themselves and you didn't want feuds in them days.

No Regrets. Happy I Came

The opportunity for free land, of course. That's why most settlers came. All the rest of the world seemed to be gone, the world we knew. Ten dollars got you started and 10 dollars was awfully cheap for 160 acres of your choice. There was no bargain like it. At least we thought it was a bargain then. A lot sure changed our minds after, I can tell you.

Minneapolis. That's where the family came from and my grandmother came right along with us. She had been bedridden for years but she died at the age of 79 and outlived her three children. She spent more than 50 years in bed, but she lived a full and adventurous life.

Her two sons and their families decided to go to Canada. To homestead in Saskatchewan. Remember, she was in bed and couldn't even use a wheelchair. But she was determined to go, and my grandfather, who was a veteran of the Civil War and had just a small pension, he was reluctant. Well, one day she was looking out the window and saw a real estate man viewing some property and she had him called in, and a few days later there was the agent at the door with a buyer and my grandfather gave in. He sold and so off we were to Canada for free land.

That was May of 1910. We got on at Minneapolis Central Station—an interesting sight. A porter carried my grandmother. She was tiny. She wore a large black cape over her bedgown and jacket, a soft mauve scarf over her waxed white hair, mauve bed slippers. And she was off to a homestead!

The rest of the family came behind. My grandfather, my mother, and Aunt Nellie. Mother with my eight-month-old brother, of course. My brother, nine, and me, 12, and three cousins.

They put Grandmother in a berth right away, and as it got dark we saw the last of the lovely Minnesota maples. The next morning, Canada. My father and uncle were waiting for us. They'd come up earlier with the two carloads of our possessions and we spent some time in the big immigration building. It smelled of disinfectant. Then Mother went to the big kitchen in the building and made us a hot meal. Then another night on the train.

Saskatoon. It was still a frontier town, as I remember, and they took Grandmother in a horse cab to a hotel. It took Grandfather, the porter, and the driver to get her in. We all freshened up in the hotel and then away we went again on the train—but what a train! Much cruder. The last station was Zealandia, just a few hours west, and then it was by construction line. So they took Grandma out of her cot in the baggage car and we had to wait in this little town until they told us that a train of materials was going out to the end of steel. That was Kindersley. They were going to put a passenger car on it for the settlers, although there was no scheduled train.

The railway, of course, was not the best. The train was slow, as it had to be because the grade was uneven, and Grandmother on her cot in the old dilapidated car was shaken from side to side. To show how slow this train went over the new grade, one salesman threw another salesman's hat out the window and the fellow jumped off, got his hat, sprinted back along the track, and caught the train.

It was almost dark when we got to Kindersley, with Grandmother still giving orders and telling people what to do. You know. Kindersley was end of rail. You'd call it a mushroom-growth town. The streets were lined with tents. They had wooden floors, walls a couple of feet up were wood boards, and a stovepipe poked out of the canvas. My dad and his brother made three tent houses for us—one for us, one for my uncle's family, and one for the grandparents.

That was how our family got to the West, to the end of steel at Kindersley The women stayed there while my father and my uncle went 30 miles further on to what is now called Marengo, where they put up homes for us. Not really homes but what were called homestead shacks. Thirty miles was a hard and long day's journey with a horse and wagon, and everything—lumber and tools and all the supplies—had to be hauled that way as the rails had not been laid yet. Everything by horse and wagon.

And when the shacks were ready, the men came and got us

and we went to our home in the West. We were to have many adventures and some sadness, and there was a lot of hard work to be done. There were hard times, like the droughts, and good times, when wheat was three dollars a bushel. But I guess you could say that what we went for and what we got was free land. It was good land. What they called heavy land.

Of course, even in those days you couldn't really live on a quarter section. This is what they told the people overseas; that they could live on a quarter section, 160 acres; but it just wasn't so. So my father had his homestead and he was able to purchase South African scrip. This was scrip given to the veterans of the South African war, and a veteran who did not want land could sell his scrip. I think my father paid 300 dollars for his 320 acres. Just imagine. Half a section. So he had three-quarters of a section. Open land. Good land. It was a chance to make a good start and we were lucky. Good times and bad times, but all in all, there is nothing to regret.

People Were on the Move

We first settled near Cooking Lake but Dad didn't like the district. I think it was just one near neighbor he didn't like, but that would be enough. There was so much land open in those days that you could go anywhere and buy it. As long as you didn't want to be too close to the railroad. Say, seven or eight dollars an acre.

So we moved. Even the house. Board by board. Dad and his hired man did it the way Boy Scouts build a cabin. They numbered every board with the alphabet and numbers so you knew exactly where N-15 went and where S-12 went. There is nothing new about that. Just common sense.

We moved about 30 miles south and Dad bought new land, put up the house, built a barn, pig house, shed with roosts for the hens, and in a month we were back in business. The only thing changed is that we had a new town to go to and my sister and I had to learn to know a bunch of new kids at the new school. That wasn't so difficult though. People did move around a lot in those days. Somebody would file on a homestead and find it was too light, too alkali, too rocky, too many trees, or even in the middle of a tamarack swamp. The smart ones went out and scouted the land. The ones in a hurry—and wasn't everybody?—they'd see that this piece here was taken up and that piece there and this piece south of there and they'd figure that if they were okay, then anything in between was okay.

City people, or people today, seem to think that when farmers went on the land they stayed. Oh no. They moved around just as much as city people. Dad didn't like a neighbor. Somebody couldn't find decent water. That was legitimate. You can't keep stock without water. Land sandy. Good for potatoes, rye, but not wheat. Wheat was what you wanted; wheat was king. Rocky. A man can't spend his life picking rocks. Let a Ukrainian, a Pole, take over the place. They didn't mind. To them it was land, better than they'd ever had before when they'd had none. I know, there are farm families who've been on that same section since 1900.

But no, the fact remains that Canadians in those days, we were a people on the move. How do you think every little town could support at least two, sometimes three, real estate offices? They didn't make their money acting as agent for the Prudential or Wawanesa. They were buying and selling farms, renting farms, trading farms. If you looked at the prairies, say from Winnipeg to west of Edmonton 50 miles from 40,000 feet high, like an astronaut, you'd have seen it like a big ant pile that you'd disturbed with your foot.

I think they liked to move. They got tired of one place, looking out of the kitchen door south toward the barn and seeing that same view day after day and year after year and knowing you'd be seeing that view until you died. I think for some people that was good enough reason for moving. After all, it wasn't a question of there not being any land. There was. I remember when the boys came back after the First World War and they looked for land, they found it. Bush land. Poplar. But it was pretty good land. It was never a question of land running out.

I think there was an excitement about it. You'd go into a new place like we did after we moved south of Cooking Lake. We moved into what was called the Scott place. My sister and I went to a new school. I was grade seven and just becoming aware of boys. My Dad would go in to town and shake hands with the livery-barn man—he was the one you got to know. Before you know it, Dad would have met four or five other farmers hanging around in the little office. Mother would want to know where the church was. We were Presbyterian. We'd all go to church the first Sunday and the visiting minister—always a visiting minister unless it was a town church—he'd announce from the pulpit who we were. After church, out in the yard Mother and Dad would meet the neighbors. The sewing circle. The Ladies Aid or whatever it was in those days. In ten minutes we'd be playing with children our own age in the churchyard and next week we'd be visiting each other. That's the way it worked.

But don't think that the prairies was fixed, there to stay. It was moving all the time, moving, moving.

3 *The Hard Land*

Yes, it was a hard land, far harder than most of the settlers ever imagined; far harder than they had been told it would be. Dreadful heat in summer, winters so cold that the mercury was a ball at the bottom of the thermometer. Trees to be chopped down, rocks to be hauled out of the soil. A hard land.

Men worked for neighbors, for the railroad, in towns, in mines and logging camps, for a dollar a day. Families just existed, somehow. But they endured. God, how they endured.

Yet the memories they have today are usually fond ones, told with humor and spirit, although sometimes they say, "How we ever lasted out those first years, I'll never know. I don't think we could do it again . . ."

Clearing the Bush Was Hard

To this day I don't know how they did it. You can visit any lodge in this province and you'll see the old folks sitting around, talking, watching the programs on television, or just looking out the window and you wonder. How did they do it? All that bush. They've got to be up in their high 80's, in the 90's, and they're just waiting in those lodges to die, but I wonder if they remember. Somebody should get them on the air and get them talking about it.

It was the bush. I can only remember that I was a little girl but we went out of Edmonton in July, my dad, my mother, my brother, me, seven, and we had a horse and wagon and the wagon, well, I'd have to say it was loaded with what the man in the hardware store in Edmonton said we should have. My dad knew nothing about homesteading. He knew less about the country. He could have gone south and then east of the Calgary line and found land just as good as he got up north but no, he had to pick a homestead four days' travel. That was 60 miles north. Westlock became our town when it was built up.

It was the man in the hardware store who helped us. He could have cheated Dad when he walked in and said he needed supplies to go north. But he didn't. Everything that went in to that wagon, everything Dad bought was needed. The man said buy three axes. Dad, I remember, said one would be enough. No, the man said, what if you break one and lose another and then where are you. Without an axe, you are nothing. The best saws. Files. Spikes. Baskets. A stove. Two stoves, a bigger one and a smaller one and stovepipes and two tents, the big one and a small one, and two draw knives and hammers and chisels and buckets, pans for milk, oh everything, and then he said, "What about a team?" Of course Dad hadn't thought of that and here was everybody getting off the trains, every day, and buying horses and we'd been camped just on the edge of town for four days and Dad hadn't done a thing about getting there. That was Dad for you.

Anyway, the hardware man wrote Dad a note and told him to take it to this man at the livery stable and Dad did get a good team. Molly and Dandy. We had them for a long time. Molly would really dig into her work and she'd shame Dandy into it because he was sure lazy in the mornings.

Then we got to the homestead. Bush. That's what we called

it then but bush today means little trees and willows. I mean big trees. Pine trees and cottonwoods, poplars, every kind of tree seemed to grow on that homestead up in the bush, and they weren't small. A man is five foot eight, right? An axe is three feet long. A day is as long as you want it to last but say, say 10 hours. And do you know how big 160 acres is? And then look at those trees. Some were only six inches through but lots, many, many, many were a foot through.

And there was one man with an axe and a team going at it and the government regulations said you had to clear five acres a year for three years to prove up, but there was no way one man could ever do that. One man going his best lick, providing he didn't break or lose or dull his axes, might, and I say *might*, clear two acres in a year. Out on the prairie, why, it was just plow and chop willow roots. But in the bush it was cut, cut, chop, chop, all day long. Then you got the team to pull the logs to a place where you were going to burn and when rainy weather or cold weather came along you burned. I can re-member my dad coming in to the shack at night and he'd say, "It's hard, Mother, it's hard." That's all he ever said.

It was the bush that did them in. When you went out in the morning it was there and when you blew out the light at night you could feel it was there. It wasn't that it was dangerous. You could find the odd deer. Somebody might see a bear once in a while, a fellow just passing through, I suspect. There was an old beaver meadow over in one part of our quarter and there were muskrats in it. The bush wasn't friendly. At home you could walk through the forest and it would be great oaks, high to the sky and round and solid, and you walked through aisles on leaves and feel at home. Here it wasn't dangerous but it wasn't friendly and the only things in it, it seemed, were those stupid rabbits. Yes, we ate them but to this day I never have felt any love for the rabbit. The Easter bunny, nonsense.

All day for Dad it was chop, chop, chop. Down, up, down, up. It never ended. He got strong though. Those wrestlers on tele-vision are positively flabby compared to him. Muscles that stood out. He certainly felt healthy. Wouldn't you? Outdoors all the time.

But bit by bit the bush went back and soon there was a clearing and in a year it would be bigger and big enough to put a fence across, part for the cow and the rest for oats and here and there you'd see the black earth where the brush piles had been. Where we'd burned. They'd burn all night shooting sparks high and if there had been airplanes at that time you would have seen the whole country just dotted with fires. Like burning straw piles in later years.

You had to be a strong man to beat the bush. I think my father found out something and it was that he was a lot stronger and tougher and a better man than he ever thought he would be. At home he was always kind of a dreamer and not much at holding a job. In Canada he found he could clear the bush and when you stood in the doorway at evening and saw what you had done, the pasture and the cow and horses and the oats, then you saw that you had done something. You knew you had done something.

Ah, Those Fine Letters Home

My brother Dan came to Saskatchewan in 1905. He took the first train—the train for passengers that actually was a passenger train— from Saskatoon, and when it got to what is near Islay today and he just jumped from the train with his two kits and that was that. The train was still moving. It was summer and he got work for himself with a farmer. He liked the country and wrote back to my father and ourselves who were all living in Somerset.

Dan was about 32 or 33, I should say, and, after being in the Army since he was 17, there was no life for him in England. There were 12 in our family. Dan was number one, you might say, and I was number 11. There were eight boys and four girls and two of the girls married but two not likely to be. My sister Florrie and me. We weren't exactly the pick of the bushel.

Dan began writing these fine letters home, all about how the country was what we call open, parkland, and the fine grass for grazing and the good weather. He didn't say you could get two feet of snow in a blizzard in the middle of June because everybody was new to that district and they didn't know. So Dan would write how he had got 160 acres of good land and good fir trees and how he was working hard and Dad would write back —and mind you, my father was a man of 55 by this time and my mother a year younger—but these letters of Dan's got my father all boiled up. He was an ironmonger in the High in our town and while he had a nice home, things were not at all good in England, and Canada seemed like a wonderful land. It was Canada, Canada, all the time Canada. His customers would come in and talk about it, and there seemed no place like Canada. Finally my father wrote Dan a letter and he told Dan to come home. He told him that something as important as moving the family to Canada was too important to be discussed in letters. He wanted us all around in the parlor and Dan talking and everybody asking about prices and the weather and the neighbors and all these kinds of things that are important.

You never knew my father. He was what they would call a patriarch. He was the head of the family and even if Jonathan was 30 and Elsie 28 and on down the line, what he said went. Besides, only two of the eight boys were married, so five were living at home, eating off his table, so he could talk like a king. Yes, like a king he was.

Dan came home. It was wintertime in Canada and he was glad to get home, he said, but he had to go back soon because he was proving up his homestead. He told us all about Canada, and we asked him all the questions and it all seemed pretty straightforward to me at the time. I was pretty young. So this family meeting was on the Sunday after Dan arrived back home, and then Dad announced that we would all go to Canada. He'd sell the shop and away we'd go and each boy would take up a homestead and we'd all live together. What Father was thinking was like a colony, a settlement of Bishops, with hundreds and hundreds of acres of land and herds of horses and fields full of cows and sheep, all in Saskatchewan.

So Dan was to go right back and J.J.—that's Jonathan—with him and Florrie was to go as cook for them, the woman around the house, and Dad would sell the shop, the house, the stable, the trap and driver, everything we owned, and off we would go to Saskatchewan to make our fortune.

In about two months a letter came back from Florrie. There were dried tear marks on the pages. She said it was terrible. Just terrible. We couldn't imagine how terrible it was. The weather was cold, terribly cold, and where they lived was not a house but a log shack and she drew a diagram to show how small it was. She said they ate porridge and rabbits and the only comfort was tea and sugar. The nearest neighbor was five miles away. And on and on and on.

The J.J. wrote a letter. He didn't say it was that bad, but he did say that Dan's thinking must have been out of joint to tell us what he did. He said about the shack and the rabbits. Hares, he called them. What he did say—what Florrie had perhaps forgotten to say—was that we should stay right where we were. England might not be all that fine and dandy, but it was far better than Saskatchewan.

Dad read the letter and said, "He's only seen it in the winter. Everything looks worse in the winter." So we went. Mother, Father, three of the boys, and myself. You couldn't pull the other three boys out with chains and the other two girls were married, but the rest of us trekked out. I think the ship was the *Tunisia* and everybody on it was English, all heading for Saskatchewan. Not Alberta. Alberta for some reason wasn't even heard of then. All for Saskatchewan. Names we'd never heard of. We only knew of Islay and Saskatoon and Regina.

We got there and we tried it for three years, but what does an ironmonger and a couple of soldiers and a couple of apprentices know about Canadian farming? We couldn't even get homesteads right together, and finally everything just split up. Dan went to Calgary and was killed working on the coal mines somewhere around Drumheller. Two of the boys went to Winnipeg and got jobs in a gravel pit at Bird's Hill before they settled down. Henny was a milkman for many years. Dad and Mum went to Saskatoon and then he and my mother went back to England. With nothing. They lived practically in poverty.

The family tried to homestead but it was just too hard. I think it was the winters, mostly. I never got used to them. I remember Mother one April looking out and saying that the flowers would be blooming in her garden back home, and there was still some snow on the ground and the ground frozen still and would be for another two weeks, maybe.

It was just too hard a country. It was too hard for us.

Oatmeal, Tea, and Rabbits

The first winter I don't know how we did it. All we had to live on was oatmeal and tea and rabbits. Oatmeal without milk. Tea without sugar. My mother used to make scones, like bannock, with only water, and that is what we lived on.

Rabbits. White rabbits. Trap them. You don't see them around anymore, but there would be a dozen at a time in them days in a little patch of bush as big as this room. Or shoot the rabbits. You'd see the two black eyes and you'd shoot between them.

Oatmeal, tea, and rabbits. They kept us alive. Sure. I don't know how we did it. I honestly don't.

Three-Time Loser

Oh, Jesus, we made mistakes, my cousin and me. Everybody did. Coming out from Ontario or Pennsylvania or that, you may have done a little farming, but coming from England or somewhere else, maybe in Europe where you farmed with a grub hoe, they made big mistakes.

You know, they didn't have then what they have now, these fine agricultural colleges and a fellow in every town telling you what the weather was going to be like six months ahead and what to plant and world prices and all that. No, none of that.

But my cousin and I, we got two quarters side by side on this land about 25 miles this side of Vegreville and it was good land. Kind of parkland, you might say. About seven-eighths open and one-eighth trees, sloughs. Well, we just left the sloughs alone. Didn't try and drain them and the trees we left alone.

The first mistake we made was that horses was a hell of a price but we wanted horses. Should have got bulls. Horses were about 200 dollars each them days. Everybody wanted them, so we could only afford two, Indian ponies, and they was too light for that kind of work. So I found I could buy a big steer for about 35 dollars, so we sold the two horses to somebody else and bought bulls. Hell, I had nine bulls and with another plow, we were in business.

You see, bulls are slower and you can't work them too well in the middle of the day, too hot, but they pull hard and they don't need oats. Oats was expensive but hay was cheap and lots of it, so we did all right. That summer and fall we broke 125 acres and that was a lot of land for two young fellows in them days.

Then in the winter I came into town and used them bulls for hauling gravel from the flats down there. I made good money and all the while old Mother Nature was doing her work, breaking down the sod, making it all crumbling and gentle so all you had to do first thing in the spring was pull two sets of harrows and we was in business. We got hold of a drill and we seeded her all to wheat.

Well, we got a fine crop. Finest in the district. That crop would go 30 bushels to the acre. And two weeks before I was to cut, you know what come along? Hail. The worst hailstorm you ever did see. I didn't get a cent out of that crop. That crop would have been worth over 3,000 dollars.

So I went back to freighting and I done good because I knew how to shoe my bulls, and so we worked good on them hills when everybody else was slipping and sliding. Oh, I made good money out of bulls. That kept us going that winter and bought seed and food for next summer.

So then we planted another crop of wheat, all 125 acres of it —and we got a whole bunch of hoppers that year. And when they was finished there wasn't much left but enough for us to get by. And wouldn't you know it, goddamn it, but about two weeks before cutting starts, frost! Frost! Went out in the morning and every kernel was black. Well, that wasn't another 3,000-dollar wheat crop, but it probably was a 1,500-dollar one and, let me tell you, even 1,500 dollars was one hell of a lot of money in them days.

So back to the bulls. Another winter. It was an open winter and I made money again and next year we seeded again and we got good rains in late May and good rains about two weeks later and a good rain about July 1. And let me tell you, that crop was just coming on like a house afire. She was a jim-dandy. Then we got no more rain and it got hotter and hotter, hotter until she sizzled, and then this wind come along, a wind from the south and west, and it sort of snapped your head back a little if you took a deep breath of it. It was that hot. You could stand at the door and see these acres and acres of waving wheat, and then there comes a time, and you notice it, and it looks like the wheat is curing on the stock like buffalo grass and you walk around it at near dark. Hell, it's too hot to walk out in the full daylight. Then you cut through it and you can see that that wheat is just burning up. You don't have to be a farmer all that much to know that the crop is finished. Just burning up like a youngster with a bad fever. So there went a crop that would have went 30 bushels to the acre and that meant there was another 3,000 dollars or more that we were never going to see.

In three years, hailed out, froze out, burned out.

My brother had left, gone back to Ontario after the second year, and so I said I wasn't going to go on anymore. I just couldn't take it. Three years, no crops, and I'll say it, that half section was some of the best land east of Edmonton, and yet I never could get even part of one crop off it.

It was mine, of course. I'd proved it up. I sold out my quarter and I sold my brother's quarter and sent him two-thirds of his money and I sold my bulls to some Ukrainians down the road who knew how to look after them and get something out of them, and I walked down the road and never looked back. I never wanted to know how that land did. For me it was a jinx, a goddamned jinx and that was all I cared about it.

A Prairie Woman Remembers

While my parents were in Glace Bay my brother Bill was born and now with three children they left Nova Scotia to come west to Taber in Alberta where Dad worked in the coal mines.

The first part of March of 1910 Dad and a good friend who was also a miner, Tom Taylor, decided to go homesteading and they walked from Taber to their homesteads about 60 miles away. They crossed bleak plains. Grass grew thick and high and there had been no animals on it since the buffalo. That was 60 miles of prairie with nothing on it but grass. Dad having trained in the British Navy could read the stars and they walked mostly by night. Dad and Tom's homesteads joined, so they became close neighbors in years to come.

Their nearest town was Warner, where they could buy lumber and nails to build themselves a tarpaper shingled shack, and they did this that summer. And then on the 15th of September they went back to Taber, where Dad worked in the mines for the winter months. This way he could earn money for next summer and he was back with his family too.

The following year, March 14, 1911, Dad and brave Mother loaded their precious belongings, like washtub and scrub board and wagon grease and their wedding gifts and precious photos of loved ones left behind in Scotland, and with their three little ones on a wagon pulled by one horse they set out for the homestead. After many miles Mother grew weary of asking how much further, and on the fourth day crossing that huge prairie, on the 18th of March, Dad said that if she looked in the distance she would see a building. Mother said later it looked like a lone toilet on nothing but prairie, and Dad said that was their new home. Mother made sure no one saw her and then she turned her head and cried.

That evening they arrived at the one-room shack. They hadn't had enough lumber to put on a roof so the wood they had brought from Warner made the walls to protect them from the wind.

Just then it started to rain so the shack was no good, so Dad and a neighbor who had come over to talk to us, they turned the wagon box upside down and Mother and the three little ones took shelter. Their wedding presents, photos, and other precious belongings went under with them.

That was the start of their homesteading days.

So, some days passed and Dad and this new neighbor who had helped with the wagon box, Paul Carr, they left for Warner to buy lumber to finish the shack and Mother had to walk a good mile to another neighbor's place to get two buckets of water—it was as scarce on our place as if we had been in the Sahara desert. Every day she made the trip.

One day when the men were away and Mother had just returned to the shack she saw fire and smoke in the distance and she had the pails of water. She dipped gunny sacks in the water and ran to meet it. It was a prairie fire and they were terrible things in those days. As the fire got close to the house Mother fought it, beating at the high flames with the two wet potato sacks, and she fought it and fought it until she was exhausted. But she managed to protect a little bit of land right around our shack and a bit of the thick grass where our horse could graze. When Dad and Paul Carr came back and saw where the fire had been they ran to the house and there they found Mother, very dirty, very smoky, very tired, but she had saved the children's prairie home and enough grass for their horse.

The following spring on the third of March they moved once again to the homestead, across those 60 miles of prairie, and this time they moved to stay. They would make it on the land or they would not.

Every day Mother still carried the water, but she also had to walk another mile to a family called Taylor to get milk for the baby. They were the only people who had a cow. Then another baby came along.

Father just had to buy a cow, so we had plenty of milk and Mother could make bannocks and scones. She also ground wheat to make porridge, and roasted ground wheat and added chicory to it and that was coffee for them. She also made her own soap and other things.

Life was terribly hard those first few years, and God must have helped them survive those first years of pioneer life.

Water was a major problem, and by this time there were neighbors all around us and they were always taking water from the same neighbor's well. So Mother and Dad decided they just had to find water on our place. Water of their own. Close to the house. So Dad took a pick and Mother took a spade and they chose a spot not too far from the house and they dug down about five feet, and would you believe it, next morning when they went back to work on it the well was full of water. It had seeped in. It was good water although it was hard.

There was great loneliness, especially for Mother. There were occasionally visits from neighbors as everybody felt so alone in the world, but I am sure many times Mother must have wished she were back in Scotland. But she had five fine children and she tried to be happy and busy, although often she would talk to us about scenes from her own home back in Scotland.

I remember the bitterness of winter and there was no wood on the prairies and Dad had no money to buy coal, so he had to drive miles to work in the mines and they gave him his pay in coal. He would work in the mines and Mother and my oldest sister would hitch up the wagon and drive miles and miles to the coal mine to pick up the coal he had earned and bring it home. But it kept us warm.

Often blizzards would come up without warning. Snow would sift through the cracks in the shack, frost would form on the inside walls and on nail heads and on the latch on the door. We would huddle around the fire to keep warm, with our fronts warm and our backs freezing, and you could count on half an inch of ice in the morning, frozen on the water pail. Frost always covered the widowpanes so you couldn't see out, and all during winter we would have to melt pails of snow or fill the wash boiler up with snow and melt it on the stove to get water for drinking and washing because our well had frozen up, and also to water the stock. I'll always remember the wet clothes hanging in lines strung around our tiny shack. If calves happened to be born during the winter months, they were carried in out of the cold and placed in front of the fire in the house.

In spring and summer we kids would go out on the prairie and pick up cow chips [dried cow dung], and we used that as fuel so we wouldn't use up our precious coal.

We ate very frugally, just the very essentials, but when Dad went to Mr. and Mrs. A. W. Bird's country store in Birdsholm he would bring back luxuries. These would be dried beans, black strap molasses, and dried apples. But I never remember going hungry. Mother grew plenty of fresh vegetables in the summer, so there always was vegetable soup all through the winter and always oatmeal, although I could never get used to it. In the summer there was a small cream check once in a while, and that helped us through the winter too. It would buy sugar and tea and we had our own eggs and meat and vegetables, so we never starved. I don't think anybody starved on the prairies.

Two Weeks, 10 Dollars

In those days I never thought of the people who had no money. A man would have to work for a neighbor for two weeks to get 10 or 12 dollars to buy flour and pork and salt and rice and beans. I knew some in that first year or so that didn't even have a horse or an ox. If nobody was going to town, they walked. More than 20 miles. In town they'd sleep in the livery barn. You went one day, came back the next. Nobody could walk 40 miles over those trails in a day. When he got to the store he'd buy his stuff and give Mr. Miller a piece of paper and on it would be written, "I'm good for 10 dollars. Will settle with you later." An I.O.U. It would be something written like that, a note from the farmer, the new settler, and that was as good as cash, that note. Everybody trusted everybody else.

Then the man would put the sack on his back with the other groceries tied on top and he'd fix up a tump line—around your forehead, a leather strap and back around the load—and start out. That load might be 60 pounds, and back home there would be a wife and maybe five or six kiddies waiting for him to come home. If he didn't they'd starve. Probably they had nothing in the house. If a blizzard came, he just had to hope that there was a trail going off the main trail and he could follow the off-trail and come to a house where he could stay.

I remember my husband and I going to town, just spanking along in a cutter, and we passed this man leaning against a tree. His load was pushed back against the tree to take the weight and he was just standing there, arms down, head down, utterly exhausted. We stopped and he said he was on his way home and his load was about 70 pounds and he was finished. I asked him why he was standing like that. He said if he took the load off he would never get it back up again. Well, there we were. What do you do? We were going to a meeting in St. John's [Anglican church], but the man had five miles to go and he wasn't going to make it. My husband—oh he was such a good man, such a Christian—he turned the outfit around and got off and took the man's load and put it in the cutter and helped him in and away we went, bells jingling, to this little sod and pole shack he lived in. And I was right, there were about four or five children.

Now that man had walked 17 miles or so from town that day with a 70-pound sack of groceries, and he was just out from London. He knew nothing about the country, he knew nothing about farming, and he really didn't know much about work either. I was pleased to see them leave the country next summer. We wanted settlers, neighbors, but these people were just going to starve. The train was through by then and they went back to Saskatoon.

The Axe Went Deep

There isn't in me the gift of telling you how it was when you walked up to a piece of land that had to be cleared and you looked at those trees, mostly poplar, but big poplars—bigger than I've ever seen since—and all you had in your hands was an axe.

It was like grain in a field, I guess. You couldn't see 15 feet into that bush and yet you'd have to start, you know. You'd have to start somewhere, so you'd walk up to the first one and say, "All right, Dandylegs, you're coming down," and you'd swing and the blade of the axe would go in deep. It was not all that hard chopping poplar. You got a darn good bite at every swing, but these trees were a foot or more through, and you just kept swinging.

There was a way of doing it: just keep going, stand back and let 'er fall, and it was up to you whether you limbed them then and used the Swede saw on them for firewood or you waited until you'd done what you were going to do that winter. I used to say I did five acres a winter. Clear it too, I mean. That meant you had enough firewood and more for next winter, good dry stuff but fast burning, and then in that space you planted spuds, all in and around the stumps.

My God, how those eyes used to grow. You wouldn't believe it. It was nothing at all to get a thousand bushels of potatoes off that five acres you'd cleared, in and around the stumps being all the same thing. No hoeing, no watering, no nothing. Just put them in and they'd come up and you'd dig them, sort them, sack them. That was the hardest part. What you'd call the harvest, but the darn things practically jumped out of the ground at you, and good! Good? Was they ever good. I could put them on the train to Edmonton, to the big hotels, and they'd just grab them. Top prices. Nobody cheated you in those days. If you gave honest measure, good value, you got the top price. Always, Now it's a mean business. Everybody out to jew everybody else. Not then. If they were Bob Harcus or Pete Thomas or Ronny Mathews spuds, those places in Edmonton would take them.

First year I cleared five acres. Next year into spuds that went. That next winter, five acres. Spuds. So I had 10 acres. Next year, five more acres. Next year, the first five acres went into grass because I was starting to pull stumps by that time. The roots start to rot, you see. So that year, five acres of grass and five cows and 10 acres of spuds. Next year, 10 acres of grass and six or seven cows and 10 acres of spuds. See how it builds up? Next year, five acres, that's the first five of 1910, five acres of oats and then 10 acres of clover and alfalfa and seven or eight cows and another 10 acres of spuds. Every year, another five acres, first spuds, then grass and then oats or rye or flax, and in 10 years you've got a big farm and people driving down the road to town they suddenly say, "Hey, look at that Pete, he's got a regular farm there."

They see a good frame house and a well and a new barn and corrals and way off, they see land and a couple of oxen for pulling stumps. I was one of the last in that district for having oxen. For pulling stumps. That good strong pull, steady as she goes. So people say, "Hey, look at that Pete, he's doing well."

And it's all here. In these two arms. Tough. Strong. You betcha.

Not a Penny in the World

We come to Calgary in 1898 and then we moved out of there about 10 miles and then my father died, so my mother she took a homestead. Oh yes, a woman could take up land then, but not many did. Not many. I don't know how she did it or how she ever got the idea she could do it. A wonderful woman, my mother, wonderful woman. Even today I don't know how she managed.

See, she had no experience. We weren't farm people. We'd come from the Falkland Islands, and if you know them there's nothing there to farm.

I don't know how in the world she ever got along. Three children, two sisters, and myself and not a penny in the world. Somehow she got a roof over our heads. A neighbor or two helped but she did it all, mostly. That's the kind of women there were then. I wish I had a picture of her to show you. Not a big woman but all this spirit. She knew she had to provide a home for the three of us and that's how she did it, right out on the prairie. She would work 18 hours a day. Absolutely.

At first she'd hire to get a little bit of plowing done when she could get a dollar or two. She'd sell eggs in High River, and sometimes women in the town would hire her for a day. She'd walk in to town, work all day, walk back. For just a few cents. Wages wasn't nothing in those days. Not too many people had money and those that had it were awfully close with it.

First she got an acre plowed and that became a garden. That's an awful lot of garden, but all of us worked in it. We didn't go to school much but we sure worked around the place. In that garden. Then the next year she got another acre plowed and so forth, and after that I was big enough to drive a team around and I plowed up the rest. I can't remember just where she got the horses. I think she must have borrowed them or maybe rented them, because I know we didn't own them. Horses in them days was expensive. So I was behind the plow. How old was I? Oh, 1905, let me see, I'd be about 10. Yes, I was 10 years old. It must have been quite a sight to see a 10-year-old boy behind a big team of horses plowing. It wasn't good land, it was fair land, some alkali, some sand, and I plowed up the whole shooting match.

Yes, I remember now. We rented the team from the money Mother used to make working for other people. She'd get a dollar and a half a day in harvest. She would cook, sometimes for as many as 21 men during harvest.

Between her and me we proved up that homestead and everybody was saying, "Oh, they'll never make it." But Mother just kept at it, working away and getting this done one year, that done the next year. A cow, more chickens, later a team. The neighbors were real good when they saw how hard we were all working, and they come and give us a hand.

It was my mother who did it. She just said she was going to have a home for us and that's all there was to it and she went and filed on that homestead. She'd never seen it but the map showed it was on a lake and she thought that would be nice. Having a home by a lake. She said, "That's the place I want," and she got it. And then she brought out all the things we had from the place west of Calgary and she rolled up her sleeves and pitched in. She worked 18 hours a day, that woman did. And when it was all over, all those years later when she had a nice farm, if you looked at her talking with other women in town on Saturday, just as quiet and gentle and lady-like, you wouldn't have believed that she could have done it.

It Took Me Nine Years

A lot of the trouble was in the government. They said a man had to prove up in three years, and that meant breaking 30 acres of land into crop. So, a lot of these poor simpletons tried it, but it couldn't be done. Something was always getting in the way. That was 10 acres a year. Imagine just what 10 acres is. Bigger than your city schoolyard.

The government didn't actuall mean you to prove up in three years. At least I never thought so. They wanted you to keep working at it and if you did five acres one year for potatoes and a garden and a bit of barley, and three acres next year, well, I always found that nobody would bother you from the government.

That was the rub. People thought they would lose their farms and so they used up their savings, went into debt to the Jew and the bank to do 10 acres a year and when they did prove up, well, the Jew or the bank they'd have so much money lent against the quarter that they'd just take it over.

If you'd be in the store and somebody said that Kelb or

Simons or somebody had proven up, that would be big news. That meant he'd done his 30 acres and got his patent, but only a few ever did it in three years. How could they? This wasn't the prairie, this was the bush—and you know what the bush was like. I proved up in nine years. Got my patent. Nobody said anything. I was working and building up a small herd and fencing and putting in a better house and all those things, and you couldn't expect a man to do everything in three years. What an Ottawa man thinks a settler can do is not what that settler can do in northern Alberta, where everything is very hard work and nobody had the money. I used to walk around with 20 dollars in my pocket, go into town, and there never was a time I couldn't have farmed out that money at 10 percent interest. Never a time. These settlers, unless they sold a bull calf, never had any money.

I never got actually moving until I got myself a wife. Then I didn't have to look after the pigs, the chickens, the milking, and the money we'd get for those things in town, that she did, I could use to hire help and get things done. I rented the first big tractor to come into our valley and you know how? Because my wife was looking after the house and garden and stable part of it while I was working on the land. A single man couldn't do it. They shouldn't have expected him to. The set-up was all wrong, as I see it.

Thirty acres of bush, well, God, man, that's an awful big piece of land and a man and a bull team can't do it. Not in three years. It took me nine and I worked hard. God, times I worked harder than any man alive.

4 Blizzards and Bulldog Flies

Dressing for Canada . . . We Didn't Know What a Mosquito Was . . . Those Flies Made Life Miserable . . . It Don't Hail Like It Used to . . . A Year's Work Gone in 10 Minutes . . . Oooh, Those Thunderstorms! . . . Summer Storms Were Real Bad . . . The Fires Burned for a Month . . . Mother Saved the Homestead . . . Imprisoned in the Snow . . . Lost in a Blizzard . . . It Was Clear and Sunny When We Left . . . The First Day Was the Worst . . . Do You Know What 40 Below Is?

How do you describe 40-below temperatures? Prairie fires that blaze day and night and consume everything in their path? Those bzzzzzzing hordes of mosquitoes? Hailstones the size of hens' eggs? The settlers put up with all these—and more. The pretty pamphlets and speeches had not prepared them for nature's fury. It was something they had to experience for themselves.

Dressing for Canada

Oh, I remember we knew nothing about Canada. When my parents decided they would come to Canada, my father went down to the library in the town and got out an atlas, and there was North America and the top half was Canada and the part

62

where Western Canada was, that was marked "British Possessions." That was good enough for my father.

But they knew Canada was cold. So when we were on the ship
—and this was in June—my two sisters, me—we wore what we'd
wear in an English summer. White frocks, white socks and
patent leather shoes, and we had those straw hats with a blue
ribbon around the crown.

But when we were getting near Halifax my mother said,
"Come, children, we've got to go and dress for Canada now."
And there we were on deck as the ship docked, with warm
woolen dresses on, heavy coats fur trimmed, and we had gloves
and warm stockings on, and it was about 85 degrees, a boiling
hot day. When we walked in the streets everybody looked at us
as if we were crazy.

We Didn't Know What a Mosquito Was

The thing I will always remember were the mosquitoes. They
seemed to be so much bigger. So much more eager to bite you
than today. I don't know, maybe it is this stuff they spray on the
sloughs that make them less.

When I was a little girl we homesteaded on the prairie east of
Calgary near the Saskatchewan border, and it was a country
of more sloughs than it has now. Of course in Sweden we never
knew what mosquitoes were. If you'd asked us what a mosquito
was, we would have looked at you silly. They never told anyone
there would be these creatures who would blind you and make
the horses go mad, and that they were with you for three
months. I'm talking about the pretty pamphlets with all the
high-falutin' words and descriptions of the country that made it
sound like paradise, something like out of Smith Family Robin-
son. They never told my dad when he went to sign up for the
trip. From what I found out, they never told him anything. Or
anybody anything.

But you just could not believe what the mosquitoes were like. My mother would send me to the slough for a pail of water. The way was through thick grass. Long grass and this is where the mosquitoes lived. You'd be wearing a long skirt and long stockings, so it was your face and your neck and your hands you had to hide. Imagine going out in June in the warm morning wearing mittens to get a pail of water. That was what it was like. You wore a mosquito netting for your face and it wasn't until a month or so that the storekeeper mentioned he had got another order of mosquito netting. Then Dad found out there was such stuff.

That first summer when my father was plowing, I had to walk on one side of the horses and my smaller sister on the other waving cloths. Bits of cloth tied to sticks to keep the horses calm enough because the mosquitoes were driving them out of their minds. To distraction. It was a common sight to see a team with three people around it, one man plowing and two others brushing off. This went on, you understand, day after day. Yes, week after week, until a time came along in summer when all of a sudden there would be less of them and soon there would be none. They'd all died.

It was funny too. Some people the mosquitoes just did not bother. I've seen a man with his sleeves rolled up and his arms black with the nasty things and yet not one would be sucking blood, not one biting, and all the rest of us would be all done up.

Many the time I've heard neighbors sitting around our stove and they'd be talking about how bad things were. And I've often heard these men say that if they had to do it again, they'd go to where there were no mosquitoes. If there is such a place.

Those Flies Made Life Miserable

Oh, the things some people did. You see, they were so terribly green. Right out from England where they may have been gentlefolk and into the wilds of Canada, and what could they know? What could ever have prepared them for some of the things they met? The terrible loneliness, for one thing.

Or the bulldogs. The bulldog flies. Big and black and when they bite, they tear a chunk out of you. My mother tells the story about a neighbor who had come out with her husband and children in winter, so she'd never seen bulldogs. And the first time she did a bunch were swarming outside her kitchen window.

Well, she thought they were bees. Never seen bulldog flies, couldn't imagine any fly that big, so they had to be bees. She thought some neighbor had lost a swarm and she'd keep them there for him until she found out who it was and he could come and get them. So this dear soul went outside and smeared the outside pane of the window with honey to keep those bees there.

I think my mother said that house had bulldogs swarming around it for the rest of the summer, making life completely miserable.

It Don't Hail Like It Used to

You never get hail like we used to. Never. Like BB shot now. Then it used to be big as eggs. Smashed everything, just everything, in its path. Near Minnedosa I saw a whole herd of Holsteins dead in a field and every one of them had been killed by hail. Them pieces as big as this, as big as hen eggs, and when they got closer to earth, somehow they joined together and you'd have a piece of ice about nine, 10 inches long. And when it hit, well, it hit. That's about all I can say. You just can't describe it today but these cattle and they were all dead. Not a moan in a carload of them and when you felt them there under the skin it was pulpy. Just beaten into a pulp.

I don't know why more people weren't killed, but I guess it was because they had sense to run with the horses for the barn

if they saw it starting over their way. The storm, I mean. My
brother had to hide under a tin trough we had by a spring out in
our pasture once and that saved him, but his team was hurt bad
and the hailstones hit that trough so hard they splashed all the
water out of it. Yeah, they hit that hard. Hard to believe, I
guess, but you've got to see it to believe it. I can't describe it. A
black cloud just coming out of nowhere and then . . . Well, we
just don't have them like that no more. Maybe when they let
loose that atomic bomb it did something to the weather—but
I hadn't seen a real hailstorm long before that, so I guess not . . .

A Year's Work Gone in 10 Minutes

A hailstorm. A hailstorm on the prairies. It was a thing we had
never experienced before, not from where we had come from,
and we just couldn't believe it. This was beyond belief.

After we began farming we began to really prosper. This was
after we gave up ranching and went into wheat and got more
land—one field was 500 acres and it was all in wheat. And I
remember this one sunny day in August. It was in 1898. You
could look out over that field and it was the most beautiful sight
in the world. As far as the eye could see that field was waving
with glorious golden grain and just ready for the harvest and
we were getting ready to cut it, getting ready to stack it.

It was just about noon and the men were coming in for dinner
before starting on that field and during dinnertime the sky
darkened and the storm clouds rolled up and there was flashes of
lightning everywhere. Tremendous rolls of thunder warned us
we were in for a storm, but I don't think anybody thought all that
much of it. It would delay the harvest, that was all.

We took shelter when the storm rolled over us, and when we
came out 10 minutes later our beautiful waving fields of wheat
were a blackened, battered mess of mud and straw. Hail and
terrible rain but mostly hail. Huge hailstones lying everywhere.

Our farmyard was strewn with the dead bodies of Mother's chickens, and the swollen river had swept away the geese and ducks that had been feeding on it. In our pasture were, everywhere, the bodies of our young cattle and calves that had been pounded to death by hailstones the size of walnuts.

All in 10 minutes, without knowing what was going on as we huddled in the shelter, all the work of a year had gone for nothing. Just nothing. Just blackened, battered crops in the mud, good for nothing at all.

Oooh, Those Thunderstorms!

Thunderstorms. Oooh! On the prairies. Nothing like them in the world. Now anybody who has ever lived on the prairies, they'll never forget them. That was in the old days, mind you.

Good God. I had a neighbor, six horses leaning against a fence when a storm came along, and every one of them was struck dead by one bolt of lightning. Six Clydesdales.

Oh, they were so bad they'd even make me scared.

No matter how good you are at words, nobody can properly describe what a thunderstorm was like in the old days.

Sheet lightning. That's what we're talking about. Now I've seen a lightning storm last all night, and every time the lightning hit the ground, it might hit a barn or a house or maybe only a little poplar tree, but it would do some damage. Those storms used to wreck the countryside, believe me.

I remember once I was in my little shack and the lightning was flashing all around outside and there was this flash that seemed to explode in the house and I felt heat go down my leg. That's what I felt, heat going down my leg. I must have been grounded all right, but after that I went out and bought some lightning-rod conductors so that wouldn't happen again. Immediately. I put up six on my house.

We got so absolutely afraid of the lightning that it made our lives miserable and when we were away from the house it was worse, that much worse, because there was nothing to take the positive stroke down into the ground.

Summer Storms Were Real Bad

People don't think life was dangerous on the prairies, but there were always things to watch out for. Our whole family almost drowned right in our own back yard.

We used to have cyclones in that part of the country. Everyone dreaded them. There was this afternoon when all the signs in the sky pointed to a cyclone. The sky was black.

Beside our house and past the barn there was this gully and my father had dug into this and made a room. This was our underground milkhouse because it was cool, and we also used it for vegetables and stuff. If a cyclone came, we got into it for shelter. It worked that well.

This afternoon we stayed for almost two hours. The twister went through the district and then there was this terrible rain storm. Lasted a long time and with it there was this terrible thunder and lightning, so it was decided it was safer to stay in the root cellar.

Then happened what never had been thought of before. Dad had dug out the cellar somewhat below the ground of the gully and back into the hill, and to get into the cellar we had to go down several steps and through a thick door which opened into the underground room. The great rain flooded our fields above the house with a great lot of water, which finally began draining off and came roaring down the narrow gully and began pouring down our steps and began to fill up the room we were in. In just a minute or two the water was all around us and we were fighting for our lives.

I can always remember, over the noise, the voice of my father rising strong and calm. He got us children to stop scream-

ing and then he told us to cling, each of us, to one of the poles
holding up the ceiling, keeping the dirt from toppling in on us.

By this time we realized the water was only going to rise to
the top of the door, but it left only a foot of air between the
ceiling and the water. What Father did was this. He took
Mother and us four young children out, one at a time. He held
us and dove under the water and out the door and swam with
us down the passage and into the gully and got us up on the
bank of the gully where we were safe. Safe but terribly frightened.

He did that with four young children and my mother. Billy
and Jim, the eldest boys, they were able to save themselves.

To this day it has always been a mystery to me how Father
did this, because the force of the water raging through that
gully was really terrific. Just to show you, Jim and Billy who
could swim were carried about 200 yards down that gully before they were able to grab something and hold on. But Dad got
the five of us out and right up on the bank immediately.

So you think life wasn't dangerous at times out there?
Summer storms were real bad in the early times as they were
very sudden and very violent. When the district became cultivated and the great prairie became grain fields, the fierce storms
got less and later they were quite mild. Harmless. I don't know
why this should be so but it is so.

The Fires Burned for a Month

I've seen prairie fires burn for a month. In the spring. You could
could see them burning 60 miles away. Red glow in the sky.
You didn't bother because it was so far away.

I've seen a big fire jump the North Saskatchewan River. That
was a half-mile wide, bank to bank, even though the river itself
might only be 100 yards or so in the middle, with sandbanks in
it too. But the buffalo chips would catch fire and smolder, and

the high wind would just pick them up and away they would sail right across that old river. Sure, in a high wind.

It was a very dangerous thing. The last thing a man would do before going to bed each night in the spring and fall was to go outside and circle around his shack. Why, he was looking out there to see if he could see the glow of a fire. Sometimes there were two or three, but if there was no wind you usually were safe. Your firebreaks would protect you. But if there was a wind, even a breeze, then look out. That's one night you didn't go to bed. No sir.

Lots of people were burned out, everything gone, while they slept. Or if they got away, when they came back there was nothing. No shack, no barn. Even the fence poles gone. Handles burned off the plow.

I never could understand how they could start. Indians sometimes would let their campfires get away from them. They weren't all that smart, you know. A couple of cowboys making supper might kick a coal into grass. That sort of thing. Settlers too. Sparks from their chimneys. And lightning, yes. Yes, often lightning. But sometimes they'd start when there was no people on the prairie, no storms and no lightning. They'd just start and I was never able to figure out how. They'd just start and sometimes you couldn't see the sun for the smoke from fires, and at night there would be a glowing in the sky here, and over there and way over there.

Let me tell you, there was nothing worse than a prairie fire.

Mother Saved the Homestead

I remember that morning as if it were yesterday. I was five years old, this was in 1909, October, and my mother had sent me out to play and look after my sister Mary, who was three, almost four, and my little brother Colin, who was not quite two.

I remember watching my father and my uncle ride away on horses across the prairie to help a neighbor fix up his house for winter. Everybody helped everybody else every way they could in those days and where we lived, the whole area was virgin prairie, around Hannah. The pioneers who came in that spring and lived in tents were now starting to finish their sod houses and get them ready to move into for winter.

So that left Mother alone looking after us three kids and my cousin and grandfather, who was in bed in the house sick after a stroke. And to top it all off, my mother was pregnant. This was like it was on the prairie in those days. Women had to do a lot.

It was a queer morning, I remember—unreasonably warm. It was getting darker and there were more gusts of wind, and this to us meant a storm coming. It was about noon when a very bad swirl of wind struck us, and this time we could smell the odor of burning prairie wool. That was what we called the kind of grass that grew everywhere on the prairie. And then I looked to the southwest and I ran to the house as fast as I could yelling, "Fire! Fire!"

If you looked to the southwest you could see this ridge of grayish-black cloud, which was rising rapidly and spreading fast, and through it you could see the occasional finger of red shooting up into the cloud.

Mother grabbed up some blankets and herded us all toward the well, which was inside the fire guard that my dad had plowed. Just about the first thing a settler did was plow a fire guard to protect his homestead and family against these fires. So Mother took us to the well where the horse trough was and she sopped all the blankets. Then she said, "Whatever happens, make the children stay right here. The grass is worn off, so it won't burn. Wrap one blanket around each child."

Then she grabbed up another blanket and a pail of water and went to try and stop the fire. One woman and one blanket against that terrible fire, which by now we could see was made up of great flames, and as it got closer it made a tremendous noise, crackling and popping through the high grass as it came closer and closer to the fire guard, and there was my mother out there, doing somehow what she could to save the house. Remember my grandfather was in it because he was paralyzed, or partly paralyzed, and couldn't get out of bed.

The little kids were pretty good because they were used to me bossing them around, and under this black smoke which filled the sky we just huddled there in the wet blankets, trying to get breaths of air with all that smoke around. And then it was over. The fire had gone past around us and we heard my father's voice calling my name. Oh, it was a blessed sound.

I found out that the men had ridden over from the other house over all that fresh-burned earth and found Mother exhausted but still fighting the fire where it persisted in creeping under the sod of the fire guard, putting out all the flames before they could start moving toward the house where Grandpa was.

That is my memory of a prairie fire.

Imprisoned in the Snow

I must tell you about our first house and our first blizzard. The house was made of logs. Everything was. The roof was poles and sod and I guess there was a layer of tarpaper too. There must have been. Dad had gone up to Onion Lake where there was a sawmill and he brought down boards for the floor and windows —although the windows were very small, but they were windows. A lot of people didn't even have that.

Then this blizzard came. It wasn't a three-day one but just one day and night but there was this terrific amount of snow, and by the time he was ready to go to the barn next morning the snow had covered the house and the wind had packed in the porch. The door. We were sealed in tight. Really.

So we couldn't get out. There we were, trapped out on the prairie because all this snow had packed up against the house and the door opened outward and so there we were, caught inside. It took Dad about two hours of fiddling around, fiddle around and fiddle around. First he got it open by pushing enough to get his wrist through and he dragged snow back into the house. Then he could push it open just a little more, the amount of the snow he'd taken out. Then a little more. Then more. Finally he could use a pot to push through and pull out a pot of snow at a time.

That never happened again. There wasn't a snow like that again that winter and next spring he rebuilt the door so it would open inward so we'd never be caught again.

There were so many things those first years on the prairies that nobody ever told anybody about. They would have if they had known, but we had come from Germany. We had no real snow there, no blizzards that I can remember, and we had to learn everything the hard way. Always the hard way. It seems to me there was no easy way then. If somebody had just put out a pamphlet in a lot of languages because there were so many of us, just saying you should do this and don't do that, it would have been easier on all of us.

Lost in a Blizzard

This was about in '06, about a year after we came, and one morning Dad says he was taking the team to town. We needed food and he needed some things, a bottle of whisky, and there should be some mail. Then he said, "I'll take Tommy. Time he learned how, he'll have to be going to town one of these days." Tommy was me. I was nine or 10 then. About 10.

We're going to the barn and Dad says it looks like snow. You're darn right it looked like snow. The first of the stuff was falling, twisting and turning in the wind, and I thought to myself it didn't look like the best day to go to town, but I said nothing. With my Dad you could get a clout alongside the ear for things like that.

Town was eight miles away and we got there okay a good bit

before noon, mostly like we always did. We had the team, and I think it was Dolly and Jack. In town Dad says to take the pair to the barn and get them some oats and he'd do the shopping.

You didn't know my Dad. Shopping meant about three hours in the bar at Silver's Hotel and then going into the general store just across from the station and ordering about two clerks to run their heads off getting his order filled while other people, people who could have been there first, stood around and looked mad. He never thought of going to the store first and leaving his order to be picked up like everybody else did, or sending me.

He was a big man with a big mustache that took up half his face, and he wore one of those big sheepskin coats. He'd got it off one of the homesteaders west of our place when the guy, a Ruthenian or something like that, decided to quit and go in to town. The man owed Dad some work for some horse work Dad had done for him and the man had turned over his big coat. It was some coat. It would have kept a regiment dry.

My father was not very popular. Our name was Miller, but in the store once I heard a neighbor call him "that damned Prussian." This was behind his back, of course. Always behind his back. I asked my mother once what Father was like when he met her and she said, "Oh, when he took me walking in the park the first time he wore a monocle and . . ." but her voice sort of trailed off. There was a sword, sort of slightly curved, in a sheath, which she said was his when he was in the Guards. I think she meant the Grenadier Guards, the Welsh Guards, or one of those regiments. They came from England. This sword, us kids thought the sheath, the scabbard was the sword part and how could it kill anybody until one day I was fooling around with it and found that if you pulled on the handle the sword itself came out and it was shiny and sharp as a razor.

So this day I hung around the store for about two hours and the storekeeper gave me some crackers and cheese for my lunch. They always did that though. He knew I had sisters at home too and when we'd be putting away the groceries when Dad came home we'd always find a bag of candy in with the rest, and that was for us kids.

About two o'clock Dad came in and I hustled over to the

livery stable and got the team and hitched them up and away
we went over to the store. It was still just coming down a little
bit, nothing to worry, but I was a little scared because there was
that feeling in the air. I can't describe it. If you've been on the
prairies you've heard people sort of sniff the air and say,
"Blizzard's coming." It was that kind of day.

Sure as shooting, Dad was ordering those clerks around and
pawing through the mail and spilling some of it on the floor,
and I could see the neck of the bottle sticking out of his big
coat. He seemed squiffed—lots of loud laughing, lots of joking.
And then we gets the stuff in the back of the wagon, it's on
runners, and away we go.

There he is, singing to the horses and we don't go half a mile
when the blizzard hits us. Slam-bang. Suddenly you can't see
50 feet ahead of you; soon it's less than that, and finally just as
far as the horses' heads and they're not liking it one little bit.
The thing to do was turn right around and head back but do
you think my father would do that? Walk into that livery barn
with all those fellows sitting around and say, or they'd know,
that he come back because of the storm. No. We'd go on. I knew
that and anything I might say would fetch me a clout, so I just
sat up there on the seat with him and I'm peering into the snow
and we're going along okay, I guess. After all, the house is only
about seven miles away by this time. Seven miles ain't so far
when you've got a good team.

That's okay—except for some reason those two horses suddenly charge off the road. It's not a road as such but it's a hard-
packed winter trail and the snow is pretty deep off it. If I said
three feet I might not be too far wrong because we'd had three
or four good snows before Christmas. Anyway, over goes the
whole rig, and that's not so bad. All we have to do is unhitch
and get a line on the side of the wagon and haul her upright
and we're away again. That's fine. We do that, except the front
runner is busted and that wagon isn't going nowhere.

By now it's blizzarding hard. Harder than I ever saw it. Dad
says we better get going and he throws himself up on Dolly just
like she was a saddle horse, and tells me to throw up one of the
sacks of grub and we'd carry that with us and let the horses

take us home. I could see he was getting a little worried. The blizzard and the cold and it was really setting in cold by that time—it was all beginning to get in behind the whisky in his head. He says nobody is going to touch the wagon and the rest of the groceries and the few sacks of coal we'd picked up, so we best be going. So we got going, him on Dolly and me on Jack. He always had a pretty full line of curses for every situation around the farm, and he went through them one by one as we went along. He also wasn't forgetting his bottle. He said once: "I'd give you a pull but you're too young. It's a bad habit to start." Later he said, "God bless Mr. Haig."

It was still daylight but it might as well have been night and then it did get darker and then it got night and it was still blizzarding. Dad was okay but my mackinaw wasn't holding out the cold like it should. Dad said, "Get down and hold on and walk," and I did and that felt good for a few minutes, but then I couldn't drag my legs much further, the snow was that deep. So I tried to get up on Jack again but I couldn't, and I had to go around to my father's side and he gave me a heave up on her neck and away we went.

I yelled at Dad that shouldn't we be at home by now. Fact of the matter is, we should have been home hours before, and Dad yelled back, "You young pup, we've been off the trail for hours now. I don't know where we are and neither do these damn plugs."

You see, in a blizzard or an emergency, horses are supposed to be able to find their way home. Just give them their head and trust to them. In a blizzard a horse has got horse sense. I've always found that in most situations a horse hasn't got the sense God gave a goose, but it is supposed to always find its way to the stable door.

In those days there were no fences. It was like one huge Herd Law all over the country, and of course there was no roads either—just trails going to the different homesteads. But in that blizzard you had to hit the homestead right on the button, straight as a rifle shot, or you would miss it by 10 feet and that could be a mile. Unless they had a light on, of course.

Somehow I lost a mitten and I was afraid to tell Dad, so I

stuck my hand in my pocket and held on for dear life with my other hand. If I knew then what I know today, I can tell you that losing a mitten was pure bad medicine. A fellow can easily lose a hand that way. It has happened, sure.

The horses were floundering but they were harnessed together, and that was one good thing because we couldn't get separated. But they were in bad shape. They'd stop and we'd have to kick them on, and this went on and on. I had to wipe a lot of snow out of my eyes every time I wanted to see, and I'd lean over a lot and clear the big gobs of snow from Jack's eyes. Dad was doing the same. He'd finished his bottle now and he kept saying to himself, "Getting mighty late. Mighty late." I thought to myself that maybe it was too late. I knew parts of me were frozen. I was sure my feet were. I was wearing shoepacks, which I don't think are the best thing unless you're walking and getting circulation through your feet.

All the time the snow was blowing hard and then it would ease off a bit and then swirl some more and I'm nodding, nearly going to sleep because of the cold, and suddenly the horses stopped. They had been stopping a lot but this time my Dad yelled, "Thunderation!" and I looked up and we're at a building. Thoses horses had their heads right up against a door. A stable.

I slid off Jack and fell down and Dad ran around to the door and opened it and we all piled in. Dad slammed the door shut and looked around in the dark and said, "Somebody's barn." I remember saying, "Isn't ours," and he yelled, "I know that, you fool." We got the harness off the horses and Dad said, "Well, if there's a barn, there must be a house, but we don't know which way the damn-fool thing is, so we got one chance in four of making it. Or three chances in four of dying out there without the horses, so we stay here."

It was the only thing to do, you know. There was hay for the horses and hay for us to sleep in and the barn was warm. We'd find out what side was up in the morning, so I just went up to the loft while Dad was feeding Dolly and Jack. I dug a hole in the hay and pulled it in after me and I was out like a light.

I don't know how long I slept but I heard voices talking, and when I backed down the ladder these two voices were talking about the strange horses in the barn. I yelled that they were ours, and was telling them about coming in in the night and not being able to find the house because we didn't know which way it was when Dad comes backing down the ladder. He's all full of the old Nick and you'd of thought he was the king of the castle and the bravest man in the country the way he told it, and these two fellows, a man and a younger fellow, are looking at him kind of funny.

Then my father says, "And what is your name, sir?" and the older man says, 'Stebbings, Will Stebbings," and he introduces his nephew who he says comes from Ontario too. Then Dad asks where they live and when he tells him, my father's mouth just falls open. You've seen them in the movies—they get told something they don't believe and the mouth drops open. This family lived 20 miles south of where we lived, a whole 20 miles. We had been going north from town and now we were south, about 15 miles south of the town. I had mentioned to Dad that the wind seemed to have shifted on us when we were plowing along, but what had happened and we didn't know a blamed thing about it and didn't even think about it was that the horses had turned around.

Dad said, "The thing puzzling me, we must of crossed the tracks and didn't even know it," and the man, the farmer, said that if we lived where we said we did, then we sure as shooting had crossed the C.P.R.

You've probably figured it out by now or got an inkling. My Dad had bought that team from a farmer south of town, a man named Woeller. Woeller had sold out, and gone back to the Dakotas in September. The farmer told us he had come out from Ontario with his nephew and bought the Woeller place off a real estate man in town—land, buildings, machinery, hay, and all. So what those horses were doing is just what comes naturally to a horse. They'd gone home, but not to *our* home. No siree. The first place they had settled in was their home, and any other place they went just didn't count. That's why they headed for Woeller's old place. It just made sense to those horses. Do horses talk to each other, discussing what they're going to do? I've often wondered.

The upshot of it was, we stayed there another day helping around the barn and doing some cooking. There was no woman in the place. Next morning it was cold and clear and we harnessed up the pair and headed north. Dad figured if the horses had made a straight beeline for the Woeller place when they turned around on us, he'd be able to pick up the gunny sack of groceries he'd dropped. We didn't see it although it should have stuck up on the prairie like a sore thumb. We never did find it and I was kind of hoping I'd spot that whisky bottle. Just for the hell of it, I guess. A souvenir. The wagon was there, we found that easy, and got the other grub sack.

When we got home Mom and the kids hadn't been the least worried, but she was sure surprised when we told her what happened. "All that, good Lord," she said. "I would have thought you would have had enough sense to stay in town and sleep in the livery barn. You men!"

This made Dad so mad that he was a grouch around the house for two days.

It Was Clear and Sunny When We Left

One day we were going to Mortlach. It was clear and sunny in the morning, and when we left at noon in the cutter for Mortlach it was getting dark and, oh, we had a dreadful time to get to town. The blizzard hit.

In the barn when we left, my father had put a foal and the chickens and the cattle were loose. So were the horses. I can't remember about my mother's pet cow she'd brought up from North Dakota. She loved it and it loved her. But the blizzard hit and we barely made town. You couldn't see and it was very cold. No, wait, we didn't get there that day. We had to stop at a neighbor place overnight and next day we made it. Dad said, "Oh, I'll go out tomorrow. The foal will be okay." There was plenty of oat sheaves it could reach. And it could suck snow that came through the holes in the roof. After the first week he said he'd make it the next week. Do you know that blizzard lasted eight weeks? Eight weeks before he got back to the farm. The colt was fine but the chickens had frozen feet and combs and they had to be killed. It blizzarded every day. Every day. I have pieces from the paper which will show what I mean. The winter of 1907. Nobody who lived through that winter will ever forget it.

Why, the railway trains would get through because they had the plows, but the farmers would come down to the tracks and pile things on the rails and stop the trains. They demanded coal from the trains, just to keep their families alive. Naturally they got the coal. But before they decided to get so desperate as to hold up the trains, they had been burning willows out of the slough—and you know that willow wood is no wood at all to keep warm. Awful wood. It was terrible.

Finally it ended. Everybody lost their cattle. Ranches lost their cattle. Homesteaders did. Everybody did. When the thaw came, there was just dead cattle all over the country. In every direction.

The horses. Finally my dad found the horses. Many, many miles away. You'd start out and just ask questions. Have you seen such and such a horse? This horse. That horse. In those days every horse was distinctive. It had a certain style, a mark, a blaze, something. Horses can survive where cattle can't. Horses can paw down through the snow, the crust, and find the prairie wool. Cattle can't. Horses in a blizzard can get their rumps to the wind and keep warm, and sometimes I've thought when they all got heads together in a storm that their breath somehow kept each other warm. So he found his horses.

Did people give up? No, they didn't. Soon as spring came they were going strong again. They didn't believe in giving up. Not in those days. They were good, tough people and they fought for what they had.

The First Day Was the Worst

As you know, there is The March Blizzard. That's what it is called—The March Blizzard, in capital letters. In the early days the settlers were more vulnerable to it than now because then there wasn't much communication—no radio, no phones, no television, no cars, trucks, four-wheel drives, no oil heating, no lots of nothing as the Chinaman said. Each farm family was at the mercy of this storm, which usually came after the first thaw and usually lasted for three days or so. Lots of snow, cold temperatures but worst of all, the high winds, and this meant blowing snow, blowing, blowing, forever blowing. So each family was a fort, so to speak.

If you know the first thaw, the bright blue winter sky fades away to streaky gray and the sharp cold has gone and there is this delicious muggy mildness that tells you spring is in the air and it's just a joy to be outside. You go outside at every chance and you want to walk the fields and see how things are, and maybe carry a gun and see if you can get a rabbit or prairie chicken for the pot. You do these things and you love the spring feeling but still, you know darn well that there probably is a March blizzard coming. To ignore this fact, of course, is wishful thinking, because these wonderful days are just the warning that winter is coming back again and probably soon.

So instead of walking around outside mooning, in the early days we got ready. We'd pack in all the extra wood we could, stuffing it all over the house, and Dad would inspect the windows and doors and if any were gaping or seemed weak then he'd strengthen them, and the storm windows were partly boarded up.

In the stable and barn, all the extra food and straw bedding is brought in and placed where you can get at it easily but the big problem, naturally, is what are you going to do about water. Water was always the number-one problem.

If the storm lasts a week perhaps, how are you going to get along without water? Well, the answer is that you can't. You need that water, so one of the older boys is given the job of hauling extra water, and I'd go along and watch and our big mare is hitched to the stone boat. Know what a stone boat is? It's a platform about four by five feet on skids and you can use it winter or summer. The stone boat will hold three barrels, and we take a bailing bucket and an axe and go down the wooded gully road to the south pasture where there is a winter spring near the old country bridge. There is an icy pool here and you've got to open it up with the axe, and when that is done the water bubbles up and runs down over the ice to the river. It doesn't take long to fill three barrels with the bucket, and back we go to the barn,and into it, and they unload the three barrels and go go back for more until 15 barrels are lined up and that should last any old blizzard.

Then everything is shipshape.

Every night before going to bed Dad stretched a rope from the front door of the house to the barn door so that if the storm came up during the night, and it usually did, then there would be a sure guide through the blinding blizzard. Because when that storm hit, everything in the world was blotted out. A Manitoba blizzard was just as bad for seeing as the worst London fog I have ever been in, and much more dangerous because when that wind is blasting down on you, there is no standing up against it without clinging to that life rope.

You could almost tell when it was coming because the morning would be dull and muggy, springlike, and then the afternoon would get darker and darker, and when it became night the wind switched from southeast to northeast and you'd see the first big flakes of snow starting to come down. Life went on indoors as usual, the lamps lit, supper served, stories and songs and the evening prayers and then off to bed. And next morning you'd look out and the world would be white, a deep blanket of snow everywhere, and the snow still coming down and you knew the blizzard had come again.

As the first day of the storm went on, the wind kept rising until it was blowing a gale and huge clouds of snow were being driven before the wind, which whirled this way and that way. By nightfall a hurricane was raging outside. Our house was built well but it would begin to creak and sway and tremble, and I remember the time my father went up to the attic where there was lumber stored, and he brought down some studs and nailed cleats on the center of the west wall in the dining room and the kitchen and also on the floor to give the whole house more stability. Those blasts were just shaking the house, and during the night we all huddled in the kitchen. We didn't go to bed because we didn't know if the house would hold together. Of course, the younger ones like me slept, but Mother and Dad kept awake to be ready if the house suddenly came apart or something, because they had to be ready to get us all out into the blizzard and into the storm cellar. But it was a good house and finally it was a fire many years after that particular blizzard that finished that good house.

The second day was much the same as the first, I guess, although the wind seemed to die down a bit. Anyway, it always seemed as if the house didn't shake as much that second day. The noise outside got less too, and inside the house we all felt better about it. Our west windows in both the kitchen and the dining room were blacked out by snowdrifts, and when we went upstairs we could see the snow had drifted so high it was over the eaves and on the roof. This was why it was so quiet in the house—because it was practically covered by one huge snowdrift.

Every day, of course, Dad would go out to the barn to feed and water the stock and usually the first day, which was the worst, he would find the water barrels frozen over and have to break them and melt the chunks of ice in the hog-scalding pot that was in the cow stable.

The first day was the worst and then the next would be less, and in about four of five or maybe even a week the storm was over. You could say that joy returned to our house, because the storm was over, we had come through it fine, and winter was gone and spring was just around the corner.

Then everybody had to pitch in and shovel snow because we had to make trails around the place, but the spring had come and every day it would melt and then freeze at night and soon the snowbanks, which were still huge, would be strong enough to bear the weight of a team and we could go to town for groceries and supplies.

Every year The March Blizzard came and every year we survived it.

Do You Know What 40 Below Is?

Even as a boy I always wanted to come to Canada. That was my idea. I used to read all the papers. The old comics. They had them in those days. Oh yes. Riding across the plains on a fiery steed. We read Butler and I believe there was a book by Warburton Pike or anyway, his journal, and Sir George Simpson and the Hudson's Bay men, their stories were published and I'd go up to the main library in old Brum and get these and read them.

Of course there was Buffalo Bill. I'm pretty sure I saw him, but if it wasn't him it was another Wild West show. There was more than one, as I remember.

Then my uncle came over. He was a first mate on a ship and we were sitting down to tea and he said, "Charlie, do you know what 40 below is?" I said no, I didn't know. He said, "Well, that's what it is in Canada." Then when my mother was out of the room he said, quietly, "Charley, in 50 below, if you pee against a tree or the side of a barn, your pee will freeze before it runs down the tree and hits the ground." Well, that shook me somewhat. That cold! Good gracious. I'm not sure I believed him but he was my uncle and a man of some consequence, and when I got to Canada I found he was right.

He said I should go to New Zealand. He said he heard they were giving the land away free. No strings attached, just sign here, Mr. Smith, and thank you for coming to our country. I never did find out if he was right, but I guess he was.

But I came to Canada and went north of Edmonton, spent

the summers on the railway or freighting, usually freighting, and the winters chopping down those damned trees and every time I had to pee I'd select a nice big tree and I'd let go and watch the pee freeze and I'd think of Uncle David and that Sunday afternoon in old Brum, but I never wondered about New Zealand. I was quite happy in Canada. No regrets. Happy I came.

5 *Golden Sheaves*

*Our First Crop . . . In Those Days They Did It
Different . . . Everybody Else Was Wiped Out . . .
We Stooked Every Acre He Had . . . A Big Man in
the District—But He Went Broke . . . A Western
Hero—the Sack Sewer . . . Now They've Got 18,000-
Dollar Tractors*

*That first crop meant everything in the world. It meant that the
wrenching tear away from the Old Country was a thing long
gone, the fearful trip to the new land now a memory. The house
might be a shack of poles and tarpaper and the barn a soddy,
but there it was—that first crop. Whether or not they had been
farmers before, it was a great day.*

*And the years went by; the district filled up. The types of
wheat improved—from Red Fife to Marquis—and prices went
up. The world wanted Canadian wheat, the best milling wheat.
It was a good time, for here was a land rich and huge and young
and eager.*

Our First Crop

When we first came to Wilcox there was nothing there but a
sign on a post by the railway which said *Wilcox* and a boxcar
where the railroad workers lived, but they weren't home and the

86

conductor said, "Well, you stay here and your car will be along in a day or two." That's how they did things in those days.

My father pitched his tent with us kids helping him and we had some cooking stuff and food because we were told in Winnipeg that this would happen.

Then our things came and my dad's younger brother hopped off the train and said, "Let's get going." My dad had left him behind to ride on the cattle car and feed our two horses and cows. We'd come from Iowa. Billy, that's my uncle Bill, the one who stayed with the horses, he had quit school to come with us and he was going to fool on his age and file on a homestead too. That didn't work out. Not because he didn't look 18 or 20 but because he couldn't prove it. I guess those land fellows weren't such fools either.

We spent our first three or four days on the prairie, just playing during the day and Dad getting things ready with Billy and studying the map and sitting around the fire at night. Planning big things. The sense of it was, there was no sense to it. We had no money; all we had in the world was in those settlers' effects; and we didn't even know where our new home was. Dad had the numbers. Where out in all that country north of there was that little peg in the ground with the numbers on it? I remember though, we were happy. Mother made a stew with the last of the meat she'd brought, and we had baked bread and pudding and coffee and Dad kept saying, "Good water makes good coffee," and he'd smack his lips and say that the country was full of sloughs full of water. "It's good land, good land."

I think now the fact that he was getting it for free and not paying so much an acre made it better land than it ever was. Also the reason was, sitting around a fire, full of good food and drinking coffee, you could see half a dozen fires around of people who would be our neighbors. My father, he always was a dreamer and he saw a whole community of white farmhouses and red barns and driveways lined with big green trees and fat cattle in the fields. This was what gave him his sense of well-being.

How could he know that Billy would run off back to Iowa before the fall came? That Jessie, the youngest, would die of pneumonia that winter and no doctor for 50, 100 miles it seemed like. That we'd live for years in a sod shack and then a tarpaper affair that wasn't any better, really, and that half our neighbors would just pack up and leave. These are all things. Like losing his best horse, a mare, a good-sized mare, in a big blizzard. You'd think a horse would have sense enough to come home. Well, Bonny didn't. And how we had a bad time, a terrible time getting just the things we thought nothing of in Iowa, like salt and baking powder and coal and wood. And even a small thing like Mother's big knitting needles being tossed accidentally into the fire one day was a tragedy. Imagine, just a pair of needles. Of course, Dad whittled her a new pair but she always complained, all that winter until spring, that they just didn't work right.

That first winter was hard. Not much snow fell; it was the wind which howled around to make it seem like an awful lot. Dad tied several ropes together and attached one end to the side of the house and the other to the little barn he'd put up of poles and a side rope to our coal pile. I was oldest, so I had to go out and do these things when Dad was away, because he worked for a while for a neighbor who was building a house. He was making a dollar a day and his food.

What if a blizzard came up? Well, it did, several times that winter, but I managed. There is absolutely nothing a person can't do if they have to. I fed our stock and watered them with melted snow, which is not a good thing to do at all, but somehow they managed and I got in the coal. I helped my mother and I looked after the two boys.

It was cold. That's what I remember about it. The water in the bucket would go hard during the night, and I remember once there was a bottle of ink. It froze solid and I had to heat it up next morning before I could do the tracings for my lessons. You couldn't see out of the windows because of the frost ferns, and when neighbors came from the railroad they'd say it was 35 or 55 below zero.

Oh, I know I'm an old woman now and all I guess I have is my memories, but I'll never forget that first spring. One morning we heard crows and then geese came over and we'd hear them at night lying there in our little house, and then there were ducks in the pond right near our house. You could almost kill them with sticks. We had some good meals of duck. They say you can get tired of duck and cleaning them is more trouble than they're worth, but I don't say so.

Then it really was spring and Dad went over to the house he'd helped build to try and buy the other horse from that man and he came back and said the man had no horse to sell. He went around to some other places but he couldn't make a deal. You see, he didn't have cash. He'd have done it for credit, like signing a note payable in the fall, but everybody was wise. My father wasn't a farmer. He'd been a carpenter in Iowa and what he was doing on a Saskatchewan farm, the good Lord only knows. Only there were hundreds like him. Today I guess you'd call them a bunch of dreamers.

There we were. And then the man in the big house sent over a note with his boy saying he'd lend Father a horse and he'd be over on Sunday with it. I must say! Things looked better after that, but when the man came he told my dad that he'd never get a crop in that year. Not even a small one. He'd have to break it and then disk it and prepare it, and it was late May by this time and there wouldn't be time because sure as God made little apples he was going to get nipped by an early frost. He said he could feel it in his bones. Dad said, "Well, what do I do?"

You do, the man said, what everybody else did around here who came late, and he told Dad to bring out his seed. Oats was the thing. There was no place to sell grain yet, no elevator, and what Dad could grow that first year wouldn't amount to more than a wagonload anyway, if that. That's what the man said and Dad stood there nodding as if he knew what he was talking about.

I'm sure you've seen pictures in your Bible of people sowing grain by hand. You take a handful and you sort of throw it out so it goes out like a fan. It's called broadcasting grain—I think they call it distributing grain too. I know it was the way the first man who planted the first fields back when man first started, that's the way he did it.

"Now," says the man, "we hitch my black with your horse

here and we'll cover this and we won't go deep. We'll just cut through the sod and down a little and lay it over this field you're going to seed. I'll do this little bit I've done and then you do the rest and then—and better be quick because I'll need that horse —you lay the sod over it."

This man did it and he showed Dad how to plow. Do you realize here was a man out on the Saskatchewan plains with a young family and he didn't actually know how to harness the horses to the plow or how to plow? This farmer showed him how. My father must have learned quick.

Dad and I spent the next day, or the next morning, sowing the grain on top of the new grass and then Dad started to plow and I must say he did well. Oh yes, he made lots of mistakes, but I think we got about four acres seeded and plowed over, just lying there black and rich on top of the ground and it looked good. The man came back on another horse, riding it. He looked it over and said Dad had done real good and he hadn't missed the horse for the few days we'd had it. But I think all those nails Dad drove on his new house in 20-below-zero weather might have had something to do with his generosity. He said we might get a crop but not to count on a good one. Naturally our little family were counting on a good one. We had to, I guess.

So that's how we planted our first crop, just like they did 2,000 years ago, when Jesus was a boy.

All summer my two brothers and I worked like Trojans in the garden while Dad built a barn for a man, a rancher, over toward there, and every morning and every night we'd look at our oats. They came up—little green shoots and then they got higher and higher and higher and in August they turned brown. Our garden was huge and Dad came home and I helped him build a root cellar and then we were told it was time to harvest. There was a store closer now and Dad went to buy a sickle, but the storekeeper told him to buy a scythe and cradle and he'd do the job quicker and better. I think then a good man could cut about two acres a day, but remember, my father was still a carpenter and this was a new tool to him. I think it took him five days. Four or five acres. It was easy for me to keep up with him tying the bundles. You tied the bundles into sheaves with straw.

How old was I? I was 12 or maybe 13.

Then one day about a month later there is this wild racket coming down the road and it is a threshing outfit. They come in and clean up our little pile of oats in half a morning, it seems like. Dad paid off their cost—and I think it was about six cents a bushel—by working on the threshing crew for a week. I think that first crop went about 80 bushels to the acre, so we had a nice pile. It wasn't enough, naturally. Dad still had to work for neighbors, but it was a start. Like my father said, it was a foot in the door.

We still only had one horse and the house was still a dreadful smelly thing, just two rooms. It leaked and the mosquitoes just were fearful, but with that big pile of oats in the shed and two pails of milk every day and that great big cellar full of turnips and potatoes and pumpkins and dried corn and dried beans— well; things looked better.

That was our first crop.

Then one day just a short time later there is a sound of a wagon coming and there's a "Hi-ymp!" and it's Billy. My father's brother. He'd come back with a load of cattle and horses all the way from Iowa, and he was home to stay. So he said. He filed on one piece next to us and bought another off the railroad next, and he said he and Dad would be partners. Where he got the money I don't know. He must have robbed a bank. Wouldn't put it past him, the cheeky beggar.

But with two men and horses and good weather right into late October the men broke up a lot of land, as far as you could see. We put up a fence around the garden and added a lean-to on our house for Billy. Did a lot of things around the place and things started to look up.

Of course, it was a long time before they had the place looking like the big places in Iowa with a wooden house and trees and a big red barn and a windmill, but it was a start.

In Those Days They Did It Different

You see, in those days they did it different. The wheat and oats weren't stooked and left out in the fields until the threshing machine came into the field. No, the wagons went out and picked up the stooks. All the stooks were taken into the yard or near and they were put into stacks so that the thresherman, always busy at that time, could drive right inside and set up his steam engine, and they'd do the threshing in one place or in as many one-places as there were stacks. So, until the threshing machine came, which could be as late as November, a fence was built around the stacks so the cattle couldn't get at them.

Now there were two ways of building a stack. One was the right way and one was the wrong way. Some farmers never learned the right way. That was to build it carefully, like building a house. Every sheaf fitted into the sheaf you put on before so they were all interlaced, and the whole thing was built up like a house even to a pointed roof. This would make it strong against the worst wind, but also it made the stack safe from heavy rain, just as if it had a wooden roof on it.

When the stacks were threshed there was a lot of straw and this, when the threshing was over, was still fenced. That was important because whether you brought a herd through the winter okay or not might depend on that straw stack. It was extra feed, of course, because hay was still the most important food for a herd. All that you needed to do when you decided to start feeding some of the threshed straw was make a road from the stable to the straw pile and start an opening through the snow and the cattle would do the rest. They'd go out each morning and feed all day and come back to the warmth of the stable. Though straw was not the most nourishing, the cattle seemed to do well on it.

But all this was long after the threshing. It was the most exciting time of the year. You see, everything that had been done for months before led up to threshing, and long before it was our time we could see the trail of black smoke from the engine against the sky on another farm and we'd rush home to tell Dad the neighbors had started to thresh.

That was when Dad would get everything ready, for it wouldn't be long before the steam engine with the separator would come clunking into our place. We had to be ready. Just had to be.

Two neighbors owned threshing machines, the Stewarts to the east of us on the river hills, and the Millers, who owned a large farm north of Oak River. Usually it was the Stewarts who did our threshing, and it was a big day when their big J. I. Case outfit moved in to our stacks. The first thing to arrive would be the caboose, the place where the hands of the Stewarts slept, and then there would be the chuckwagon where the men ate. It was a combination of a dining room and a kitchen on wheels. With a stove, cupboards, bins, dishes, water cooler, a big table, and benches. It was usually run by a woman with a girl helper.

Those women made big meals because the men worked terribly hard. Big platters of bacon and eggs, maybe four dozen fried eggs and bacon cut thick. Pancakes. Lots of maple syrup and plain syrup. Gallons of coffee. Sometimes they'd be feeding up to 20 men and they had a long day ahead of them. Working 12 hours was just child play, and sometimes if they had a farm to clean up and they could do it in that day, they might work 16 hours and nobody complained.

In the dinner time, at noon, they'd come in and there would be plates piled high with roast beef and ham and pork and potatoes and turnips and carrots, and usually there was a big thick pudding and they poured syrup on that and coffee or tea or milk if the farm had cows. At supper it was usually cold. The men were awfully tired and they'd just clump into the cook car and eat, and though it was supposed to be a lighter meal than dinner, there never was a time when I saw them leave anything. They always cleaned it up and you'd see a man walking out the door with the last two pieces of cold beef and he'd be chewing away at these. Maybe not because he was still hungry but because he just didn't like to see anything left on the plate.

Then you'd see them sitting around their bunkhouse or lying on the ground, maybe standing, and they'd be having a cigarette, although cigarettes weren't too popular then, but a cigar. A lot of them smoked pipes. Then it was time to go to bed.

That was the life of a thresherman—sleep, get up, eat, work, eat, work, eat, sleep—and they made from a dollar to two dollars a day. It all depended on your job, naturally. Some got more. A lot of them had little homesteads and that money, even though it wasn't much, helped them get through the winter. Some were farm boys from across the line, Montana and places like that. The railroad brought in harvester trains with people from the Maritimes and college boys looking for a lark. But that was a bit later. Most of the early crews were local men or fellows from south of the line.

Us kids used to get our first view of the Stewarts' separator coming early in the morning. We'd see the big monster coming down the river hill to the bridge, and that was the signal to us and we'd take off down the river path to watch the outfit cross the bridge. The neighbors had put special timbers in the bridge so it was reinforced so the engine could get across it, because the people who had put the bridge in had never built it for such a weight. Even so, the engine would have to be uncoupled and the hitch to the separator lengthened by logging chains so only one of the two heavy units would be on the bridge at one time.

If we were lucky the steam engine man would let us get up on the engine after it had got across the bridge, and we'd ride on it like heroes up to where our stacks of grain were. That was grand for us.

You see, the stacks were built in pairs, in a line, two by two, each opposite the other one, and where the separator was placed, that was called the set. A small farm would have only a few stacks so it would have only a couple of settings, but a big farm would have lots.

When the separator was in place, the wheels were in blocks and the big rubber belt would be run out and the engine would back up and get itself into place. The belt was about 100 feet long. They had this long distance so the sparks from the engine wouldn't catch fire to the stacks of grain or to the straw which had been threshed, or even to set fire to the stubble if the setting was in a field. Then they mounted the belt. That was tricky. It had to be just right, just the right amount of pressure. Then the straw wagon would come up and they'd feed the straw into the firebox to get more steam up, and the water wagon would come up and water would go into the boiler. When it was all ready the engineman would give a toot-toot. We always waited for that toot. *Toot!*

The pitchers would be up on the tall stacks and they had a tough job, for their job never ended. They fed that thresher from both sides, and they kept up a steady pace because you had to keep the machine going. That was important. Then the engineman would push in his throttle and the big belt would jiggle and throb and start to turn, and the separator man on top of his machine would give a signal, and the spike men would get all set to go on the sheaves. Dad would come alongside with his grain wagon and my brother Jim would be right behind him with his wagon to take the grain in bags where it would be taken to a safe place and kept until we could take it to Oak River and get our money for our year's work.

There was an indicator on the engine, and when it showed that the drive wheel was turning at 150 revolutions a minute the engineman would signal to the spike pitchers and away they'd go, throwing in the cap sheaf and then one after another, down would go the sheaves. Down below the band cutters, two of them, one on each, side, would cut the twine on each sheaf and throw the string away and a man called a feeder would guide the sheaves into the machine. This was earlier times because later on these three men were replaced by a self-feeder, and there were other changes too which I will tell you about later.

Soon you'd see the first bit of yellow straw coming out of the spout of the separator and you knew the threshing was really on then. Then the first drizzle of grain would start coming down the spout where the bagger was. He'd hold open these big bags and when they filled up he'd slip another in place and then tie up the first bag and pass it on where Dad would put it on the wagon to be taken to our own granary. These bags were heavy and it was hard work. In fact, everybody but the engineman and the separator man worked very hard, but they got the most pay because they were the most expert or, better still for them, they owned the outfit or had shares in it.

This went on until those two stacks were finished and then

the outfit was moved a short distance. So it went, do two long stacks and then move on until that farm was finished. Then toot-toot of the engine and move on to the next farm. This used to go on for weeks.

Progress is something they all had a lot of in those days. We shouldn't think we have a strong arm on progress. Why, most of the inventions that are important today were thought of long ago or started long ago, and men in the big plants in the States and Canada were always trying to make things quicker and easier in farming. Quicker and easier meant more money, more profits, for the farmer and the manufacturer who sold him the machines.

One big change in farming in the early days was that they stopped building stacks side by side, although some still did, of course, but they worked out a method where the sheaves were stooked in the fields. You've seen pictures of huge fields with thousands of stooks, all in long rows stretching away. Then they'd have racks with a team of horses to each, maybe five or six in a big outfit, and they would go around and pick up the sheaves, the stooks with their racks and bring them straight to the separator and pitch them down on to the self-feeder and im- provements to the machine would slice and get rid of the binder twine and that was that.

Another thing they did was put on a grain-loader attachment, which delivered the grain unbagged into the waiting wagon and you just hauled it to the granary, or they could put it directly into a granary if there was one right there. This cut out the bagger. All the killing work that went into wrestling those big bags around. Wheat is darn heavy stuff.

That was the way it was in the early days, long before the smaller separators and the gasoline and diesel tractors. This was when the day began about four o'clock. The engineman went out to the field in the dark to light his fire and start getting up steam and when he did he'd let out a bunch of toot-toots and you'd hear it and know it was time to start getting out of bed. Of course, the women in the cookhouse had been up long before that frying bacon, baking biscuits, doing all those things.

But these enginemen. They liked to get the reputation of being the first to get up steam in the morning and there would be several outfits threshing in the district. In the early-morning air, in the autumn, cold usually and still very dark, the stars out, you'd hear the toot-tooting from our place, from way over there, from up to the north and often a very faint toot-toot-toot and you knew that had to be many miles away.

It was a good time of the year. Harvest time.

Everybody Else Was Wiped Out

How did I get started? The hard way. The first year I got out here, first, I had to find a homestead. It was 1910. I came in March. Got off the train in March, and the fellow in the land titles office said all the places were taken up and he was right. But there was one. Not a full homestead, 160 acres, but 117 acres because part of it was chopped off by the big lake. Nobody had wanted it but I took it.

The first year I broke 27 acres. I had nothing, so I picked rocks for fellows all around here and at the end of the summer I had enough money to hire a fellow to break 27 acres for me, at two and a half an acre. That was doing it the hard way, but the only way I could because I had nothing. No money. I went away to work and next spring I came back and I planted wheat on those 27 acres.

Then, all along here, everybody froze on the 12th of July. Everybody except me. It was because of the lake. The warmness coming off the lake kept the air warm, and so I didn't freeze. Everybody else wiped out. You could smell the stink of rotting grain all over. My crop went 50 bushel to the acre. Number one. No dockage. It went hard [the top grade].

I didn't even have to haul it to the railroad. The municipality told me they'd pay me two dollars and 40 cents a bushel. The very top top price for seed. They would sell it to the frozen-out farmers for seed next year. One farmer got 30 bushel, another farmer 40, another farmer, a big farmer, he'd get 75 bushel. One farmer got two loads. He got 150 bushel.

That year I was able to build a good house, a barn. You could get a good house for a few hundred dollars, a good barn for about 200 dollars.

Oh, I was rich. I was in clover. In those days dollars was worth a lot. Dollars are nothing now like they were then. Dollars are like nickels now.

We Stooked Every Acre He Had

We lived in Winnipeg. A big house on Cornish Avenue. My father was an important man in business there. Land. He owned chunks of it all over the place, out Portage Avenue, Fort Garry. Where the university is now. I was not his favorite son, I'm sure of that.

He was a hard man. He believed his children should work and he saw that they did. His father had had a tough time, coming out from Collingwood, Ontario, and not doing so well in Manitoba. Farmed at Stonewall. Had a butcher shop in Selkirk. Finally settled down to working in a flour mill, and my dad said he'd never wind up like that and he didn't. By the time he was 40 he was wealthy. And he wanted his family to be like him. A hard man. Right to the end.

This was in 1911. I was 16, tall and skinny, and I guess he got tired of seeing me lounging around on the porch in the hammock or coming in from a hard afternoon's tennis, so one night at the table he told me he was going to send me out on the harvest. Not did I want to go, but I was going. He said he'd stake me to clothes, work clothes, and next morning—no, the morning after that—there was Billy Thompson with me on the C.P.R. morning train heading west. I'd talked Billy into going with me. I remember we treated it as a lark. You know, if we wanted to, we could always quit, but that wasn't how my father played the

game of life. When I opened my bag and took out my clothes
once we got settled on a farm south of Regina, there was a letter
on top of my clothes. Five dollars, in one-dollar bills, and a note
saying I was to stay until after the harvest was finished. I
thought that could mean anything. If we got on with a farmer
with a small farm that could be three weeks. Well, a big farm,
longer. But he'd underlined "stay away." He was a hard man. A
just and fair man but hard too.

We got off at Regina and a man in the station said that there
was a hiring hall for farm labor not too far away. It actually was a
big livery stable, and when we got there it was milling with
men. Talking and joking and we learned the going rate was a
dollar and a half a day and found. Farmers would come in and
they'd walk through these men and they'd touch a fellow on
the shoulder, and he'd follow the farmer and he'd touch another.
This way the farmer got his crew together. Each farmer would
take three, four. Two sometimes. Well, it went on and on.
Through the afternoon and fewer and fewer men were left, and
then there was just a handful and then, blazes to glory, there
was just Billy and myself. Now I can't say this wouldn't have
been different in any other place. All those other men were
bigger than us, and most wore their work-clothes. We were
dressed like dandies.

It became a matter of pride. Damn it all, were we going to be
the only ones in that whole barn who couldn't get hired? Well,
it certainly looked like it. I admit I was a bit ashamed. Yes, I
was. I guess I was pretty much of a lounge lizard in the eyes of
those farmers. They could spot a green one a mile away. Then
there's a wagon coming and a man calls out, "Hey, you two, hey.
You want work?" We ran over. I guess that gave us away, being
too damned eager. Yes, sure, yeah. He said, "I'm paying a dollar
and you'll work for it."

Well, we had to take it so we hopped in. He said his name was
Davidson and he farmed outside of town. We got there in the
dark and this was in the middle of July, so it was pretty late. He
had a shack. A log shack. There was one bed in it. His. A bunk.
A table. Two chairs. A shotgun and a rifle on the wall. Some
clothes of his hanging up. If you didn't leave the door open

there was no light. He had no window. He cooked us something on the stove, a kind of stew, and Billy and I poked around in it and I fished out a few broad beans and chunks of potato but that was about all I could go. He had a big cream can there and he fished out some water in a ladle. For us. He seemed to get all the nourishment he wanted just sucking his big mustache. Suck, suck, suck, I'll always remember Old Man Davidson for that. The water was warm and skunky. Slough water.

That night we went to sleep on the floor. Did I say it was a mud floor? And bugs. Crawling things. I said no sir, no sirree, and next night I slept under the stars, out with the gophers and the other animals. I didn't care what they thought of me. I was too damned tired to think of them.

Next morning. You know, there is something about a prairie dawn. Just something in the air that you can't buy in the city for a thousand-dollar bill. He fed us. Actually he could stir up a pretty fair pan of porridge. That comes from being a Scotsman, I guess. Right out of the wilds of the Highlands. Porridge, bacon and eggs, coffee and bread. It wasn't a bad breakfast, and better than we'd been led to expect from last night's performance with the stew pot. His shack was in the northwest quarter of his land, squeezed in there against the road allowance, and the rest was grain. Wheat. Waving wheat. Golden. And there was 640 acres of it. That man had one of the finest pieces of land I have ever seen, then or since, and he got about 639 acres of good wheat land out of that section.

He handed us each a three-tined fork and he said we had to stook it. How? I said. He went over to the first sheaves, not 20 feet from his door, and he showed us how all right. Pick up the first sheaf, fork through the top, and pound the base into the ground. Do that with the second. Then build your stook up, 10 or 12, built so they'd shed the rain. He threw the fork at me and went to get his horses. He was cutting with a four-horse team, all geldings which he kept in a sod stable. He was about four days' cutting ahead of us, and we never did catch up. I don't think we could have been expected to. It was devilish hard work. I would have quit a hundred times that first week but I

Throughout the world, in newspapers, magazines, pamphlets, and even on decorated wagons, Canada was publicized as the land of plenty, the last frontier. (Public Archives Canada, C 9671)

The lure of the land proved irresistible to those who had heard that Western Canada was a country of great riches. (Saskatchewan Archives Photo)

DEPARTMENT OF THE INTERIOR.

Dominion Lands--Sub-Agent's Receipt,

No. 61607

Amount, $ 10⁵⁰   *Saskatoon*   Sub-Agency *Aug 21* 19 06

RECEIVED *from* *Albert Andrew* *of* *Saskatoo* P.O.

the sum of *Ten* Dollars in payment of

homestead entry fee for *N W* Section *16* Township *33* Range *28* West *2ⁿᵈ* Meridian

NOTICE.—This payment above acknowledged is received subject for its acceptance by the Agent of Dominion Lands at _____ who will refund it if it cannot be applied to the purpose for which it was made owing to the land not being vacant and available.

Robt Mc Calvert

Sub-Agent.

A 10-dollar receipt from the land agent in Saskatchewan allowed a homesteader to begin proving up his 160 acres. (Saskatchewan Archives Photo)

In Moose Jaw, a flourishing city in 1908, homesteaders-to-be lined up by the scores at the Dominion Land Office to file on free farmland. (Saskatchewan Archives Photo)

Well dressed, well fed, ready for any hardships, two Russian families pose
aboard ship en route to their new futures in Canada. (Public Archives
Canada, C 38706. John Miller from Page Toles.)

Part of the vast immigrant flood, these Welsh Patagonians leave Liverpool
with dreams of prosperity in the Canadian West. (Public Archives
Canada, B 4588)

Families arrived by prairie schooners from the American Midwest. Many were experienced farmers, and they prospered. (Public Archives Canada, C 37957. Glenbow-Alberta Institute.)

A Barr Colonist camp near what is now the city of Saskatoon. (Public Archives Canada, PA 38667)

Many settlers preferred mule trains for hauling household goods, food, and tools across the prairies to their new homes. (Provincial Archives of Alberta, E. Brown Collection)

One symbol of the West was the soddy, often a settler's first home. Made of sod cut from the prairie, thick and sturdy, it was warm in winter and cool in summer. (Provincial Archives of Canada, E. Brown Collection)

Built of logs chinked with mud, a tiny shack such as this often served as home and hearth for years. (Provincial Archives of Alberta, E. Brown Collection)

Many Russians, Ukrainians, and other Eastern Europeans built thatched-roof homes in the new land, like the ones they had left behind. (Provincial Archives of Alberta, E. Brown Collection)

Women learned to cope with the most primitive living conditions on the prairie. (Public Archives Canada, PA 30820)

A few posters and a calendar brightened up the log walls of this settler's cabin. (Public Archives Canada, C 38696. Glenbow-Alberta Institute.)

A pint of home brew and some cards relieved the monotony of two young bachelors. (Public Archives Canada, PA 38702)

As farmers prospered, they built new homes. The Rogerson home north of Morden, Manitoba, features the new style of architecture; the original homestead squats in the rear, looking like a shed. (Public Archives Canada, PA 11445)

In new homes, the drawing room, cluttered with furniture, knickknacks, and pictures, was usually used only when visitors came to call. (Provincial Archives of Alberta, E. Brown Collection)

The first "crop" for many homesteaders was a huge pile of buffalo bones, worth about seven dollars a ton. (Saskatchewan Archives Photo)

How the West Was Won, or What the West Was All About: grain as far as the eye could see, and beyond. (Provincial Archives of Alberta, H. Pollard Collection)

knew I had to live with my father that winter and he was a hard man.

Our muscles cried. We had to help each other get moving in the morning. But then it got better. It got easier. We toughened up. I know I felt better, and day after day I'd go down those rows. Stooking is mindless work, you know. You fit into a rhythm and you just keep going and then it's dinnertime. On big farms we'd have just sat down to a big meal that the women had been working on since 10 that morning, but we had to go in and do it ourselves. Billy would leave half an hour early to get the fire going, and it didn't matter too much because it was always stew anyway. But we got the stew going better. We told old Davidson we needed better grub and he didn't bitch. Next time he went into Regina he brought out more. Plenty of meat. Tins of things. Tomatoes and peaches and peas and things like that. It was still stew but it was much better and we just ate like hogs. I've never eaten so much in all my life. I went up from 135 pounds or so to 155 and I was hard as nails. If anybody had said boo to me I'd have knocked him down. Billy and I used to wrestle after supper at night, just for the sheer hell of it. That shows you what shape we were in. Nothing to think about but work.

We stayed with old Davidson and we stooked every goddamn acre he had, and when a big windstorm came along in late August old Davidson said we'd go out and repair the damage. Not one of our stooks had toppled and that had old Davidson shaking his wooly head. We stayed until late in September with the threshing, and I knew my old man would be sending out the Mounties darn soon for us. Missing school, you see. That's bad in a Scottish family. Education is the big thing. In fact it's everything. So about September 20, I walked into the house with about 80 beautiful Canadian dollars in my pocket. Old Davidson had paid us two dollars a day for threshing.

We were lean and hard and tough as nails and happy as the day is long, and while we didn't go back the next year old Davidson had asked us back. It might have killed his black old Scottish heart, but he did invite us back.

He took us to the train in Regina and even waited on the platform with us until the train came in and then he shook our hands. He was a little man, actually, when he stood up to us on the platform, and he shook our hands and then he said, "You're both good lads."

It was like winning the medal for the 100-yard dash at the track meet. I've never forgotten old Davidson. I've often wondered, too, what he did with all his money. He must have had a granary full of it.

A Big Man in the District—But He Went Broke

My brother Wilf lived up in Neepawa but he worked our district. He came back to it because he was born there and knew everybody and I guess he figured he could get all the business. Oh, he got all the business and he'd be working well into winter. Into late November. But after three or four years of running the steam engine, he sat down and figured everything out and knew he was going more in the hole every year.

It was a lot of things. You had competition. A man with an outfit might come in to your district, and if you were doing oats for four cents a bushel he might say he'd do them for three and a half cents. Well, he might have been doing it for three and a half, but he must have had a magic formula. Maybe it was just a poor crop year and there just wasn't much to pick up. Prices low. That happened a lot. The farmer was at the mercy of the East and the world market. You might have a breakdown and maybe that would take a couple of days to get going again. Let that happen three or four times a season and you were in trouble. You needed good men too. You needed a good man on the engine and a good man on the thresher, and if you didn't have them you could be in trouble. You couldn't do it all yourself.

Then there was the harvester boys. The railroad used to bring them out from the Maritimes and Quebec and Ontario. A lot would be university lads and they'd just be on it for a lark. A dollar a day and found [room and board]. Those fellows didn't know how to work, or they didn't want to. Or if prices were so low that the farmers weren't willing to pay the going rate, then the harvesters just might walk off the job and where were you? You had to have about five or six wagons going if you were threshing in the field. From stacks by the barn was a different proposition, of course. You could make money at that. But you couldn't trust the harvest boys, but that was the only labor you could get.

Moving was another problem. Getting one of those outfits out of one farm and down the road and set up on another, well, you could do it at night but the men did have to sleep, so mostly you did it in the daytime. If you had one farm here and another five miles away, that took up a lot of time. Anyway, though, it was long, long hours. Too long it sometimes seemed.

Naturally, in each district the wheat and the oats and the barley and the flax, it didn't all ripen at once and if you were field threshing, then you were picking up and setting down all the time.

But you were a big man in the district. You owned the steam engine. The thresherman. If there was a dance some Saturday night, you bought the whisky. I've seen my brother come home after a week away because they didn't work Sunday. Sunday was for washing up and gathering your strength for the next week. He'd have rolls of bills. He carried them in a couple of socks and he'd throw them out on the table and count them and I didn't know what he was thinking then, being just a girl, but he was probably thinking how he would make his payments and would it rain next week—you couldn't work if the grain was wet. Or would his crew run out on him. Or maybe it wasn't worth it at all, being the big thresherman of the district, but I've always noticed this. There is a kind of man who always wants to be the big shot. Maybe the hotel owner in a town or the owner of the best store, and that is what he wants to do because it makes him feel the big shot. That was the way my brother felt. That pile of money on the oilcloth on that table was a shot in the arm to my brother, even though I guess he knew he wasn't going to make a go of this threshing business. And he didn't. He lasted about four years and then he was dead broke.

A Western Hero—the Sack Sewer

When it was harvest time the gangs used to come into town, and the farmers used to come in to hire their crews. I mean the farmers who had bought a big traction steam engine, maybe a Hart-Parr, and a threshing machine, and they'd go around the district threshing on custom. The going rate usually was three or three and a half cents for wheat and two, two and a half cents for oats, barley. That was a bushel, bagged and loaded. A custom crew would need at least 20 men and as many as 28 or 30, and they traveled around the district, doing each farmer in turn. If he was smart, a custom thresher tried to get his key men to come back every year, his steam engine man, his thresher man, his sack sewers, and he might pay them a bonus. But some just tried to hire in the streets and in the saloons. They'd start hiring as soon as they heard the harvesters were drifting into town.

These were all kinds of men. I can show you pictures of crews that were all young men and you see them all standing there in front of the outfit, arms crossed, hats off, and you'd think they were some championship football team. Strong and good for the rough work because harvesting was rough. Oh yes, very rough.

Then there would be crews with mostly older men. These older men might be drifters, or they just might be farmers of the district who would be working off part of their own bill by working custom. Sun-up to sundown. Dollar and a half a day, everything found, bring your own blanket. They'd thresh from first crop, and I've seen it as early as July 28 and right through to mid-November. Six inches of snow on the ground, all the geese gone south and bitterly cold. These older men, some threshing outfits liked them because they were stayers, good for the long haul. No horsing around. Just work, work, work.

Sewing men. They didn't look different. They dressed the same. Same old clothes, same hat, same boots. The only thing you could tell what they were was that they had their sewing needle stuck through their hat. Like a feather. Like a Robin Hood feather. They built up reputations. Like a race horse's performance. The first reputation was, when the grain was coming down the spout, could they keep up? Yes, if they could, then they had a reputation. Could they stay the route, the season? If they could, that was something else. It didn't matter if they drank. Drinking was done only on Saturday night and Sunday was washday, day off, so it didn't matter.

If a man could do 600 or 700 bags a day then he was a sack sewer and a valuable man, but if he could do a 1,000, 900 a day if he was needed to do it, then he was a real man. You'd call him a superman today.

I'd go and watch the sack sewer. Each outfit had two and the outfit that did our district had two, and one always came. His name was Ely. I got to know him real good. He was from the States, Idaho, and he worked on winter wheat down there until it was cleaned up and then he'd come up to Canada and work for this thresherman named Vickers. I'd go over to where the outfit was working after I did my chores in the morning, about nine o'clock, and I'd just hang around, sit on the ground out of the way and watch Ely and talk to him and he'd tell me where he'd been and what he'd done. He'd been a sailor, to Australia and Japan, and he'd worked on the Mississippi, and he could pick up a blacksmith's hammer and go to work anytime he wanted—but in the summer he always went with the custom gangs. He made more money than the others. I don't think he made all that much more, but even if it was just a quarter a day that would be enough. Quite enough. You see, it would show his superiority.

The way they worked, there was a man called a sack-jig. That's what we called him. Other parts of the country might have had different names. He would watch the sacks as the grain came out of the funnel and when each sack was just about full he'd hit a divider board and that would put the wheat into the next sack he'd got ready. Then he'd pick up the full sack and shake it, jig, jiggy-jig sort of, and that would settle the grain in the sacks. Then he'd swing it out in front of Ely or the other men. They each sat on a box or a chair and they'd go to work and they had the sack needle. It was about so long. Ely would whip the line around one end of the open sack, you see, and this double half-hitch would make an ear, a carrying hold for the sack when it was finished. And then he'd stitch across the sack with his needle, in and out, in and out, as fast as it was possible to do, maybe 10 big stitches, every one pulled tight, and then he'd fling in two more half-hitches on the other end and the trick would be done. It looked easy but you try it sometime.

Then he had to pick up that sack and carry it across to the pile or to the wagon box where it would be loaded. Those sacks of wheat would weigh easily 130 pounds and usually more, but they handled them like loaves of bread. Hour after hour. Maybe 700 or 800 in a day. What's 800 times 135 pounds? You figure it out, but whatever it comes out to, that is an awful lot of grain to handle in one day. And if they got weary at the end of a day they never showed it. Of course, I never did see them at the end of the day because I'd have to go home and get the cows, do my chores, wash up, help my mother, slop the pigs, all the things a boy had to do around the house or in the yard.

Ely was my hero. Of course, he had to go. Progress. Progress was what farming was all about in those days.

Now They've Got 18,000-Dollar Tractors

Oh, I guess the young bucks wouldn't understand. When I drive over to Kindersley or Rosetown to visit with another old-timer like myself, I see them in their 18,000-dollar tractor-combines with air-conditioning and radios, just sailing along as though nothing can stop them, and I think of the way we used to do it and it wasn't all that long ago. The world has been around a long time, so 60 years is pretty much a drop in the bucket to it, but they look at you funny when you tell them about threshing in the old days.

We'd pick up the stooks and bring them into the yard and then we'd wait and wait until the threshing outfit came along. There were a few in the district, but you have to remember that not many fellows had more than half a section, so that meant a lot of moving the outfit, setting up, threshing for a half a day, a day or so, and then moving on. Like where a fellow has 1,500 or 2,000 acres, 15 quarters, then it was only one or two quarters.

I've seen us threshing the day after Christmas with the Dooley outfit at 18 below. I've seen it into the middle of February and the district wouldn't be cleaned up and it would be 30 below, and one man would be on one stack and he'd call across to the man on the other stack and he'd say, "Hey, your nose is frozen," and the fellow would look over and yell back, "So is yours." These old-timers with what looks like bad skin on their faces, that's just from being frozen over and over again. We thought nothing of it—middle of February and 20, 30 below. Now the boys have got it cleared off before the first frost and wishing the time would get along faster so they could get at curling. They don't know anything about threshing these days. And because it was always so late and so cold, we always had to take a poor grade at the bins. It wasn't fair but that's the way it worked out. Now they've got 18,000-dollar tractors, combines, and just sail along.

6 Man and Beast

*Where Have All the Buffalo Gone? . . . "Here Lies
the Western Farm Horse" . . . Green Settlers and
Wild Broncs . . . Stubborn, Worse Than Any Mule
. . . Our Canine Postman . . . That Dog Was Brave
. . . You Couldn't Buy a Cat . . . Eulogy for the
Coyote . . . I Went Hunting Wolves . . . The Prairies
Did Not Teem with Game . . . Gophers Go Where
People Are . . . Big Rabbits, Good Eating . . . Ducks
Are Stupid Creatures . . . Prairie Chickens, Thick as
Fleas . . . Dumb Birds Make Good Dinners . . . A
Strange Custom of the Past*

*Probably there is not a pioneer living now who ever saw wild
buffalo, but many remember their whitening bones on the
prairie. Old men today can tell you the exact date the last wolf
was killed in their district—but the coyote, like death and taxes,
is still with us.*

*You can still hear, too, debates about the relative virtues of the
ox versus the horse, with the horse winning. There are also
stories about the flicky-tailed gopher that decimated crops along
the road allowance, and about the plentiful rabbits and prairie
chickens that provided many a meal for the family.*

*Yes, all these prairie creatures were cursed, tolerated, or loved
depending on their effects on the settlers. Today, they no longer
play a significant part in life on the prairies. But they are not
forgotten.*

108

Where Have All the Buffalo Gone?

The atmosphere then was much clearer than it is now, and you could stand on a little rise and look way off, far away into the distance, and in the spring the prairie would look sort of white. You know what that would be from? The bones of buffalo. The prairie would give off a whiteness from these old bones and they would be everywhere, just everywhere.

If you lived near the railroad you could sell those bones. Five or six dollars for a wagonload, I believe, and they were shipped off to Ontario for something. I just don't know what. They made something with them, but six dollars for a wagonload or a ton, whatever it was, was not very good for a 60-mile round trip. We never did it.

And buffalo wallows. My dad used to hate them. You never see them today, I don't suppose. But them days at the turn of the century they was everywhere. They were round, about so deep, about eight feet in diameter, and the buffalo rolled around in them to clean his fur of lice or ticks, and he'd gradually wear the ground down. Well, as deep as he could climb out of it. One wallow, one buffalo, although a lot of buffalo would use the same wallow. They were everywhere and they made it hard when it came to plow your land. To break your land. It caused a lot of cursing, them wallows, I can tell you.

But the buffalo, all gone when we got there. Gone for many years. I'm a bit of a historian, you know. I read a lot, anyway. What I can't figure out is how, if there were millions of buffalo, where did they all go to? A buffalo is a pretty big animal. I know some were shot for winter food and the like and for buffalo robes, but how could millions go? Just in a few years.

Those books will tell you of herds that took all day to pass a camp, tens of thousands of them. What happened to them? Did they all decide to go down to the States and get themselves killed off by those crazy Americans? Like when my dad came out here. He still expected to see buffalo but they was none. That was about 1890. But there was the bones, and for weeks they used buffalo chips for making campfires so the buffalo had been here.

So what happened? I dunno. I never read me a history book yet that even had one good explanation. Not one.

"Here Lies the Western Farm Horse"

You know, the farmer didn't have too much luck.

First, when they come out they all had these bloody small horses. Indian ponies, the ones that the Spaniards turned loose or they run away and drifted north. Then the Sioux and the Blackfoot and the Cree got on them and you never saw so much fighting and killing and hard riding in all your life as when those Indians got horses and guns. But that was long before my time. For the work they had to do in Saskatchewan and Alberta, these horses were too small. You could ride one 80 or 90 miles in a day. They'd go forever but you couldn't use them on the plow. Heavy work.

So they brought in horses from Ontario. Draft horses. Your real farm horse of them days, and some of the ranchers and some farmers, they brought in stallions from England and other parts of the world. Your Percherons, Clydes, some Shires, although they wasn't all that popular, and they started to breed. Breeding up. Breeding your real big horses to cayuses and then breeding that to Ontario stock and going on and on. They did this and by the time they got them bred up to the job, we—without a word of a lie—in the West here we had the finest work horses in the world.

And then the tractors came in and the horses were worth nothing. The tractor came in slowly at first, because they were still sort of experimenting with them. But when Ford and Rumley and a few of them other outfits got the tractors working good, then everybody wanted tractors. And the horses, worth nothing. Only poor people used horses by that time because everybody

who could afford one, why he got himself a tractor and sometimes two, and him and his son could sit up there on the seat and
do the work of one hell of a lot of horses and a lot of good men.
You know that, eh?

Tractors was good, but when they came along, you could put
up a marker and cut on it: "Here lies the western farm horse. A
good and faithful animal." It's true. Anybody who doesn't admit
it isn't just thinking right.

Green Settlers and Wild Broncs

There was two Irish brothers came to the town of Laverna,
which was opening up about 1907. The engineer of the railroad
had named the townsite for his daughter. Her name was Laverna. And these two brothers, Huntley, Steve Huntley and
Dave Huntley, they stood about six foot three and weighed
about 250 pounds apiece. They were good men to work for and
they took me on.

The settlers around there, they were coming into the country
and they needed horses and they had to buy their horses from
the ranchers down around Maple Creek. These ranchers used to
bring herds in and these horses were right off the range. Wild
and green as grass. They used to give these horses to the Hunt-
leys to break so they could sell them to the settlers—and most
of these settlers didn't know the front end of a horse from the
rear.

So you can imagine me breaking these range animals, a four-
horse spread with two old horses on the outside and a couple of
these wild ones inside, and they'd never had a strap on them.
But we'd drive them around for a while until they got the idea of
what the harness was all about.

Then we'd harness them up to the wagon itself. Alone. These
horses, mind you, they were still wild. We'd go together, three
of us, and we'd have double trip ropes on these broncos, and I'd

be hitching up the last tug and the chap who didn't have the reins would yell, "Let 'em go, Jack!"

Away they'd go and I'd grab on to the end of the wagon as she flew by, and those wild broncs were just piling it on. We'd let them run for a while, and then the one with the reins would yell, "Whoa!" and yank the trip ropes and down those two horses would go, right on their noses, right into the sod on the prairie. Well, it only took twice or three times going down on their faces that those broncs got the idea pretty firmly into their minds that "Whoa" meant stop. Those trip ropes sure did the trick. They knew what "Whoa" meant.

Then the next thing I'd hitch up the horses to a breaking plow, Steve and Dave helping me, and I'd take them out and break land, half a mile to a side, up and over, and the lather would be half an inch thick on those horses. They knew what harness and a plow was, and they were ready for sale. They were still wild as off the range now. They'd just learned a few things.

As I said, the settlers were coming in and they needed horses. Well, the ranchers had horses. If a settler was smart, he'd ask to see these horses work in harness. "Sure, sure, we'll show you," and he'd get a couple of boys to hitch up a pair of these horses that we'd broken a bit, and they'd pull a wagon around the town a bit, and the driver would yell "Whoa" and the horses would stop nicely. They didn't know the double trip was not on them. They'd turn corners fine too. The plowing had taught them that. So, as it usually happened, the poor settler would pay down his money and buy a wagon and away he'd go. Happy. He'd got a team.

I hate to think what happened to that man once he got that pair of broncs out on his homestead. Probably a lot happened. After all, those horses were still nearly as wild as they would have been off the range. They'd only been a little bit educated and not half enough for a green settler.

They was getting up to 200 dollars for those horses, and that was a very good price. A very good price. And the farmer couldn't come back at him. After all, he'd inspected the horses and seen them demonstrated and he'd bought them. Oh, it must have been tough on him.

Stubborn, Worse Than Any Mule

I never liked oxen. They were stubborn. Worse than any mule. They did pretty well what they wanted, and if they felt like pulling they'd pull, and if they felt like lying down I think you could kick them until doomsday and it wouldn't make much difference to them.

The flies bothered them a lot and where a horse would take it, endure it, and go on even though it was torment for it, the oxen were just as likely to pull off into a slough and just stand there. You could have a wagon full of goods. Didn't matter to them.

A lot of times you had to lead them. They wouldn't be driven. I remember from the time I was about 10 until I was about 14, there I was in my little sunbonnet and in my brother's overalls and boots, up and down, up and down, leading those oxen. Every summer, every fall, every spring. I wanted to go to school but I couldn't because of those oxen.

You would hear arguments though about whether horses or oxen were best. I'd say that if you ever had good horses then you'd never want oxen, no matter how good they were. Horses were good for the long haul. With oxen they kind of petered out during the heat of the day and we'd plow from five in the morning until about 10 and then from about four in the afternoon until seven or eight. The heat just got to them and they ran out of work. Not with a horse. A horse would go all day and when it was tuckered out, then it let you know because it wasn't pulling, but it would work through the day, heat, mosquitoes, flies. No, there was no doubt in our minds. It was horses, and as the country grew up you'd notice that more and more people who had used oxen were switching over to horses. But I remember seeing oxen used as late as 1920.

One thing you have to remember. Horses were a great deal more expensive than oxen. After all, an ox was nothing more than a big steer and slow as molasses in January. I could get very affectionate about our horses, but when we had oxen they were just dumb animals, steers, as far as I was concerned.

Our Canine Postman

In January of that very cold winter, one of the team of gray mares that my father owned died on us. My father hauled it out into the field and left it there. There was nothing else you could do with a dead animal.

It wasn't long before the coyotes discovered the carcass, you see, and there were sometimes two or three around gnawing at the frozen meat and making the night melodious with their howling. We didn't mind. Then one day I looked out and I saw a black animal at the carcass, eating there, and we recognized it as our cousin's black dog "Shep."

We went out and he was quite friendly and we petted him and he came back to the house with us. Then Dad got the idea of making him a collar with a pocket for a letter. It was a very, very cold winter and my cousin's place was quite a long way away, so there was no visiting because the snow was very deep. So Dad wrote a letter and put it on the collar and turned Shep loose, and soon he took off across the prairie in the direction of his home.

We watched next day and sure enough, there he was back at the frozen horse, and sure enough, there was a letter in his collar. A reply to ours. All that winter as long as the supply of horse meat kept up, we exchanged letters with our cousins. Not every day, of course, because Shep made his trips quite irregular, but quite often, Shep was a good postman that winter.

That Dog Was Brave

This happened when Mr. Lenda was away with the herd and she was alone in the cabin with just a dog. Her small children too, of course.

This cabin had a porch across the end with a window and a

door opening on to it. One night, a good moon, the ranch dog became restless and started to growl way down in his throat. She let him out and he was soon chasing wolves away from the door, and each time the wolves would let him chase them further until the dog realized he'd chased them too far and he came right back to the door. Mrs. Lenda got up and looked through the window and saw two big wolves creeping on their bellies toward the dog, one on each side. The dog was up against the door, so she opened it just a bit and the dog came in.

She kept that dog in for the next three nights, and then she figured the wolves must have been gone, so she let the dog out. Soon she heard him chasing the wolves. She heard only the dog because the wolves never made a sound.

I guess the wolves figured it was time to end this fun. They probably had other places to go than hang around the cabin. This time he chased them only once and they made up their minds and one suddenly turned on him. Well, the game was over. He slashed the jugular vein close up behind the jaw and the dog just managed to crawl back to the cabin. Mrs. Lenda found him next morning. Dead.

That was when the wolves left. They'd had their fun.

But what courage a civilized dog can have, chasing wolves away to protect his master's wife and children.

You Couldn't Buy a Cat

Do you know another thing there was a great scarcity of? Cats. Yes, cats. I don't know why. I guess nobody thought of bringing them out with them. I know they brought dogs. There were lots of dogs, but no cats.

There were mice, of course. That first winter I could look out the window of our little log shack, and I'd see one or two running on the snow. There was one that used to come right up on the windowsill and then, being mice, they got in the house.

Out on the snow they were fine, but in the house they were not fine.

I asked my husband, I said when he was going to town next with a load of wood, would he please bring me back a cat. For the mice, I said. He said he would, but when he came back he said there were no cats to be bought. Anybody who had a cat was keeping it. You couldn't buy a cat.

Immigrants who came in from the Old Country or from Europe, you could see why they wouldn't bring a cat, but people who came from Down East, Ontario, or the south, why, you'd think they'd bring a cat. But no. I guess everybody thought there would be plenty of cats in the country. But there wasn't. Oh, a cat was worth its weight in money.

Later, of course, we did get a cat or two. They'd stay in the house all winter and then in the spring they'd go outside and turn wild. You'd never see them. Wild. Then next fall back they'd come. After a while there were plenty of cats, but in the beginning you couldn't buy a cat—not unless you wanted to pay a lot of money for one.

Eulogy for the Coyote

I never had it in for coyotes. Some fellows did. There was two brothers and their cousin, and they'd spend all winter ranging from Crane Lake south over the tracks and right into the hills looking for coyotes. They were bonkers about it.

They had three hounds, and they could run down a coyote and chew him up pretty badly before the horses could get up to the kill. That's why I think there was a bounty on the critters then and the pelt wasn't worth much.

I saw them hounds work once. They chased a coyote, he was a dog coyote. Right up to a stack where I was pitching hay once onto a rick and I saw them coming aways. That coyote had some plan in mind, something to do with hiding in the stack or something, but when he saw me that changed it all, I guess. When he'd run right up to the stack he turned around and those hounds were just a-running and he sort of crouched down, snarling, his teeth showing and I guess he said to himself, "Well, I've done my running and this is the end of the road. I'll die fighting." If coyotes think that way, and I think they do. Anyway he didn't have a chance. Those three hounds hit him all at once. Piled right in on top of him, snarling and snapping, and by the time I'd slid off the stack and kicked my way into the fight, it was all over. But I sure admired that little fellow. They're not very big, you know. Most of that bigness look is all hair. Yep, I admired him.

Sometimes the boss would send me along the river scouting, just seeing where his cattle were and what they were up to. I'd take along jerky, some flour and grease and coffee and sugar and some onions if the cook had any. I liked to eat them raw. In those days they said if you ate onions raw it was good for the complexion, the face, and I had a few pimples. Like most kids. I'd be less than 20 when I worked for that ranch. I'd camp out at night beside my fire and there'd be nobody around for 20 miles each way. The whole country was open then, if you didn't count the odd homesteader who was just a nuisance. They never stuck it out. Stuck up some fence, ruined a good spring, and left a bunch of tin cans and bones and old boots lying around their soddy. But anyway, just me and the stars and my little friends, the coyotes. One would start over there. North. Yap, yap, yap-yap-yap-yap-yap. No howling and no barking. Just a sort of yap. Then over here, south, the answer, and then they'd all be talking back and forth to one another. They smelled me, the horse, the smoke, the bacon grease, I don't know, but here they were having a chat about me. Say they started at 10 o'clock. Well, at 11 sharp they'd quit. Snap, just like that. It was the funniest damn thing.

I used to have to hold my tongue. We'd all be in the saloon or the café and they'd be talking about running the coyotes down with the dogs or getting a rope around one and his partner, him getting his rope around it and then pulling it to death. That's what I said, tearing the poor creature apart. I hated that kind of talk.

I figured the coyote did more good than harm. I never saw a coyote kill a steer or a colt, and if he could go into a yard in broad daylight and snaffle off a chicken, then more power to him. That's what I thought.

Anyway, these two fellows were telling how they'd torn apart a coyote and how the poor thing was snapping at its own guts which were hanging out, biting at something because of the pain, and I said, "Ever try that with a big wolf?" That's all I said. Just that.

Later, we're riding home and the foreman, Christie, he came up alongside of me and he said, "If I were you I wouldn't make any more remarks like you did back in town." I told him I didn't know what he was talking about. He said about tackling a wolf with ropes. He said I was being sarcastic and mean with those two boys and he said, "Do that again and I might have to give you your time and that ain't even your own horse you're riding. That's the brand." He meant the ranch owned it. I said something like, what the hell, can't a guy express an opinion. And he said, "No. You got to have the right attitude to work for us and maybe you just ain't got it." Something along those lines.

Just about that time I said to hell with ranching, if that's the way they look at life. Anything I've heard or seen since hasn't changed my mind a whit.

I Went Hunting Wolves

When I got off the train I didn't know what station I was at. I just got so tired of riding on that train I got off and it happened to be Maple Creek. I was never so tired of a railroad in my life.

By the way, do you know what I call the C.P.R.? The Robber of Canada. Never in the history of the world, I'll bet you, has one company taken so much from a country and given back so little. The Robber of Canada. Think about it.

But anyway, I got off and I went over to the Commercial Hotel. I don't think it is there anymore. Most of them old buildings burned down at one time or another. But I was in the bar and standing there is a man who stunk to high heaven. An old man. Grizzled. I remember his beard was all stained dark brown with tobacco juice. I guess he drooled in his spare time. We got talking and he'd done everything, been everywhere, to hear him tell it. Steamboating on the Missouri. Killed a man with a fence post at Fort Benton. The Klondike. Worked on salmon traps in Alaska. Been to China, Hong Kong. Ranched. Owned a hotel at Regina. I remember all this because he was an interesting old fellow. And when I asked what he was now he took out a big roll of bills, and I mean a big one, and he said, "I'm a wolfer."

There were wolves in the country in those days. In Montana too, across the Medicine Line. That's what the Indians called the 49th Parallel. Why? I really don't know. Somebody said it had something to do with Sitting Bull escaping across after Custer. There were wolves all through the hills, I'd say, up to the South Saskatchewan. They weren't your big, mean, old timber wolves, but more what they called a lofer. A range wolf. Smaller than a timber wolf, I'd guess, but at least as big as a good-size collie dog, and they'd snap a dog's front leg just like that, and then go for his throat. They could do it to a couple of dogs before you could say lickety-split. Not that I've seen it happen, but I've heard it.

Now I was just a young Scottie. I'd gone to the agriculture college in Edinburgh for two years, and then my father had given me money and told me to hie myself off to the colonies. When I landed up in the creek I was 19 and raring to go. This was 1906. The summer before the bad winter.

So this old-timer he asks me if I want to go wolfing and I said I did, and we toss a few more back and go around the corner and up the street to the Chinaman's and have some bacon and eggs and he tells me how. A good horse. He told me to go see Mr. Deacon at the livery barn. Traps. He'd help me with them. Poison. That was the tricky stuff and he'd take me out tomorrow and show me how. Next day he showed me how to set traps and put poison, strychnine, pellets of the stuff, in dead meat. This was the real stuff, I thought.

He asked if he could sleep on the floor of my room at the hotel, and I asked him what about all his money and he said he feared he'd be robbed. It didn't look like a rough place to me. He snored all night, ground his teeth and ki-yied like he was riding a bucking horse. He slept and I saw the dawn come up. He was a character. He died down around Shaunavon years later. I saw him on the street once when I went down there.

Well, this isn't much of a story. I went out, new horse, pony for packing traps, 30:30 which was too light to carry for wolves anyway, but he said to buy it, and he told me to work between the track which was Maple Creek and the forks, which I'd say was 70 miles northwest. Up near where Leader is now.

I spent all summer out there. Rode hundreds of miles, slept under the stars, lived on prairie chicken and rabbit and slough ducks. I got an antelope with a very, very lucky shot once, and I tracked and trapped and worked like a dog and you know what? I never saw a single wolf. I never smelled a single wolf. I never trapped, poisoned, or shot a single wolf—and what is more, I never even heard a single wolf howl. I could have got coyotes but I thought they were worthless, so I just spent my time riding that whole country. I'd see Indians sometimes and stop at a ranch here and there, get some grub from them, and when I rode into Maple Creek in September I didn't have a single pelt. Not nary a damned one and I didn't care. You know why? I had the best life any young lad could have had, the life you read about in books, at home, in school, Scotland, and it was a wonderful country.

It got so, I didn't want to kill a wolf. I almost felt they were like me, wild and free. Let her buck, cowboy!

The Prairies Did Not Teem with Game

People today who think the prairies were filled with game, well, they are mistaken. I traveled for miles and across land as flat as this floor and you'd never see much.

Of course there were ducks. When I came there the prairie was filled with sloughs. Every depression had water and every depression had ducks, but just a few geese. There were ducks, but that's about all.

A few deer, but you'd only see one occasionally. Rabbits, but not too many. Plenty of gopher, lots of gopher. More than you could handle. You'd think with gophers there would be fox, but no fox. Sometimes you'd see a coyote or come across the den, and you might try to dig out the young ones if it was the right time of season. There was no bear. You'd see the odd herd of antelope, but old-timers said where you might see a herd of 500 a while back, now you might see only 25. Never get a shot at them at all.

Of course the buffalo, they were finished by the '80s. I never saw a live buffalo. They were the main thing on the prairies. When I got there, just the bones, lying around, the prairies white with them, as far as the eye could see, buffalo bones.

You read stories about the prairies being filled with game. Well, it just wasn't so. The buffalo, they were gone, and all that was left was gophers.

Gophers Go Where People Are

When we first started farming at Vermilion I can't remember ever seeing a gopher. There were no gophers. I didn't know what a gopher was. It was only after the settlers came in that the gophers came. I'm sure there never were any here before that.

I can tell you why. There was this lady, that bunch that came from South Dakota that came near us, she and I were walking down the trail one day and I saw this little brown perky animal just by the field and she said, she was so excited, she said, "Oh, look at that dear little gopher. That's a real South Dakota gopher."

That was the first time in my life I'd ever seen such an animal or even heard of one.

Well, you know what happened. Those dear little gophers nearly ate us out of house and home. They were everywhere. Millions. Billions. All over the prairies and everyone filling his little belly with wheat and oats. I remember they got so bad that the government put a bounty on them. For a gopher tail you got a penny. My eldest son would snare them and shoot them, and he'd get enough in the summer to buy Christmas presents in the winter. He might have 300 or 400 gopher tails. He'd take them into Lloydminster to the government in a shoe-box and collect his money, and I don't know who counted those tails, one by one, but it must have been an awful job.

One year the government in Regina had this big campaign against the gopher and my two sons got medals for killing so many gophers. I forget how many but it was an awful lot. But the more you killed, the more there were. I think the best way was to poison them with poisoned grain, but some people didn't like that because you killed birds too. Those red-winged black-birds. Such beautiful birds. They were killed along with the rest when they ate the poison set out for the gophers.

I'm sure gophers only go where people are.

Big Rabbits, Good Eating

We lived on rabbits for years and then they died. Just gone. It was a disease. A long name. I've heard it, but it was explained to me that everybody's cells are dying all the time, but just as fast the body is producing new ones to keep you going. Finally in these rabbits, the new ones stopped producing. I think I've got that right.

But those rabbits. They were millions. I believe it. We used to have them in our fields where the stacks were. These weren't your Peter Cottontail type of rabbit. A little brown fellow with big eyes and a twitching nose. The Easter bunny. These were what we called the big snowshoe rabbit. I guess it was a hare. I may be wrong but I think some of these rabbits went as high as eight pounds, and I know my father used to go out with the stone boat and the shotgun, and you'd hear banging all afternoon and he'd come back with that stone boat loaded. Maybe 150 pounds of rabbit. That might be 20 rabbits. We had one of these big pots, about two feet across. My sister and I used to call it the missionary pot because it looked like the ones in the picture books, the kind where the African natives used to boil up missionaries.

Well, we boiled up rabbits. Dad could skin a rabbit faster . . . well, almost faster than he could take a tight glove off his hand. A few cuts with the knife, whacks with the axe, whack, and zip and off it would come. I forget what he did with the skins. I think he did something. The Indians, maybe. But the rabbits went into this huge iron pot of boiling water and they cooked and boiled until they were a sort of mush. Bones, eyes, guts, meat, and everything, and when it was all a mess Dad would throw in two buckets of oats or barley and the whole thing would go for the pigs. They loved it. A pig doesn't care what he eats.

What was left we fed to the chickens and they ate it all too. Those eggs Dad sold in town when he hauled wheat, and it wasn't hard selling the chickens either because they were so fat. We didn't eat those eggs or those chickens. It was just some reason Mother had.

We did rabbits though. Mother would take a big plump one before it went into the pot and she could do more things with that meat. Roast it. Boil it. We ate hamburgers from it 50 years before I think I ever knew there was such a thing as a hamburger, like they sell in the restaurants. Stews. I think they made the best stews, with carrots and peas and potatoes and a gravy. You got it out of a bottle. A slim neck and a fat part underneath and it came from England and it made the best gravy. I haven't seen it for years.

But you could have too much rabbit. I used to throw away my sandwiches at school if my mother had put rabbit meat in them. Sometimes I could trade them.

But there were millions. Millions, all white against the snow but you could make them out. They weren't quite that snowy. They wouldn't fool a wolf or a fox or a coyote. Then they'd be gone and in a few years they'd be back again, millions of them. Now they tell me there are none left anywhere.

Ducks Are Stupid Creatures

The country was alive with ducks. They came down from the north and by the millions too. They'd decide to have a palaver in every slough, feeding, talking, telling jokes, all this sort of thing, and every day winter would get a little closer. Day-by-day thing. Even when the last crows had gone and they knew the score, there would be a slough full of big fat mallards and when there was ice around the slough, there they were. Like gypsies at an overturned food wagon. Next day, more ice. Next day, more, and slowly that ice would creep in on them until there were thousands of ducks just all jammed in that little area maybe no bigger than a city lot.

Usually we got our mallards all in one crack. It worked this way. Ducks are stupid creatures. No matter what others say, ducks are stupid. Not one of them had sense enough to say, "Hey, let's get the hell out of here."

You waited and there was always one morning when you knew winter had come. You'd get a few neighbors and your shotguns—and a lot of us had big 10-gauge shotguns in those days, real barnbusters—and we'd sneak out on the ice slowly, sneak slowly, and then we'd all jump up and yell, and you never saw anything like it.

In one huge flock, maybe thousands, they'd get up. All at once. The sky would be black with them and there would be half a dozen old 10-gauge cannons blasting right into them and there you had your winter ducks. It was a poor hunt if you couldn't get 50 or 60 each. It was like throwing a handful of wheat against a wall. Every grain that hit was a dead mallard or a wounded one. Then we'd have the rowboat and we'd push it out to the water and spend the next hour throwing dead ducks out on the ice, wringing necks, cleaning up that bit of open water. And that's the way we got our ducks for the winter.

Then somebody had to clean them, but that's another story. 'Twasn't me.

Prairie Chickens, Thick as Fleas

One day I went to the shipping office in town. Man named Cook. I got tickets. I thought I'd appease my wife. Send her to England. Her and the baby and the boy three. Next morning I put the envelope on her breakfast plate and of course she was tickled.

She said, "Well, you'll be left here with these cattle and this farm and how will you eat?" and I said I'd get by. She said for me to go out with the .22 rifle and shoot some prairie chickens and she'd fix them up for me, so I went out and I shot 46 prairie chickens around the place. They was thick as fleas, you see, and she spent all that evening and that night plucking and cooking these prairie chickens and we froze them solid and put them away and she said, "Well, at least you won't starve anyway."

From the time she left until the time she came back I ate prairie chicken, and when she got back I still had a few left. That's how thick the bastards were on the prairies in those days.

Dumb Birds Make Good Dinners

We were poor off as mice in a stone church. I worked for 50 cents a day for a neighbor, buying flour and grease and beans. Thank God we had a good stove and firewood. Neighbors would give my wife old clothes, scraps and such, and she'd dye them, making pretty colors, and make comforters and rugs and trade them in the store and get a little trading out of that.

A neighbor had this big oat field and I'd take the oldest boy with me and we'd go down to this field and there was a prairie chicken on every stook. And I'd use a three-tine fork for aiming and I'd set it up and put the old .22 on it and whang away. God, there isn't a dumber bird in creation than a prairie chicken, and any evening we'd get 15 or 20. They went a long way, roasted. Soups. Nourishing but plain fare.

Another thing was partridges which is a bird right alongside the field chicken for dumbness. They'd roost early, head under wing, in poplar trees and you just shoot away at them at the bottom one first, then the next and you'd wind up with a pile of five or six under that tree. Too dumb to fly away.

We didn't pluck them. Skinned them. You could do five or six skinning while you were plucking one.

It all made good eating though. Birds, potatoes, rutabagas, onions, scorched barley for tea. There was a trick to living in those days. You ate what you had and then you told your belly it was full and content and forgot about it.

A Strange Custom of the Past

One thing you never see anymore. Wild animals. I mean bears chained up outside restaurants or saloons. I don't really know why they were chained up because if a fellow is going to have a meal at a restaurant or have a drink in a beer parlor I can't see that having a bear on a short chain outside is going to influence him in any way, shape, or form.

But when I was a young buck, 70 years ago, there were quite a few of these desperate creatures chained, and now when I think of it I think it is the worst thing I ever heard of. But in the old days it didn't seem to be as bad.

I remember getting off the train in Calgary and walking down Eighth. This was about 1908. When I first got there. I was looking for a store to buy a pair of work boots and I went into this shoe store and there was a bear in the corner. I thought I was seeing things. But there it was, a brown bear. Brought in, I guess maybe north of Edmonton. I never saw bears around Calgary.

Wolves too. Coyotes. You'd see the poor animals in pens, chained up and usually no water in their dishes and God, you wept for them. But people didn't seem to care. Indians would dig up a den of young pups and sell them for 15 dollars to merchants. People who wanted to attract attention. Those would be wolves. I imagine coyotes would come much cheaper. I've seen red foxes too and a few badgers. Now there's a fellow you don't want to tangle with. A good big badger will take your best big dog apart with no trouble at all. Your dog when it is all over will look like he's been through the knives in a reduction plant.

The thing was their spirits, broken. Nothing worse than seeing a bear with nothing to live for. A wolf, on a short chain and some bastard may have pulled his main teeth and all you remember when you've walked away is those big, those great big yellow eyes staring at you. Insane eyes.

But as I say, you'd see these tied-up animals quite often. I've seen them in a farmyard. A bear chained to a big post in the yard. No chance of ever getting away. Now why in hell would anybody ever want to do that to a live creature? They say the wolverine is pretty bad medicine but I still wouldn't do it to one of them—not that I've ever seen one.

We've changed one way since those days. We're kinder to animals. You might say there are better laws to protect a dog against its owner now than there is to protect a wife against her husband.

7

The English...

A Bit of England on the Prairies ... The Days When
Oxen Gave Milk ... It was Terribly Hard Work ...
The Bachelors Were So Pitiful ... So They Went
Back Home ... You Can't Give an Englishman Ad-
vice ... Some Farm! Some Experiment! ... Remit-
tance Men of Kindersley ... Tadpoles in the Tea ...
Two Whores and the Englishman ... Become a
Canadian as Quick as You Can

Some came out as remittance men, youths and men of good
families who would pay money quarterly to keep their wildness
in the West. Some came out because there was a depression and
jobs were scarce. Others came for adventure, while perhaps the
majority came because they felt they could improve themselves
in the new country.

Times were hard for them. They tended to congregate in loose
colonies and stay apart from their neighbors when the best thing
they could have done was assimilate and learn correct farming
procedures. Times were hard for them. Great numbers migrated
into the towns and cities and carried on at their old trades as
bank clerks, stone masons, carpenters, surveyors. But thousands
of others stuck it out on farms and succeeded in their new-found
lifework.

128

A Bit of England on the Prairies

I think you might have laughed your head off at it. I know I still do sometimes when I think about it. About the time I visited Canada.

One morning at breakfast when my mother was opening the mail she read a letter and then she said, waving a letter, that this was from her cousin Grace who lived in Canada asking if I would like to visit them. She lived, Mother said, on the western plains near a place called Swift Current. Well, we very well know where Swift Current is today, but in those days it could have been a place on the moon.

For some reason I said yes. I didn't say yes right out loud, but I sort of accepted it in my mind. But I wanted to think it over. My fiancé had been killed in the South African War, which had ended just a couple of years before, and I was restless. He wasn't actually killed; he drowned while swimming on a beach while he and some other officers from his regiment were on leave. Anyway, as a young girl will, I was quite crushed. Still was, three years later. I think we all took things like that so much harder in those days. Love was to be forever, to be eternal, and that sort of thing. When I think of today's young people . . .

Well, a week went by, let's say, and I brought the subject up to Mother and said yes, I'd like to go. I'd driven over to our library and asked for the map of the western plains, as we called them, but there was nothing on them to give an inkling, the slightest, as to where this Swift Current might be. Then the librarian gave me Captain Butler's book, which was popular in those days. I spent two hours or so in the ladies' reading room going through it and there was nothing of Swift Current in it. Of course, we know that Swift Current didn't come along until 25 years after Captain Butler's journey, but then, how was I to know? But everything sounded so exciting.

Anyway, I wrote cousin Grace saying I would like to come and, rather timidly I must say, asking about their ranch and the country and what balls and galas they had. Just the things a girl of 22 would ask. Right smart, within a month I'm sure, a letter came back. Come, come, and she told about the country, how it was ranching and prairie, as if I really knew what prairie meant. If she had said prairies were something like moors I might have understood a little better. She said they dressed and life was carried on in our English style and that they had a big house and so on, but I noticed, or I remembered later, that she didn't mention any galas or teas or balls. But she did say that if they could find a safe horse for me that I might go hunting with cousin Harry for coyotes. He had, it seemed, a couple of grey-hounds and he went after coyotes. We all know now what coyotes are and I'm fond of them, but I didn't know then. I rather imagined them to be something like foxes, but of course they turned out to be small wolves.

So I went, trunks and bags and hatboxes, to Liverpool, to Quebec, aboard a train where one got lovely and well-served meals and watched this vast, this terribly lonely country go by the window. When you went to bed at night it was there and it was still there when you opened your eyes. But it was all a new experience.

Cousin Harry met me at Swift Current. There was a station, a water tank, I remember, some corrals, a town of sorts and that was about all. But I was so tired of that train, it moved so slowly, that I would have welcomed a stop in the Gobi Desert. Cousin Harry, whom I'd just met once, at their wedding, and I was a child, he had the back of this vehicle piled high with groceries and packages, and the first thing he said when we went on the road to the north was that if I was in their new country I must learn to use the proper speech and what we were riding in was not a surrey but a democrat. He said it was an American buggy. What did I care? Hah!

We drove and drove and drove and if I'm not mistaken the train had got in about six o'clock in the morning and it was about noon before we got to their ranch. Their farm. What shall I call it? Well, it wasn't Fairview Farm like we had in the Old Country. In the first place, there wasn't a tree in sight. Some willows along a kind of creek but that was about all. There was a barn made of sods and a pigpen and a chicken house and corrals and other buildings around and what I now know to be a typical western layout. But in those days it looked very forbidding. I remember how dry and light the air was and how far you could see, miles and miles and miles.

Cousin Grace greeted me and I must say, old Harry had done right by her with the house. It was two stories of frame construction, but it was bigger than any house I'd seen on the drive from the town and besides, it was painted. It was painted white and it looked very nice and cousin Grace was very nice, very gracious, and she said that day I would just rest and not do much. I was glad to do that, believe me. My bones ached, every last one of them. Besides, cousin Harry had hired a wagon in the town to bring out my trunks and we'd left it far, far behind. I believe that it was pulled by oxen and you know oxen. Slow, dead slow. Two miles an hour if they feel like it.

Cousin Grace had a maid she had hired out from England. I think she paid her three pounds a month, which was about 15 dollars in our money then, which was good, I thought. She also had an Indian girl about 14 that she was training. She had an Indian name but she was called Elsie. The priests at Regina had sent her along.

They had a good table, I must say. Beef. Always lots of game. Good bread and scones and pastries and lots of butter and delicious berries that grew wild. You know, saskatoons and the like. It was the first time I'd ever seen them. Or blueberries for that matter. And wild plums. Plenty, oh plenty of good vegetables.

And the thing was, out there on the bald prairies, these two lived like they were in the heart of Dorset. Everything was done just so. Linen, cutlery, candles, times to do this, times to do that. When I look back on it I think that if they had put their time and energy into honest labor of being Canadians and pioneers they would have lasted longer.

What cousin Harry did, I don't know. He was up and gone before we got up, riding the range or going to town or chasing those coyotes with his damned dogs all the time. When cousin Grace and I got up, we naturally dressed in morning dresses. Then breakfast in the big room. No mail to open, no newspapers to read. No gossip. Goodness, their nearest neighbor was six or seven miles away, across two creeks, a gulley, a coulee, and a ravine away. Don't think the prairie is flat. Not in that country. Like the lines in an old man's face. So there we were, two English creatures in a fine house with our eggs, our scones, our curled butter, and our India tea. My dear, it was ludicrous.

Then, at 11 every morning we'd each go into our rooms and we'd change. Perfectly all right if you were in England and being driven to town for some shopping. But on a prairie farm? Oh! Oh! Change into a nice street suit, an outfit quite proper for going into the town and visiting, and then we'd sit on the porch and talk some more about nothing, and the maid would bring us some tea and biscuits and, as I recall, the next big decision would be where to walk. Would we walk west or east? Or would it be north or south? The road ran north and south and it was easier walking so we would go that way usually, but we never stopped to talk to anyone who might be coming along because my cousin never, no, but never, ever talked to her neighbors.

I asked her once and she said, "Oh, they are not the sort of people you talk to. We don't actually have anything in common. You wouldn't like them, I'm afraid. So I just nod to them and they pass by. It's better that way."

That's the gist of it. That's why there were no balls or galas, although in the country at the schoolhouse, which was about six miles away, there was a dance quite often. I know because the maid and Elsie used to get taken to them by the cowboys. Not rough cowboys actually, either. Some were English lads who had come out for fortune or adventure. I think my cousin had four cowboys and two were Englishmen. But, oh no, I wasn't allowed to talk to them. If they'd been wearing Christie stiffs and spats I suppose it would have been all right.

Anyway, we'd walk out over the prairie and then we'd walk back. Then it would be time for a nap or a bit of sewing in our rooms and at four o'clock, I would change into a tea gown. We'd meet in the big room and cousin Harry would come in, "By Georging" it and "By Joving" it all over the place, and he might bring us a bit of gossip and things might get a little livelier and we'd have tea. I poured.

Teatime past, dinner was served at eight. Dinner at eight. Wasn't there a play by that name once? We dressed formally. Yes, I'd put on a formal gown and all we didn't have was a butler and footmen and a three-string orchestra playing through the curtains. Oh, it was ludicrous.

These Englishmen! Why couldn't they forget all that non-sense? It never made the slightest bit of sense, you know. They had neighbors but no friends. They couldn't have friends be-cause they had this silly notion that because they were English-men they somehow owned the earth. Their conversation made no sense. They had come from Bath. Now Bath is a rather social town, as I'm sure you'll agree if you've ever read any Victorian literature. Always the mention of the season in Bath. Well, they talked about dances and parties they had been to, as if they had occurred the night before or the week before, and actually they had all happened five or six or 10 years ago.

And as Mr. Pepys used to say, "And so to bed."

I used to sit at my window and look off to the south and there was a light there. Six or seven miles away but you could see in-credible distances in those days, and here was this light, just a tiny light, but it meant there were people out there, laughing and maybe singing and enjoying themselves, and I wouldn't have minded if they had come out of the Glasgow slums. I would have liked to have gone over and seen them. I would have walked all the way. But it couldn't be done. I was a guest and in your host's home you act as the host. When in Rome . . .

The upshot of it all was, I finally took the train back to Winni-peg. I told them thank you very much for the visit, I enjoyed it, la de dah dah dah, you know how it is, and I went to Winnipeg and I got a job there. In the library, there, you know. Right downtown, by the city hall. The pay wasn't anything but I enjoyed myself. I really did. Despite the Sommers and their ridiculous ways I had come to enjoy this country and in not too long a time I met a man, Will, the man who was to become my husband.

He had a farm at St. Francis and he was in the city to attend some political convention. A delegate. Politics was rather rough-and-tumble in those days and Will enjoyed it. We met at a friend's house on Scotia Street and he took me home, and as time passed we saw more and more of each other. Then my friend and I went to stay on his farm for a week during our holidays and, bingo, as they say, we tied the knot.

A year or so later we came to Alberta. Will said that Alberta was filling up with independent people, people who had had enough of the stupidity and foolishness of the old ways and who were not going to take any more of the economic nonsense that was being fed them in other places, and he wanted to be a part of it, the new land, and so we came to Alberta.

And my cousins on their ranch—or should I call it a rawnch? —they went belly up the next year. Not even their toes wiggled.

The Days When Oxen Gave Milk

I remember my dad telling a story and my, he'd laugh every time he told it but it was about this couple who came out from England and they were in Regina or someplace, but I think it was Regina and they were buying their outfit. Horses, cattle, furniture, food, all the things they needed to go out on the prairie with that fall and starve.

I guess he was one of these guys who always consulted his wife on what to do. Should we do this, dear? Should we do that? What they both knew about farming you could probably put in a teacup. Probably came from the chimney pots of Lancashire.

Anyway, as my dad would put it, they came to buying a team to haul their wagon and do their breaking and it was a choice of getting a team of horses or oxen and he asks his wife what it will be and she says, "Oh, I think you had better take the oxen. The milk will be so good for the children."

It Was Terribly Hard Work

Leicester. That's where I came from. Never even had seen London. Sixteen, just between that and 17. The war was over, the South African affair, and all the veterans and no jobs nowhere and everybody was coming to Canada. That was the place to go, everybody figured. So I come out and worked for 10 dollars a month for some bloody old farmer from five in the morning until nine at night.

I'll tell you how bad it was. From the time you blew out the lamp chimney until you lighted it next morning to go to work the glass didn't have time to cool down.

That was at Rapid City. Farmer named Landley. I was a farmer's boy. My first job. There wasn't any welfare office to run to in those days and I only had 20 dollars in my pocket and 5,000 miles from home. So you did some quick thinking and decided that no matter how bad things were you stayed with the job you had.

I got the job through a bloody sky pilot by the name of Weekes. He dealt in mugs like me, needing work so shipping them off to Canada. He'd put advertisements in English papers, you see, and say that he would get jobs for young Englishmen in Canada. You would work on the farm and learn farming in one year and then you could start your own farm. So I wrote and an awful lot of others wrote and he wrote back, a letter all full of big promises about good wages and all that. Most of it was lies.

You see, this Weekes fellow and I guess others like him, they put ads in Manitoba and Saskatchewan papers too and they'd say they could provide good workers, young Englishmen, for farms. So the farmer would send Weekes some money and I never found out how much but he was damn glad to get a husky young man for 10 dollars a month when the going rate was 30 dollars. Then Weekes would take 15 dollars off of me. That's what I paid him. He'd also get a rake-off from the steamship company that took us across. When I sailed on the *Tunisian*, the ship, it was jammed with people going to Canada, the West, and down in steerage where they put us there were an awful lot of chaps going to Manitoba and Saskatchewan to learn farming and get 10 dollars a month. A lot of fellows who'd never seen a farm, a lot of lads from the South African War. So this preacher was getting money from three places and making a fortune.

It was the same set-up as that Barr fellow who started the colony at Lloydminster although Weekes just dealt in young men. Barr hooked in whole families and skinned them clean. They was both preachers, Weekes and Barr.

Well, when I got to Rapid City I saw the set-up. I was a slave. That's all you could call us. I stuck it for four months and then I quit and in that time I learned nothing about being a farmer except that a farmer has to work awfully hard. At work at five in the morning, quit at nine at night If it was a rainy day and you couldn't get out in the fields he had a dozen jobs for you to do, hauling manure out of the barn. When he went to town on Saturday afternoon he left enough work that would take a man three Saturdays to do. No such thing as rest.

Landley was a mean, rough old scissors-bill, let me tell you. Those were pretty crude old buggers. Cheap labor it was. No better than slaves. A man doesn't mind working but they worked you until you dropped.

So we had a row and I quit and went to work in a store in Minnedosa. That was easy and I stayed six months, then I went into Winnipeg and I heard they were looking for men at Lac Du Bonnet, on a dam. So it was winter by then and I hiked seven miles down the lake and 14 miles through the bush, and I came to the place they were building the dam. The foreman said, "You don't look tough enough to work on the rock pile." You see, the only place they needed men was on the rock pile it was so tough. I was only 17 and I said I'd try it.

I got to work and I could handle it. It was terribly hard work, that it was, but they treated you like a human being and paid 17 and a half cents an hour. That was five times better than 10 dollars a month, working 14 hours a day and it was fine with me. See, an Englishman wasn't afraid to work. When I finished I was making three dollars a day and that was good. Canada looked like a pretty good place to me.

The Bachelors Were So Pitiful

Our district west and north of Kindersley, it was full of bachelors. The homesteaders. Englishmen. Perfect gentlemen, almost every one of them, but my goodness, what a life they had.

Oh, it was dreary. It was pitiful. The poor fellows, they lived on jam and graham crackers, pancakes. They didn't know what to buy to eat and they didn't know how to cook it if they had it and in the end run, they didn't have the money to buy nice things anyway.

There would be a family here and a family there and in between would be a lot of these English bachelors, half a dozen of them, and I think they'd all get together some time in the week to decide what home of a family they'd visit on Sunday night. To get a home-cooked meal, some decent food. My mother used to bake wonderful bread from our own wheat and she'd give them each a loaf of bread and they'd go home happy as a lark.

You see, the homesteading regulations said they had to live on the quarter six months of the year. So the fellows who lived in eastern Canada, Ontario, or had come up from the States, when summer came they could head back to where they had come from and get work, work for five months and a bit, and come back to spend their six months' winter in their shacks and with the money they could pay some neighbor, like my father, to break up the acres they had to break each year. And, of course, they always had enough money left over from working in the summer to get them through the fall and winter. But not the English boys. They were too far from home. Half of them didn't know how to work anyway.

They had been told in England, through the propaganda, that in Saskatchewan and Alberta, you just had to come out, stay on your quarter for six months for three years and then sell it for a fortune. It just didn't work out that way. A lot of them would have liked to go back home but do you know, they just did not even have enough money to pay their passage. They were stuck out here.

No, it was a grim life for them. Oh yes, a lot did prove up the land and some of them are still there but it was very, very hard on them.

They would come to my father. Of course, he was a good farmer. They would borrow a team and they wouldn't even know how to harness it. They'd say, "What will I do now?" or "What do you think I should do?" You know, there are certain things you just automatically do on a farm if you're going to farm it and take off a crop, but they knew nothing. They didn't even know enough to pick rocks off the land they'd got broken. Things like that.

I remember our first Christmas on the prairie and we had two bachelor brothers in for dinner. There were no turkeys on the prairies at that time. Roasted chickens. But all the trimmings.

We had a big dinner and there were popcorn balls and home-made candy and it was a happy, noisy day and we were happy and the Englishmen were happy just to get out of that awful cold little shack they lived in. I'm sure they were very lonely and frightened by that vast cold country they were in. One of them brought me a tin of English biscuits that his people in the Old Country had sent him for Christmas. They were a distinct luxury to us.

One of them had a beautiful voice. He provided the entertainment. Without accompaniment. He sang "Land of Hope and Glory" so beautifully that I cried. It was though he was singing it just for us and out of the prairie, and then another song he sang was "Off to Philadelphia in the Morning."

They stayed late but finally they had to go and I know they hated leaving our warm house, going off to their old cold shack and probably nothing to eat but crackers and syrup or jam.

I used to feel so sorry for those boys.

They were so pitiful. My mother, she worried over them and she babied them and they came to her with all their troubles. They talked about home to her and she'd give them tea and biscuits and they'd sit and talk with her.

When the war came a lot of them joined up. Just to get out of there. A lot of them never came back either.

So They Went Back Home

It was too hard for many. You see, most of the people in our district were from England. They weren't farmers. They didn't know the first thing about farming. They were, I guess you could call them, useless Englishmen. They just couldn't take it. They'd stay a year or two, sometimes three, until they got their land proven up and the money they got selling it, that might take them down to Edmonton and back home again. Canada was never home. Home was always England. So they went back home.

There were trails between every homestead. You just couldn't get through most of the bush without trails, it was that thick. Oh, you could walk it, yes, but try and take a round-bellied horse through the bush and you would go pretty slowly. So you'd cut these trails. House to house. I remember once my mother handing me a bottle and telling me to go to Ramsdens and borrow some vinegar. She needed it for cooking or cleaning, I think. So I went down the trail and when I got there the Ramsdens were gone. Just left in the night, and they were our good neighbors. Just gave up. Couldn't take this country any more. It wasn't until we went to the post office next week that we found what happened. Yes, they'd just left. Mr. Ramsden told the postmaster he'd sell his team and wagon and the few things they'd piled in it, sell them in Edmonton. Might get them as far as England and home.

You Can't Give an Englishman Advice

I can remember about 1905. I'd come back to Winnipeg and spend a few days just going around to the hotels, the bars, and having a great old time because I'd been on the road for three months I'd meet the immigrants who'd be waiting around for their goods to catch up with them or they were just waiting for the little birdie in their ear to tell them to go.

I never saw a bunch of jaspers so full of questions. Of course, being only 20 I liked to play the big shot. Here I was traveling on the road, hitting half the towns, and so I knew something about the West.

Why, people would ask me about the Indian rebellion. The first time a Limey asked me I had to think and then I asked him what rebellion? It turned out he was talking about Louis Riel. They wanted to know if the Indians were still savages. Nothing savage about our Indians. If you ever wanted to see a beaten-down lot just look at our Indians and I told 'em so. I told 'em the Northwest Rebellion was 20 years ago and I didn't think more than 60 or 70 persons had been killed in it anyway. My father had been in the Winnipeg Light Infantry in that thing and he always said it was a farce. Anyway, I think these Englishmen wanted to think the Indians were wild and wooly.

I'd ask them where they were going and they'd say some place like Swift Current or Maple Creek. I'd tell them they were crazy. I'd say you won't do much farming at Maple Creek. That's ranching country, I would say. If you've got 20,000 acres you might do okay. Or why Swift Current? It never rains there, and the winters are so cold they'd freeze the nuts off a brass monkey.

I'd think I'd be giving them good advice but you never can to an Englishman. I remember one saying to me, "Oh, it shawn't be cold where I am." The poor damn fool. Thinking he could tell a prairie winter what to do.

I'd tell them that between Winnipeg and Regina there was still plenty of good land. You know, the road was through from Saskatoon to Edmonton by that time and the railroad was going through even then and there must have been millions of acres with grass and water and plenty of wood, all they could ever use in a lifetime. But no. Maple Creek. Medicine Hat. All along that line, so bare that you could see an antelope's ass bobbing away five miles away. But always the fellow would wind up saying something like: "Oh, but I've got a letter from cousin Bertie and he says it is perfect country." I'd hear that over and over.

So, here were these dumb Englishmen. You couldn't tell them a thing. I know, I know, I was only 20 but I'd been on the road for two years by that time, and maybe a shaver of 20 doesn't know as much as dear old cousin Bertie, but I know they were passing by millions of acres of fine land, good deep prairie loam, for land that was semi-desert. That was the too bad of it. The too bad of it.

Some Farm! Some Experiment!

Remittance men? Sure, I remember them. There were quite a few of them. There was a place a few miles east of town where a fellow had set up what he called an experimental farm. It was just an ordinary homestead but the fellows that come to it didn't know what it was.

This fellow from England, named Hanson, he came out and filed on a quarter, and he got this idea of bringing out Englishmen and teaching them how to farm. As far as I could see, he didn't know much about farming himself but he advertised in London papers, putting in an ad saying he was a successful farmer in Alberta and he would pass on his secrets to young Englishmen.

It was a racket. Come to Canada and learn farming and some father who had a son who was raising hell in Merry Old England would say, "Hmmm, for 30 or 40 dollars a month I can get this fellow off my hands." And he'd do it. And the son, well, it was okay with him. He was going to the Wild West. The Wild West was big in those days, everybody who wasn't here thinking all we did all day was ride horses, shoot buffalo, and fight Indians. So they came. Of course, some of them weren't remittance men but just ordinary English boys.

Hanson built a house of 21 rooms for the Englishmen to live in and another house beside that for him to live in. It was a sight, yes a sight you wouldn't believe, to see him plowing a field and

15 or 20 young Englishmen following him around like a lot of fools watching him. Then one of them would be given the reins and he'd plow a bit and then another would take over and then another. This would go on all day, this whole gang of fellows following this plow and it was just the darndest sight you ever laid eyes on, let me tell you.

When it came down to actual working, well, you can imagine. Say 20 men on one farm with just so much to do and Hanson only had 160 acres, so most of the time everybody just stood around watching one person work. Twenty men watching Hanson milk a cow, 20 men watching Hanson showing them how to hoe potatoes.

Why, the only person who actually worked on that farm was my oldest sister, who would go over once a week and do the men's laundry. She worked about 12 hours, using the old scrub board, you know and Hanson paid her a dollar. He certainly wasn't spreading his money around.

Finally these fellows would get sick and tired of Hanson and his farming school and figured out they were learning nothing and they'd get out on their own. Some would file on their own homesteads or go to work for somebody else where they'd really learn what farming was all about, or they'd go to work on a ranch. Some, I guess, went into Calgary or Lethbridge and some, of course, went back home. When the Great War came along an awful lot of these fellows hightailed it back for home to join up and I don't think any of them came back. My guess is that they all died in France.

But when things got low for this fellow Hanson, with his students leaving him, another bunch would always show up and for years he had a pretty good racket going for him. But for all they learned about actually running a farm, why, I think they'd have learned as much chasing gophers.

When all was said and done, this Hanson fellow was probably doing Canada a favor. Yes, I know what he was running was a racket, but in the long run he was responsible for bringing a lot of awfully nice fellows to Canada. These remittance men weren't as bad as some folks made out. Some liked to raise a bit of hell in town but more often than not, a lot more often than not, they were just good fellows and those that stayed around, why, they became good farmers. A lot of them made out awfully good in the long run.

Maybe it was just Hanson we were jealous of. Here he was living high, wide, and handsome and taking them young Englishmen's money and having a big old laugh at the rest of us working our backsides through our overalls.

Remittance Men of Kindersley

Just about this time I was cooking for four remittance men near Kindersley. About 30 miles from there.

I tell you they were quite a crew. They weren't wanted at home, in England. Paid to stay in Canada. They had been Oxford and Cambridge men.

Oh my, let me tell you we lived high. Peaches and cream for breakfast. We never wanted for nothing. Anything I asked for for cooking they'd get. They paid me 25 dollars a month and that was all I wanted. I was living just like a king, nothing to spend it on, and I was high, wide, and fancy free and if I wanted a drink why I'd just take one. The bottles of whisky just came in a steady flow from Kindersley.

The way they worked it, my remittance would run out but yours would be coming in, and when yours was gone then the other fellow's check would come in. It worked out fine. They never ran out of money.

Oh, they had homesteads but that's . . . they never did work on them. Nothing. All they ever did was go out in the bush and bring in poles and set them up as steeplechase. They all had real good horses and they'd spend a lot of time jumping. Riding. They rode to foxes. Except their foxes were coyote, chasing them across the hills.

This Chris Murr. He decided he was going to go back to the Old Country for Christmas. Well, he went back and he said he'd be gone three or four months. Well, before the end of January he was back in the shack.

"Well, what happened, Chris? How come you're back so soon?" somebody said.

"Well," he said, "I'll tell you. We're sitting at breakfast one morning and I turned my head to say something to my sister sitting next to me just at the time a maid put a cup of coffee between us and my head hit the coffee and spilled all over her and I yelled out: 'Jesus Christ!' Well, my mother fainted and my father jumped out of his chair and he ordered me out of the house and when I went back to get my things they ordered me never to come back again. And I got an increase in my remittance."

Yes, they lived good. They all had big remittances and they weren't afraid to spend it. I'll tell you what they did once. I had a mouth organ and I was sitting outside the shack once, playing away on the old thing, and one of these fellows came out and he said, "For God's sakes, throw that bally thing away." I said something about it's nice to have music around the place, and you know what they did? They all piled into the wagon and they went to Kindersley and they were gone about a week. When they came back, do you know what they had in the wagon? A player piano and a big box of rolls.

But they never had to earn a living. Their folks just sent them money to stay away. They didn't farm, they didn't do a thing but drink and ride their horses and eat my good food. They were fine fellows.

Tadpoles in the Tea

My father always wanted to go to Canada. Ever since he was a boy. It was his dream. He'd had a lot of bilious attacks and the doctor said to him one day, "You know, if you went to Canada you'd find that you'd be a lot better." Well, he didn't need any coaxing and soon after that he picked up one of these pamphlets about the Barr Colony coming over. So my mother and father went to London and interviewed the Reverend Barr, who was organizing the big colony, and decided they'd come.

During their first summer on the prairie, when my father would be away for some reason and we were living in a tent, my mother and us children, she'd hear the coyotes howling about and she said it always reminded her of that trip to London. They saw the Buffalo Bill Wild West Show and it was all about the West, Indians, and wolves howling.

There is divided opinion on whether Mr. Barr was honest. I know that the settlers hated him and how badly he had organized the colony. You know, I think it was 1,500 who came out on the boat. I know we paid Mr. Barr for new army tents and the ones he gave us were old ones and they leaked like riddles. We didn't get as many McIntosh blankets, rubber groundsheets, as we paid for.

The boat trip? It was the *Lake Manitoba*. I remember they fed us ling cod at almost every meal and not one of us have ever eaten any ling fish since. The food wasn't anything too good. An awful lot of people were sick. The *Lake Manitoba* was an old army boat and there was no ballast, only our luggage, and the captain told us when we got to Saint John that all the way over his heart was in his mouth because had we hit a bad storm we would have keeled over.

When we got to Saskatoon our trunks and boxes, that luggage which had been in the hold, hadn't arrived with us. It didn't arrive for some time and then we found that water had leaked into the hold of the ship and all the contents were damaged. Mildewed badly, stained with other colors. I remember a parasol my mother had packed, a lovely thing of shot silk, mauve, and when we finally unpacked it it was stained black.

Saskatoon was just a straggling village, and of course a lot of people brought money out. My father didn't. He was just a postman outside of London and he had to borrow the money to bring us out. But there were a lot of educated people and moneyed people and the people of Saskatoon soaked us right and left. The price of horses went sky-high, oxen too and wagons, plows, everything you needed. And food, of course. It was all so high that a person, a family with just a little money, was in a very hard way. They took advantage of us.

We had to buy cayuses that they'd driven up from the south. These were half-wild range horses and we were expected to drive across open country, practically untouched prairie for 200 miles, with these wild things hitched to our wagons. Luckily my father got two that weren't bad but some people had terrible troubles.

A lot of people had oxen and they had trouble with them. First they were slow. We could go 20 miles a day and it took us two weeks to get to the colony but the oxen people took a lot longer. It was in spring, see, and evidently there had been a lot of snow and the creeks were full and these oxen wouldn't cross. They'd just get down on their knees and nothing would make them cross. So the men would make a raft or there would be a raft there and they'd have to unload the wagon and raft it across and then carry the women and children across. And then the silly oxen would get up and pull the wagon across. Oh my. Goodness.

They had a very good system. The federal government had set up marquees every 20 miles and there was a big pile of straw there and lumber and they'd told us in England to bring empty mattress cases and we'd fill the mattress cases with straw and then put them on the lumber which we put on the ground and then we put the rubber sheets down, then the mattresses and our blankets and we slept well. We slept in our own tent but those that hadn't got even the old leaky bell tents they could sleep in the marquee. Then in the morning we'd put the straw back on the pile and away we'd go. A very good idea.

I think the first night on the trail was the worst for my mother. My father was always enthused, but this time Mother wasn't so sure it was such a good idea coming to Canada. We'd stopped and Dad went down to the slough and filled up the kettle and put it on the fire. Mother made us a good meal on the little tin stove we had bought, and then she made a big pot of tea. It seemed like a good time. Then she poured the tea into our nice cups she'd brought over and the cup was full of tea and tiny dead pollywogs. Tadpoles. Of course there was no tea that night. Mother was pretty discouraged. From then on Dad dug a hole beside the slough and the water seeped in and it was clean and good. No pollution in those days, except tadpoles.

On the ship the men had picked out the homesteads from a big map that Mr. Barr had so everybody knew where they were located. But in the lectures about Canada they gave the settlers on the ship they did a very stupid thing. I can't think today why anybody ever did it but they said that four men should get together and amalgamate. That was the word they used, "amalgamate." It meant four men would get together and take homesteads together and make up a section. This would mean they could pool their labor and help each other, but it also meant that they would pool their money. That was the stupidest thing of all. Whoever thought that up doesn't know anything about human nature. In the foursome that Dad went into, one man's name was Drabble and the other Simpson and I can't think of the fourth.

Dad and Simpson and Drabble went out to their section south of the colony place and the fourth man's wife was sick in Saskatoon, so Dad figured it would be best to build his house first, a sod shack, so she would have a place to recuperate. She was coming with other people soon. So Dad and the others started that shack.

They worked that day and then the other two said they would go back to Saskatoon to get the rest of the goods we'd all shipped to Saskatoon and didn't get. They didn't leave right then. When we got up the next morning they were gone, taking their wagons and horses and also Dad's wagon and horses. But they also took the plow we had bought and all the other things we'd bought in Saskatoon to go farming with.

Do you know, my father never saw those two men again. They just disappeared. Gone. We had no horses, we had no wagon, we had no plow or other things to farm with. Dad had hardly any money left and we were miles from the settlement, 200 miles from the railway, thousands of miles from our lovely home in England, out on the Canadian prairie.

That's what amalgamation did. It wiped my father out before he even got started and remember, the money that he'd invested, it wasn't his money. It was debt money. He'd borrowed it. He had to pay it all back.

I think that was when Father decided to abandon the homestead he'd picked out because it was too far from where the town was going to be and so he went in to see Mr. Riddington. He was the government man from Battleford who recorded the homesteads and Dad picked one only five miles north and west of the Barr headquarters.

I don't know where Father got the money to start again but he managed to borrow some. Not much. You didn't need all that much. Dad cut the poplar poles from near. They weren't straight like pine but we managed to put up a small house of logs and we went up to Onion Lake to get boards for the door and the window frames. That's where a small sawmill was. The roof was poles and then sod piled high on top and Dad didn't know how to mud it so he got some Indians to come and mud the house. That meant filling in the chinks with moss and other stuff and then plastering mud over the chinks to make the house secure. It was a very cold winter that year, but there would be chinooks and every time there was a chinook things would melt and the mud would drop out and the chinking. I've seen us sitting at the table and the wind would be blowing through and I've actually watched in the little bit of tea at the bottom of the cup little shards of ice form. In the house. Believe it or not. Yes, we were healthy, never a cold, never a fever.

We had no money that first year, not two nickels to rub together. A neighbor woman taught Mother how to make bread because in England you bought your bread, you bought your cakes. No butter. Bacon fat on our bread but that didn't hurt us.

Then Father would work the farm in the summer. You had to stay six months a year for three years. After that he'd take us into the village, which is the Lloydminster of today, and everybody was building and Father found he had a very natural ability for carpentering and he built a little house for us and he made good money and we got along.

Of course, a lot of people quit even before they got to the prairies. They just went as far as Winnipeg and stopped. Some quit in Saskatoon. Others, oh quite a few, they got as far as the townsite and looked around and they'd spend a night or a couple of days and back they'd go to Saskatoon. No pioneering life for them. And others quit after a year, sometimes because the women were crying and moaning about the cold and the hardship, how lonely it was, how far away from anything. But you know, the railroad came through there in 1905. What a grand event, what excitement! And then we were very close to everything. You could go anywhere. And, of course, prices went down. No more freighting by wagon 200 miles from Saskatoon.

The years went by. Dad wasn't a natural farmer but he stayed on the farm. The church was built early. Then they had a school over a store and then a proper school. A hall. Hotels, stores, doctor, everything. Dad got the farm built up and we stayed on the farm all the time and it was a good life. Nobody who stayed ever regretted leaving England. They all came to love Canada, the prairies. I know I loved the prairies, the town, such good people for friends and neighbors. I've never regretted coming.

Two Whores and the Englishman

There was an old man named Rogers, very religious, very English and he had one eye. It had been knocked out and the eyelid stitched down over the hole so he looked at you with this other big eye and he was very, very vain. Very pompous. Everybody in town knew him. He was a big man in town. A big businessman.

He was a big horseman and he always had three or four men working for him, looking after his horses and this old man Rogers was always looking for a good buy in horses. He'd go a long way to look at a good horse and he was a good trader and buyer and he was very vain about that too.

One day Bert Hemming and I spoke to him and told him there were two important young ladies in town. We told him that

these two ladies were the daughters of a very important businessman and politician in the city and that as we didn't have a
buggy we were looking for somebody to drive these two lovely
young ladies around the town and show it to them. Show them
the town as they were visiting there. We said we wanted somebody to entertain them who could entertain them the way they
deserved to be. Well, he said yes. And, of course, everybody in
the town was in on the joke.

These women. Well, they were the new prostitutes in town
and there was old man Rogers, all religious and an important
man, there he was with these two women. You know, as long as
he lived in that town, to his dying day, he never lived that down,
him driving through the streets with his fine horse and buggy
and with these two girls in their fancy clothes and bonnets and
ribbons and the whole town looking at him and laughing their
heads off where he couldn't see them. Oh, it was grand.

Become a Canadian as Quick as You Can

My uncle was a wise old duck. He brought me up. Father was
killed in India, adjutant of a regiment, safest job in the army, but
he got it. Mother just drifted away. It was one of those kind of
families. Victorian morality wasn't all it was made out to be.
Look at old bunny-lugs, Edward the Seventh. Actresses and
whores and duchesses all his life.

But anyway, I grew up in Galloway. Taking lessons in a fine
but small school, very strict, headmaster who lived by the cane
and the Golden Rule and Latin verbs. Driving across the hills
in my little pony cart each day. I lived on the farm. The byre-
man, who is a cowboy in Canada, the plowman, the farm boys,
I hung around with them and while I was learning my Latin
verbs so I could forget them I was also growing up to be a
farmer. And a jolly good one too, I thought.

I'll make this short. I went to Oxford. That was where I was expected to go because of my father's connections. Then because I had no training for anything remotely connected with making my way in the world and because it was 1899, I joined a border regiment. Off to South Africa, boys. And there I was, the lowest of the low. A subaltern. Bottom rung. When we beat the Boers, if that's what we did—and I was never quite sure—I went home to Uncle.

We sat down in the parlor, each with a glass of whisky and he with his black twist tobacco, and I can remember his words. He said, "Of course you know you're quite useless. I can't hire you at 10 shillings a week to clean out my cowshed or be my groom. You're kin. And there's nothing more useless any time than a scholar, which you are for some reason, and a soldier, which you've been." Those were what he said, approximately.

I told him I knew and I said I'd been thinking of moving to Canada. "Good man," my uncle boomed. "Couldn't do better."

He took my glass and filled it up again and then the old bugger, crafty as they come, he gave me his line. I knew by the time he'd finished that he'd been doing some thinking about it. First, Canada, because he'd gone out there for five years about 25 years earlier. He still called it Canada West but it is what we call Ontario. So he knew the country or, looking back on it, the old bugger thought he did but he didn't. Not by a long shot on a rook's eye.

He said he'd make me a contract. Not in writing. He called it a father-and-son contract. I was to go to Canada and he'd give me 200. That was a lot of money then. Call it a thousand dollars and you'd be closer than not. I was to go to Winnipeg or whatever place in the West I wanted and I was to invest the money. He said I'd probably get 5 percent and that was when money in England was only earning 2 percent and so I asked him how he knew about the 5 percent.

He said, "Wrote Mr. Evans. Have his letter here." Mr. Evans of Edinburgh did his banking, so the old bugger had been thinking. How did he know I wasn't going to get my left leg shot off?

Then he said I wasn't to buy land right off. Don't do that. Reconnoiter. I was to spend one year in Canada working. If I wanted to be a carpenter then I was to go to work for a carpenter. If I wanted to go and be a butcher then I'd probably make a good butcher because I knew cattle and hogs, but he said it would please him if I became a farmer. As a farmer himself, I guess. Like father like son, or uncle and son. I said I'd like to be a farmer and he said then, "All right, fine, lad, hire yourself out to a farmer or a wheat farmer and then a rancher and then a cattle farmer." But I was to wait at least one year and look over the land before I drew out that money.

And I remember him saying, "Keep your money. Don't be in the bars with all those young fools from this country who go out there and just want to ride the country and shoot and hunt. The country's full of the damn fools as it is." And then he said, "Remember one thing. Become a Canadian as quickly as you possibly can. Even quicker. The Canadian is a rough-and-ready lad and he's quick to shake your hand and be your friend. He's also quick to take offense and if you're putting on airs, strutting around in your finery, he'll soon find a way to put you on your backside in the nearest puddle. In front of half the town too."

Let's see, I was 24 at the time but here I was like a child in the classroom. I can't remember minding it. Somebody had to tell me these things.

He told me that England was finished. Since Napoleon England had been God, England had been everything, trade and commerce, navy ruled the world, money was power and England had most of it, now it was finished. Class war, he said. Not between the plowman and the chap in the big house. That never existed except in novels. Between labor and capital. There was the rope that was going to drag England down. There was no place for anybody in between in this coming struggle, this fight. Everybody in the middle would be finished.

"Emigrate!" he shouted. Pound of stick on floor. "Emigrate!" Pound of stick. "Canada!" Pound of stick.

He said in a year I'd have saved maybe 300 dollars. He had to convert dollars to pounds for me. And with the other 1,000 dollars I'd have something.

"By God, my boy, you're a lad with stuff in you and a lad with stuff can do well in Canada. You'll become a landed proprietor," he said. Pound of stick on floor. By a landed proprietor he meant a good-sized farmer. He said he'd come out and visit and I could show him my acres of wheat and my herds of cattle.

Then he said, "Two things more. I won't tell you about the winter and I won't tell you about the mosquitters." He called them mosquitters.

Maybe, just maybe, if he'd told me all of it I wouldn't have come at all. But I don't think we had moving pictures in those days so he couldn't have warned me. Nothing but moving pictures can tell what those bastard mosquitoes were like.

I went to Canada. All English. God, how green. How green were these colonists. Clerks, teachers, cooks, and cabbies, people who had never smelled a plowed field or good cow manure. All they knew was London fog and smoke. I pitied them. Not the front end from the rear end of a cow would they know. Try and milk a bullock, probably.

I went to Winnipeg and didn't like it and I went on to Oak Lake and had a mind to stay there but didn't, and I wound up in Regina. It was a funny little place, not quite at all what I'd imagined a prairie town to be, and I hired on with a family. Irish, west of the town. A good-sized farm. Irish. Not Ulster but southern Irish. God, how they hated Englishmen, and why they took me on I'll never know—except maybe because I was tall and husky and knew my way around.

They'd come to Ontario about 60 years ago. Their grandfather had. Both of these were actually born in the bush outside of Toronto, but Irish as paddy's pig. Talk about the Tories and the Corn Laws and the Famine and the English, and you never heard such hatred. There I'd sit with them night after night and there was no use me defending the English because at school and prep and Oxford, I hadn't ever heard of the Corn Laws. But, by God, I know what they are now. I think the Irish by their very nature bring a lot of these things down upon themselves. A treacherous lot.

I worked with the father and his loutish sons for six months and I should say that one of the big lummoxes did take a swing at me with a pitchfork once and he got knocked spinning for his trouble. Then I went to a spot called Eastend and spent six months learning a bit about ranching, but I decided that country was not for me. I could have married a little school marm but I didn't.

Then I went to Saskatoon and worked six months and then I figured, well, 18 months have gone and you've done more than your apprenticeship. I really had. What's more, I liked the country. I thought of going back and seeing my uncle and then said to hell with it. This is where I want to live. I always thought just at dawn, and just at sunset, the prairies were beautiful. Pity we didn't have any good landscape painters around.

Then I went back to Regina and bought a driver and buggy and spent a month just driving around asking about land. By this time, you see, I had about 1,500 dollars. I was a wealthy young man.

Out west and north of here I bought a good farm of 320 acres from a land company. Five dollars an acre. The ad in the *Leader* said, as I remember, "Here's A Real Snap!" I put 500 dollars down. I picked a piece on the edge so I could homestead on that part that just touched the company's land. That gave me three-quarters. I hired a man with a Rumley to do me plowing and by God but he turned that land over, those furrows just rolling out like the waves of the seas. I did the disking, the harrowing.

I had about 150 acres broken and ready for spring and that winter I worked for a lumber yard in Regina and batched and in spring I moved up my seeder and four good horses and what else I needed and a load of lumber and a couple of kegs of nails and tarpaper. By this time, you could see, I was pretty deep in debt but I knew what I was doing. I made sure I got that new Marquis wheat that was being talked about and I seeded that and I got a good crop. About 38 bushels to the acre and that was the finest wheat I've ever seen. They still haven't matched it, in my opinion. Hard and wonderful for milling and it made the finest bread in the world.

Well, when I cleaned off that crop in October I had enough to pay off the land company, enough to buy my implements, enough to build a decent house and a barn and use the shack as a granary and enough to think I was king of the world. I was. There never was any doubt in my mind that this was sure as hell a wonderful country. Through the years we've had good years and some real humdingers, disasters when the black blizzards came and you couldn't see the allowance road for blowing dust but all in all, I did pretty well.

I was a young farmer and I had working capital and I think that's what made the difference. I went into it pretty big right off the bat and it was that uncle of mine, the old bugger, that taught me the right lessons for Canada. Sure did.

8 ...And the Others

They came. Polish, Ruthenians, Russians, Rumanians, all the others from that huge area we now refer to as being behind the Iron Curtain. The Canadians, the English, the Americans, the Scandinavians, and the Germans referred to themselves as "white" and the newcomers as "foreigners."

Their arrival by the thousands caused bitter debate in Parliament as many members felt these "foreigners" were devaluating the pro-British currency of the West. One member rashly said, "Canada is today the dumping ground for the refuse of every country in the world." On the other hand, Sir Clifford Sifton, Minister of the Interior and in charge of immigration, felt that a man in a sheepskin coat with a strong wife and healthy children was an asset, for they would make the West strong and prosperous. The two sides were generally far apart, but the anti-Ukrainians could just as well have worried more about the United States and her policy of Manifest Destiny than about a stolid, quiet people who only wanted peace and prosperity. And freedom.

I Wanted Freedom and I Got It

Where I came from, originally it was a Livonian fortress and then it was taken over by Poland and then taken over by Russia so it was a Russian city.

I was born of Jewish parents and at the age of four I went to more or less an ecclesiastical school and then as the years went by I moved on up to the gymnasium. A classical school like a high school but run on military lines. You wore a uniform, semi-military.

In the country there was a lot of unrest, talk of revolution, preparing for the 1905 war with the Japanese. We saw what was going on; the young people I had known were all revolutionaries, and the oppression was terrible. You daren't mention the tsar's name in any way for someone, if they heard you, they would report and no one ever saw you again. You were just taken away.

Some of these young people, my age, were hanged. Shot. And I myself have seen the Cossacks on the horses galloping through the streets. They had whips with a ball on the end and were flailing away at the people in the Jewish section of the city. For no reason.

No, you couldn't call it a ghetto. You had freedom. If you lived outside this Jewish area you could move in, move out of it. But it was more or less where our people gathered together, our stores, our churches, the things that the Jewish people would do together.

And there were very frequent assaults by groups of Russians, not soldiers, who called themselves the Black Hundreds, Russians, peasants or working people, who were supported by the government and they used to raid the Jewish quarter.

The Cossack business got worse and worse. I knew several neighbors of ours, one was shot and the rest we never heard of again. And all they did was that they were opposed to the oppression of the Jews. But you must also know that the Russian people themselves were oppressed. They were nearly as bad off as we were.

Well, finally the decision to leave Russia was made by me. I didn't want to live under this oppression. I wanted to be free. Do you know, I always filled my pockets with stones when I walked to school to protect myself. I could show you scars I have today from beatings.

So I told my parents I wasn't going back to school. I was leaving. We had all the books of the great French and English writers but what impressed me most was the books about North America, the books about the Indians and how a person could get up on a horse and ride wherever he wanted, ride all day. Land of freedom. The Wild West, oh yes. We all dreamed of the freedom, a man jumps on a horse, rides all over the prairies, nobody bothers him, he was his own boss. I decided that's the life for me, that's where I'm going.

And that's why I wanted to go to Canada. To get on a horse and ride around and be free. So that's how I came to Canada, at 16. The only fuss was from my mother and father. The Russians let me go. I think they would have liked to see us all go.

But when I got to Canada in 1905 I quickly realized there would not be any horses to ride on the prairie and no red Indians to shoot, but that was all right. It was freedom. I wanted freedom and I got it.

A Lesson in Government Policy

Man, read your history books! It's all in there somewhere. Sure. There was racial discrimination against us. This was in the late 1890's and the early 1900's. The government had all those lands in the West to fill. The C.P.R. was dying to get those millions of acres filled up with farmers. All through England they advertised. Scotland and Ireland too. They wanted Englishmen in the West. Keep Canada British. Their motto. Their slogan. All through England there were agents.

Well, the Canadian government contacted these people through their London office. They said, for every adult over 21 that you sell a ticket to for western Canada, we'll pay you a bonus of $4.80. About one pound in those days. That was a lot of money whichever way you look at it. For every person under 21, half a pound. A bit of distinction there, wouldn't you say! What's the diff between a husky lad of 20 and one of 21?

Anyway. If some family was thinking of immigrating, and the three places were New Zealand, Australia, and Canada, the agent would hustle Canada. See, New Zealand is these two little islands way down here, and who wants to live nearly to the Antarctic. That sort of thing. Australia is mostly desert, full of kangaroos, and it's too far from good old Leicester too. Now here's Canada. Right here, just across the ocean.

So they want Englishmen. They'll also pay the bonus for Frenchmen, Dutch, Belgians, Scandinavians, and Germans. Bring them all in. Fine, they're good for the country too. So agents in those countries get that bonus.

What about us? The Polacks. Hunyaks. Russians, Ukrainians, Hungarians. What about us? Aren't we good enough? Apparently not. We aren't considered preferred immigrants. I believe the word "desirable" was used. Who is better? An Englishman who has sat on his butt at a desk in some shipping office on the Thames all his life and suddenly decides he wants to go to Canada and become a wealthy farmer and land owner or a Polish peasant whose ancestors have worked the land for generations and is a farmer, through and through? Who is better for the land? It's like the old story, if you want to put it that way. Put a thoroughbred dog and a mongrel on a small desert island and go away for a month. Come back and who is dead and who is the survivor? Well, maybe that's not the best example but in the West it was the mongrel dog and the Polack peasant who survived more than did the pedigreed dog and the Englishman. But no, no bonus for ticket agents who sold tickets to people from behind what we'd now call the Iron Curtain.

But by God, they came. Boy, did they ever! Quite frankly, I don't know how they survived. I've heard my parents talking about it and frankly, it's all rather unreal to me. I couldn't have done it. You couldn't have. I don't know anyone who could. Think, dropped off at the side of the railroad with maybe only a boxcar as the station, no station agent, no nothing, no store, no-body to tell them what to do, where to go. Just a piece of paper with the number of their quarter section on it, and my mother says there they are sitting there and the train's gone, way on to who the hell knows, and soon there's this wagon comes along and there's people in it and they are Polish. My folks are Polish. So, they go along with them. They help them get started.

They became good farmers. Drive through Saskatchewan today. On your right, on your left, all farms and good farms and they started out as sod shacks built by immigrants from Poland, the Ukraine such as it was then. Russia. Peasants. Damn near serfs. They did it.

Sure, they were crude. They couldn't speak English. Did you expect them to? Hell, they couldn't even read and write in their own language. Did you know that there was between 85 and 90 percent illiteracy in those countries at the turn of the century? That's the way the tsars and the landlords, the barons and the kings, kept them down. So they came to this country and 50 or 60 years later English is still a new language to them. Admit it, English is a hard language to learn.

They weren't wanted here. I'm sure they were looked upon as something, somebody to be exploited. And they were. They were. Until they learned. But they came, come hell and high water, and I'm sure you'll admit, because you have to, that Canada, the West, is a better place because of it. Right? Right!

But you can't get around the fact that in the early 1900's when Canada had a national priority to fill up the wheatlands of western Canada, you can't get around the fact that the government practiced a deliberate policy of selective immigration against the Central Europeans. It's all water under the bridge now, but it was there.

When the First Foreigners Came

It was about 1905, in around there, when the first foreigners came into our district. They were mostly Polacks. Polanders. Up until then we'd had people from Ontario and from the States, English families, people from Germany and Scandinavia, but then the Polacks started to come in. Not a lot at first, just one or two because the land was pretty well settled, that which wasn't was all bush, poplar. But they'd go to the immigration hall in Winnipeg and they'd send them out to look at what was left, whether it was poplar or swamp, and they usually seemed to take it. They'd get off the train and take a buggy from Scott's Livery barn and away they'd go down the mud roads, and 160 acres of free land looked pretty good to them. After all, they only needed 10 dollars for a filing fee and most of them had a little money.

Some weren't good farmers. The ones that were did very well. One chap Danylchuk said he'd done all his farming in a steel mill in Cracow. Gives you an idea. Another thing, most of them that had done farming had done it on five acres. That's what a peasant had in Poland or Russia, if he had anything at all. I think most of the men had been with big Russian landowners. But they worked hard and they learned, and if you could get one for a hired man you were lucky. I know my father used to say he'd take a local Bohunk over a man from Winnipeg any day. That's what we called them, Bohunks. Today it's an insult, they don't like it, but then it was the same as calling a Scotsman Scotty.

There were schools dotted all over the country. That is one good thing about having a country settled first by the English, Germans, and Scandinavians. Schooling comes first. The little school where I went we had a different teacher every year from Winnipeg. But many of the Polack kids never went. There must have been a whole generation of those kids who grew up never knowing how to read and write or do their sums. That's about all education was in those days anyway, the three R's with some history and a bit of geography thrown in. If you could find Africa on the map you passed geography. That was about the size of it. Oh, I know that the Manitoba School Act said that every child had to go to school. A hundred ways of getting around that and I think the one that stuck up like a sore thumb would be the one that said the child didn't understand English.

They could. Eaton's catalogue English, we used to call it. Learned their English out of the catalogue.

From the very first they lived with their animals. This used to shock some of the old-timers and I should say an old-timer was one who came in early, about 1880. An old-timer was one who came up by boat, taking the railway through the States and then coming up the Red by boat, but most of them came by the train. Say 1890. So they had a 15-year jump on the Polacks.

The houses were small. It seems to me that they were incapable of thinking big. Like a family might have father, mother, six children, and a grandmother, and they'd have the same size of a house, about this room's size, as a family with mother and father and two kids.

They cut poles out of the bush and laid them one on top of the other and that was the walls, and they laid smaller poles together, side by side, and that was the roof. On the walls they plastered them with a guck of straw and mud and lime. The roof had straw on it and then dirt, about a foot of dirt. You'd be surprised how cozy they were.

I remember going to one place at night. It was only about seven o'clock but the house was dark but I thought, oh well, maybe they are in bed but let's see. I knocked on the door and the man came and he invited me in. His name was Fred; I said why they were eating in the dark, and he said, "Kerosene gone." I said sure, I figured that, but didn't they have candles. "Oh sure," he said, "for Christmas." See what I mean when I say they were frugal?

You never got to see their women. I mean, not to know them. If you visited them, there they'd be in the house, bare feet, hankie over their heads, and always working in a corner, back to you. A woman of 35 looked 50. In town they stayed in the wagon or walked about three feet behind old Nick or Pete. Just like an Indian squaw. But I have a feeling that when nobody was around they ruled the roost. They worked hard. Every year or two there was another kid. The way those families worked, the next oldest kid looked after the younger one. They were careful with their kids and they were well behaved. When they started coming to our picnics on July 1 that must have been the basis for a lot of discussion in those houses before they decided. They did what they were told. They were the best behaved kids on the lot. One word from the mother and that was it.

They liked music. To my surprise I found they made their own violins. You could buy a violin at Eaton's, two or five dollars but no, they'd spend a whole winter working on a violin. Sounded just fine. When they started coming to our dances, and this was some time after, after the first school burned down and we built a two-room one, they could sure make the night lively. Their violins. Maybe half a dozen of them and that was all you really needed. Not for the kind of dances we danced.

Oh, they were a good bunch and they worked hard and the thing was, as the years went by, you began to notice things. Not that their language got any better, because they'd always speak broken English as long as they lived and their women would always wear the babushka and look old. But if you looked around their yards you'd see things. They started buying good equipment. They still must have lived on nothing, everything out of the bush and off the farm, so they were plowing everything back into the farm. Then you'd notice that if there was a bit of land near going up for sale, the chances were 10 to one they'd buy it. They always seemed to have money when they needed it.

There was more and more of them coming in too. Gradually a lot of the first old-timers, the ones who had been there first, they began to leave. Move further west. Two this year, three the next. I think most of it was that the older ones just thought that the district was turning into a Little Russia, and I guess it was. Poles and Ukrainians.

A funny thing though. They left the municipality to us. I don't think there ever was one of them as reeve, although a few became councilors but not at the same time. They began to concentrate on the school board. That was their baby. It was because they finally realized the importance of education. Not for us. One of us could still leave school at grade eight and go into the city and make good. But if you had a "ski" or a "chuck" on the end of your name and you went to the city, you were on the end of a pick and shovel for the rest of your days. Or you stayed on the farm. They knew this. Oh my but how they knew this. So they wanted the best school, the best teacher, the best of everything for their children, and by God that was why they concentrated on the board. Good for them. I always said when people complained that the Bohunks were taking over, I'd tell them that if it was good for their kids then it would be good for our kids.

Finally I went west too. South of Swan River. It wasn't the best but it wasn't bad and I don't know why I did it. Especially at my age. I guess one of the reasons—and I don't know how big a reason it was, but it was all part of it—I guess I got tired of having the neighbors across the road and down the road and up the road all Ukrainians and Galicians and Polacks. I think it was a slow process but it seemed to get me down after a while. I think I stuck it out as long as anybody.

But what am I talking this way for? They were good people.

The Old Customs, the Old Ways

When we came to Regina we came from Rastadt. I remember it. I was 12. Rastadt was a colony which had been in Russia oh, maybe 100 years. From about 1810 or so, I think. Germans were given land in that part of Russia, the steppes, and I think we were to build towns and teach Russian peasants to farm. Which was done. I remember we'd pledge honor to the czar and czarina in the village school, but Father would tell us at home we were still Germans. Remember that, he'd say, you kids, you're still German. This was after 100 years.

My father was a blacksmith, a cabinet-maker, and he played the organ. He was known as an educated man. He taught us Latin at home. We spoke German and Russian. I believe he used a small farm too. He rented it. Everything was in rubles so I can't tell you how much for.

A lot of people from the German colonies in Russia, South

Russia, were going to America. That was the United States and Canada. Some were going to Siberia where there was good land, but my father chose Canada because people from the village had gone. Right here to Saskatchewan. They wrote and said, "Come to our village and be our blacksmith." So we went. This was about 1910. First by train to Odessa and then to Berlin and then to France and on a ship. It was a big ship. No storms. My father went to a class for learning English. A schoolteacher from one of the colonies taught it. For free, I guess. I don't think my father learned anything. He said he would be a blacksmith and would learn as he earned money.

But in Regina Dad worked as a cabinet-maker. There are still lots of pieces around that people can point at and say, "Old man Stark made that."

There were lots of Germans in Regina; we stuck together for a long while and got together Christmas Eve for the Christkindel and St. Nikolaus and the whole thing. That's a ceremony, a kind of party for the children on Christmas Eve where good boys and girls get gifts and pats on the head and bad boys—never girls, always boys—I think got hits with a stick. Christkindel was a girl who dressed up in white with this white thing over her face, and she'd bring little gifts and cookies to the little kids.

By gosh, I can still remember me and my pals screaming when old St. Nick would get after us. He was a man, not a girl, and most of the time we were bad and we'd sure get hit. We sure would. This guy wore old ragged clothes and a mask on his face and he was the tough guy. We knew who it was. One of the Schuler boys.

Then we'd open the gifts. The boys got gifts too, even if we were bad. It was a game. A ceremony. A Christmas thing, something German, which our grandparents had kept up in Russia; our parents had, too, and now they were doing it in Canada, in Regina. It was a good thing, this keeping the things of the homeland going.

After a while we didn't say much about these things. They just died out, you could say. There was just too much doing in this new country; everybody worked so hard. Now I can hardly remember the times on Christmas Eve when we'd pray to the

Holy Jesus child in his crib and then Christkindel would come in and see the children. It was a long time ago. We changed to the ways of this country. It was a good thing, but you should still keep some of the old culture and ways too, I think.

Peddlers Had a Lonely Life

In southern Manitoba there was a lot of Jewish peddlers. They'd go out through the Mennonite country, where the Russian villages were. Out on Monday morning with their wagons and their goods and peddle through the countryside and come back in Friday night, wagons full of eggs and butter and other barter. Of course, they shipped it all to Winnipeg.

There were about four or five of these men in our town and they had a lonely life. Alone all the time, on the road, going from farm to farm and village to village. Mostly barter. The peasants didn't have money but they had produce.

Before my time they did it with a pack on their back. How they bartered for stuff, how they carried it, I don't know. The horse and wagon was the next step up. This was the best way they knew to make a living and the next step would be a store in town, in Brandon, in Morden, in Winnipeg. Then they could settle down.

They were just like you and me, like everybody. They wanted the best for their families, for themselves. A little store, a home, peace and quiet. Most of them got it too, I think. Some of the men I got to know got stores finally after they'd saved so hard and worked so hard over those years. I know one of the men in our town, his son became a King's Counsel and another owned a big men's clothing store down on Hastings Street. Some of them did real well.

There would be maybe 20 or so families around. They kept pretty well to themselves. Religion? Oh, they had a temple in Morden and Jewish families from all over would go there. But they had a killer in our town. You see, Jews will only eat meat a certain way and so the steer would be killed and then dressed and the killer would come along and he cut the meat that was for the Jewish people. Kosher, oh yes, kosher.

I think you'd be surprised if you went around and asked a lot of the Jewish merchants and storekeepers today how many got their start as peddlers. Of course, the fellow would have to be at least 80, maybe 85 or so, to have been a peddler. And another thing, it might not be any use asking their sons in the stores if their father had been a peddler to the Mennonites. He might not tell you. Might not like to have to admit it. It's like the son of a junk dealer who was asked what his father did and he said his father was in the waste iron disposal business. You see, ashamed of his father. But nobody need be ashamed of those men. They were considered good businessmen, working for themselves, working hard, long hours to get a start. They were all fine fellows, the ones that I knew.

They Resented the Americans

Oh yes, there was trouble between the Americans and the other settlers and I remember hearing of it along the Soo Line and the main line but, well, I think you could call it natural.

Some of those settlements, those communities in Saskatchewan, had been settled all in a piece by Canadians. Down Easters. Yes, Ontario people and they were a combination of Presbyterians and Methodists and a lot of the old memories died hard with those people.

To them, every American was a Yankee. It didn't matter if he was Swedish or Norwegian or German, he was a Yankee. That's how they'd been taught and their fathers had been taught and so forth, right back to the American Revolution. To them the Americans coming in taking up new land on the prairies were still revolutionaries, against King and Crown, so to speak, and their eyes showed them to be traitors. Yes, I know, the revolution was in 1776 but their ancestors were the third of the American Colonies who went north into Ontario. They were proud to be called United Empire Loyalists and they stuck by it, although it was their great-grandfathers who had done the running up into Canada. You go down to parts of Ontario today and you'll still find this feeling.

There was money involved too, you see. These Americans were selling their farms for 100 or 150 dollars an acre and coming up to Canada where the pickings were easy and buying off the land companies, Luse Land, Hopper, others for 8 or 10 dollars an acre and from the railway sometimes cheaper. They had money, they had the latest farming equipment, and what's more, they were good farmers. When they got off those freights, unloaded on the right-of-way, they had the best mowers, binders, plows, and good horses, horses that really knew how to lean into the collar, big horses but ones with stamina, and that was darned important. They had good cattle too. They knew what they were doing.

But resentment, yes, resentment. Oh, little things. I've seen my dad refuse to lend an American neighbor some piece of equipment, something that would save him a long trip to town that day in bad weather, saying it was broke or he didn't have it, and all the time it would probably be sitting there good as gold. There never were serious things. No barn burnings or having a horse hamstrung. No, it was all small stuff. Petty stuff.

But the Americans didn't complain. They tried to be good neighbors. When there was a bee they were there, first to come, last to go, and they did their share. They helped build the curling rink in town, as I remember, although I don't think they knew what a granite rock was at the time. They joined the glee club and the town band. Oh, they were glad to get them in the town band. The more players the merrier. They didn't ask for the town to grant them land for their church, Lutheran, but bought it like any storekeeper and they were good churchgoers. If they got on the school board they did their share. They paid their taxes, such as they were.

Sometimes though, when I think about it, maybe it wasn't

the American Revolution and the War of 1812 that caused the resentment, but the Americans coming in and having all the good equipment and having the first steam tractors in the district, the first hard-rubber ton-and-a-half Maxwell trucks, and the Tin Lizzies and scooting over the roads while the Canadians were plodding along behind old Bessie. I think that might have caused some of the problem. If that's the case, then you could put it down to jealousy, but one thing they conveniently forgot was that to get those Maxwells and the threshing outfit, they had had to work pretty hard for them, pretty hard.

The Scandinavians Were a Good People

Of all the new people coming into our district I liked to see the Scandinavians. They were the best. Clean, resourceful, intelligent, and eager. They had all those qualities.

They were able to take adversity, hardship, and they never whined. They mostly spoke some English or it was just amazing how fast they picked it up.

The best of the best were the Norwegians. They settled in well. They got a house up fast. The men were good axemen; yes, they knew how to use that big American axe, and they built good log houses and barns. If I went back there I think some of those buildings would still be standing today. Maybe in use. They built them like fortresses.

The Danes were good. We got a few. The parkland type of country didn't suit them too well, and most of them moved to towns and got into dairy and cheese and butter, but they were good. So were the Swedish people. A lot of them worked in the bush in winter and made money to carry themselves over for the summer. I once saw a Swedish family come in from Battleford in a wagon and half that wagon was cartons of books. They were intelligent.

We had a few Finns. I'm not sure if they are exactly Scandinavian or more Baltic, but I'll call them Scandinavian. They weren't farmers so much as bush people. As I recall they did a fair amount of quarreling among themselves. They seemed generally to be short and stocky men and very strong. They could work all day.

All these people were very good to their children; they insisted on them having good schooling. One Christmas I was visiting a Norwegian family and they had a Christmas exactly as they had had it for years back in Norway. I thought that was nice. Keep to the old ways. Be Canadian but keep the old traditions. Some got together, some families inviting other families who were having a hard go of it. They seemed to help each other. They stuck together, not like the English who were always so independent and they knew everything but knew nothing and a lot of them failed. If a Norwegian or a Danish fellow didn't know something about the country or plowing he'd come over and ask and he wouldn't mind being shown.

They were always cheery. I liked that about them. They paid their bills when they sold an ox or a horse or got something for their grain. That way the storekeepers didn't mind giving them credit. Everybody got some credit, naturally. You had to in that country. But if you tried to pay off every year, some of it, most of it, then you got just that much extra credit and that helped a lot when the going got tough.

They were good people, the Scandinavians. I remember once my wife had too much wool and the store wouldn't even take it in storage. I said we might as well burn it, what use is it to us? She said she'd give it to a Norwegian family that lived over by the lake. I drove over with these bags of wool and gave them to the woman. She took these bags of wool and made them into yarn and about a month later, one Sunday, she and her husband drove over and they gave us two lovely wool sweaters. Knitted. One for me, one for my wife. They didn't have to pay us. It was just their way.

Then there was a fellow named Larsen who used to drive a mile out of his way to ask us if we wanted anything in the store and even if we didn't, he'd still drive another mile out of his way on the way back to deliver us any mail. But they weren't the best farmers. It wasn't their fault. So one by one they moved away, to Edmonton for work in the city. Some went to Prince Albert where there was plenty of lumber work, and I don't think that by the First World War there was too many left. It was not a place where you could be confident that, from year to year, one year was going to be better than the next. Nature had too many dirty tricks for that.

Every Chinese Restaurant Was Called "The Royal"

There was never enough Chinese in any town or even in the bigger cities to cause any trouble, although I'll say this: there always were enough white men around who would have caused trouble if they'd been given half a chance.

I think the only Chinese I knew growing up and being a young man were the ones who ran the cafés in the towns. It seemed every Chinese café was called the Royal Café. I can remember a string of them across the West, all the same. Booths on one side, the cash register just as you went in the door. That would be on your left. The counter and a kitchen in the back. Try as hard as I can, I can never remember how many others would be in the kitchen in the back. There might be two, a cook and a dishwasher, or there might be 10.

You were always hearing about how hundreds of Chinese were being smuggled into the States, and then into Canada, to do cheap labor and take the jobs away from the whites. The fact is, I don't know of any white, unless he was a Greek—and then he's more Asiatic too in some ways—but I have my doubts that whites would want to own cafés, restaurants. Long hours, you see. Poor pay as far as I could see. They got kicked around quite a bit too, you know.

I've seen it happen when a harvesting crew came to town, or maybe there was a railroad gang going through, and they'd come in to a Chinese place and eat a big meal, topped off with pie and ice cream, and then they'd just walk out. The Chinaman would be screaming, but there was never any of this stuff about chasing them with a meat cleaver. That was for the comic books. No. I guess the poor devil would just chalk it up to loss and with his profit being so low, I guess that day was just a write-off.

There was one thing though. They were great gamblers, great poker players. There was this café, and I think it was in Kindersley, where the old Chinaman would pull the shades of his front windows down about 10 o'clock and lock the door and the poker game would start. It was just part of the town's activities and it was this, I heard, that started the expression "He doesn't have a Chinaman's chance." If you got in a game with a couple of them, say a seven-handed game, you might just as well turn your bucks over to them right there. I played in a few of those games. A lot of whisky was drunk.

There was one family in Brandon that had a Chinese cook. They were supposed to be the best, but they really weren't. It all depended on how they were taught. If they were taught by the lady of the house and say she did lamb chops a certain way and said, "Now, Wing, this is the way Mr. Brown likes them," that was the way they did them until they died. Vegetables. Stews. Porridge. Rice pudding. It didn't matter. Once they were taught they never unlearned and if they went to another family that's the way they did it. You liked it or lumped it.

They got about 15 dollars a month, I think, and they became devoted to the family. I knew another family in Regina and they had one and it was the same. He used to go back to China once in a while and you'd think he'd spent all his money on the family because he brought everybody back a present, and an expensive one too, although I imagine they were pretty cheap there then.

This was about 1911, when I was doing the books for this family. That was where I learned about Chinese food. They had girls in the house and one of the daughters, Vera, she told him she was bringing some girls home for lunch on this Saturday. Dinner was at noon on most days and was the big meal except on Saturdays. That was the prairie style. I was visiting so I was invited, and we sat down to about eight plates of goodies.

I looked at it and said to myself, "Hell, there's not enough there to keep a sparrow alive," but when we dug in we found we couldn't finish it. Little bits of pork fried in sauce. Fried noodles and vegetables. Stuffed shrimp. All these things you'd never find in Regina, so I guess they came from his own stock down in the cellar where he and his cronies would get together and feed up. It was a treat. I never saw the same things until about 1944 when I came out to Vancouver to visit my daughter and we went to Chinatown.

All the years I lived on the prairies I don't think I ever saw a Chinaman taking a job away from a white man. I seen lots of Chinese laundrymen but who'd want that job, 12 boiled shirts for 75 cents? And what white man could do 12 boiled white shirts even in a whole day? The last light on Railway Street would be in the laundryman's place and there he'd be, working away. I never saw a Chinaman working on the railroad except the odd one in the boarding car with the gangs, and that wasn't such a good job either. In fact, it was a hot job. Some towns and I've seen a lot of them, some had a Chinese market gardener. He'd come around twice a week with a horse and wagon and sell door to door. However, I never saw a Chinese wheat farmer and I don't think I ever will. Nor a hardware man. There was the odd grocer around, but just small stuff.

I remember once at Dundurn there was this Chinese fellow and I don't know if he had a bakery and sold groceries on the side or if he had a grocery and did some baking, but he made good doughnuts. I've seen as many as six or seven cowboys riding down the street with this fellow's doughnuts. He'd go out and cut willows and skin them and then he'd thread the doughnuts on the willow and you ate them off the stick like eating an ice cream cone. I think he sold a dozen hot doughnuts for 10 cents. Something crazy like that.

There was a lot of Chinese people in Calgary and in Edmonton, and while I haven't been there I think in Winnipeg too. Some of them got rich. You know, there was a caste system among them too. Like in India, only not as worse, I don't believe. But if you were a Gold Rush Chinese that meant you were top of the heap because your father's father's father came to

California for the 1849 gold rush, and then came up to British Columbia for the one in 1858 and on into 1865. If you were Railroad Chinese that was pretty good too because that meant you'd come in for the building of the C.P.R. and I guess they could say they helped build the country. I know they did all the dirty work in the Rockies. No, not the Rockies. The Fraser Canyon and through there. Rock work and dangerous. A lot died and they buried a lot just beside the track. Then the third level, the bottom of the heap, was anyone who came in after that.

One thing, you know. You never saw any of their women. I'll betcha that there weren't three Chinese women in all of Calgary and they were kept out of sight. They used to say that a China- man and an Indian woman made a good combination. They had goods sons. But a Chinaman and a Negro, that wasn't so good at all. I remember when I worked up at Prince Rupert a prostitute told me the Chinese guys were always after them to marry them. I guess some did.

But I'd sometimes laugh when I was with this English family in Regina when I was a young buck. The boy they'd gotten, he'd come from Vancouver and he'd been taught to cook roast beef as tough as leather. The fellow, Nesbitt, he liked his beef rare. Do you think his wife could get it through that boy's head to cook that roast rare? No sir. No. As I say, once they learn they stay learned.

You know. If you think it over, and I have, I wouldn't like to be fighting them in a war.

Two Pumpkins for the Hungarians

These are the stories I tell my grandchildren. You never find them in the history books and I think they should know.

Once when I was 10 my father decided I would move into town, Whitewood, to be with his brother because he had plans for making a doctor of me. He nearly succeeded, but that's another story. Anyway, he wanted me to board in town where he felt I'd get a better education.

It was 50 miles and halfway along the horse went lame and as we had to stop somewhere, Dad pulled in to this farmyard. It was, believe it or not, a Magyar's home. Imagine, a Hungarian and his family on the bald prairie, and he wasn't doing so well. I always associate Hungarians with riches, wealth, big houses, dashing horses, bright and snappy uniforms, and waxed mustaches. Too many books. This fellow wasn't doing so well but he invited us in. The usual thing. Poplar logs, a chimney made of mud and prairie rocks. Saskatchewan style or Saskapoosh plaster, as we called it. But inside, let me tell you it was another world. This was the world he came from.

There were carpets on the floor. There were tapestries on the log walls. There were lamps, the kind that are so thin that you can see through but it is still china. Translucent would be the word. And bookcases made of planed logs and filled with books, sets of books. All leather bound. Oiled and dusted, and you can see that those books were read. A big table of oak and six chairs. You would have thought the inside of that shack was a castle. At my age it made a fantastic impression. I'm 76 now and I've seen a lot and did a lot, but I can't remember anything that has impressed me quite as much.

Here was a family who had spent a lot of money bringing some of their best things out from the Old Country and they were living like paupers. Oh, I guess they could have sold some of these lovely things, but there are people and then there are people and the old ways. The old things were important to them.

The husband spoke fair English. Not good. He and Dad stabled the horse and I looked at his two kids and they looked at me but that was as far as it went. It was suppertime and so we were asked to stay. Sowbelly. Have you ever eaten sowbelly? Two inches of greasy fat and a sliver of meat. Boiled. Boiled potatoes. The man said they came from their garden. Sowbelly and boiled potatoes, four people's shares divided among six of us, and Dad and I were so hungry we could have eaten the arse off a skunk. And the table. Linen. The very purest white. China, straight from the Austro-Hungarian Empire's greatest days. Who was it? Yes, fit for the Emperor Ferdinand. And silver cutlery. But sowbelly so bad it practically made you gag and potatoes. Okay, potatoes were fine. It's the Hollywood movie business maybe but I think it might have been reasonable to expect a string quartet to be playing in the background, over in the corner where there was a heavy drapery. Behind their bed.

How did we know they were Hungarians? Oh, the man told us. He was proud of his being Hungarian. Magyar, he called himself. Proud as a peacock and next morning Dad, I could see, was thinking, "Now how much can I pay this fellow so his proudness won't tear my head off?" It was ticklish, I know, but finally he figured cash money wasn't the thing. Payment in kind. He went to the wagon and brought in two huge pumpkins that he had brought along for my uncle in town. He put them on the stoop outside the door and he didn't say anything. Then he brought out a sack with five pounds of pork sausage in it that my mother had made. That was for my uncle too. I half expected him to go off the deep end and bring out the crocked butter and eggs that my mother had given him to swap at the Whitewood store, but he didn't.

He shook hands and I shook hands with the boy and the girl and then we got up on the wagon seat and Dad said, "Hrrrup, hup!" and away we went. Down the road Dad said, "Feel sorry for that chap. He can't last."

When my uncle drove me home for the Christmas holidays, I used part of my allowance to buy a big bag of hard candy for the man's two kids. I was going to get my uncle to pull off the road and I'd give it to them. When we got close I could see the snow drifted up over the steps and there was a place where a wolf or some coyotes had peed on the corner by the door and I knew I was too late. The family had gone, with all their nice furniture and white tablecloth.

Proud to Be a Canadian

When I moved in to this district it was solid Ukrainian. I'd say it was more than two-thirds Ukrainian and all the grown-ups, hardly any of them spoke more than a few words of English. This was bad because all their business they had to do, it was in English, of course. They couldn't read nor write either, of course.

So I decided it would be a very, very good thing to make them realize that they'd have to learn some English. I decided that I would hold a school for them. The grown-ups. Sunday was an open day for me so that was the day I held classes and I had about 12 of them, and some came quite a distance. They were so anxious to learn. The first thing they wanted to learn how to do was write their own name. You see, these people weren't only non-English speaking, but they were illiterate in their own language too. I said, yes, of course. I told them I'd teach them to write anything.

I started them on the alphabet and we were doing fine and then, of course, spring came and they needed every hour on the land. So we shifted the class to a night class and we kept that up.

And it so happened that that summer there was a federal election and I was a polling officer and on election day all my pupils came. They were scared so they came in a bunch. You see, they'd never voted in Russia. So I told them what to do. I said you go in there and there's a pencil and you mark the man you want. They knew politics a bit by this time and they had learned enough from me that they could probably figure out the names all right. There was one man named Nikolai Hukaluk and he went in behind the curtain and, by gosh, he was there an awful long time. Half an hour. People waiting. Fussing. Complaining. Finally he came out and he says, "Here!" He hadn't marked it. He'd written his name in big letters across the ballot. I guess I just didn't get through to him. But he handed me the ballot and he said, "Now, that go to Ottawa."

You know, I never forgot that. Nick was so proud. For

generations his people had been peasants in the Ukraine and now he was taking part in the electoral process. Proud as he could be. He was now a Canadian.

9 Growing Up on the Land

I Wasn't Culturally Deprived . . . Mary Down the Badger Hole . . . Well, You Just Worked, Hard . . . The Early Years Come Back to Me . . . Happy with Two Bits a Day . . . Children Just Kept on Coming . . . Why Did We Need That Spring Tonic? . . . The Great Pedal Organ Caper . . . Looking After 30 Head of Stock . . . Fun Was What We Made It

Unlike today, children of the early 1900's were expected to take their place in the family work pattern at an early age. At four years a boy or a girl could be seen helping to fill the big woodbox by the stove. At six they milked their first cow. It was a proud day when an 11-year-old took his first turn on the hay rake behind a pair of cayuses and the girl presented the family at dinner with the first wild berry pie she had made. And so it went . . .

But they had their fun, lots of it, and they played many of the games that farm, town, and city children still play—when there was no work to be done. Their young minds were, well, call it programmed if you will, to the Protestant work ethic, a type of thinking, an attitude toward life that dominates their thinking and their lives even today, 60 or 70 years later.

I Wasn't Culturally Deprived

I don't think we were culturally deprived. I know I wasn't. A Negro family a few miles away had a big Christmas party one year when I was about ten and I received a slate off the tree. With that slate and wet cloth I spent whole winters in our shanty drawing what I saw.

I drew the Indians who came to the door begging, and the teamsters and their oxen who went down the trail, and I can still hear the language of the men. I still don't know which made the animals go, the goad or the language. I couldn't use their language but I filed it away for future use, but it never seemed to come in handy. I drew oxen and wagons and carts and horses.

Occasionally somebody would stop for dinner or for supper and the night, and they might have a Winnipeg or Regina newspaper. We learned to read from the advertisements for stoves and linen goods and boots and real estate. That seems to be about all they sold in those days. By myself it seemed that I learned enough so I could go on to reading the news in the Regina paper, and I believe they even had funnies in those days too. This was at the time of the Boer War and I couldn't pronounce it; neither could my mother. To this day I have to catch myself from saying "Boe-err."

My mother taught me to cook. That would be the home economics part of my education. Rabbit and prairie chicken and sometimes some beef and plenty of oatmeal. Rolled oats and beans. It was my job to pick out the hard, blackened beans and then she'd take them and put them aside. She'd take six black beans and two black beans and say, "What do they make when you divide them?" and quick, I'd say "Three." Multiply would be 12; add would be eight; subtract would be four. You could do the same thing with eggs we found out in the nests by the slough from the hens that would go there and get broody.

My uncle played the flute and we'd sing the old songs. That way we got another side of the cultural thing. Of course, we also sang without the flute. Supper, usually bread and lard, saskatoons in milk, lots of tea, and then singing for a time, a few verses from the Bible, and then to bed with the chickens. That was our life.

When I went to school—when the men got together and built a school in the fourth year—I was ready. I could read, I could write very well and do my sums, I could draw and sing, and I was as good a class storyteller as anyone. That's one thing we did. After singing "God Save the King"—or was it the Queen?—in the morning and the Lord's Prayer, one child would have to tell a story. We usually made them up but they were quite good. Story-time, the teacher called it.

I learned a great deal about life on the prairie in those days, and nobody told me I was deprived so I didn't know it and life was very good for us. We enjoyed our home and our parents and our playmates and school and nobody told us we were poor as church mice.

Mary Down the Badger Hole

We made our own fun on the farm. We had to. Nobody else would do it for us and we had the run of the whole place.

I remember once one summer my sister Mary and I were playing hide and seek, and when the places to hide had kind of run out I had fooled her by going through the garden fence into the field and hiding in a badger hole. Badgers, as you know, dig very large holes. Big at the opening, and they go down big for a ways.

That gave her the idea and when it was her turn to hide she sneaked through the fence and crawled down this big badger hole. Of course she was a lot smaller than me and she went right down, and when I called, "Ready or not," and started looking, of course I couldn't find her because the last place I expected her to hide was a place I had just hidden.

But what happened was that she had got her clothing caught

on some part of the hole and she was stuck down there, and when she yelled I couldn't hear her and finally I became scared. I got desperate and I ran for Mother and neither could she find her. We were both getting scared and Mother grabbed me and said, very earnestly, "Is there any place you have showed her where to hide?" Remember, she was a little girl. That was when I remembered the badger hole.

We ran through the garden to the hole and sure enough, there she was with just her shoes showing out of the hole and we had to dig her out, a very dirty and very frightened little girl. But we were tough kids in those days and in a few minutes we didn't think much more about it and went on playing as we had before. Mary was not the kind of little girl to become easily frightened, and she was always getting into danger and mischief, even around a farmyard.

Kids had to make their own fun in those days and falling down from the hay loft into the manger or just getting out of a field when an angry bull was chasing us was just fun to us. Except for the badger hole. That was kind of serious.

Well, You Just Worked, Hard

One sure thing about those days, we sure knew how to work. It wasn't exactly that we called it work, it was more like just part of our lives.

If I'm not mistaken, I couldn't have been more than six when I put my childhood things away, my toys and slingshots and my pets, and the only time I looked at them again, I guess, was when I dug them out again and gave them to my kid brother to play with.

It was the same with girls too, you might say. Yes, the same with my sisters.

Even before five or six, though, we were doing things around the yard, hunting up broody hens and getting them back to the henhouse, and going for the cows with Spot, our collie, and handing my dad things when he was fixing a piece of machinery, oiling it, replacing a part that he'd fixed. He did his own black-smithing. Everybody did, but not the hard parts. Or in the summer I'd load up my little wagon with two stone mason jars, one of water and one of lemonade, and with sandwiches and cake and cookies I'd go out to the field where the men were working and give them afternoon lunch.

Of course, you never went between the barn and the house but what you didn't pick up a load of poplar wood for the woodbox. If you came in without it you got a glare, and maybe if my mother was in a snarky mood you got a clout on the ear, which you tried to duck and she'd say, "C'mere, you," and give you a worse one. Wonder us kids didn't get ear trouble that way. Even if you could only manage a few sticks you brought some-thing. I've seen my two-year-old sister Mary toddling along with one little stick in her arms and getting a pat on the head from my mother.

Of course there was the water to bring in, and a milkpail full of water is pretty heavy for a five-year-old. I mind how at first I'd have to carry that pail with both hands and the pail banging between my legs against my knees and the water slopping all over. I was so small I couldn't get it up to put it in the stove reservoir—my mother would do that.

When I was seven or so, there I was, winter or summer, milk-ing my one cow, and then it got to be two cows and three, until by about nine I was doing a man's job with the cows, milking, carrying the pails to the house, getting the De Laval separator turning.

I've seen me on the summer fallow at 11 years old, hardly big enough then to get the harness on, and me with a four-horse team, and at seven in the morning seeing all the other kids going down the roads to school, where I should have been going ex-cept Dad said the field had to be done, and that was that and I did it. I remember there was one kid named Jim Davis who used to go by just like he was a cowboy. On a Shetland pony. I'd ask Dad for a Shetland pony and he always said, "A Shetland pony shouldn't be for children. There's no meaner horse alive. Good only for a cart," he said. "Half the horse bites in this country are from them little bastards." At the time if I was big enough to handle harrows and a four-horse team, then maybe I was man enough to handle a Shetland pony, but that's one thing about my father: what he said stood as gospel and that pretty well was that.

I was a field pitcher when I was 12 but, of course, this was when I began to shoot up. A field pitcher is the poor fellow out in that big field who hasn't got a team and wagon, so all he does from start of day is go from one rack to another helping other fellows load, and when their load is three-quarters done he's the one who still stays on the ground while the other fellow had the easy job of catching the sheaves and building his load. Then he walks on to the next wagon and starts all over again. Then, half an hour before quitting, he hightails it for the yard and starts the windmill so the trough will be full, and goes into the barn and forks down the hay. There's about a dozen other things he does too.

I didn't mind it so much. One thing in those days, and maybe still now, you were proud of your strength, proud you could work like a man even though you were just a boy in years. But actually you were a man because by the time you were 13 or so and had the knack for farming, which you would pretty well have, there wasn't much you didn't know around the place.

By this time, when you would be 12, you'd pretty well given up the business of school. There didn't seem to be much sense to your going anymore, and each year you stayed away, the harder it got to go. What 15-year-old fellow wanted to sit with a bunch of 11-year-olds when he went back, if he did go back? I don't think there were any laws about when a fellow had to go to school or when he didn't. I know lots of boys in our district never went beyond the third or fourth grade. I got to the sixth and I could read and write and do arithmetic. Usually a fellow married a girl who had gone through, right through, and maybe into town for what they called senior classes, and if it came right down to a lot of figuring, she could do it. A lot of those farm wives did all the figuring, books, elevator accounts, all that in those days. As far as I know there was no income tax then. That would have floored everyone.

At 13, you pretty well considered yourself a man and certainly old enough to tell your old man how he was running the farm wrong. That's when you sure found out fast that you weren't as big as you thought you were.

At 16 you'd start courting or sparking around the district, usually in your own shiny buggy with your own horse because that was something like a car for a young fellow today. A young fellow in those days liked to have his own rig. Gave him mobility, you might say, like taking the Benson girl on a Sunday evening down the road along the creek, something like that. Or there was a lot of visiting too on Sundays. Maybe 10 or 15 young people would get together at one place and sit around and laugh. They've done it enough at our old place. It all depended on how the old folks looked on such goings-on. If they were the kind that would go to prayer meeting on Wednesday night, choir practice on Thursday, and church twice on Sunday—if there was church twice on Sunday—then the chances were you never went to that farm.

About 17 or 18 if you'd decided you were going to be a farmer and in those days, most everybody did unless they tried to get on the road [the railroad] or work in town at something, then you'd start looking around the district for a quarter section or a half, something you maybe could buy. If it meant renting it on shares first, that was usually okay but it had to be in fairly close because you were going to be using your father's equipment for awhile. And anyway, half the time you'd still be over at his place helping out. Of course, there were plenty of times when he'd be over at your place too. That's the way it always worked out unless the father and the boy had a falling out—and that happened too, believe me. Father didn't want the boy to leave and the boy did. Boy tired of his old man's ways and figured he could do it better, and maybe in a lot of cases he could too.

But all through this, what I've been saying is this. It was work and it was hard work. You built up your muscles early and that muscle inside your head soon became used to the idea that on the farm you worked and there was no room for slackers. You've got to remember, there was no machinery then. I mean equipment that worked by turning an ignition key. It was horses and bull labor and you worked and you expected to work, and not just because it was expected of you. You kept on working from about the age of six on, and you were part of that farm's vital machinery in that if you fell down on your job, took sick, ran away, then that farm wouldn't run so good because a smart part of that machinery was gone and that was you. You worked hard, and I'm telling you that as the truth.

The Early Years Come Back to Me

Memory of events, persons, and places of the early years come back to me easily now, although I might have trouble remembering what I did last week. Those early days are so much clearer now than my later years. I guess most old people find this is so.

I can remember back to when I was four years old. I remember my first spring, but I remember the terrible winter before it too. In those pioneer years winters in Manitoba were really bad. I don't know if they are as bad now. The great freeze started usually in late October and lasted until early April, and the only livable place during that time was inside the house or in the school. It was sometimes down to 60 degrees below zero.

Inside our house it was far from pleasant. Our place was built before the railroad came, and most of the wood and supplies had to be hauled in from Rapid City, which was 20 miles away. Our house had two stories and was well built and snug against rain and snow, but the terrible cold seeped through into every room except the kitchen, freezing everything. The kitchen stove was kept filled all winter long with wood, and that wood was stored up for a year in advance because once winter came, there was no way you could go into the woods and find firewood. The kitchen was the best place in the house.

Then came the living room. The fire was lit in it after dinner to warm it up for the supper meal, which was the only meal we ate outside the kitchen. Breakfast and dinner, at noon, we ate in the kitchen like most farm families. Like all farm families, I guess.

When I was four that was my first winter I slept downstairs in a bed. I had always been in a crib in Mother's room before that. Her room was off the kitchen and now I shared a bed up in the North Room with my brother Billy, who was six. Nearly every morning we'd wake up to find frost on our curly hair. Billy's hair was dark and mine was quite goldy-like, but first thing in the morning we'd have the same color hair, a sparkling white.

There was no plumbing in the house and it was too cold to go out to the backhouse, so every room had a chamber and it was our job to empty these every morning, although it was difficult sometimes because the contents of these chambers were often frozen. I didn't like that job.

That winter, when I was four, I was given another chore and that was filling the woodbox. First thing after breakfast Mother would bundle me up, earcaps and wool mittens with moccasins over heavy duffels on our feet, and then we'd go out to the big pole tepee where our wood was stored. These tepees were quite familiar in Manitoba farmyards of those times. One tepee would be one year's supply of wood, cut, dried, and stacked for the following winter. This work was done late in the fall. The wood was cut by bucksaws as there was no such thing as electricity or engines. I'd make many many trips from the tepee to the kitchen until I got the woodbox filled, and that would last for another day. This was a job that had to be done every day except when blizzards threatened, and you could sort of feel them in the air. Then Mother would make sure that I brought in a lot more wood and it was stored, piled in her room against a wall.

Children over six years old had to go to school. I was too little, but I used to watch with envy when my older brother Jim would bring the jumper around to the door and all the kids of the family who were old enough would jump in and Jim would drive off with bells jingling across the snowy fields to the little school. I always wanted to go with them but my mother would always say, "Never mind, Johnny, you'll grow up soon enough."

Those days when the other children were at school and I was at home with my mother helping and doing the chores I remember now as the most valuable of my whole life. She was a busy woman with seven children. She was small and very elegant and dainty, and she was too young to go to school in

Ontario before the family came to Manitoba. Then when they did get a school set up in the district where the family lived, she was too old to go. But she taught herself to read and write and she could write beautifully. She read so well that the minister often asked her to read the Scripture in Sunday school and church.

When she told us stories, we really climbed with Jack up that beanstalk to that castle in the sky, and when she read the Bible, the heroes came alive and were right in the room with us. My grandmother once said, later, "Lizzie knows more of the Bible and of Shakespeare and *Pilgrim's Progress* than all the rest of the family put together."

I know now that she never liked the pioneer life, but she did it as a labor of love for her husband and family. It's amazing to me now that she lived through 17 years of hardship and toil and childbearing and a terrible climate when you consider that when she was a teen-ager she was considered a consumptive. Eventually she did die of that disease.

It was that winter when I made my first trip with my parents as Mother wanted the first family group photo taken, and we had to go to the town of Hamiota, which was nine miles west of Oak River. This was in the winter of 1895. I was four years old. The trip made a deep impression on me. I remember being decked out in a new suit, which my mother had made. We ate breakfast by lamplight and the January sun was just peeping over our bluff when we got into our two-horse bobsleigh, which Father was using for this trip.

This contraption was sort of a double bobsled arranged tandem under the grain wagon box and held together by a king-pin and by side stakes in the bob-sills. The high spring seat for the driver was hitched onto the main box near the front of the wagon box, and a second tier was added as a wind break in case a storm blew up. Just back of the driver's seat was our comfortable nest and it had two low benches lined up on either side of the wagon set upon two thick horse blankets, and under each bench there were two big hot stones to keep the feet and legs warm. Can you picture the arrangement? This was the way people traveled in those days, in the worst of weather, but they were tough and they made it.

Mother and me and the girls sat in the back under two big buffalo robes, Jim and Billy sat up on the spring seat with Father, and away we went dashing down the road to the trail to Hamiota. It was a cold morning and the air was clear as could be, and as we got closer we could see the tiny village, the town of Hamiota, from more than 10 miles away. Even today I can see it as it lay there gleaming under the morning sun, sort of silhouetted against the blue sky, and I saw two pearly gates. I remember asking Mother if that was the place in the sky where heaven was and she said, "No, that is Hamiota, where we will soon be, and those two big towers you see are the grain elevators." The pearly towers I saw were the grain elevators.

That's the only thing I remember about that trip.

Happy With Two Bits a Day

When I started out first of all to be my own man I was about 11 years old. I shoveled grain for a threshing crew outfit which was hauling it in wagons. Five wagons on the rig hauling grain and I was at the bin and I had to keep up with those five wagons, throwing it back into the bin, with a big scoop. I got two bits a day, that's what I got.

That would be 12 hours a day. They had a ruling, the government did, that 10 hours was a working day, but that didn't stop this threshing rig from working 12. No, you worked 12 hours if you wanted the job.

You started at seven in the morning and worked until eight at night, and I've seen us work until 11 at night. Instead of putting me with a team of quiet horses to haul, they give me the heaviest work in the whole crew and I was only 11 years old. How did I stand it? I can't tell you. Course I was a strong little beggar, but that was work that maybe a full-grown man would have caved in under before noon. There's not a young person in this country could do it today.

The going rate for men was a dollar and a half, but because I was a boy and couldn't speak up for myself much I got 25 cents a day. Oh sure, I thought it was not enough money, but I wanted to be on my own. Course I lived at home but I wanted my own money to spend the way I wanted. But oh, when I think of it, they was mean to kids. Twenty-five cents a day, that's what the farmer paid me. Of course, what I didn't tell him was that I was tickled to death to get the work. Things have changed, haven't they? Darn right they have.

Children Just Kept on Coming

Once my mother got going, she had one every year. She had 11 children. The people down the road had 12. I have known women to have 15 children and when the oldest was 20 years old, maybe 10 or 12 of those children were still alive. Some of them would be having children of their own. Remember, it was nothing for a girl to get married at 15 and a boy too, although the girls seemed to get married earlier.

Yes, big families. They just kept coming and coming. They certainly didn't have the pill or any other of the doodads they have now. If you didn't want children I guess you didn't do it, but as you know, those winter nights were long.

You don't see those big families except among the farmers now. Most people in the cities and towns today, two children. Maybe three at the outside. But I remember going to picnics or places where you'd meet people and my sister would be introducing me around, and she'd say, "This is Mrs. Jones. She's got seven," and then, "Meet Mabel Brown, she's got six," and so on. She could have said that Mrs. Jones lived near her and her husband had two sections of land or whatever, but no, everybody was introduced by the number of children they had. This is today, in the last 20 years, so farmers still have big families.

Everything was done by midwives. But were midwives all that necessary? After you've had six children in eight years, really, is a midwife necessary for the seventh, eighth, and so on? I don't think so. The women, although many could keep very nice figures, the women became in fact like baby machines. Just out it would come and nothing unusual about that. Somebody would say at the store that the Sycamores had a new baby and nobody would be the least surprised. The only thing the man might ask would be, "A boy?" Boys were wanted. Girls were to be married off, sent to teach school. Maybe one to stay around the house as an old maid. It was always handy to have a spinster around. People after a while actually forgot she was there, but she did all the work. I'll tell you it wasn't much of a life being an old maid on a prairie farm. Live and work until you die, and that was about the size of it.

Sometimes it was quite surprising how many children lived. It seems there always was some kind of illness going around. One year, 1908 I think it was, it was diphtheria. Another year, too, it was diphtheria. Then there were the diseases that all children get—smallpox, scarlet fever, things like that. Of course, the influenza was very bad some years and a lot of people died, but I don't think you heard too much of the children dying. They seemed hardy, these children from big families. They seemed to survive better. They'd come to school with hardly anything warm on, the girls maybe only in thin stockings and a wool scarf wrapped around them and their hands just blue with cold, and the same with the boys, but they were hardy. They were strong in those days.

Of course there were some who didn't have big families. North of us were some Scandinavian farmers and they didn't have many children each. But the Scotch did, the Austrians, the Germans, the Polacks and, of course, the Ukrainians. I often thought some of these people didn't know what caused babies. I have honestly thought that since.

Now that I think back on it, maybe it was the Scotch that had the biggest families of all. But they didn't stay on the farm long. Away to work for somebody else. Work on the railroad. The girls to the city to work as shopgirls or in offices when not too many girls did that. They'd go to business school first, which were first starting up. A lot of the boys went into railroading. The C.P.R. because that was our station and they could get a recommendation to the roadmaster from the station agent. Some boys went to Wesley College and became student ministers and this was the way they spent their summers. They might not have believed in God and salvation but it was one way of getting an education. As I remember the Scotch, they were very strong on education. Education was a big thing with them. It was with the Germans too.

Those big families. Maybe women were more used to the idea of having children in those days.

Why Did We Need That Spring Tonic?

Every spring, just as sure as you'd see the first crow or hear the first meadowlark—"Yes, I am a pretty little bird"—you know how their song went, up and down. Well, just about that time it was time for spring tonic.

I don't know why Mother felt we needed a spring tonic, why every kid in the country needed a spring tonic, but we all got it. She'd mix up some sulfur and molasses, a batch of it, and I still don't know how it was done because I vowed I'd never give my children such a horrible mess. But for three or four mornings, we'd line up before going to school and have to swallow this big spoonful of sulfur and molasses. Ugh. I can still taste it. The molasses, I suppose, was to kill the taste of the sulfur, and what the sulfur did for us I'm afraid I'll never know.

The Great Pedal Organ Caper

In the fall of 1896 I was born. Right there on the place my father had north of Crane Lake. He delivered me when my mother took to her bed. No doctor in them times. Washed me and weighed me on a trout scale. Six and a quarter pounds. He said I come out like a trout, just a-flopping.

There was no road then like there is now up to Leader, but when I was about nine he started to send me over the old trail down to Maple Creek. I think it was about 18 miles. My father was crazy about the London papers. *Punch* was one of them. He'd been a gentleman in England, and now he had cowshit on his boots, two other kids besides me, both smaller, and nothing but a bunch of cows and wild horses and he'd hire on with one of the ranches. That was the old Lister ranch that got split up when they went broke. For years old-timers when I was growing up would spin yarns about how those Englishmen who had the ranch pissed their money right down the drain. They didn't know nothing about cows.

When I was 'bout nine my father told me I had to get the mail. There should have been mail service, but for some reason there wasn't, and I'd hike into Maple Creek. Sleep in the livery barn and come back next day. I'd get a cup of tea and a hard biscuit in the morning from the old nighthawk at the stable and that would see me home.

One day the postmaster said for me to go over to the freight shed. There was a slip in our box telling me to do that. Something for us. It turned out to be a pedal organ sent out from the Old Country, and when I saw it I thought how was I going to get it out to the ranch. It was a Foster. Three feet long, three high maybe, maybe 200 pounds, and all nicely done up in cherry wood. I was walking, you see, so I got a screwdriver and took that thing apart. There are dozens of parts in an organ, pipes, valves, tubes, dowels, parts glued together, pedals, bellows. You never saw such a mess when I had it all laid out on a floor in a room in the station. I forgot who the agent was then, but he'd just come around and shake his head. "You've got one big whopper by the tail," he'd say and then he'd come back. Fascinated.

I had a sack and the first trip back I put in some small parts and hiked home, and I think for about three months, every time I went to the Creek I brought more pieces home, piece by piece. All these little pieces. God, when I think of it! I must have been crazy. A nine-year-old and you know, by God, I had never seen an organ before.

Finally I got the last stick home, a big glued piece, and I did it with a travois. Two poles, one cross-stick, the piece tied on top, and I trailed home like an Indian.

I'll just say I put it together. I took quite a while but it wasn't as hard as I thought. When my mother sat down to play it for the first time it worked. She played a hymn. Then she played "Rule Britannia." Then she played "God Save the King." Then she got up and she kissed me on both cheeks. I'm glad my father wasn't there. He'd probably have fetched me a clout on both ears and a kick in the ass to boot. He was that kind of a man.

Looking After 30 Head of Stock

My sister would be hardly nine, eight years old, because she was younger than me, and my brother was nine. They had to look after 30 head of stock, water them, tie them, clean them out, go to school and do their lessons, and also do all the other work around the farm that was expected of them. At that age.

Imagine the kids of this day. These kids, it would have been better today if they had had something to do. There wouldn't have been these hippies today, I can tell you. And every one of those kids in our family made something out of their life. Yes, sir, they all turned out well. Very well.

Fun Was What We Made It

In the early days youngsters entertained themselves. At Christmas you might get a toy or you might not, but if you did it was usually, if you were a boy, some little wagon or something that your dad had whittled out for you after you'd gone to bed. A girl might get a rag doll. That was about the size of it.

You made things. We made our own bows and arrows and we got pretty good with them. We could never quite get the right kind of wood for the bow that would give the arrow just that right zip. No, we didn't play cowboys and Indians. Not that I can remember. I imagine that came along after the silent movies came along, and that was quite a while later.

We made our own baseball bats and a ball. The bat, well you know how it was made, and the ball was leather stuffed with rags and sewed up tightly. You could hit it quite a long way. In our town there were a lot of Americans, those who had come up from Minnesota and Illinois and places like that. If the town had a lot of Americans, then everybody played baseball. That was their game. If the town had a lot of Englishmen, then you played soccer. Kick football.

We also played tag and hide-and-go-seek. Stuff like that. Pretty simple stuff. We didn't need a lot of swings and turn-abouts and sandboxes and a supervisor to make us happy.

You hear about young folk today as being pretty wild, but as

I remember it, we were a pretty good bunch. We all grew up together and there was no this side of the tracks and that side of the tracks. No snobbery is what I mean. The doctor's son and the drayman's son or the grocer's son and the poorest farmer's son would be good friends and all part of the gang. There was only one gang in the town, mind you, and if something went wrong our parents quickly knew where to look. It wouldn't be anybody but us kids raising the ruckus.

And then most kids around 10 or 12 years of age had a horse of some description and we used to go rousting around the country. There were darn few roads in those days, mostly only the main line road graded by plowing up four or five furrows on each side and throwing the dirt up on the center with a grader, but we didn't stick too much to the roads. It was off into the country, into the bush.

We'd shoot gophers and badgers. A badger hole could break a horse's leg easy as snapping a match stick. We'd hunt ducks. Sometimes we'd ride eight or nine miles down the line to the next town and spend a nickel or so for candy in the store. We did a lot of riding, riding on the prairies.

The creek was two miles south, and in the wintertime we'd go down there with our skates and skate for miles. Somebody would carry a small sack and at noon, yes, this would be on a Saturday—never Sunday for we had to go to church—we'd stop and build a fire and cook up some meat and eat our bread from the sack. That was a lot of fun too. Cold or not, as long as there was no snow on the ice that was the most fun in the winter.

Curling was big in our town but that was for grown-ups. The club in our town had a building they put up every fall and took down about the middle of April and it had two sheets of ice, but some towns just curled out in the open. They had bonspiels which were fun to watch for us kids.

Our fun was all of our own make. Nobody helped us and nobody told us what to do. If we were doing wrong then somebody came along and told us not to, and that's about as far as it went.

I remember about 1906 or '07 a fellow coming to town with an old Edison gramophone and he set it up in the church hall, records for an hour or so entertainment, and people came and

Against an unlimited horizon, a new settler breaks prairie sod for his first crop. (Provincial Archives of Alberta, Photograph Collection)

Looking like a great roaring beetle, the steam tractor revolutionized farming, breaking and cultivating more land than 10 teams could do in a day. (Provincial Archives of Alberta, H. Pollard Collection)

Opposite page, top: In the early days, harvests were truly outstanding, making the promoter's boasts come true. Center: A harvest gang breaks off work to pose for a picture. Many harvesters came from the East on special trains to work the fields of the West. Bottom: Like a great army on the march, a long line of binders hitched to new gas tractors moves through a grain field in 1911. (Public Archives Canada, PA 32612; PA 38655; PA 29941)

Below: Smaller than those today, and of slightly different shape, grain elevators, those symbols of the prairies, line up along the railroad tracks at Lauder, Manitoba. (Public Archives Canada, PA 70871)

Homesteading was hard and money uncertain, and many farmers worked in the coal mines during the winter to provide a few extra dollars for the family. (Public Archives Canada, PA 38662)

In northern areas, farmers worked in the woods, getting out logs for lumber, railway ties, or cordwood. A hard life in a hard land. (Provincial Archives of Alberta, H. Pollard Collection)

Some who came to farm stayed to ranch, and many a small valley had its spread, house, barn, corrals, and a way of life unique to North America. (Provincial Archives of Alberta, H. Pollard Collection)

A tough breed, the Alberta cowboy differed from his American counterpart only in that he did not carry a Colt revolver. (Provincial Archives of Alberta, E. Brown Collection)

Rails opened up the West, and the builders were an ingenious lot. The Canadian Pacific came first, followed by the Grand Trunk Pacific, whose bridge-building crews are shown here spanning a shallow river valley. (Public Archives Canada, PA 38622)

Teams of horses, men, shovelers, Fresno scoops, mechanical monsters—all went into building the bed for the railroad. One day crews working in the flatlands southeast of Calgary laid eight miles of bed, an astonishing feat. (Public Archives Canada, PA 38679)

The corner of Portage and Main, Winnipeg, 1872. Peter Broadfoot led this small wagon train out of town. (Public Archives Canada, PA 66785)

The same corner, 40 years later. Winnipeg, known as the Gateway to the Golden West, was a large trading center and entrance for the tens of thousands of immigrants who passed through to the West seeking their fortune. (Public Archives Canada, C 34023)

Lloydminster in 1904. Shacks, soddies, dugouts, stables, houses went up on the frontier as each town opened up for business. The sign above this door seems like an afterthought. (Provincial Archives of Alberta, E. Brown Collection)

Left: a typical prairie town, circa 1902. Right: The general store, which tried to meet the settler's every need. (Public Archives Canada, C 63573; PA 29444)

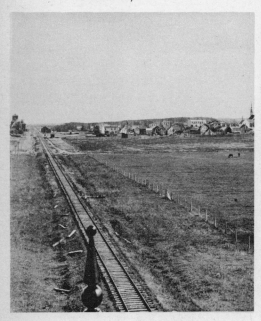

paid a dime or a nickel and just sat and listened. Us kids thought that was wonderful. We'd never thought such things existed before. Oh yes, we enjoyed it, just sitting there listening.

Of course, the Swiss Bell Ringers were of the early days. They cost money too. Once every year they'd come, stopping at every town on the Soo Line. Well, it was a group of people and I'm not sure they was Swiss, but they had different size bells and they'd play tunes. They was a big event. The Swiss Bell Ringers. A real event.

The circus? Yes, oh yes, the circus. It came to Milestone once or twice. The advance agent came through and there was nothing to talk about except the circus for weeks before. Ringling's. Oh yes, the big tent. I can remember we had cisterns at our house and all our water was rainwater. Well, a man from the circus asked my brother and I where there was water, and we said we had lots. So we carried water to the elephants the whole day long, eight or nine hours, two pails at a time, across the tracks, back to the house, across the tracks, all day, and when we finished the man in charge gave us each a ticket to the side show. The side show. Not the circus itself. We showed them to my dad and he hit the roof. He went over to the circus man and he came back soon with two tickets to the main show. He was mad, them trying to slough us off with a 10-cent ticket after we'd carried water all day, and precious water at that. He wasn't having none of that.

Theater? Oh, we had the odd company that used to come. Dreadfuls, you know. Melodrama. The villain and the mortgage and the pretty farm girl, and in those days it was all pretty wonderful. But even then we weren't usually allowed to go to the theater. Even something like a villain and the farm girl was considered a little risqué for us. No, we'd mostly go to the bell ringers. I wonder if you could get a kid today to cross the street to see some bell ringers? Yet the farmers and their families used to come from miles around to see them. Sometimes in very cold weather.

Yes, mostly, we made our own fun. We'd build dugout forts on the prairie and snow forts in winter. We didn't do anything really wrong. Nothing destructive, you understand, although there might be a little hellery on Hallowe'en Night. I remember once some of the older boys put an Adams Wagon on top of the livery barn. Took it apart, hauled it up, put it together again, and nobody heard a sound. Everybody knew who did it.

All in all, I'd say that we were pretty good little boys. The words "juvenile delinquent" took another 50 years to get invented.

10 Wives, Widows, and Whores

How I Learned to Make Bread . . . Mother Was a Midwife . . . Some Women Couldn't Take It . . . I Told Her No . . . Grandma Shanks Got Things Done . . . So We Got Married . . . I Ran the Farm . . . Mother Called Them "Fancy Girls" . . . Whipped Cream on Everything . . . I Wanted to Get Off That Farm . . . A Good Day's Work in Two Hours . . . The Strongest Woman I Ever Knew . . . The Hard Way to Finish High School . . . A Married Woman, at 15 . . . That's the Way Things Were Done . . . The Spirit of the West

Some of the women who came to Canada couldn't take the hardship, the poverty, the cold, and the loneliness. And some left, either forcing their husbands to take the family home again or leaving by themselves, alone. But for every woman who quit, there were thousands who stayed with their men and took it.

They looked after the house, cooked, sewed, mended, tended the garden. They helped on the hay rake, milked cows, made butter and traded it and eggs after a long ride or walk to the village store. They walked beside the oxen and brushed off the flies in the long July afternoons; kept the home fires burning during the bitter prairie winters. They bore the babies and did whatever was necessary to give the family its sense of cohesiveness in a large and lonely land.

One man said that the men who failed were usually men without women. In addition to the homesteader's steadfast wife, there were teachers, girls who came for adventure—and hus-

*bands, prostitutes who regularly visited the railway towns.
They were all women of courage, strength, humor, and determination. And I can't think of one woman I met who didn't say she
would do it all over again.*

How I Learned to Make Bread

Oh, I'll never forget that first year. I made a perfect fool of myself. A perfect fool.

Bread. My husband said a family needed bread, and I had a
recipe book my mother had given me and it told how to make
bread. But I just couldn't do it. I tried and tried but it wouldn't
rise or it was sour or like lead or big air holes in it. Always something wrong. Well, my husband said, "Why can't you make the
barmy stuff?" and I said I had never been taught. After all, in
the town I had lived in the baker came around with his wagon
and his hot box every morning and you just went out to the lane
and chose bread and scones and whatever you wanted. Well
Weyburn certainly wasn't England. I'll say that again. My husband told me to ask the neighbors and I said I didn't like the
neighbor women. And I didn't. They were coarse. I wasn't
putting myself on a pedestal. These women were coarse, gossips.
Almost strumpets. Some of them, anyway.

We got this farm paper and there was a column that gave
advice and it was printed by a woman called Millicent Miller.
I'm sure that was the name. You wrote her a question and she'd
answer it, so I wrote this woman—which wasn't her real name,
I found out later—and lo and behold in about three weeks the
paper came back and there was my letter printed, and with my
name on it. Well, you can imagine how I felt. Other letters she
printed had initials, like G.T. or B.R. I thought she'd do it with
me, but there was Mary Watson, Weyburn, large as life. But
there was a recipe to make bread, which as far as I could see

was the same as the one in my book. So I just forgot about it that day. I didn't tell my husband, that's for certain.

Next morning there is a knock on the door and I look out and there's a Mrs. Ratigan on the stoop. I knew her. She was one of the coarse ones. Irish. A big woman and even though I didn't have much to do with her on our street I believed her to be capable. She just looked like she was. In the store she was always wiping some child's nose or slapping another, but they obeyed her and that was something. Children were as much ruffians in those days as they are now.—

When I opened the door she just barged in and said, "Mary Watson. Weyburn. Bread. I read it," and she sat down. Then she said, "Nobody ever learned to make bread out of a book. It takes a mother to teach her daughter. Where's your mother?" I said in Guildford in England and she said, "Fine. Leave her there. I'll be your mother this morning and we'll make bread."

And we did. She stood beside me and told me how to mix and how to pour and how to get the heat up and how to punch and poke. When it was rising wè sat around and drank tea and I even thought of giving her something in her tea out of my husband's cabinet, but decided I wouldn't. Then she said, "The Good Lord never said that a person always has to have Irish coffee. There's Irish tea, too, you know, dear." I laughed and got up and got the brandy. I was getting to like her and when I came back with the bottle she poured a great whack in it, smiled, and said, "If you weren't Anglican I would have said you were one of the true faith."

She left about three in the afternoon. There wasn't much left in my husband's bottle but I didn't care. He'd forget about that when he saw that I'd learned to bake bread and buns. There were four nice loaves and some buns waiting for him under clean washcloths on the kitchen table when he came home from the store. I was that proud.

He never knew about the little ad I'd put in Millicent Miller's column in the paper. He only found about it years later and he said that half the town must have been laughing at me. I said no, I didn't guess so. I got some very nice smiles when I went shopping after that; people talked to me and I met some nice ladies. And besides, Mrs. Ratigan told me that day if anybody laughed at me for what I'd done, she said she'd conk them on the snoot.

Mother Was a Midwife

Well, my mother was a bit heartbroken at first, you know, when she found she had to leave her nice home in England and come out to Canada, but she was a very brave woman. She didn't care if she had to live in a gopher hole. She'd have dropped everything and come out here because she wanted to live with him.

What she did shows you the kind of woman my mother was. She went around with her family doctor back in England for a long time to learn how to deliver babies, because she knew she was coming to a place where there were a lot of women and no doctors. She delivered all the babies in the settlement while she was there. She was a marvelous woman. A wonder woman and she never boasted about it.

The nearest doctor was at Moosomin and that was far too far away to come for a baby, so Mother would pitch in and do the job. She delivered whole families, getting up at all times of the night when somebody came and said she was needed.

There were very few doctors in that part of Saskatchewan at the time, very few. Once one moved into a town only about 12 miles away but Mother told everybody not to go to him. Said he was nothing but a horse doctor. Wanted to give pills to everyone.

Yes, she was midwife. Delivered all the babies. Very capable. She never had any nursing training but she was nurse and doctor too. People used to come to her with other things wrong with them. She'd fix them up. If she could.

I remember once my sister fell off the swing. She was just a little thing, about two years old, and she shoved a piece of wood deep into the ball of her foot and they couldn't get it out. But Mother just put her teeth on it and pulled. It came out all right. So you see, she wasn't only a midwife but a nurse and doctor too.

Of course in those days there was no such thing as a hospital. Unheard of. There would be one in the big towns, in Weyburn or Regina or Saskatoon, but the small settlements they had no hospital. Babies were all born at home. They had to be. Where else would they be born? Right in the mother's bed. Most babies were born in the bedroom or the kitchen, plenty of hot water and clean sheets, and the midwife there.

Of course that doesn't count the times when the husband himself delivered the baby. No midwife around. Couldn't get there or there was none.

But most settlements and towns had one or two women who were midwives. They had no training but they had it up here, up in the head, experience and common sense and kindness. A wonderful woman, my mother.

Some Women Couldn't Take It

A lot of women should never have come out to Canada. Like in my own family. We lived among the chimneypots. We knew all our neighbors and they all knew us, and we were closely knit in our town. Then Dad comes home one night from the mill and he's got a handful of the pamphlets telling about homesteading in Canada and he said, "Mum, we're going to Canada."

He knew nothing about Canada. Not even where it was. He knew you just got on a ship and sailed away and then you got 160 acres and you farmed it. Now, that much land was an estate to an Englishman in a town. So off they went, kit and kaboodle, Sunday dresses, best linen, family cutlery, and my God, things you would never use in a hundred years. My father even went down to the High Street and bought a great big dagger.

And finally you were out on the bare prairie. In a sod house and where were you? Nowhere. Your nearest neighbor, the Jacksons or the Meltons, miles away across the prairie and every sound outside at night was a grizzly bear.

Some women couldn't stand it. What happened I don't know, but after about a year my mother had to go home. She couldn't take it and somehow or other we raked up the money and she went back to England with the baby. Dad and the rest of us stayed; we never saw her or the baby again. I don't know how much Dad grieved. When a man is working six months away from home in town at a dollar a day and six months on the homestead, working before dawn to after dark to prove up, there's not much time to think, is there?

I wonder if anybody saved those pretty pamphlets?

I Told Her No

One day my employer said to me, "Tommy, you and Mary"— the hired girl, a peach of a girl, slightly red-haired, half-breed— he said, "you and Mary go into the granary and start fanning the oats." He had a fanning mill. Do you know what a fanning mill is? Good.

So Mary began to turn it and there was a big pile of oats and I had a pail and I began to fill it up. We kept working and got smothered in dust and then Mary all at once stopped and she looked at me. I said, "What's up, Mary?"

She said, "Look, Tommy, will you marry me?"

I was dazed. I had a girl in England and I said, "Well, look, Mary, I'm engaged to a woman in England. I plan to bring her out here and marry her."

She could talk good English. She could talk Cree too, of course, and she said, "Never mind that. If you will marry me I'll give you 240 acres of land." That was her half-breed scrip they got after the Rebellion. "I'll give you 15 head of horses and 10 head of cattle that I own."

Now I had 160 acres and with her 240 acres and horses and cows I could have been a rich man, right away. Four hundred acres of land, everything to start with and it would've taken me years accumulating that much. I could have been rich, in the terms of the country then, right away.

Well, I told her no. That I had this woman in England and I was afraid I couldn't.

Mary Brett was a lovely girl, she was wealthy by the standards of those days, and yet I turned her down. When I told her so, she didn't say anything but just began to work the mill again.

If I had married her my whole life would have changed. I would have had a running head start in life. Do you think I was a fool?

Grandma Shanks Got Things Done

In every community, wherever people gathered on the prairies, there was someone who was a leader. Not a leader in today's sense of the word, perhaps, but a leader who was called in to get things done. In our community that was Grandma Shanks.

When sickness came—measles, mumps, or whooping cough —Grandma Shanks was called in because a doctor's care was hard to get or pay for. Also, we had more confidence in Grandma's remedies and her nursing. She had raised a large family of her own and under very pioneer conditions. Her knowledge and experience of children's ills was beyond that of most family doctors, at least around our part of the world. For all intents and purposes she had been the doctor for the entire settlement long before any doctors had been available in our part of Manitoba. But I'll say this for her, if she was called and the trouble was beyond her skill, she was the first to call for Dr. Crookshanks, who was over in the town.

As a maid, a bonnie Scottish lass from Aberdeen, she decided instead of going to finishing school in Edinburgh that she'd visit relatives in Canada. Imagine. That set her future. She married

William Shanks and they settled down in Ontario, but as in so many of these cases, they needed more land than they had there, and here were all the promises of free land in Manitoba. Land for the asking. So the whole family moved out west.

Of course, she wasn't head of the Shanks family then, but as the years went past she became the head and she had to be obeyed instantly. That was the way it was. And not only was she the head of the family but she was the dominant force in the political and religious life of the district. This woman, among all those big and strong men.

It was because of her that the first church was built in the community. It was because of her that the first school district was organized. The men came to her when they wanted to be nominated to local office. This bonnie Scots lass.

Grandma was deeply religious and was brought up in the Scottish Presbyterian Church. Know what that means? To her John Knox and John Calvin were the two great heroes of her faith, so it was through her wishes that the first minister for our district came right from the Old Country. Straight from Scotland. He was the Reverend Hosea from Edinburgh and he was our minister and also took churches in settlements around. By doing this, bringing in her own minister, so to speak, she was firmly established as the ruler of religious life in our district.

I'll give you one example. When Mr. Hosea left us, she arranged for another young man to be brought out to fill the vacancy. He was staying with us until the manse could be fixed up for him and his young bride. One day Grandma saw smoke coming out of the outhouse and she saw the young minister coming out of the outhouse and this is how she discovered that he was a smoker. Not long after, the church board met again and the young man was fired and another young man brought in. I asked Grandmother if the young preacher had been fired because he smoked, even though Grandpa Shanks smoked a pipe and my father often smoked cigars. She said: "To me, smoking is a sin because I think it is harmful to health and also wasteful. There are others who think differently and to them it may be no great sin and maybe only a sociable habit.

But deception is very wrong, especially to one who would teach others or to one wearing the cloth."

Did she mean the young preacher was fired because he smoked or that he was fired because he smoked in secret in the backhouse and therefore was deceitful?

So We Got Married

I myself did this, so it is a true story that I am telling you.

My brother came out early. We're from Parry Sound and the farming was hard there. When he bought a farm south of Russell it was just a farm. A house, a poplar pole barn, and not much more and the family had no stock. They really weren't farmers and were going to Edson, which was supposed to be a new and booming town. The man thought that his old trade of shoemaker would be good. Cobblers don't make farmers, remember that. Farmers make farmers and thank the good Lord there are enough born into this world every year.

My brother, sure, he was a crab, as we'd say. Fifteen years older than I was, but he did get himself a wife. By advertisement. Oh, it was done a lot in them years. There were newspapers in Winnipeg and he put in this advertisement and got himself a wife, and in four years they had two youngsters. She was a Polish girl. Mary. Strong and of good soul.

My brother wrote me to come out and get my roots down in this district, but he expected me to work for nothing. It was no life, so I went into town and worked at one of the livery barns. I was 22 at the time. On Saturday night of my 22nd birthday, of that week, Mary came around to the barn and left me a birthday card.

Then Dan got all tangled up in a four-horse team and a breaking plow and that killed him. When he didn't come in Mary went out and saw the horses standing in the brush and she knew what happened. It took a couple of neighbors to get him loose. He was dead anyway. Bled to death, but I think he died of other things too because that 12-inch plow, the point, was in his side.

We had the funeral and it was put on by Dan's lodge, all the men. They wore black suits. It was held on a Sunday. Mary said, after all, it was no time to take a day off for a funeral. That was something I had never thought of, making all funerals on Sunday instead of Tuesdays or Thursdays or when the time was decent.

I drove Mary home. There was no people at the house. We were too far out and the cemetery was in town. There was cows to milk so I did the barn work and then I went up to the house. I wasn't going to set out the milk pans that night. I just put the milk into the pig trough and what was left I just threw away. You see, something was on my mind.

I went to the house and I asked Mary what her plans were. She said she had an aunt in Toronto and a married cousin someplace in New York and that seemed to be about it. I asked her if she was going to leave the farm and she said, "Where would I go?" She had been a governess or lady companion or both in Winnipeg for the Stratton family, but what could she do with two little kiddies?

So we had supper that night and when the kids were in bed I said that the best thing would be if I married her. I remember her saying, "Yes, I've been thinking that myself. We're the same age. Dan was too old for me and I think we can make it work. There's no reason why not. We shouldn't let Dan's death stop us, because there's this farm to run and I'd rather have people talking about our marriage any way they want to than have them talking behind my back about you living here and working on the farm." That's not really what she said but that's what she meant.

Next morning after chores I hitched up and we drove into town and got married. Nobody said anything. Nobody to this day. I went around to the livery barn and picked up my bedroll and my rifle and my chess board and a few other things. Then we went to the store and bought some things and then back to

the farm and we were married people. I think that's all I need
to tell.

Accidents happened. A woman couldn't be left on a farm
alone and there were a lot of weddings, quick-like. I know that
today people would be shocked. It just wasn't done. Even then,
in the city, it wouldn't be done, but out in the bush, you just
made up another set of rules and that's the way it was. I know
several cases of men marrying their brothers' widows.

I Ran the Farm

Got married. Went to Winnipeg for the ceremony and then back
again. My huband had the nicest home in the village built for
me. Of course his father paid for it. It just happened his father
was a very wealthy man in England.

My husband when he was on the farm, he never did anything.
In fact, he never even blacked his own boots until he went into
the Boer War. So you can imagine. But he wanted to farm. I
knew more about farming than he did.

Some men should never be farmers. Some men are city people
and they should never have come to the Saskatchewan prairies
where life was so hard. I practically ran that farm. I'd had all the
experience ever since I was a small child.

I ran the farm for three years when he was overseas. He
wanted to go off to war so he did and left me alone. You couldn't
get proper help. I remember I had one old man as a hired man.
He was cranky. He was cruel to the horses in this way. He
wouldn't get after the horses when he was on the machine in
case he got toppled off the machine. But when he had them tied
up in the barn he'd take the bullwhip to them. I remember that.
I could hear this lash going and I stopped that. That's the type
he was. He left me in the middle of seeding. It was an argument
over the cows.

We had another man there who was a huge great hulking fellow but he was a little bit simple, you know? But he was an educated man and the poetry he used to write, love and hope and fear and all this nonsense. All that, over and over again. In the cow barn he'd put the milk pails down and weave back and forth and give out with this poetry, bellowing in a loud voice. I had a hired girl and she came in one night and she said, "I think he's lost his mind."

Anyway, the poet left and I got a Russian. He was big enough but he knew nothing about farming. This man was willing, mind you, but the things he used to do. He'd try and put a hay rick through a gate that would barely take a wagon. Drive it full tilt at the gate. Wreck everything. He didn't know about the young colts. He'd leave the halters on too tight until they practically had grown into their cheeks. I had to keep watch on everything on that farm all the time.

By the time I finished I bought another half section of land. I put all the money from the wheat back in the farm. I knew my husband was no farmer, never should have been, and I wanted to have as good a farm as I possibly could when he got back. I put a 30-foot extension on the barn so the cows didn't have to winter out. All the buildings painted, house and everything. Two henhouses put up. I bought sheep and built them into a good crop.

So when my husband came back there was a better farm than when he'd left. Much better. Then things started to happen.

I bought a sow and I paid 50 dollars for her and we put up a fence between the boar and the sow and her piglets, eight of them, and the first day my husband was home he saw this fence and he said, "What's the point of that fence being there? It just means more walking around to feed them." So he pulled it down and that night the boar got in and killed those eight little pigs. That was the start.

When the price went up and it was two dollars a bushel and our wheat was all threshed and ready to haul and I told him he had better haul it to the elevator right away, to market, and he said there was all winter to haul the wheat. By the time they hauled it that same wheat was 50 cents a bushel.

He had friends who'd play cards with him. They'd gamble

with him. They'd go swimming with him and is it any wonder I got sick of the farm? I knew what to do, you see, but there was nobody to help me.

There was enough wheat left in the bin to pay the second installment of the half section of land I'd bought and so what did he do? He took that money and he bought the first car and then he bet with his friends he could go from our place across the Indian reservation with potholes and rocks in just half an hour. He did it. He smashed the car to pieces. He liked a good time.

Things went from bad to worse, going haywire, and I could see it. His father sent out 3,000 dollars to save the farm and that went. And then when we hardly had enough money to buy the bare necessities of life he went into town and bought a piano. That did it for me, I think.

There are some men who should never be allowed on a farm. My husband was one. Oh, well.

Mother Called Them "Fancy Girls"

We had this little store in the valley and all our goods came in by C.P.R. because there were no roads to speak of. The C.P.R. was the beginning and end-all.

Mother was the real businessman of our family. She was a real go-getter. My dad managed to keep the store going, which was an accomplishment in those days because he never had any money for stock. The only money he made was when he sold the store twice, to two different fellows and they couldn't make it go and Dad took the store back from them. He'd got his down payment and then a while later he got his store back. We lived, free rent and wholesale groceries.

My father was never much good at collecting bills. He'd give out the credit and the wholesalers would expect my dad to pay the bills when October came, and my dad expected the farmers to pay their bills at the same time too, when the crops were sold. But not all of them did and my mother was all the time pushing him to collect. He usually did, eventually.

My mother was the backbone of the family. My father had a heart of gold and was a wonderful man but, as I said, not too much of a head for business. My mother was different. Here's what she used to do.

She used to take trunks, four or five big trunks, and go to the city wholesales. She'd fill those trunks to the brim with fancy clothes and hats and dresses and underwear and shoes that she'd ordered before, and they were waiting for her to pick them up. Then she'd get on the train and visit big towns and smaller towns all over the country, and over into the mining country of British Columbia too. This was the early 1900's.

She'd go into these whore houses—she called them sporting houses—and she'd sell them—she didn't call them whores but fancy girls—and she'd sell them fine cloth and lovely dresses in all colors with lace and doo-dads everywhere and hats that looked like they had flower gardens growing out of them. Underwear, fancy underwear, and stockings and shoes.

They loved to see her come. In some towns those girls weren't allowed out on the streets, or maybe just for two hours of one afternoon a week, but like any other women they loved pretty things. I guess you might say it was all part of their business too. Anyway, they waited for the postcard saying she was on her way and they looked forward to seeing her. They couldn't go anyplace to get the latest fashions, so there was Mother. And her trunks.

Still, a staunch Presbyterian, she'd never really admit that there she was, selling her fancy hats to the prostitutes, but one day she sort of came right out and said it. She said they were the only ones who could afford it. No, she said they were the only ones who had any money. Same thing, I guess.

A wonderful business woman.

She was funny too. She belonged to the Temperance League. That was a big thing in those days. She wouldn't allow any liquor anywhere, and we had a small boardinghouse affair next to the store—a few tiny rooms with beds in them for traveling salesmen and travelers who'd come. If she found liquor when she was cleaning up one of these rooms, and even if the man was in the next room, the kitchen, having breakfast and chatting with Dad, she'd march through, right past him with his bottle in her hand, and pour the thing right down the sink. She was a strong woman. They had to be in those days.

Whipped Cream on Everything

I'd been in the country a few years so the young girls who came out as brides from the Old Country, the cities, or Ontario, would come to me and they'd say, "Oh, what will I do? I can't bake, I can't make sauces, I can't give him anything that's nice except meat and potatoes. What will I do?" They would say they couldn't make the stove work or the wood was green, oh what would they do?

I'd tell them, "Look, you've got a cow there and you've got cream, haven't you?" "Oh yes." "Well, cook your cakes and pies and make your sauces and whatever your little heart desires, and then pile up big gobs of good thick whipping cream on everything and he'll never notice that what's under it might have gone wrong."

It worked. I never lost a marriage among all those girls. I knew it would work because that was what I did when I got married.

I Wanted to Get Off That Farm

I was 16 and my father's hired man because he couldn't afford a man. So there I was, a girl of 16 doing a man's work. Or supposed to be. I hated every minute of it and the work was so heavy it was turning me into a man more than a girl. But I had to do it. There was no other way for it.

So one day we're building a stack of stooks in the field by the road and a man in a buggy comes along. He stops and asks where he can find such-and-such a girl for she'd agreed to work on his farm during the stooking and the threshing. His name was Mr. Honey and he was from Binscarth. I told him and he went down the road. Soon he came back and said the girl had left for another job the day before, and would I like the job? He said it would take a month to clean up his place, and I knew by that that he had a real big farm. I forget how many sections he and his boys farmed, but they had their own threshing outfit and crew. He said if I came he would pay me 20 dollars a month. Well, 20 dollars a month was a very fine wage in those days. Real good pay.

I knew I would have to work very hard, up before five in the morning, cooking, baking, but he said there would be a girl of 14 to help me and a boy of 16 who would do heavy work. You see, his wife was dead so I would be in charge.

I'd have given anything to get off our farm, so I thought quickly and I said to Dad that if he let me go I would give him the 20 dollars that I earned and he could hire a full-bodied man while I was away and get twice the work done. I said he might even have some money left over.

My father didn't care much for me, he just wanted the work out of me, so he said all right, if I gave him the 20 dollars I could go. You know, of course, that meant I would be working 15 hours a day, six days a week, for a month for nothing. But that's how much I wanted to get off that farm. So I ran to the house and I gathered up my few belonging and got into Mr. Honey's buggy and away we went. As we drove away I was thinking that just an hour ago I had been sweating in the field pitching those sheaves and that I had an ingrown toenail which was making me squirm and hurt and Father was yelling at me and now I was in a fine democrat and going off to a big farm and my first job.

Every Saturday afternoon Mr. Honey would come into the

kitchen and he'd say, "May, come and trim my whiskers." I had to get the clippers and trim his whiskers and his hair; then he'd put on a white shirt and he'd ride away for the weekend. The first time it happened I said to his daughter, the 14-year-old, I said that her father had a woman, sure as the dickens. She said, "Don't be foolish." But that December she wrote to me and said her father was getting married. A Miss Tibbetts from Fox-warren.

Then next summer he came back for me to work for him, and I told him that I would have thought that now that he was married his wife would be doing all the work. He said, "Oh no. My wife can't make the bread and make the butter and make the meals for a bunch of men like you can." So I went with him that year again and got 20 dollars. I gave it to my father again.

A Good Day's Work in Two Hours

While I had the livery barn the prostitutes used to come in. They always used to travel in pairs.

They'd always come to me to see about the hayloft. I don't know if they did it other places, or if others did it other places, but they wanted to use my hayloft. The barn was near the station. Convenient.

They offered to pay me for my hayloft, but I'd say to them they were making a living, a quiet living, and just as long as they didn't set fire to the place they could use my barn. Five dollars a time, they charged.

It worked this way. They came up from Saskatoon at half past 12 and the train from Edmonton came down at half past two, so that gave them two hours to work—say an hour and three-quarters.

They'd make 25 to 50 dollars each in two hours. A good day's work. Of course they had a couple of hours' train travel too, but that didn't bother them.

How did they contact the men in town? They didn't have to contact them. They was on a schedule. The schedule was written right there on the blackboard of the station—when the Edmonton train came in, when the Saskatoon train went out. And everybody knew they were in the hayloft. Three times a week —Monday, Wednesday, Friday. Like clockwork.

I knew more about what went on in that town than the policeman. Much more, I'm afraid. Everybody knew what was going on, of course, but as long as I didn't take any money for it, nobody blamed me. That went on for quite a while. I never went up into the loft to see just how they worked it, but they did fine. Just so nobody lit a match or the men didn't urinate in the hay after, they could do what they liked. I didn't care.

The Strongest Woman I Ever Knew

I'd like to tell you about my mother.

We'd get in our usual supply of flour every fall. I'd go into town and buy it, haul it out, and this time because I was busy I carried those 12 bags into the kitchen and every one weighed 98 pounds. Ninety-eight of anybody's pounds. I stacked them in a corner of the kitchen and I said I'd carry them into the loft after dinner and I went out to the barn and I was away no more than 45 minutes. I swear it.

When I came back Mother was making dinner. I looked in the corner and the flour was gone. Huh? She just kept stirring and said she'd put the stuff upstairs in the storeroom. What had she done? She'd carried every one of those 12 bags up a very steep stair and crossed the length, 18 feet, of our loft, and piled those bags. Mother at that time was 52 years old, little, but she was the strongest woman I have ever known.

The Hard Way to Finish High School

It was perfectly scandalous how some of those important people in town used to take advantage of the farm girls.

We lived too far out of town to go back and forth every day, but we did want our education. We had to have it if we were going to ever get a good job in Winnipeg in an office or a business, so we had to attend high school. In those days most farmers were poor and my father just couldn't afford to pay my room and board in town, but there was one way of doing it. A family in town would take you in and you would look after their children and do a bit of work and you could go to high school.

I wanted to get the last two grades that I needed, so this family agreed to give me a place. I won't say who it was but it was in Strathclair and it could have been the home of a banker, a lawyer, doctor, a businessman. People with big homes who needed a bit of help. The woman told my mother: "Oh yes, we'll give Belle a good home and treat her like one of us."

You had to get up early and make breakfast for the family. When you came home from school at lunch you had to make lunch and there were the breakfast dishes all cold and dirty in the sink waiting for you. Back to school and home to do dinner and there were the lunch dishes in the sink. So after dinner you did the dinner dishes along with the lunch dishes and then cleaned up the baby and did some washing and some cleaning and other things and I don't know what not. You were a slave. That's what you were. All these fine people in their fine homes and they treated you like a slave. It's a wonder you could stick it out for the year, but you had to. Then next year they'd get somebody else to do their dirty work. It went on all the time.

How was a person able to do the studies? You had to do that, you know. There was always plenty of homework and nobody got out of it.

And I remember another thing about that fine house. I had beautiful hair, lovely, lovely hair. Dark brown and it used to just shine. I went home for Sunday dinner not too long after I started at this house and I was scratching my head. My mother asked me what was the matter and I said that I was itchy. Mother said, "Come over here." Lice. Just full of lice. It was that bad that Mother just took the foot of that long hair and brought it over this way and cut a huge chunk of it right off. And then we had this heater and she took that hair and shook it over that heat and those lice, you can't imagine how many, they just fell in and burned to death.

That's the kind of a house those people had. But I had to go back. I had to get that year and I had to stay someplace, but by God I worked. And I never forgot how hard those people made me work either. Them, their fancy ways.

A Married Woman, at 15

There was this chap. Joe. He was an Irishman but he'd been in the Argentine and then he came up to Canada. I hired him, put him on the ranch to work with the Indians looking after my cattle. It was pretty country, little lakes, rolling little copses, and he didn't have too much to do. One day when I went out to visit him he asked me where he could get a woman. "Where can I get a woman?" he asks.

I said in a joke that there was an Indian family over on Section 34. My home place was Section 32, so they were neighbors. I mentioned this family had three girls. So this wild man rode over there and scooped up this girl. She was 14 and he put her in the buggy and he heads off to Lashburn to see the minister. Just like that. Just scoops her up.

He was going straight to Lashburn to marry this girl. Did he ask her? I don't know on account of the lingo, but he was going to marry this Indian girl. He didn't even give it much thought. He was an intelligent man. He was educated in a Jesuit College. He was crooked, a Catholic renegade, unscrupulous. If you haven't found out by now that there is a difference between

Irishmen and what there is in the rest of the world, then you haven't found out anything.

Anyhow, he got this girl and she began to scream and squawl, I guess, on the way. She began to cry. Any girl of 14 would, no matter what you were going to do. So he got tired of this and he brought her back and he grabbed up another of the Indian's daughters. This was the oldest, she was 15. Oh yes. Into the buggy she went and she didn't scream or anything; she didn't know the first goddamned thing about what it was all about except she came back a married woman.

At that, Jack, who was the Indian, and his wife they were honored that a white man would marry their girl. They were tickled pink. And Joe taught her English and stuck with her and he took her all over the country on his travels and to the celebrations we used to have. He made a real white woman out of her.

That's the Way Things Were Done

I don't know who first got their hands on a copy of Butler's book on the Wild West, but all the young men in our town read it and they all wanted to come out to the Northwest Territories. Make their fortune.

This book by Butler caused a lot of excitement, but looking back on it I don't know why it should have because he had been writing about another time. Anyway, you know how a bunch of young men are when they get their mind on something. Instead of going to Montreal or Boston or Maine where a lot had gone to before, they all began hightailing it out to the West.

Mind you, I was just a girl of 13 or so at the time when my two brothers left, but in two years I had my schooling, and what was there for a girl to do in a small New Brunswick town? So nothing would do but that I go out and spend the summer with Ted and Will. My brothers. They had taken up land near Moose Jaw. North. And they'd write and say in fun that they couldn't stand their own cooking, so why didn't I go and cook for them? I wrote I could do that and they wrote back and said come soon, come as quickly as I could, and one of them would meet me at the town. I did. I went.

But before I did I had some adventures. My mother packed me a great big hamper of food. There was chickens and pickles and bread and pies and milk—everything to keep me going because it was four or five days across the country. I also had a big suitcase of clothes, you know, and when I transferred at Montreal I had to pay a man to carry all this and I gave him 25 cents.

It was a hard trip, I can tell you. The seats were hard and made of wicker, and they wouldn't fold back like some do now, so you had to sit up all the way across the country. And it was *rough*. The train seemed to go slow. It was always stopping. Sometimes it would stop for an hour, sometimes more, and there was nothing to do about it, not even somebody you could ask about it. And then in some towns they would throw rocks at the train and some windows were broken. This was because in the year before a few trainloads of harvesters had come out from New Brunswick and when the train stopped, these men and boys would run through the town and grab things like food off the shelves of the stores and run back to the tracks and jump on the train when it started to move. This train I was on had a lot of farm workers on it, too, for the next year and the people in the towns had found this out and were waiting. No, I wasn't hurt. Nobody was hurt, but it was an exciting time.

Then we got to Kenora and I started to get my things ready because I thought Moose Jaw was right near Winnipeg. But I found it was many hours away. I stayed the night in a waiting room in the Winnipeg station and finally got to Moose Jaw.

That's about all my life. I cooked for my two brothers, cleaned house, and one day a neighbor who had lived in New Brunswick near us came over and in the autumn I married him. We had three children and they married and had families of their own and I have great-grandchildren now. My husband died 10 years ago. We went through the good times and then the dry years and we stayed on our farm when everybody was leaving to go north or to British Columbia. It all worked out pretty well. My daughter comes round and takes me to the hairdresser once every two weeks and I watch television and sometimes visit and I live alone here and everything is pretty good with me. I have no complaints.

Did I know I was going to get married when I got on that train? Well, all I can say is I hoped something. There was nothing for a girl in New Brunswick, what with all the boys leaving, and I think when my parents put me on that train at Saint John I think they hoped I'd come back with a husband in tow. I did, you know, and they were mighty glad he was a New Brunswick boy. It sort of made it easier all round, wouldn't you say?

I know just sitting there on the train, no games to play, no cards to play with, there were three other girls like me going out to the West to visit or cook for their brothers and I know they had marriage in mind. I mean, you don't fish in a pond with no fish in it, do you? That's what put the idea in my mind. Them. I honestly admit I didn't have it at first. I think my mother did but not me. I was just going out to see my brothers and the country Mr. Butler had talked about. But you know, the more I thought about it, the more like a good idea it seemed to me. Now that's the plain truth about it.

So when John came over that night, riding that big black horse of his, I must admit I looked at him with a rather sly eye. Will it be him? I guess I was asking myself that. I liked his looks and so I put my best foot forward and that was really all there was to it.

He might not have known he wanted a wife right then and there, but he seemed to get the idea quickly enough. Anyway, he was back again the next night and in the meantime I'd done my share of thinking too.

That's the way things were done in those days. You might say that's the way they had to be done.

The Spirit of the West

A few years ago some friends sent us a Christmas card that I'd never seen before. It showed a man in a big floppy hat and work clothes, and he was leaning on his plow handles and the reins were draped around his neck and he was looking out toward the horizon. You know the kind of scene I mean. They sometimes have ones like it with soldiers on war memorials. Anyway this scene had under it, "The Spirit of the West." Well, I say, not quite. I'd like to see beside that man a drawing of a woman, about the size of my mother, little, and she's got a big cast-iron frying pan in her hand and she's looking out to the horizon too, and then it really would mean the spirit of the West. She was a great old gal. Died at 84. Chipper until the day before.

11 *Ribbon of Steel*

Colonist Cars, a Depressing Experience . . . Railroading—a Way of Life . . . The C.P.R. Was All . . . The Evening Train Was a Big Event . . . Everybody Was Building Railroads . . . A Dollar Here, a Dollar There . . . A Very Short Railroad Career . . . How They Got the Freight to Francis . . . A Defense of the C.P.R. Land Policy

The toil-weary farmer returned from town after a futile attempt to get a bank loan. He saw his wheat crop burning up in the August heat. His daughter was pregnant by the hired man and on the house door was a note from his wife saying she'd run off with the neighbor down the road. The man clenched his fists, looked at the indifferent sky, and cursed: "Goddamn the C.P.R."

Funny? Kind of. Irrational? Yes. But that farmer meant it because he had to have something to attack, and for four generations in the West the C.P.R. with its overwhelming presence has been there, big as a hip-roof barn and easy to hit. Hit, perhaps, but hardly dent. The C.P.R. has always made a good target for the West's major grievances and complaints—high freight rates for grain moving out and their necessities coming in, poor service, Eastern Canadian economic arrogance, and the belief the dice were thrown against the West by the fact of Confederation.

This is not the place to debate these charges, but it is true that the railroad was the major instrument used to open up the West. Where the C.P.R. went, the settlers followed. These stories tell the impact, each in its own way, of the railroads on those settlers —on their lives, their future, their hopes and dreams.

223

Colonist Cars, a Depressing Experience

Rough broad seats. No upholstery. You just had to sit on those beds. And my, they were hard. Right across the country, from Saint John in New Brunswick right across to Regina, where you caught another train. That was a colonist car for you.

If a person came back from the grave and saw what people travel in today, on the C.P.R., the C.N., and what we had to travel on then, they would think they were in heaven.

The colonist cars were named that because they carried the colonists across the country. You came by slow boat. Everybody was sick. My mother was deathly ill for 10 days. Could hardly raise her head. Then you got off and you stood in the immigration shed at Saint John or maybe Halifax, and you went through immigration. If you had consumption or something they could send you back. They could send a mother back and the father and kiddies would go on. It was very sad, some of the cases you saw. Very sad. It made you want to weep. Why they couldn't have gone through the inspection at Liverpool or London I just don't know.

Then you got in colonist cars. They were all named. Named after deer, buffalo, Canadian animals. I think this was so if you lost your car at some station you could find it again.

But what about those who couldn't speak or read English? There were an awful lot of them, you know. Thousands. We'd call them Central Europeans today. We came out in the spring and the men, these Polacks, they all wore big sheepskin coats and a lot of them had big mustaches. They had flat faces. They didn't look too intelligent. Yes, the women never said anything. They just trailed behind the men carrying big bundles tied into blankets. The children all seemed the same size. I mean you'd get the impression that all the women had one baby a year. They all dressed the same and the children said nothing either.

They must have been petrified. Imagine you or I getting off a boat at Montreal and getting on a train, traveling hundreds of miles and not knowing a single word of the language. As far as I know, nobody who worked for the C.P.R. spoke Russian or Polish.

A big stove at one end with a scuttle of coal. Everybody did their own cooking. I don't know where we got the food at Saint John but maybe we just weren't that hungry. Every so often along the line somebody would meet the train and sell bread and meat pies. Things like that. There were also places where you could buy milk. That was for the babies. There was a lot of young children on the train. You could also buy candy, chocolates. Women would come aboard or you'd meet them outside and they'd have a basket of hard-boiled eggs. Everybody did their own cooking. First up, first turn. It worked that way all day.

Day after day, day after day. We were going from Toronto to Winnipeg and it seemed as if all those trees would never stop. Once in a while a little town, like there were trees and then suddenly this little place and more trees. It was depressing. Was this Canada? Where was all we heard about? I think if I had known more about it I would have cried. I know my mother did and I think my father looked pretty grim. I think everybody looked pretty awful.

There was nothing to do. You were mixed up, English, Scotch, Polish, and Russian; nobody mixed and there was nothing to do. We had no cards, we didn't have any checkers. Just those hard seats and then at night the trainman would come through with this thing and he'd light the lamps, but that made it worse. It was no fun. I mean, there was no adventure.

At night was the worst. The cars were full and babies were crying and I can't remember any blankets. It seems nobody told anybody to bring bedding and all our bedding was in our trunks. Our trunks were not on the same train. These trains ran across one after another and if you got on, say, number two there was a chance your stuff would be on number four. It was a mix-up. Some people didn't get their baggage for days, weeks.

You pulled the boards down into a sort of bed and two people slept there. A man came along with a sort of a hook on a pole and he pulled down an overhead thing which became a bunk and the men slept up there. That was for two men. They shouldn't have called them colonist trains. They should have called them cattle trains. That's what we were like.

When the train stopped you could get out, but there was not

much time to walk around. Usually you were waiting for a special train to come through, maybe a mail train. But sometimes way in the bush you'd stop for an hour; nobody could figure that out. You'd wake up and there you'd be stopped. People would be muttering, babies crying, it was awful and there was just no sense in complaining. What if one person complained, or a hundred? What could you do against the C.P.R.? Nothing. You were in Canada and at their mercy. At their mercy.

I'll tell you this, like the girl who had to milk 10 cows when she was little and after that she hated them so much she never drank a glass of milk again, that was like me. I could never stand the sight of a train again. Never.

Railroading—a Way of Life

I joined the railroad because my father was a railroader. It just came naturally. Railroads all his life, railroads all my life, railroads all my son's life.

That was the way it was with a lot of families in the West. Some families were just naturally farmers. They'd be farmers in Ontario and now they were farmers in Manitoba or Saskatchewan. Others would be storekeepers or run the implement shed or the livery stable or maybe they'd put up a hotel or buy a hotel. But if you were a railroader, the whole family could be railroaders.

Of course it was all the Canadian Pacific Railroad in those days. The C.N. was nothing. It had one little line up north of Portage, which I think was called the Canada and Northwestern or the Manitoba and Northwestern, but in those days the C.N. was all in eastern Canada. It was called the Grand Trunk then.

You could start out working around the station handling freight and express, keeping the place swept, keeping the fires going in winter. There were a lot of stoves. You could work on the track. On the gangs. Hard work, that, very hard work. Or you could start in the city or town in the roundhouse, wiping. Oiling. Call boy. Then you'd get up to be brakeman, front-end brakeman, then fireman, then maybe locomotive engineer. A locomotive engineer was sort of like the king of the castle. Him and the conductor. The conductor was actually the more important person because he had all the paperwork to do and all the figuring. He made the most money. If you were a conductor you could throw a fellow off a train. He was like a policeman. If he said something the crew jumped. He was, his word was, law.

But you came from a railroad family and you got to be known as that. The other kids knew it at school and it just seemed right that you'd go on the road. Although there's one thing. If you belonged to a railroad family, you knew what that meant. Why, it stands to reason. It meant you got the first kick at the cat. If you were 14 and a job came up, your name would be ahead of other people whose name might be on the list. Your dad always had a word to say, sort of nudge the superintendent in the ribs, and you'd get the job. See what I mean? It was who you knew, not what you know. Of course, at that age what does any kid know about railroading?

Well, actually we did know quite a bit. Railroading was the talk around the dinner table. Eating. When my dad and another man would go out hunting, they'd take me and we'd be waiting in the punt for the ducks and the men would talk about railroading. You think railroaders don't gossip? My, my. They are worse as old washerwomen for gossip. They knew everything that was happening on their line, what was happening in Winnipeg, what was happening in Windsor Station [Montreal], they knew everything. So I guess we did have railroading in our bones.

All across the West you'll find, still, big families and there might be six boys in that family and three of them work for the road. With us it was always the C.P.R. It was our life, you might say, with three of my brothers with the road and two sisters, one marrying a telegrapher who became a station agent outside of Winnipeg, and another who became a big shot in Regina. It worked that way too. The girls married railroaders.

You might say the C.P.R. liked it that way. Kept everybody closer together. I guess they could keep an eye on us all. One big family.

The C.P.R. Was All

The C.P.R. practically ran this country in the early days, you know. Why, there was nothing else. Nothing. There was no roads, just trails across the prairie, and it was that way for quite a while after the car came to be.

There was the main line of the C.P.R., which came through Rat Portage, which is now Kenora, and through Winnipeg, Portage La Prairie, across to Brandon and over through Regina, to Medicine Hat, which was a pretty important place in those days, and then up to Calgary and into the mountains at Banff. So you can see until the new railroad came through Saskatoon and Edmonton about 1905, the C.P.R. had the whole West to themselves.

They had the passengers, they had the through freight. They had the stop freight. You know what that is. Local freight. I've seen as much as 30,000 pounds of way freight dumped on my platform from one train, and that was on a branch line. A lot of it was machinery but an awful lot of it was stuff I had to load and cart into the station storage room too. It was a hard life. Then they had the telegraph line too, so anything that moved in the West—passengers, people, freight, coal, grain, lumber, messages, and telegraphs—they all went over the railroad. And the mail. All of it.

And they gave good service too. Better than they give today, so I've heard.

We also took charge of tickets too. I remember an Austrian girl came down from the hotel. A maid. She came down with her trunk an hour before the train came through for Winnipeg, and she wanted to go home. In that hour besides all my other chores

I got her ticket made up for across the country, down to New York where there was a ship leaving in a week, and had her ticketed right across the ocean and right to Austria. That only cost her 65 dollars. I guess you could call us travel agents too. We could send anybody anywhere in the world, so long as they had the money and there was a ship or a train going there. Anywhere in the world. All those tickets and schedules were right there in my office.

When I started out I made 30 dollars a month. I was an assistant. I'd be sent all around the country, mostly Manitoba, relieving men who were sick, men who were on holidays. Or if a station became vacant I'd fill in until they got the right man. Most stations were like all the others. On the main line you had a lot more traffic and the colonist cars too. Immigrants. Lots more freight and more messages. Most of the big towns were on the main line.

There were a lot of branch lines and they were nice places. Some of the towns were booming and you'd get a lot of freight. Through Plum Coulee we got a passenger train once a day, each way, and then there were two others. Wednesday and Saturday, out of Winnipeg. Down to Deloraine.

When I got my own station, about 1906 or so, I got 35 dollars a month. That wasn't much but we got by. Everything was much cheaper. We paid five dollars a month for the stationhouse and it was a good house. We got our kerosene and coal free. I'd burn a carload of coal a winter. It was good coal. Pennsylvania coal. There had to be a fire in the waiting room and fires in the house and in the freight shed too. It kept you busy every day. There wasn't time to do much fooling around, but I used to go moose hunting every fall. Always got my moose.

The C.P.R. kept the road in good shape. At every town about eight or 10 miles apart there was a track crew. That was the foreman, the first man, and two others, but in wintertime only the foreman and the first man worked. They looked after a certain amount of track, about eight miles.

The section men had it pretty hard. A lot were bachelors. Foreigners. They had to patrol the track every day, doing all the changing of the ties, changing the rails, doing all the construction work, and you know how much those section men got? They worked from seven in the morning to six at night and they got one dollar and 15 cents a day. They worked hard. There are a lot of men in Canada today, old men, worn-out men, who worked on the section gang for the C.P.R. But often it was all they could get.

It was huge. A tremendous company. It went from way east of Toronto right out to the coast and they had thousands of men. Thousands. There can't be many men my age, over 80 or so, who can't say they didn't work for the C.P.R. for some period, some time.

I know families where all they know is the C.P.R. Five generations of Canadians, all working for the C.P.R. From locomotive engineers when they were putting the track through, or boys like my grandson, who is going to make his career with the C.P.R. in the restaurant end of it, to telegraphers to station agents, men who worked their way through school on C.P.R. survey crews, firemen, conductors, all families who say if you ask them, "Oh, I come from a railroading family." They don't mean the C.N.R. They mean the C.P.R.

Well, look at me. Believe it or not but I can remember when the engines between Rat Portage and Winnipeg burned wood. Cordwood. Six-foot lengths. Contractors would cut the wood and pile it at stations along the way and the train would come through and fill up the tender with wood. That was quite a ways back before the turn of the century. Back about 1890. Wood in the engines. You'd have thought that had disappeared a long time ago. Why, on the prairies they used coal, but I can remember wood and that goes back a long, long time. I tell people that and they find it hard to believe.

We worked hard for what we got. The pay was pretty low. When I retired in 1947 I was making 165 dollars a month. I got a house, of course, but 165 dollars makes for a mighty low pension these days.

Happy days? Yes, I would say happy days on the railroad. We worked hard. We were contented but we worked hard. The boys of today don't know what hard work is. But I would say happy days.

The Evening Train Was a Big Event

Everybody went down to the station for the evening train. One up at night, down next morning. You changed from the transcontinental at Regina to our branch line. It was the thing to do. Meet the train.

When we were kids we'd stand right where we knew the baggage car would stop, so we'd let the big engine go by us— although it wasn't really that big when you look at the ones they used in the mountains after that. Then the door would open and we'd yell, "Got any, Mr. Davers? Got any?" We meant convicts because that's where they kept them when they were taking them up to Prince Albert to the jail there, in the baggage car. They'd be chained to the wall and when the door was slid open and we boosted ourselves up, hanging there, we could see any prisoners they had chained to the wall. It was quite a day when we saw a prisoner, and sometimes there would be four or five.

My big brother who was bigger, he had a small wagon, big wheels at the back and smaller ones to front and he'd wait too and if a traveler came along he'd ask if he could haul his valises and boxes to the hotel. The hotel was next to our opera house. If the traveler said yes, that meant my brother would make himself about 25 cents for hauling his sample cases to the hotel. Travelers, if you don't know, were salesmen who traveled around the country by train in them days selling to the stores. Then when the bags were on I'd follow Del, my brother, and get a nickel for helping him do the work, pulling and seeing the bags didn't fall off and carrying them into the sample room at the Pioneer.

Everybody else just stood around and looked. My father he used the train as an excuse for a stroll after supper and you got to see everybody who got off the train. There'd be travelers, like I said, and people coming to visit or getting on to go further up the line, people from the Old Country looking for farms or work in town. Farm hands. Quite often a minister. The Salvation Army band, part of it, from Regina used to come up the line every summer playing once in every fair-sized town. There would be women who'd get off and get right into a carriage and be driven away and you know who they were, don't you? Fancy ladies coming in. Our town had one brothel. And then there would be just ordinary people from the town who'd been to the city, to the dentist or just plain visiting. We always got our first look at the new teachers every fall when they got off the train. Somehow you could always tell them. Up from the Regina Normal School, some of them.

You've got to remember nothing but nothing ever happened in a small town. If you had a runaway, somebody's democrat flying down the street, that was big news and you'd talk about it. That's why the train was so important. It was the only thing that ever happened in our town regularly. You could always count on the train. It's not hard to close your eyes and think back and see it, big and black with red coaches, in summer or in winter. It was always there and always on time.

Everybody Was Building Railroads

Railroads. Branch lines. Followed them right through. What the hell could you do? First four or five years you weren't going to make any money on your place. There was no way of that that I could see.

I'd go into the bush in the winter. Jesus, man, that was hard work. Cold. Winters were colder than they are now. Know that? Fifty below. We were among the trees so it wasn't too bad, but I'd come out of there with maybe 200 dollars and maybe not even that, and I'd help my brother fix up things. Barn, house. Log house, not a frame one. You were pretty big stuff when you got a frame house. Lot of fellows I know never made it. Just proved up and got a loan from the bank on their homestead, a mortgage is another way to put it, and then they were hell and gone out of the country. Or 1914 came along and saved a lot of fellows from going off their nuts. They joined up something wild.

Anyway I came out of the bush in '05, spring of, and I gave my brother 200 and I told him to plant the crop and do what he could around the place. We was farming right close, side to side, end to end. He could do what breaking he wanted and I said I was going to work on the railroad. That was J. D. McArthur's outfit and they were at Battleford and heading to Edmonton. Jesus, but he was a tough one. Not him. We never saw him but once. But his superintendents and foremen! Tough. We put that railway through in one summer, all the way.

There was two big events in Alberta's history in 1905 and one of them is the Canadian Northern coming in here, just where you crossed the tracks getting here, and the other was Alberta becoming a province. I was in on both of them, but the thing I remember was the railroad coming.

There was every kind of men on the job you can remember and we highballed her. One man told me, a fellow who thinks he's a historian out at the university, he said that they put it through so fast that they were putting the tracks on the naked grass, right on the prairie, but that isn't so. Sometimes it seemed so, but I can say it isn't so. We did lay down a grade, and the ties and steel were to specifications. But if old McArthur—he was from Winnipeg and in charge of the line, building from Winnipeg right on through—if he could have got away with it I think he would have. Man, he was a terror. A real terror.

We lived in tents and there wasn't a one I don't think that didn't leak. When it rained you put your finger up to the leak and you ran a little trail down the inside and the rain would come in and follow that line so it wouldn't leak on you. Some lived in cars, boxcars, and others just said to hell with it and made a tent with blankets and toughed it out that way.

A dollar and a half a day. That came to 30 dollars a month. Something in around there. And found. Food. There was lots of it but it was poor food. Poor beef when we got it, but mostly beans and bacon and molasses and pork and things like that. They used to bring the hogs into camp and slaughter right there and just leave the guts lying on the ground stinking. One time another fellow and me couldn't stand the smell any longer and we got shovels and buried it. The foreman or superintendent comes along and says, "What's the matter, don't you brickheads think I know how to run a camp?" I figured if I said one word he'd send me for my time and I didn't want that. I wanted that money. It was the only work in the country.

But we got the job done. One thing, there was no rock work. No rock work on that line until they got to Jasper and we did it all with scrapers, teams. The hardest thing was cutwork through clay bank hills. Little hills. It was easy country to build in and we had one fellow, a New Zealander, who was in charge of a big pusher. He had eight mules in front and 12 in the rear of this big scraper and I still remember that fellow, the way he handled those horses was a real marvel. He should have got three dollars a day and a cook all for himself, but I think he only got a dollar and a half just like the rest of us.

This fellow from New Zealand, my but he was good. When there was a bit of a break other fellows used to drift back and watch him on the cuts. I forget his name but I'll never forget him. I asked him once where he'd learned to handle horses and he looked at me kind of strangely and said, "Why, I just picked it up over here." I asked him how long he'd been in Canada and he said, "About a year and a half." When I told the other teamsters that they just shook their heads.

Everybody was building railroads in them days or had the plans in their hip pockets for one and everybody was going to be rich, but when it all boiled down to what was what, only the C.P. and the C.N. made it. But if you wanted a job it was the railroad and they worked you.

We didn't mind it. Didn't think of it too much, I guess. Young, strong, and besides there was no such things as unions. When I hear on the radio about a grievance committee and a board of arbitration, I just have to stop and think because in those days there was none of that. The boss was running the show and it was his job to make money or lose his shirt. If he didn't like your work or the way you handled a team or the way you wore your lid, then he coul fire you. He'd say, "Get walking down the grade," and that meant you were out. Seemed reasonable at the time.

You got a lot of people in those camps. Twenty languages.

Twenty kinds of noses. The Hunkies did the bull labor and they loved it. Just like a Swede doing rock work. Those Hunkies just loved to get a good dig on that shovel and let her fly. They'd work all day and work hard and if there was a downpour they'd always get in about three more shovelsful before they headed for the shelter, just to show the boss they were willing. They needed the money more than we did. None of them had nothing, just strong backs and weak minds.

Germans. If they'd be around any time they usually wound up as straw boss. It's in the character, you see. Gotta be pushing somebody around. When I went in the Kaiser's War I sure found that out.

Englishmen. Not tough enough. Scrawny. Spindly. Always complaining.

I got on best with the Americans. They were just a good bunch of fellows, ready for a joke, a laugh, a tumble, a wrestle and me being a Yankee, although when I was just a kid of eight we came up to Canada—a long time ago at that—they still knew that and I got along well.

Funny but there was a few Chinamen. Out from British Columbia and they were good workers. They just went along, day by day, moving a bit of dirt at a time but it got moved. If you worked alongside one, at first you wanted him to speed it up. But then you noticed after a while that he may just be going along nicely and you're going a good lick, but he was staying even with you. They sucked on opium. I don't know where they got it but they had it and they'd be on it all through the day. This picture you get of Chinamen lying around in opium dens looking dead is all wrong.

I got to know this one fellow pretty well and I know he was eating opium all the time and I didn't say anything, nothing at all. It was legal in those days, you know. One day I'd given my knee a pretty good clip and was in awful pain and he takes out this little tin box, like an aspirin box, and he asks me if I want one. I say sure, why not, and so he gives me one and then he says, "No, two." So I do. I guess I just swallowed them.

I'll never forget the sensation. For the rest of the day I was six inches off the ground and laughing, hollering, and for sure some fellows thought I was off my head. The Chinamen knew though. To them it was a good joke. I liked them.

At nights there'd be fights. Planned fights. Bare knuckle. Stand-up fights. John L. Sullivan stuff. Fierce. A broken nose was nothing. If you had a broken jaw you collected your pay and took the morning speeder into Battleford. They bet on these fights and no purse to the winner. Fighting for the sheer joy. You won't see much of that now. Not even the ruffians down here in the street do it anymore. The world changes. I liked it in the old days. Horseshoes and tug-of-war matches and cards. There was cards and some of those fellows really knew how to play. The Chinamen could play good.

Oh, it wasn't such a bad life. It was hard and people were cruel to each other, but we didn't mind it. It was kind of what most of us were used to. A fellow had to look after himself. If he didn't, probably nobody else would. There wasn't any la-de-da about it. Stand up straight or get out, I guess you could say, was the slogan.

A Dollar Here, a Dollar There

Who were the richest men in those early days? Why, I say the C.P.R. conductors. They were absolute lords of the train. You stay on, you get off, you get a berth, you don't—they had the say.

And money! Why, many's the time I've traveled from Saskatoon to Regina or back again for a dollar. One dollar, mind you. I've traveled from Ottawa to Winnipeg for five dollars. How? Why, you just got on the train without a ticket and you met the conductor between the cars, on the platform, and you gave him a dollar and when he came into the car to collect your ticket, stamp, punch it, whatever they did, he'd just pass you by. You see, he had your dollar in his pocket. A dollar went a long way in those days. What was it? Maybe worth 10 dollars in today's money.

Oh yes, many times I traveled around the country and the most I ever gave a conductor was a dollar.

I look at you and I consider you an honest man. I feel that myself I'm an honest man. I feel an honest man can look at another man and tell whether he is honest. So . . . ?

So the C.P.R. knew what was going on, so they put spotters on the trains. You can't blame them. They were losing a lot of money. But human nature being what it was, or is, they had to put on spotters to watch the spotters. Oh my, I tell you, it was lovely. I don't know if they put on spotters to watch the spotters who watched the spotters who were supposed to be watching the conductors, but it was one way of filling the trains, I guess.

I never paid more than a dollar to travel between Saskatoon and Regina and that's a couple of hundred miles, and my money never went through a ticket wicket. It went in the pocket of a conductor.

A Very *Short Railroad Career*

I was born below Barriefield, near Kingston, and I guess I came west in 1903. Winnipeg. Looking for a job like everybody. I was around Winnipeg for a while and, then like a fellow often does, I ran into a school chum and he was a brakeman on the C.P.R. He said, "Oh, I'll get you a job. I think there's a job out in Medicine Hat, they want a wiper in the roundhouse."

So we went down to the station and I signed up as a wiper at Medicine Hat and they gave me a pass, so I rode on the cushions out there. Had a nice ride, saw a lot of country. Left my stuff at the station, walked over to the roundhouse and found out that my job would be 11 hours a day at 11 cents an hour, which gave me a dollar and 21 cents a day. Well.

What about room and board, I asked. Oh, the foreman said, go over to this boardinghouse, Mrs. Such-and-Such, it's cheap and it's where the railroad men go, so I went over there. She said she could fix me up but I found out that my board and room would be one dollar a day. That would give me 21 cents a day to go on.

Well, sir, I was just a young fellow of 18 and I had always wanted to be a railroad man and I thought this opportunity looked pretty good, but I walked right back to the station and picked up my stuff and I left town. That ended my career as a railroader.

How They Got the Freight to Francis

There were always ways to do things in them days, ways to get around things. Like the time the first two carloads of freight came over the Arcola line of the C.P.R., or better still, when the first two carloads of freight didn't come in to Francis, which was a new town on the Arcola line, and the people needed things that were in those two cars.

This is the way it was told to me by Ben Holden of Indian Head. Late in the fall of 1903, the first week of November, the construction crew of the C.P.R. was laying the last rails into Francis before closing up shop until spring. They weren't going to work in the winter, but the rails were in to Francis and there were two cars spotted in the Regina freight yard for the town-site of Francis, one of coal and one of implements and tools. The people of Francis needed that coal and those tools. They asked the C.P.R. and the C.P.R. said, "Nothing doing," and that was that.

So Ben Holden approached the engineer of the work train that was clearing up around Francis and there was a conversation and it must have gone something like this: If those two cars are loaded and waiting in Regina and there are no bills of lading and no destination marked for them, then he would see the yard switchman and he would arrange for him to let the engineer out again onto the Arcola line. No questions asked. The engineer said he couldn't afford to let even a fireman into this little scheme, so he would have no fireman. It would be just between the engineer and the switchman and the engineer told Holden, "You will have to fire for me." It was agreed. Then Ben got busy and lined up some of the homesteaders to be ready and raring to go when that engine with the two cars pulled into Francis.

They agreed on a night and that night Ben was in Regina and he met the engineer and I'll have to say the word, the word is hi-jacked, they hi-jacked those two cars out of the small city of Regina. Off down the line they went to the townsite of Francis and Ben, who'd never fired an engine in his life, he fired it for that engineer whose name I do not know.

When they got into Francis the homesteaders were on hand and waiting and it had all gone as they planned it. They tore into that unloading like mad, just dumping everything, coal and implements, right out on either side of the track. The engineer, he was alone by this time, so he must have been driving and firing at the same time as he sneaked backwards into the Regina yards just before dawn.

I can still see big burly Ben as he told me this story. It was one of those experiences that most of us would have liked to have been in on.

A Defense of the C.P.R. Land Policy

Nothing wrong at all. Absolutely nothing and I'm not talking as a man who spent all those years with the C.P.R. Sure, the C.P.R. picked up 25 million acres of land for building the line through to tidewater. Well, what other way could it have been done? Canada had no money. So, give out land which was going to waste anyway. Hell's bells, man, the West had so many millions of acres of land they didn't know what to do with it. A few settlements, a few forts, a sodbuster here and there, and that was it.

Do you really know how much of that land grant was actually good for farming? Well, hold on to something. Less than half. I know, I know, they swapped land, poor trackside land, along the main line belt, for good land other places, but it still didn't come up to 25 million.

What throws a lot of people off is the word "prairie." Miles and miles and days and days of flat fertile land, like a pool table. Horsefeathers. There are ranges of hills on the prairies. You can go through miles of what would be called desert in California and Arizona. It's still there too. Sandy soil. Rocky soil. Light soil. Hills and valleys, deep trenches, gulleys, coulees. The badlands. Hundreds of square miles of badlands. Land too light for farming, land which is semi-arid just as the Arctic is, just as the lands in Africa you're reading about today are. Unfit for human population.

Let me tell you, the C.P.R. may have got a land grab, if anybody wants to use that term, but it wasn't what everybody thinks. You read the records of the company in Windsor Station and you'll see memos where the big and high mucky-mucks thought they had come out on the short end of a very twisty stick and they were going to lose their shirts on the land alone.

But with what they had, they did well. They finished selling that land not so long ago, I think, and they filled up the West. Remember, not everybody was homesteading, filing a 10-buck bet that he could beat the government on a homestead. Thousands bought good C.P.R. land at very, very reasonable prices and very happy many of them were with the terms and the treatment from the mighty monster of the West, that's what it has been called; very happy they were with their deal. They thought . . . my own grandfather did for that matter, he thought he was really putting one over on the company.

I realize that these railroad big shots were a bunch of pirates. Should have been sailing the Spanish Main. But remember this, they got the job done. I am not defending their financial morals, if there is such a thing, but I am saying that they got the job done. I wasn't around then, but I don't think there was a big song and dance about the land the C.P.R. got. Then. That was just the way it was done. Ottawa was broke. No credit. But lots of land. Okay, so they paid them off in land. I'd of done the same thing. Just makes sense. Play them as they lay. A gambler's term. Right?

12 *About the Town*

At first, most villages and towns were situated where a trading post had been, where two main trails intersected, or where two rivers joined. Later it was the railroads that created settlements so that farmers could haul grain to the tall sentinel-like elevators.

As the land was taken up, the villages grew into towns and some expanded into cities and as today, essentially, their one main purpose was to provide the farmer with goods and services.

The heydey of the towns was in the first four decades of this century and since the last war the small western town has been diminishing. Today, some are literally ghost towns, stripped of the once- or twice-a-day rail service and inhabitants driving 40 or 60 miles to the big town down the road with its supermarkets.

But when they were young those towns thrived, bustled, whooped, and made joyful sounds. People were proud to say they came from Shoal Lake, Manitoba; Dundurn, Saskatchewan; or Cayley, Alberta; all towns that are quiet now but once, not all that long ago, were the strong heartbeat of the district.

An old-timer will say, "I remember Saturday night around here back then. Why she was just a-raring to go. Nothing like it now. Everything is all changed."

242

The Men Who Built the Towns

All these towns along the line and, for that matter, they were built, a lot of them, by men who had had their big dream fail on them. They came out as farmers but you know, not every man can become a farmer.

They sold everything. The house. The business if they had one. All their furnishings although some of the stuff that they did bring would astonish you. They were allowed to bring so much and the rest, freight, was cheap. So people bought pianos and huge oaken tables and eight chairs and a setting of Royal Doulton for eight. Things like that. I've seen men bring their swords and sabers from some war. What did they expect? Red Indians. Swords, sabers, guns of every description. Four-poster beds. And they came to the West and what they knew about farming a gnat could put in its eye. Farming in those days was not all that scientific, but a man had to know what he was doing and if he didn't, he was lost. There were men farming 20 years after they had homesteaded who never should have.

They mostly had trades. Some were pen pushers, of course, and not much good for anything. But there were many who had good trades and had been masons and surveyors and carpenters and butchers and shoemakers for years in the Old Country, in Europe. The smart ones of these, they went into the towns and just continued on in the trade they had before. So while the government was moving might and main trying to get farmers, it was also bringing in the men who would start the businesses in the towns and the towns became cities and that was the way the West was built.

My First Memories of Calgary

We came west in '85. My father was from Ontario and then he went to Birtle in Manitoba where he was land agent. I was the first white child born in the Shoal Lake district, which is part of Birtle. Then he came to Calgary as land titles officer. That was a long time ago, I was only three, and I think Calgary only had about 500 or 600 people. I can just barely remember.

We had a stage drive from Birtle down to some station on the Canadian Pacific Railway, which was very new then, and then we came out across the prairies. It took about two days, I remember that, and the smoke pouring out of the chimney of the train's engine and the little stations we stopped at and people getting off. These were the settlers.

My first memories of Calgary? It was a November day, a lovely sunny day and my father met us and he shoved me up on his shoulder and we went over to the Royal Hotel that was just a block from the station. As far as I can remember, all of Calgary was just canvas and log shacks. My father got us a small house at Centre and Seventh, across from the Presbyterian church. Gradually that little corner built up and I think that was the first center of civilization in Calgary, just around where we were. But frame houses were going up all around and every week you looked, there was another house up or somebody putting up a store or a shop or something and, of course, there was always the Hudson's Bay Company and the big steps where the Indians used to hang around. The Indians never gave anybody any trouble.

About all I can remember else was there was a meat shop with a stuffed goat up on top of it and Mr. Linton who used to sell stationery and toys and my dad bought me toys there. He had a big life-size picture of Queen Victoria with a light blue banner across her chest, and those are my first recollections of Calgary.

Oh, another thing I remember. In my mother's trousseau was an ermine jacket and it was made for me into a nice winter coat. I remember having to go past the Indians on the porch, and every time I went by they'd laugh and point, hi-yi-yi-huh, at me, as if the sight of a little girl in a fur coat was the funniest thing in the world.

Well, you must remember I am an old lady of 94 and these are things that happened to me when I was three. That was a long time ago.

Towns Needed the Railway

Towns couldn't exist without the railway. I only know one town in the West that made it on its own, without the railway, and that's a place south of Winnipeg called Steinbach. Full of Mennonites and they were a pretty independent bunch and they made it without it. But everywhere else, you had to be on the railway.

In those early days a man might try and start his own town. Oh, it happened often enough. A quarter section would be enough. Half a section would be better, and best on a river or beside a coulee or where two roads met. But this private enterpriser, whoever he was, would start the town himself. He'd have it surveyed. Streets, avenues and likely as not he'd put up the first store to attract the settlers who were starting to come into that district. If things looked good, a blacksmith might come in next and a lumber yard next, and you could be sure as shooting that the fellow who was selling those lots, he'd be spreading the word around that a railway was coming. Well, he would be half-right. A railway was coming but was it coming through the town? Could you step out of your front door and see the morning freight come through? That was the big thing. Likely as not the railway would run their line through, maybe two miles away. Even one mile away was enough to kill a town. There was nothing to do but for that town to move over.

If you read the book about Morden, which is a town in Manitoba, it shows you what can happen. A man named F. T. Bradley figured he would be the father of a new town. Of course, he was going to clean up selling lots too. The place was on the Calf Mountain Trail and there were a lot of Métis living and farming around. Then white settlers began coming in because it is wonderful farming country. He named his town Mountain City, and he worked hard making it boom. He must have been something of a talker. Soon there were stores and businesses and two hotels. One was the British Lion and the other was the Travellers' Home. There was two general stores and a hardware and tin shop. A grist mill and a sawmill, blacksmith, harness shop, schoolhouse, homes, and even a Presbyterian church. Then the government decided this looked like a good spot and they built a big courthouse. Bradley thought the C.P.R. was going right by his town.

The C.P.R. had other ideas. I suppose they could have bent the line but they didn't. Why should they? They ran their line through their own holdings. After all, they wanted to sell lots too. So they plunked down a station five miles away from Mountain City and called the place Morden.

There was another town called Nelson in the same fix as Mountain City. This was even bigger, I believe. Some said about 800 people, but it had been by-passed by the C.P.R. same as the other. In fact, Nelson was an incorporated town. Well, there was pleadings and visits to the provincial government and all sorts of goings-on but the line was in, it was going to be Morden as the section house and water tank and station and that was that.

Businessmen in those days were just as sharp as they are now —they saw the handwriting. So, one after another, they decided to move to Morden and the railway. Move their business and their houses and get over to the new townsite before somebody else got there before them. Their buildings were raised up on skids, oak beams, and several teams of horses would be hitched on, and with the snow on the ground and those teams pulling steadily, they could cover that five miles in one day. And this went on, even moving the courthouse. But it had to be done. No other way. Everyone needed that railway. In a few years you could walk on the ground where Mountain City and Nelson had been and find no trace and you walked down the streets of Morden, according to the pioneers, and it was a booming place, absolutely everything you needed. There was no reason to go to Winnipeg.

This is not true through Saskatchewan and Alberta for the main part. The reason? Well, in most areas the railroad came first anyway. The railway first or at least the survey of the railway came first and people knew where to take up land and where to build towns, usually buying the land from the C.P.R. Like when the main line went through in the 1880's there was no real settlement anywhere along there. Homesteads here and there because the federal survey had gone through a few years before, but no towns. So the line went through and the C.P.R. said, "We'll put a town here and here and one here," so many miles apart down the line and the people came and made towns. So you didn't really get that problem anywhere except in those places where a lot of people had come before the railways came.

Election Day in a Prairie Town

There was towns where elections, they were the big thing. Every fall, November, another election and they were real humdingers. Two or three men running for mayor, a dozen for four or six council seats. Everybody wanting on and they used to run regular campaigns. These were ding-dong affairs, mostly. It wasn't personality affairs like if two men were running for mayor and one would say, "You're a rat," and the other would say, "And you're a rascal." They were probably good friends, probably did business together, towns being small places, and one might be the preceptor and the other a vestryman, both in the same church. They weren't out to throw each other's reputations against the wall like mud.

Issues, though. There could be issues. Prohibition when it was a local thing could be an issue. I remember one where it was a question of making the cemetery bigger by buying three more acres of land off the C.P.R. at 30 dollars an acre. Whether to build a bridge over the coulee and extend Main Street south. A new town hall, maybe. Things like that. Small towns in those days never had very many big decisions, not like today when a town might have to float a bond for 800,000 dollars for a new high school. Why, in those days 5,000 dollars would have been an issue big enough to bring out every voter, even if those who were invalids had to be carried to the voting booth on a door. Yes, I've seen that. An old man carried to the town hall on a door, a big husky man on each corner and a bunch of kids coming behind hooting and hollering.

Election day. Or come election night. It wouldn't take long to count the ballots. Probably no town had more than 400-500 voters, so the clerk would probably have his assistants finished with the count about nine o'clock. A crowd would be around the town hall or the hall where the voting had been and he'd announce the vote. Who had won, by how much, and who had lost. Council too.

Then there would be the parade. Torchlight parades, through the town. I believe most of us soaked an old broom in kerosene and lit that, and away the crowd would go, first to the mayor's house, and the town band would be out. Hell, every town in those days worth its salt had its town band. That was one of the first things you formed. Drums, saxophones, tubas, trumpets, flutes, everything, the darndest mixture you ever saw. It was amazing just how many men played some instrument. How many could play three or four. So off they went, the band in front, to the mayor's house, the new mayor or the old mayor, whatever, and three hearty cheers and the band playing something suitable. Lots of ommp-pah-pah. Lots of noise. Then to the three or four houses of the councilmen and like the mayor they'd come out on the steps and wave, and more cheers.

It didn't matter if the man you voted for had lost. You joined the parade. No skulking in corners; you went along. The parade and the band was just as much a part of the election as making your vote was.

No thought of hanging anybody to a lamppost. This was Canada and everything was done fairly and squarely. If you won, good, and if you lost, too bad and wait until next year.

Then the men would go to the saloon in the hotel, and sometimes the mayor's election officer would come along and buy a drink for the boys. A round on the mayor. More cheers. But if he didn't, no matter. Maybe he was a prohibitionist. In a lot of towns you could split it down the middle on that subject. It didn't matter anyway. By midnight everybody would be home in bed anyway. That was election day, I'd say, in most prairie towns.

There Were Always Lots of Girls

Oh, yes, the girls. There always were lots of girls. Edmonton had quite a few. There was no time I couldn't go to at least one house in Red Deer. Calgary had quite a few and so did Lethbridge. Out on the point. Trail, Nelson, Kasle, they were mining towns and mining towns always did have a lot of prostitutes. There was this one place in Trail run by an Italian woman and there was a sort of a lane running behind her place. You went down this lane or trail and there was a backhouse there and a little rope. It was attached to what looked like a little clothesline to the house and you gave it three little pulls. Tinkle, tinkle, tinkle and if there was no answer you stayed off. If two tinkles came back it meant come on in. No tinkles usually meant that one or two of the town cops were in mamma's kitchen drinking her wine and she didn't want any dude barging in, not until she got them out of the way. You can't blame the cops. They didn't make much money. Even the famous and glorious Northwest Mounted Police weren't all that holy.

Yes, it was a dollar but in some other places in the same town it was two dollars. In a way it was the same difference as going to Chinook Centre for your shopping or going to the Army and Navy Store. You got about the same product but you got it in nicer surroundings.

I should put in Kamloops there. It was a good town too and quite a few houses. On the way back I'd stop over a day in Revelstoke. I covered a lot of country.

I think it said in the paper a few years ago that the last wide-open house in Trail just closed up. In those days, three shifts, the houses were open 24 hours. The madame when she closed up, I think it said she went to Spokane to retire. A long and happy life to her, I say. It was a rough business at times and they had to be good businessmen.

We Had a Town Pasture

There was no such thing as a dairy in our town. That came later. Probably a dairyman in those days would have gone broke.

Everybody had their own cow and there was this sort of a town pasture. You might call it a community pasture these days, but it was where everybody put their cows. It had a wooden fence around it and you paid the helper at the livery barn I think about 50 cents a week, and it was his job to take the cows to the pasture and bring them home for evening milking.

It was up to you to see the cow was tied outside your house in the morning so the hostler could pick it up, and it was your job in evening time to get it when the herd came through town. You did this by the bell. Every cow had a different kind of bell. Some would go clink, some would go clank, one would go thunk, another would tinkle, and you'd hear your bell coming with the herd, and you'd go out and open the gate and there would be your cow, heading for your gate. She wanted in just as much as anything. She'd go around the side of the house, her old bag swaying, and whoever did the milking would get out the stool and away you'd go. That was the way you got your milk.

Some people separated. Some just used pans and some didn't use anything, but just the milk itself. So much for the house, the rest for a pig and some for the chickens everybody kept. A couple of people might have two or three cows and they would be the ones you'd buy butter off of, and they made a bit of a living off that. Not much. Butter might have been 15 or 20 cents a pound and that was a lot of work for 15 or 20 cents.

I can still hear the clinking and thunking of those bells.

Of course in winter and windy days, days when it looked like snow, everybody kept their cows in the cowshed and fed him hay you got out of the big slough on the other side of town. So everybody, you might say, had a dairy of sorts and I do believe it was that way even in places in the old days like Calgary and Edmonton too.

Freedom of the Press

In our town there was this weekly newspaper, the *Mail*, and the editor was C. W. Holmes. When Holmes and a chap named Seager opened the *Mail* in 1906 their first editorial said the paper would be a strictly independent business, and maybe it was Holmes' independence the businessmen didn't like. In late 1908 he had taken a pretty strong stand on some issues affecting the town and who was running it and where it was going. A lot of prominent men didn't think much of this—in fact, they didn't like it at all. They could see a lot more editorials they didn't like coming off the press.

Well, they got together and being businessmen and well acquainted with how things went, they formed the Milestone Publishing Company Limited on February 1 of 1909, and it had a capitalization of 5,000 dollars with 100 shares at 50 dollars each. The top man in this new company was Dr. Cook and the vice-president was Pat Murphy and so on down the line, all prominent men in town.

This company was their way of raising money to buy out the *Mail* or to buy off Mr. Holmes so there would be no more editorials. So they sent a delegation to see him one day just after the new company had been formed. He said yes, the price was fine and he accepted and took his cash price and left town. He went to Rosetown and became the editor of the Rosetown *Eagle*.

Anyway, the businessmen moved fast and they moved the *Mail*'s printing equipment over to the Enos Harvey building which they bought and they brought in a man named C. B. Milberry as their new editor and he lived upstairs while the business was downstairs.

His first issue came out real early in February and it carried a fine editorial setting forth the general policy of the paper and he ended it with what you might call a slogan: "A progressive paper for a progressive district."

A Strike in Winnipeg

In those days in the winter there was nothing else to do, work in the woods or work for the railroad. I was in Winnipeg and it was winter and I had no work, nothing doing but hanging around and saving what money I could.

It was 1906 and the street railway strike was on. I had come out from England the year before and it was in Winnipeg that I saw my first electric streetcar. Boy, I thought that was something. The strike. Playing football with the collection boxes. Putting two cars on the same track and running them against each other. Then they turned one streetcar over right on the main street.

The company had 500 scabs from Pinkerton and 500 scabs they'd brought in from Montreal. Then there was the police. The strike went on for three days and things got worse and the police grabbed a bunch of them. This was the first time I'd seen a union at work, fighting a company and the police. The police the first time grabbed about 40. Now these weren't streetcar workers. Maybe only a couple were. These were the people of Winnipeg who were all for the workers. All for the strike. Everybody wore cards on their lapels saying "I Walk!" To show they were for the strikers.

Then Sharpe, he was the mayor, he read the Riot Act and while he was reading the Riot Act to all the strikers and the citizens in front of the city hall, this happened. They were building the C.P.R. hotel, the Royal Alex, and they had put a wall of bricks around the construction site. So a big bunch of us ran down and yanked off bricks and ran back and threw them at the police. And at the back of the police the ladies of easy virtue from down on Point Douglas, the red light district, they came up and they had bags of eggs and they threw them at the police. These women they were enjoying their leisure moments too, throwing eggs. Quite a time.

They used to have police court three times a day, morning, afternoon and night and they just convicted them right and left. Daly was the magistrate. They fined them for everything.

Three in a crowd. Against the Riot Act. Just walking out at night. If they wanted to fine you they'd fine you.

Then the strike ended. The workers got a good deal. A good raise. But the trouble was, like most bloody unions, the next year they went on strike to get a lot more and this time the people felt they had enough, they were well paid. So the people didn't get behind them and they lost that one badly.

I Had to Go to Town

About once or twice a winter I just couldn't stand the sight of all that snow for another minute and I'd go into town. I'd tell my wife I was going and when I came back I'd be back. She never liked it, I think, but she never fetched me up on it too hard.

She had the children and the house to look after and I had a hired man and he looked after the cattle. That's about all there was to do in the winter.

I would walk down the street and if I didn't see any one of three or four pals of mine, fellows who'd come over to this country with me, I'd go into the hotel and I'd have a drink. If nobody I knew came in, I'd have a few drinks and then likely as not I'd head for home. But if I met one of my pals we'd go and have a drink and then a few more. And then likely as not, another pal would come in and we'd start up again, and then another chap might come in and we'd have a party and it would go on. I've seen it go on for as much as a week. Just bellying up to the bar and you could drink as much as you want and not get drunk and then go to the restaurant or the dining room and eat, and you'd have a room and you'd go to sleep. Same thing next day. And the next.

I remember once, there was this woman in town. A lovely woman, from England. Quite the nicest woman in that whole district. She'd go to Ascot, that type. Four-in-hand. Coachman, gray coat, gray topper, bugler in gray behind. The Royal Family there, you know. She met me on the street one afternoon and all she said was, "Ben, why don't you go home to your wife?" That's all. I was shocked. I suppose I could have asked her what goddamned business was it of hers but I didn't. I was so surprised and shocked that I went home. Right there and then.

I guess it took something like that to get a fellow up and moving, out of town and back to the drudgery of the farm, the snow, the cold and those bloody cows. It wasn't an easy life on the prairies, let me tell you.

The First Baby Won a Lot

I don't know where it started, but there was this thing that the first baby born in a new town, on a new townsite, the town or the developers or the C.P.R. would give a free town lot.

I have known several people in later years who told me they got a town lot. What they did with it, I never knew. In fact, I don't know whether it was put in the baby's name or whether it was just handed over to the father. The father, I imagine.

The Western Town: a Bird's-Eye View

There really was nothing to them small towns back in those days, out on the prairie. Why, I heard once that the C.P.R. set up over 800 of the things in all the time they were going, and that's all they wanted them for—for loading grain.

But these small towns. When the elevators came along, then that's when you knew where the towns were. Long distance away. I remember down the line from Canora I said to one agent, I said, "Shorty, you got electricity now, so why don't you put a electric light up on top there so we can see the way to town at night?" I thought it was a good idea but he never did. Just like railroaders—and I was brakie myself when I was young—they were all hemmed and hawed in by more regulations and rules than you could ever count on your best day.

But these small towns wasn't much. I been in a dozen of them.

There always was the big store and that usually was the first one in. It would have painting on the front, like "Douglas & Sons. Est. 1899." Just so you'd know you were there first. Like as not it would have the post office, although politics being what it was in those days, maybe the government would give some widow lady with no money the post office and she'd set it up in her front parlor. Nobody ever made no money being post office in them days. Then there would be another couple of stores. All on this one street. Always a blacksmith shop and maybe with a lean-to and in there he'd have a harnessmaker. But he'd do more fixing of harness than making it because there was Eaton's, you see, and there was no way a single harnessmaker could beat out Eaton's in harness and things like that. Why, old Timothy had a whole factory down east just filled with Italians, and all they did was make harness. If you wanted harness for a bull team, then that was another matter. You went out to the Galician settlement, wherever it was, and you dickered with them and they made it for you.

Lumber yard. Sash and door. Shingles. Many's the dollar I spent in them places. I guess in Saskatchewan the big one was Beaver Lumber but there was others, of course. They were usually over by the unloading area, by the track; and if you were in a big town like Weyburn or one of those, the railroad would probably run a spur in for you. Depended on how many cars they spotted for you a year. It was a competitive business, lumber, and when we were young bucks we used to go down to the yards when they had green lumber come in and shoot at the cats. Cats love green lumber. No, I don't know why. But there was always cats and we didn't give a hoot whose cats, if we saw one we'd blast at him. But there's more hiding places for a cat in a big lumber yard, more than Beecham's got pills, so it wasn't always that we'd get one. Anyway, sooner or later the town cop would come along. Now, during the week he was usually just a local fellow. Maybe a farmer from out of town. All he had to be was big and quick. Most of his work was hauling in the odd drunk on Saturday night and letting him go next morning, but he'd say to us, yep, he'd put his hands akimbo and he'd say, "Put away those goddamned snaggers and get off home before I ram one down your throat." Now that was tough talk in those days. Then we'd head for home.

When I was older, about 18 or so, I learned to swim. The railroad was a great user of water, you see. All those steam engines and those boilers just souping up the water and all across the country the C.P.R. had built dams. Dammed up a creek, a river, a coulee. Usually a coulee, and in spring she'd fill up real good and you'd have a kind of lake. If the town was nice to the railroad, said pretty please, they'd sometimes let the town or village build a park, some grass, a few trees, and a little beach, and there would be picnics there.

I remember one town in my boomer days—and I'm not going to name it because what I would tell you about that town would frizzle your hair and curl up your toes—but the townsfolk got to work and by golly, when I got there, and this was before the war, they had a park and a little place you could buy ice cream and pie and soda pop on Sundays. A few English sports—or Scots or Yanks, they was all in the district—but whoever, they'd laid out a fine little golf course, nine or seven holes, I forget which, and they had this nice little beach. But the goings-on there at night in the summer. You talk about girls today getting in trouble. In a family way. Today is nothing. Hardly a girl for four towns around got through to 18 without having a baby or having it taken away from her. Abortion was quite a thing then. Any doctor would do it if he figured there was good enough reason. That's what I'm told. I never had to pay out but I know fellows that did. Oh, the moaning and giggling from the bushes down at that park at night. I'll tell you.

You know, these Golden Agers and the folks I go and visit in the lodges, they're always looking at the telly and saying,

"Tut tut. Isn't that awful?" Well, I say, awful my ass, because they knew what was going on when they were young ones. You knew the score when you were 10 or 12. And I don't mean in the towns. I mean in those country schools that were all over the country. Lots of monkey business. I can't talk about the city but I'm sure. I'm quite sure. Look, human nature doesn't change.

Anyway, you get the idea. Things don't change. But them small towns did. Drive through a lot of them now, the ones I knew, and they just ain't there. An elevator and the agent comes every Thursday or Tuesday to handle the business, but no store, no post office, no machine shop. Nothing. Just a few little old houses that could do with a bit of paint, and there's a lot of old people in them and you know what they're there for? Waiting to die. But you'll usually see one thing. A church. Maybe two. One, for sure, a United. Take your pick on what the other might be.

But in my day, my father's day, right up until the late 20's, I guess, those were going concerns. You could go in on a Saturday night and you might have to park a quarter of a mile away if you were late. The town was going strong on Saturday night. There might be a show, moving picture show. In the church basement, the town hall, somewhere where there was room for a screen, which might be four white sheets sewn together and attached tight to a two-by-four frame, and the projector. A lot of people went to see that. Two bits for adults, or maybe 15 cents for adults, 10 for kids.

There was a lot of drinking too. Every town had at least one boot and some had a couple and you could buy a pint, 50 cents bad, a dollar good. If you felt rich you bought the dollar brand. It wasn't a full pint as today but the American pint. Most boots I knew were Americans although they bought their stuff from the Ukrainians, who half the time were even scared to come in to town. They'd send their kids in with an ox and wagon on Friday afternoons. They were a funny bunch.

In one town along that north line I went to pick up a bottle one night after we'd booked in and the boot's name was Larsen, a Minnesota Swede who played at farming and made a fortune in booze. He said, "Clark, forget the dollar stuff tonight. I've got the real stuff here. Two dollars." Well, I felt stakey that night, just paid and all that, so I handed over the money and took a swig. I think it was five minutes until I got my breath and I asked him for Christ sakes what is it, and he said, "Pure alcohol. Right out of the spout, double distilled." My God, I asked him to give me a bottle, a vinegar bottle, something big, and I washed it out and poured in the alcohol and filled it up with water and then, by God, I could get it down. That night I got in three fights. There was something about me. People I'd been friends with they just wanted to knock me into the ditch. The fellow I played outfield with, he hauled off and he did knock me into the ditch.

Things weren't all that quiet in those small towns. A lot of drinking.

Some philandering too. By that I don't mean the squealing in the bushes down in some park but a man and a woman, each a mate of somebody else's and carrying on right in a town with only three streets crossways and four streets up and down and everybody knowing everybody else's business. But they did it and they did it with a vim and vigor, let me tell you. Oh sure, there was lots of skulking around, but they managed to meet. If you were ever out, maybe out of town with a dog and gun and looking for some mallards or chicken or something and you saw a buggy, a closed-in buggy, over on some trail or some trail leading into the bush, you didn't have to go over and lift the curtains. You didn't know, maybe, who was in that vehicle but you knew what was going on.

I got in a few scrapes. Nothing serious. When anything looked like it was going to happen, I just left town. I could work both ends of a freight, and there wasn't a steam engine or internal combustion engine I couldn't run, so I could always get a job. I used to have papers from a Chicago school of correspondence, all duded and fancied up, saying I was a master mechanic. Well, I was. I could do anything but I sure didn't learn it from those Chicago people. I paid 10 dollars for that certificate in its leather holder, and it came in the mail.

But I always liked small towns. I'm sorry they're all gone. You know what killed them? The automobile. Pure and simple. Just stands to reason. You live in Saskatchewan, now all you have to do—and all you had to do since the 20's—was to zip down to Swift Current or over to Moose Jaw, Regina, and I don't care where else, Biggar, Melfort, Battleford, P.S., Saskapoosh, and your wife can have a permanent wave and you can see a good show, have a good meal, visit friends, and get a tool welded, or whatever fancies you, and remember, this was in the 20's. Cars would go 25 or 40 miles an hour and today, if you can find one, Old Dobbin still has a five-miles-an-hour single shift. Good roads. People moved from the small towns. Why should they stay?

But the old towns. All gone. I can take you especially south of here and you will see where the streets were, where the avenues were, where the livery stable was, the general store, everything, and now there is nothing but a lot of old people and they've given up the ghost too and yet, 50 and 60 years ago, they was going concerns.

The churches were strong then, you see. You belonged to a church or you were a heathen. But more than that, the churches were where you met the girls. That's where everything started. What went on from there was up to you and her and how closely her ma and pa were watching. They had church on Sunday and you went, whisky jag over or not, and they had whist parties. Ever hear of whist? Bridge knocked that game all to hell. Once it was whist and then it became bridge, contract bridge, night and day. A real madness. Like chain letters and other dumb things the women get involved with. And the churches had harvest suppers and other fun and games, and the young people put on plays, pageants, readings. Or they'd sponsor some preacher from down east or across the line, and he'd come and preach for a week, and that could sure get the district riled up if he was a real comer-on.

I don't remember any hatred. I mean the Anglicans or the Prots. they didn't hate the dogans. They had picnics together. If a family got burned out, everybody pitched in. Time after time I've seen it that a family would get burned out and everybody would get together, donating this and that, and that outfit would be in better shape one week after that fire than they were before. I mean in material goods. Beds, blankets, furniture, dishes, and somebody could always come up with a house they could use. Or they'd haul in a big granary from some farm and fix it up and that would get the family through the winter. Groceries too. Preserves. People really dug in.

Talking about fires. First thing a town did even before it was a village or a town, the chief cook and bottle washer, which meant usually the first storekeeper, he'd call a meeting and clapping his hands, he'd beller, "Boys, we got to get us a volunteer fire department." Why? Well, one why is that he had the biggest investment in the town, so if he had a fire he was protecting himself. This was back about 1905 to 1910 when I was booming around. A lot of these small towns were starting up through Saskatchewan and Alberta, and through the parkland, south and north and west, and towns were beginning to feel their oats. New business and maybe a bank and if you had a bank then that was big stuff, and the next thing the city fathers would be looking for would be a police barracks, then a courthouse, then a 100,000-dollar electrical plant. If you didn't get a check rein on them pretty soon they'd completely lose their minds and start asking for a university and the Parliament buildings—and here they were, two streets this way and two avenues that way, stuck out on the bald prairie with one passenger train a day each way and a freight. But a lot of these early boosters were Hoosiers and I guess they figured that good old American know-how would do the trick, so there they was, cheerleading just like at the football games on the telly.

But getting back to the volunteer fire department. Yeah. Yeah, them. They had them and I belonged to a couple and you practiced two nights a week. One town we practiced from seven to eight and then we drank hootch, and if the fire hall had started fire at 10, we would have been too drunk to save it. But we did save some. Every town used to have its fires. They wouldn't often save the house itself. Or the livery barn. Or the ice cream parlor or whatever was going up. But they could save the buildings on either side of it, and I guess that when it all boils down to maple sugar that is what the game was all about. Boy, we used to have fun. We were kind of town heroes. The school teachers and the clerks and the lawyers, they could play in the band or sing in the Presbyterian choir but it was the he-men, the drinkers, who wore the big red hats. Yeah!

Something to Think About

Now you ask me, an old man, what I think about coming to a village of a few hundred people and seeing it grow up into the city of Edmonton. Half a million people. Well, I haven't thought too much about it because it pretty well happened without me doing too much about it and I never had much education. But I read and I watch the politicians and I keep pretty close track of them and they're all a crooked lot, believe me, but we put them in and then I think of what Gladstone said. He said that in every controversy the majority always eventually turns out to be wrong. Well, anyway, getting half a million people in one place, all close together, and well, if there's a war, that's a pretty good way to drop one bomb and get them all at once. That's the general idea of cities and civilization today, I'd say. You think about that.

13 *Buyers and Sellers*

Mother Had a Stopping House . . . Ever Heard of a Jewish Farmer? . . . When the Rawleigh Man Came Round . . . Weigh Scales, the Farmers' Protection . . . In the Days of the Commercial Traveler . . . My Office Was Under My Hat . . . Credit Was Where You Found It . . . Then Along Came Eaton's Catalogue

The increase in immigration in the West was astonishing— 50,000 in 1905 and nearly 400,000 in the peak year of 1913— and with the increase grew the commercialization of the West. There was Mother and her stopping house, but that was a form of private commercialism that died in a few years. The first automobiles foretold the end of the famous (and infamous) traveling salesman. Jewish peddlers moved to the towns and in the great, churning brain of the Eatons' commercial body the mail order catalogue was taking shape, a catalogue that would change the West's buying habits. Forever and ever.

As you read this chapter you will perhaps note that nothing changes—or the more things change, the more they remain the same. Money was the name of the game—the making of it and the keeping of it—and it has ever been thus.

Mother Had a Stopping House

There were stopping houses all over the prairie. Or they might be called halfway houses. My mother had one. It was just your own home, that was all, but if you were in a place where it was natural for travelers to stop for the night after traveling all day, then it would be called a stopping house. You put a sign over your front door or on the fence saying "Bernard's Stopping House." The sign meant that you charged. That you just couldn't put up for the night free.

If you were trailing a herd you could make 15 or 18 miles a day, so a house say 18 miles out of Swift Current would be a stopping house. A man on a horse, much more. A wagon, not so far, of course. But there was always quite a bit of travel in those days, and it was an easy way to pick up a bit of change. People would rather sleep in a house than under a wagon or just wrapped in a blanket. Especially women.

In my mother's place the women slept in the front room. Then when the sun came up, that became the restaurant where she fed them. The men slept in the stable and the last thing my dad would do before going to bed when we had men in the stable was to go out and yell: "No smoking. Him I catches smoking I'll thrash."

In the morning there was a big pot of porridge. You never thought of sugar and cream or milk on porridge in those days. You salted it and ate it with a spoon. It was thick and filling and Mother might be apt to put in a few raisins or in the fall some dried saskatoons or blueberries, if we'd been out to the bushes picking. With the porridge there was pieces of salt pork. I believe you might call it fat belly. Salt pork and tea. That was breakfast and that would be about six o'clock in the morning, summer or winter, and that would usually have to carry the travelers on to the next place at night. At night Mother made boiled potatoes and salt pork, bread and tea. She made lovely bread. But I used to hate the smell of that pork frying. It had an awful smell. The house always stunk of it except in summer when Mother had an outdoor kitchen at the back and she'd do it there. The smell also reminded me of the squealing of the pigs when my father was butchering. They'd squeal, and the squeals would get smaller and jerkier as they died, and when they stopped you knew the hog was dead. Oh well.

The price was a quarter for breakfast and a quarter for supper, and for sleeping inside the house that was another quarter. So you can see it wasn't all that cheap to travel in those days. Remember this was 70 years ago and 25 cents would buy a lot more than it does today. Mother used to get paid in English shillings, American money, German franks, all kinds of money. In those days it was all good. Somebody would take it. You were never stuck with it. Banks, even they could issue their own money. Bills, of course.

There was a cupboard that Mother kept as a store. She bought in town at the regular price, and then if anybody wanted anything I guess she just tacked on 25 percent for her trouble. Maybe 30 percent. She had thread and buttons for emergency repairs, and some cloth, gingham as I remember, and tins of tomatoes, stewed tomatoes, jellies and soda crackers and cheese and sailor's biscuits. Things people could buy for a lunch snack on the trail. She also had bicarbonate of soda and some of the jellies for bee stings and patent medicines and things people might not have but might need. She also carried mosquito netting. Greeners starting out from town—well, after one day of those mosquitoes on the prairies, they were ready to pay good prices for mosquito netting. It was always a good seller, and so many times people wouldn't even know there was such a thing. Mother would suggest it, explain what it was, how it was draped down under the hat, and they'd grab it. At good prices.

My mother was the businessman in our family. All my father wanted to do was go to the Chicago International and buy the best mare and the best stallion there was on show and come back and breed horses. He talked about breeding the ideal horse for prairie work. Strong, intelligent and with stamina, staying power. He called it The Great Prairie Horse. He did breed horses later but nothing like what he dreamed of. Just horses.

The little money that Mother made kept the family together. God knows, the farm didn't bring in much. Hardly worth the trouble. Father was just not a good farmer—mind way up there floating along with the clouds. I suppose Mother took in an average of a dollar and a half a day. The potatoes came out of our patch and the flour came from the mill. Dad would take what little wheat he did grow to town and the miller would grind it. There was a split, one-seventh to the mill. You could buy rolled oats in 80-pound sacks for practically nothing. If somebody wanted milk, we had a cow. The pork was off our hogs, so there wasn't much overhead. Just a lot of sweat; Mother over the pot at five o'clock in the morning and the last plate washed at eight o'clock at night. Anybody who stopped in after seven o'clock wasn't fed. That was a rule. That way, Mother got rid of quite a few tins of stewed tomatoes and sailor's biscuits. They'd make a meal out of that. Mother had her head screwed on right. I could write a book about her.

Ever Heard of a Jewish Farmer?

My people never intended to live on a farm. Who ever heard of a Jewish farmer? They just don't make good farmers. Why, I can tell you, my friend, where my parents came from, in Russia, of course, Hebrews couldn't even own land, so how can you expect, I ask you, how can you expect that a man who wasn't ever able to own land, how is he going to become a farmer? Ridiculous.

No, they came because they had skills. People need suits, don't they? A bohunk can get married in his overalls but when it comes to his burial, ah, then they want a suit. That's where we came in. Tailors. Jewelers, watchmakers. Wasn't every second-hand store in Winnipeg a Jewish store? You bet your life. Jewish people want their own food, so bakeries, butcher shops, of course. Teachers. We made good teachers when they let us teach, but we taught in our own school too. People laugh now but that old man with the old wagon and the old horse going down the back lanes picking up bits of copper and brass and old clothing and everything else, and throwing insults at the kids that are throwing rocks at him and yelling "Sheeny," he did all right. My son the doctor, my son the judge, my son the owner of that apartment house at Cathedral and Main. That's what you get for picking up old junk.

They came off the train at Winnipeg and that was as far as they were going to go right then. No fancy trunks, no valises, no silks and satins. No, just what they had. Everything in a big blanket and the blanket drawn together and pinned with a big pin. Maybe two or three of them. I know, I've seen the pictures. And six kids. Always six kids. Nothing else. The Cossacks said, "Take your family, Jewboy, and go." You think the Russians were the worst. They were bad but the Poles were the worst. Believe me, my family knows these things.

They'd tell the land agent, "Yes, we're going to live on a farm in Canada," but when they got to Winnipeg, that was the end of the line until . . . well, until somebody would say, "Your uncle has a nice store on Broad Street and we'll send you out there to learn the business." The boy would say, "What business?" and they'd say, "He's got a grocery store. Pack your clothes. Poppa will take you to the train." Off to Regina. Or they'd say, "He's a pharmacist." Not a druggist, no, no. A pharmacist. High class. The kid, maybe 14, he'd say, "But I'm not a doctor. What do I know about that?" and they'd say, "It's decided. Pack your bag. Rudie will take you to the station." And away the kid would go to Weyburn or Swift Current or Edmonton. It all worked out.

Girls stayed home. If it was a boardinghouse, a roominghouse, they made 10,000 beds and washed a million dishes until the great day. Oh, the great day! Marriage.

So you see, it was a ghetto. North of the C.P.R. tracks, over toward the river, down to the Salter Street bridge. But not the kind of ghetto you're thinking about. There were Poles and Ukrainians and English mixed in there too, along with Magyars and Icelanders and Greeks and a few Negroes, porters on the C.P.R. and the C.N. There were about 100 churches. Without a word of a lie. Maybe 100 churches and every one had a hall in the basement and every one was competing at least once a week, some concert, some poetry class, some dance, some yukky thing. Selkirk Avenue. I can't describe it in those days. Garlic, I remember that. Road apples that deep on the street. I guess those guys over at city hall they figured we could clean off our own horse crap or maybe nobody paid their taxes.

Nobody spoke English to each other unless they had to for some reason, which I don't know why they would except a Russian and a Jew, if they wanted to deal in second-hand coats or canvas or something, then it would be in English, and some of the broken English such as you never did hear.

But that was a long time ago. There's no ghetto now. Not as you know a ghetto. We've all become rich. Who needs it, but I can remember in the early days when I was just a kid, nobody ever needed to go downtown into Winnipeg. It was only about 10 blocks south, but who needed it? There was Eaton's downtown but didn't we have our own stores? And besides, in Eaton's whoever heard of bargaining, bargaining, for God's sakes, over something that was going to give the storekeeper a 25-cent profit and he'll yatter 10, 20 minutes. I can go through the whole routine now. My mother, I've seen her do it a thousand times. You weren't buying if you didn't cut the price down. She'd rather walk away. But they're all rich now.

It used to be the boys were in gangs, and if you were a Catholic and went to Holy Name, or whatever the school was, you had to join up in a gang and fight your way home after school. Same with the Jews. Jewish school, out at six, and they fought their way home with everybody after them. Everybody fought. Then on Saturday they'd get on the grounds of the high school over there and play baseball together.

But before the war when I was young, the North End, well, it was like a railroad station. Lines used to shoot out every way, you see. You'd have an uncle at Melita and he's a merchant. Not a grocery store man. A merchant. Class, you see. So you'd be sent out there to learn to weigh butter and count eggs and watch those farm women didn't cheat you blind. Or to Regina. An uncle has a hardware store. Send Isser out. Fifteen dollars a month, sleep in the back and call the policeman against robbers and in 10 years, maybe, just maybe there might be enough money in the pot to open up a store somewhere else. So he becomes a hardware man. Bright kids become doctors, dentists. Look at the clinics you see everywhere. Some of those names might not be Jewish, but you look you-know-where and there's your answer. Sometimes it was smart moving to a new city to change. Change. Why not? If people's prejudices won't change, then change something else. Believe me, my old friend, it has happened.

But no farmers. Sure, buy from the farmers. Buy from the farmers, sell to the restaurants, ship to Toronto or Vancouver. Be up to your belly button in turnips, carrots, Morden area apples, and crocks of Elm Creek butter, but a farmer! Farming? Who needs it.

Jews aren't farmers. For the city, they always have been, I think.

A Jew has to talk to people. The more he is talking, shouting, arguing, fighting, eating, the better he is. The city, the town, is his home. He's got to be with people. A farmer talks to his horses, the gophers. A Jew would go nuts. Believe me.

When the Rawleigh Man Came Round

My mother liked to see the Rawleigh man come around. He had a horse and cart and all these little boxes and compartments built in, and they were filled with things to sell, things that women on those little patchy farms were always running out of. Oh, everything, you know. Needles. Thread. Soap. Mother made her own soap but she liked his soft, quiet kind too, especially for the baby. Patent medicines, stuff for the stomach, and if you had a sore on your lip he'd sell you a bottle of gooey stuff to clear it up.

He really had an awful lot of things, things that you couldn't always get in the store in town or in the catalogue, and he came once a month. Dad used to say he was like an old lofer, a wolf that made a trip around his territory once a month.

But our hired man liked to see him. His name was Angelo. A nice old man who didn't have much to say. When he worked with the horses he'd talk to them in Italian.

When the Rawleigh man came round, Angelo would buy as much vanilla extract as the Rawleigh man—his name was Sangster—as much as he would sell him. Oh, maybe four or five bottles. That might be all Angelo's pay, but he'd buy the bottles. They made him drunk, you see. The extract was mostly plain alcohol. I don't know why but it was. The Rawleigh man, I'll bet, sold more bottles to cowboys and men like Angelo than he ever did to farmers' wives. That's why he carried so many. He was just about being pretty close to being a bootlegger, that Rawleigh man.

Weigh Scales, the Farmers' Protection

I thought it was only in our town. I thought we were the only ones to have the bright idea. Since I've been doing some reading in western Canada histories I find that lots of towns installed their own weigh scales and that's a good thing. Was a good thing. The situation has changed now. It changed a long time ago.

In the early days the elevators cheated you. You got short weight. If you can find an elevator agent alive today—there must be some and they've got to be as old as me, 92—and if you say to him, "Johnny, did you ever give short weight?" and you ask him to look you in the eye when he answers you, if the man is an honest man you'll never get a straight look.

The reason? Reason is simple. Listen to me. An elevator agent was hired by a Winnipeg elevator firm. It was his job and he did what his bosses told him to do. They told the agent to give short weight. You came up with your wagon. You hauled in the winter, boxes on sleds, and you might see 40 or 30 sleds at the elevator if there was only one. If there was more than one, you could usually tell the most honest agent because he would have the most loads waiting. I won't use their names because they might come out and shoot me, but some of the biggest names in Winnipeg today made their money on short weight. So? So.

We all knew this. Everybody knew this. It was no secret. You couldn't look over the agent's shoulder. He was in his little room and the check he made out, after he'd weighed your load and graded, it was the check you got. There was no fooling around. That's what you got and sometimes, especially early in the winter, you went right up to the bank or the store and cashed it and you were very glad to get it. You believe me about it.

But finally we'd had enough. We were tired of being gypped. We knew how many sacks we had and how much each sack held and we weren't unintelligent men, you know. You understand. There were some fairly intelligent men among us. Me for one. I was farming because I liked it, not because I expected to make a lot of money. If I had wanted money, I would have stayed back in Durham.

We decided two things. We had to have our own scales and we had to force the elevator agent or agents to give us a tally before our grain was dumped. Compare, my boy, compare. That was the whole secret.

We got the scale easily. I believe we got it from Galt in Ontario, where a company made a very good scale. It had a capacity of 8,000 pounds, quite within our needs. I forget what it cost, but about 40 farmers in the district, from every point of the compass, got together, and I think the bank backed us and it was no problem. We set the scale outside the livery stable—this was in Riley—and it was simple after that. The elevator companies didn't like it, but at least when we did this we showed them we meant business.

Later when the co-op came along and we all had the co-ops and bought binder twine and other supplies, anything that a farmer wished, then the co-ops took over the scales from the livery barns. I'm speaking of Alberta and Saskatchewan as a whole, not just our town. Or the co-ops set up their own. Anyway it worked. The co-ops were a good thing but they didn't have the fulfillment that many expected them to have. A lot of people thought it was the dawning of a new day and it wasn't quite that.

Not nearly. A lot went broke and I think that was because of poor management. Because farmers aren't storekeepers. But they kept the scales. Now, I suppose, a scale is a museum piece. There's no need for them and hasn't been for a long time. What the scale did was this. It started keeping the elevator companies reasonably honest. Reasonably honest. We had no say in what grade we'd get for our crop, but we could work from the other side of the line. That's what we did and it worked out pretty well. Pretty well. Not perfect, but not too bad.

In the Days of the Commercial Traveler

In those days all the commercial travelers traveled by train. At any one time there might be 2,000 men traveling through the West selling their goods. It was a lonely life.

You take a thing like dry goods. Well, a man selling dry goods might have 10 big trunks, and every one of those trunks would have to be put on the dray and taken over to the hotel. We had two hotels in our town and each one had big rooms, which they called sample rooms, and this is where the traveler laid out all his goods, everything that was made of cloth, from children's socks to sheets to, well, you name anything you want.

Why, I wouldn't be surprised if some of those trunks didn't weigh 250 pounds, and it all had to be lugged, packed, unpacked, taken back, put on the train. These men did that every day of their lives. They'd be out on the road maybe five months at a time, and then back to Winnipeg or maybe it was Toronto or Montreal. Maybe a month at home, and a lot of them had wives and children, and then away it was again, out on the road.

They wouldn't go to the small towns too much because a small town might have only two general stores, say, if you were in dry goods. If you were in hardware, a town might have only one hardware store and maybe an implement shed where the owner might buy a few things off you. They pretty well had to stick to the bigger towns and hope the storekeepers from the smaller towns would come in. They'd sent out circulars, you see, saying when they'd be in such and such a town, so they had to keep to a pretty tight schedule. A thing like a train derailment, and we had a few in those days, or a bad three-day blizzard—and don't think they didn't happen—that could throw a man's whole schedule out of whack.

Of course, some had it easy. Suppose you were a hardware man. You couldn't be lugging boxes of tools and nuts and bolts around, so you had a catalogue and the merchant chose out of that. Naturally he'd pretty well know just about what he wanted, what he was low in, before the commercial traveler got there anyway. Sometimes it was just a case of the two of them going over to the hotel bar and the traveler buying the storekeeper a drink and the storekeeper giving him a list telling him what he needed. Prices didn't change much in those days. There wasn't inflation and a price was a price and that was it.

You'd think that if a stove was a stove and a nut was a nut and a bolt a bolt, then they wouldn't need traveling men. They'd just send in their orders twice a year and everybody would be happy. I'm sure that would have worked fine except for competition. You've heard of that. There were always three or four or five men on the road selling the same stuff. There would be a company in Winnipeg, one in Toronto, one in Galt, and one in Hamilton, and they all wanted that western business. That farmer business was important to them. That's why they had the commercial men.

Of course, with the dry-goods people it was different because styles and fashions seemed to change every year or two, just like they do now, and besides, the storekeeper would want to feel the fabric. But with hardware and groceries, things like that, it was the competition that did the trick.

They were good men. Yes, good men. Sometimes there was one who would drink too much, but then again there were some who never touched a drop. Not a drop. But some you would see in the bar every night. It was sort of like a club to them. They had nothing to do. Couldn't sit every night in your room and read, and what is there usually to do in a small town at night?

There weren't picture shows, you know. Nothing like that. So some would just stay in the bar and drink beer or whisky. Whisky was pretty cheap in those days. Ten cents a glass, 15 cents a glass. Around there.

Too, they knew everybody. When you've been making the same rounds for 10, 15, 20 years, you've pretty well watched one of those prairie towns grow up. Sometimes they got to know people so well that they would be asked out for supper at somebody's house. I imagine that was a big event in these men's lives. Reminded them of home.

Sometimes if a man was laid over Sunday in a small town, because some of the trains on the branch lines didn't run on Sundays, if it was a nice day he'd rent a buggy from the livery barn and take one of the waitresses from the hotel out. Out for a drive. Along the river or something. What went on out there, well, that wasn't any of our business, was it?

But they was all good men. They worked hard for their living and I don't think they made much money. Commission. All of it was commission. Expenses. They got expenses. Do you know you could get room and board, a good room and good board, in a nice hotel in those days for about 15 dollars a month? I know, I did. So a traveling man's expenses wouldn't be too high.

When cars came along, that finished the traveling salesman on the train, except for the fellows with the big trunks. They still had to use the train. The others, say three fellows from Winnipeg knew each other and one was in farm machinery and one in notions and one in hardware. They could get together in a car and, why, they'd just cover that country real fast. Maybe three towns a day. Two at least. Just skipping over those prairie trails. They all carried catalogues and they sold by catalogue and their job was a whole lot easier.

I think it was the last war that finished off the traveler. I don't believe there are any more. All you have to do now is look at the catalogue and then pick up the phone and there's some fellow sitting at a desk and he just takes it all down. That's the way I think it is done now. But the traveler was part of the history of western Canada. There were times when sometimes as many as five or six would get off the same train, all ready to do business the next day, and they sort of added a bit of life to the town. Towns were pretty dead in those days, you know. They helped perk things up a bit.

They gave us a few laughs. There was one called Ned Mitchell. A Scottish fellow. He worked for a big company out of Winnipeg and he'd come around two or three times a year. Two times. Everybody knew him because he'd get in the bar and start telling all the jokes he'd heard around the country during the six months that had gone by. He was more fun than two monkeys in a barrel upside down. Somebody would start him off by buying him a drink and he'd tell a couple of stories, and then somebody would tell the barkeep to give him another and this went on and on. I remember once a fellow asked him about all those jokes about the farmer's daughter and the traveling saleman. You know those jokes. Well, they had them then. I remember Ned laughing and he said, "Friend, I haven't even been on no farm in all my life, and I wouldn't even look at a farmer's daughter unless she came to town." That was Ned for you. Some of those fellows were real characters.

My Office Was Under My Hat

After leaving Saskatoon by democrat and team a fellow by the name of Smith and myself arrived in Scott on July 4 of 1908. I was sent out by the Farmers' Lumber Company to start a lumber yard, and Smith began a butcher shop. But he left a couple of months later.

There was a crowd always coming and going all the time and the steel of the railroad was roughly four miles east of where the town was going to be, and they were waiting for heavy timbers to build a bridge across Catherwood Coulee. Finally on August 7 the first train came puffing into town carrying among other things a small shack, which turned out to be the station for the agent, whose name I don't recall.

I also received the first carload of lumber on this train from the Farmers' Lumber Company. Now I was in business and I meant to build an office and a shed, but the demand for lumber was so great that I immediately sold all of it to the settlers and townspeople—so I didn't get my office. I sent word back to the company and I received six more carloads of lumber the following week and I sold them. Every week after that, more carloads came in for me and I sold all of it and I still hadn't got around to putting up a place of business.

In the meantime A. Senger of the Sturgeon Lumber Company came in to town from Battleford with four wagonloads of lumber about August 10, and he built a lumber office for his company on First Avenue. So while I was the first lumber dealer in town I wasn't the first to have business premises.

The Farmers' Lumber Company kept sending me material and I kept selling it faster than they could supply it, and it was a while after that that I built an office. In the meantime, I guess you could say my lumber yard was the spur track down by the station and my office was under my hat.

Credit Was Where You Found It

It was hard times those years. You only had money in the fall when you could sell something. Nobody had much money and we had none. I was living with my brother at the time because I hadn't built my house yet. We went to town, oh, about 25 miles, this spring day and we had orders from his wife for 60 dollars' worth of groceries.

When we got there they refused us. What? Oh, credit. They refused us credit. There was two stores there, Snyder and Armstrong, and a store down the street. Forget the name. I don't know. They'd give credit to others but they wouldn't to me and my brother. I hadn't had a crop yet, but he had and he'd of paid them in the fall.

When we couldn't get credit at Snyder, we said we'd try the other store. We went down there and they knew we'd been getting our groceries at Snyder's and paying cash for it so they said, "No, you been getting your groceries up the street, so you go get your credit there."

We both had families, babies had been born, and we couldn't go home without anything and have our children starve, so we went back to Snyder and Armstrong and they said, "Did you get it?" and we said no. They sort of smiled at us.

I didn't say this but my brother did and he said, "By God, we're not going home without them groceries. We're gonna bust in to get it. We'll wait around and then we'll bust into your damn store tonight and we'll get it, and I don't mean maybe. We got kids out there and we need 60 dollars' worth of groceries and if you don't want to sell them to us in an honest way, then we're gonna steal 'em tonight. And I'm telling you I'm not kidding you." He was mad.

The storekeeper said, "Give me the list," and my brother give it to him and he handed it to his helper and he said, "Fill it out." That's all he said. In fact, when the final reckoning come that bill was worth about 70 dollars. About 10 more dollars.

So anyway we got through that time, and we got a crop and we were going to put our order through Eaton's this time. Between the two of us the order was more than 400 dollars and that was a lot of money in them days.

So we went to town and we went to Snyder's and by this time we owed them 300 dollars, because during the summer we still needed groceries and I guess they just couldn't turn us down like they had tried to do for some reason that one time. So we paid them the 300 dollars and I offered even to pay interest on it but no, they turned me down. They wouldn't take interest. They seen how we were at least honorable and paid our bills.

That made me feel better about Snyder and Armstrong so I said to them, "Look," I said, "here's an order all made out for 400 dollars to Eaton's, where we was gonna buy instead of you. If you can match their prices you can have this order." One of them took this big long list and he looked it over and he said, "We'll meet these prices." So they got 700 dollars out of us in one

Curse of all settlers were the roads. In spring, as shown, they were quagmires; in summer and fall, dusty and rutted. In winter, they were barely discernible under deep snow. (Provincial Archives of Alberta, E. Brown Collection)

Sunday was the day for automobiling, to show that fancy new contraption off. It soon proved itself useful on the prairie, with the great distances to be covered. (Provincial Archives of Alberta, E. Brown Collection)

Picnics—right on the prairie grass if there was no pond or stream handy—were a summer adventure. Food, feasting, and fun for everybody. (Public Archives Canada, PA 37806)

Fall suppers were another feature of Western life, with entertainment after. The money raised went to a charity or town project. (Provincial Archives of Alberta, E. Brown Collection)

Left: Every town and village had its baseball team and rivalry was intense. This team could afford uniforms. Right: These young ladies of Edmonton, dressed in their finery, were known as the King's Daughters. (Public Archives Canada, PA 38582; Provincial Archives of Alberta, E. Brown Collection)

Hurrah for the military band! It provided music at dances, on special occasions, and even on Sunday afternoons in the park. (Provincial Archives of Alberta, E. Brown Collection)

A plainsman with his Indian companions in downtown Edmonton, 1898. Townspeople were used to sights like this. (Provincial Archives of Alberta, E. Brown Collection)

Posed as if for a postcard but nevertheless on duty is Corporal Johnston of the Royal Northwest Mounted Police. (Provincial Archives of Alberta, H. Pollard Collection)

day and that was a pretty good day's business. From that day on, they trusted us and we trusted them and they never lost on us and we never lost on them. That's the way a lot of business was done them days.

Then Along Came Eaton's Catalogue

Lord, Eaton's. Good gracious me, yes, I remember Eaton's. Mail order. The catalogue. I can still hear my father. His brother used to call him a store boomer. Boomer was a word for a railroad man who went all around Canada and the United States working on railroads. Mostly telegraphers and brakemen and jobs like that. Not too many engineers and conductors. They were big men and they stayed put. But these boomers, they always boasted about how many lines they had worked on. Well, Dad was a store boomer. We had stores all over the West, it seems. Lord! Morris, Manitoba, and Carman and Portage. And when the settlers started to move into Saskatchewan, Dad headed west with them. He'd buy a store with the money he'd got from the last one or he'd put one up. Buy and sell. Buy again. My goodness. The man thought he was making money. Well, just ask my mother. He wasn't.

Then Eaton's came along. Everybody seems to put Eaton's and Timothy together. He was the start of it all down in Ontario. Old Timothy's store they sometimes called Eaton's. Then they came to Winnipeg and I think this was about 1905. Or 1906 or 1907. I was helping around the store at the time. Clerking. Doing a lot of packaging. Dad would get in bags of salt, boxes of raisins, soap flakes, and I'd make them up into one-, two-, and five-pound packages. That's the way we'd sell. But along came this great big store on Portage Avenue in Winnipeg. I do believe it was the biggest building in the West at that time. It must have been. Lord, but it was a big one.

But what Eaton's did, which I remember most, was bring in

mail order. Ordering by mail. It's nothing now, I know. In the country you do it every week and think nothing of it. You do it in the city too. But in those days it was something entirely new, although Dad had heard about it. I think it had been done a lot down in the States before that. Most things that were done in the West in those days had all been done in the States long before. Like farm machinery. New kinds of plows. Binders. Threshing machines. It seemed most of our ideas came from the States. Not from England.

Dad first heard of the mail-order business of Eaton's when the train came in and there were four or five big bundles of books. They weren't the big mail-order catalogues you see to-day, but they were big enough and they were addressed to everybody in the district. You see, Dad had the post office in the back of his store, so he'd be the first to know.

He hired a girl named Teresa Wyatt to be the postmistress. She was one of five Irish sisters who had come out to Canada a few years before to live with their two brothers north of the river. Bachelors around had snapped up the other four. Some-how Teresa hadn't made it. But she would later. She got a few dollars a month and her board and room and a chance to see all the bachelors who came to town.

So Dad looked at the Eaton's catalogue and he said it would be the death of him. It looked that way. It had everything in it. Oh Lord, what was in it you could write down in a month of Sundays. Every dry goods you could imagine—ladies' shoes with instructions how to measure your foot to get the right size, kitchen pans and pets and cutlery and harness and grub hoes and axes and camps and boots for the men, overalls, jackets, bells to put on your cutters and pumps and guns and everything galore. The only thing as I remember that they didn't have was groceries, but there I could be wrong. Maybe they did have groceries. Of course, the very first catalogue didn't have all these things but they soon did.

They had a one-price system. There was page 110 and on it was ladies' nightgowns, several kinds, two or three colors, white, pink, blue, and the price. Now the price was the price. No haggling. Eaton's wanted that price and if you wanted that nightie, then that's what you sent off. In country stores there was always the price marked on it and the price the customer had in her head, and the real price might be somewhere in between. That's called haggling. You'd haggle.

But that didn't work very good either because Eaton's price was always less than Dad could sell for. This is the way we saw it. It was explained by a drummer who came once and Dad invited him for dinner. He didn't do this often, just to specials. There was something he wanted to find out from this man. This drummer said Eaton's had the whole West as customers, the whole West, from Winnipeg to the Edmonton-Calgary line, and they bought up in quantity. A factory making nightgowns, they could buy everything that factory made in six months, five months, and so they could sell cheaply. They'd still make a darn good profit. Large turnover. It didn't matter what line you were in, hardware, notions, dry goods. A large turnover was the thing.

So there was Dad, and the good Lord knows, storekeeping was his whole life. It was what he had learned from his father in the Ottawa Valley. They had a store there. Now at age 50 or so he was faced with the Eaton's catalogue, and what must have made him mad was that each and every one of them was going out through the wicket of the post office to every person in the district and that post office was in his own store. He couldn't hide them. He couldn't burn them. Having the post office, that was a sacred trust in those days. When you had it you were marked as a man of the community. Lord, yes. Besides, said the old lady in the shoe, if you had the post office it meant that when people came to town they had to at least come into your store. I don't think the post office itself paid more than 20 dollars a month. If that. Maybe less.

They could sit out there in their log houses, their shacks on the bald prairie with the wind whistling through the cracks, and they could look at that catalogue with every consarned thing in it that man could think up to make, all the good things and all the trashy frivolous things too. Let the wind blow. They just got out their pencil and marked in what they wanted. Bolts of cotton, hames straps, patent medicines, axe handles, anything you wanted. They filled in the slips and that was that. No waiting around. No taking a substitute for something that Dad or Carter didn't have. Carter was the other storekeeper in our little town.

And Lord, I can remember when it first dawned on Dad what was happening. You see, you didn't send money through the mail to Eaton's. They didn't want money. Postal orders. That's what they wanted. It was down there in black and white. I think it said "Send No Cash." So these people would come in to Dad's store and he'd see them going down to the back to the wicket and he knew darn well that they were buying postal orders in his own store to send off to Winnipeg. To buy things that were on sale not 10 or 20 feet from them, right in Dad's general store. I guess if there had been such a saying then, Dad would have said, "They've got me coming and going." He might have laughed later, but it was no joking matter then. That's the way it was. Of course, way back in Winnipeg Eaton's didn't care, although they must have known what was going on. They weren't that stupid.

Dad hung on. Had to. In fact, he didn't do all that bad. People who bought from the mail order maybe did so only three times a year, twice a year. At the most maybe four times. They still had to have groceries. Staples. A shovel might break and they had to have a shovel, so they'd come in. They had five crocks of butter they wanted to trade off. Well, old Timothy in his big mansion in Toronto wasn't in the business of buying crocks of butter put up by farmers' wives for pin money. Dad did that. Barter, trade, and once a week he'd ship off the butter and what eggs he'd collected to a wholesale house in Regina. The family would come to town and the kids had been promised a little bag of rock candy each, and so the family would come trooping through the door with its bell dinging away and the kids would get their candy. If they bought a big order of groceries, the kids got their candy free. Do you know that in those days a little brown bag of rock candy would last a kid a week, two weeks? Lord, yes. Pleasures came along few and far between. Few and far between.

The store or Carter's, it was still a meeting place. People

still had to buy a lot of things that Eaton's didn't have or wouldn't ship, or they couldn't ship in less than three weeks even though we had daily train service. When people needed it, they needed it. And there were some families who were friends of Dad's, of my mother, they'd known them since they'd come to town right from the beginning, a few years back. Maybe they attended the same church. Church of England. They still dealt at the store.

But receipts did go down. I could tell by the way my father and mother discussed the books. Every month it was less. You couldn't give up the post office. That made no sense, my dad told me. I suggested it. Carter would probably be glad to get it. Somebody else might bid for it. The store was still a social center and there was that big box right inside the front door which Dad had put there and it was filled with books and magazines. Books people had brought, English and American magazines, the *Family Herald*, the *Weekly Free Press*, and people could take books and magazines home to read. They were expected to bring others to take their place.

The catalogue hurt other people too, you know. Just not the stores. The harnessmaker. He couldn't compete with harness and straps and things that were made in big factories in Pennsylvania with big machines and sold by Eaton's. The town carpenters made some very fine pieces of furniture, but they couldn't compete with the sideboards and the tables and chairs that Eaton's could ship out from their factory in Hamilton or wherever it was. There was just no way they could do that. Working alone in their shop. Even with the freight, Eaton's could do it cheaper. So, you see, it just wasn't our store that suffered. But you couldn't say it was happening by actually seeing it because people were pretty close-mouthed about their business in those days. But you knew. You knew. I don't know any stores that actually went bankrupt. Went out of business— I do know this. If a store closed down in some town, for some reason, like as not that place wouldn't open up again as a store.

But I suppose it all worked out for the best. The best. Eaton's gave good service and they shipped pretty quickly. They had this money-back guarantee. If you weren't satisfied with the goods you could ship them back and get your money back or what you really wanted. They did a lot. No credit, though. No, old Sir Timothy was too canny a Scotsman for that. Dad gave credit. He gave a lot and he carried a lot of people, but again, he was a little storekeeper in this little town and he pretty well had to. Well, he didn't have to but it was expected of him.

Looking back on it—and by the way that store was the last one Dad ever had, and I don't know whether it was because of Eaton's or not—but looking back, Lord, there was something that Eaton's could not provide. Couldn't do. Smell. The smell. Of kerosene, paraffin, raisins, dried prunes. They used to call dried prunes C.P.R. strawberries. Of flour. Of the oil that Dad used to put down on the floor once a month. The smell of those ship's biscuits the bachelors used to buy because they didn't bake bread. I guess the smell of people, too. Not many farmhouses had bathtubs, you know. It was a dib and a dab out of a bucket on Saturday night before coming to town. That was about all that was done. People would die today if they knew how many baths we took and the amount of underarm deodorant was sold. None. A little warm water and soap, that was enough. But all these smells and the manure and straw on the boots tromped all over the place, that gave a country store the right smell. I always thought it was a friendly smell. When I worked in that store up until I was 18 I don't think it ever offended me. No, I don't mean that. What I mean is that when I went to Normal School when I was 18 and then went away teaching, I missed that smell and when I went into somebody else's general store wherever I was teaching, that smell always reminded me of my home.

14 Oh, the Prairie Schoolhouse

The surest way for a lass in the West to get married was to become a schoolteacher. It didn't take much—usually just a grade-nine education, a temporary teacher's certificate, an appointment to a small country school—and then the bachelors flocked around. She could pick and choose.

And today, throughout the West, there are still many, many elderly ladies who will say, "Oh yes, I was a schoolmarm, oh yes. We had gay times in those days." A little smile will flit across the mouth and show in the eyes. They weren't well paid and living conditions often were dreadful, but it was exciting, it was adventurous.

The children of that era remember the schoolteachers too, and the lessons, the picnics, the fun, and all the things they used to do in the little prairie schoolhouse.

The Very Best Time for Us

The best time for me going to school was in the spring when me and my brother and my sister Elsie, we'd run over this big field of rubber ice.

There was this big field and in the spring you'd see the water come up over it. It would flood it, you see. Then at night it would freeze and in the morning we'd run across the ice to the school and every step we took, well, the ice would go down and then come up behind you. Down, up, down, up. It was fun. You could only do it in the morning in the spring when the ice froze. Not in the afternoon because then the ice would be melted. Again next day, the same, running all the way, down, up. We'd get to Southmere School all tired out, but it sure was fun.

Another good time would be when we'd get to school in the winter and the teacher would be in the school and she'd say, "No school, children, not today. Go home." That meant it was too cold to have school. The teacher knew that all the fire in the stove wouldn't warm up the school, so she'd be standing there in her coat and hat and she'd say, "No school today."

Then we'd go home and that was when Dad wouldn't put us to work. He always let us play those days. I mean, if it was that cold he figured it was too cold for us to work outside. The rest of the times, Saturdays, we always worked. My father was a hard man. He had all of us milking when we were only seven and eight years old. Everybody had to do their share, he'd say, and he never let up on us. That's why I liked it on cold days, because we didn't have to work.

Sometimes we'd be going to school and it would be awfully cold and we'd say to each other, "I'll bet you the teacher will send us home." A lot of times we'd be right. In the country you get so you can pretty well tell how cold it is, just by the way your boots crunch on the snow. If it made a hard, brittle crunch that meant it was pretty cold, I'll tell you. It never seemed to hurt us anywhere though. I mean I never got a frozen nose or ear, although I've seen cows with their tails frozen off.

Just a stump and in the summer they couldn't swish flies off and that was bad for them. A boy from down the road had the job of cleaning out the stove and lighting it. I think he got 25 cents cash. A quarter in those days was a lot. It could be more than his father had in his pocket at any one time. Usually the boy got the fire going and the first hour might be cold, but you pack 30 or 40 kids in nine grades into one of those little schools and they warm up pretty soon.

The grades were all in rows. Like near the windows on the east side there would be the grade ones, and it would work over there to the right where the older ones were. It didn't matter, actually, what age you were for the grade you were in. There could be 14-year-olds in grade three along with kiddies eight years old. The ones whose folks came up from the States and bought land, they had good schooling. So had the ones from Ontario or those who had had land around Winnipeg and then moved further west. But what we used to call the Polanders, from Europe, they didn't have much schooling. Not our kind of schooling. They didn't most of the time have the English to understand the lessons. That's when you saw boys of 14, bigger than the teacher, in the same row as six- and seven-year-old children and you kind of felt sorry for them. They didn't have time to study at home either, I'm sure of that. When we'd be coming back from town after selling grain and it would be dark, just after milking, maybe seven o'clock, you'd pass their little houses, the Polack houses, and there wouldn't even be a light on. They'd gone to bed to save kerosene. So how could the kids study? It's no wonder a lot of them quit school. Not so much the girls, really. They stayed on but the boys they just stayed a bit, and then after a year or two they just left and went, maybe to the farm to work or to the city or maybe into the bush to cut wood.

But we had fun in that school. In both schools I went to. With all those children the teacher had to be thinking of doing things all the time. The older ones would play word games on the board—I knew about that game of Scrabble long before I ever saw it played on a regular flat board. We did that at school, although each letter didn't have a number, a value. The team that made the longest or best words won. Then the other team had to stay after school and wash the blackboard and pound out the erasers and things like that. We also had spelling matches. Ones for the little kids where the word "horse" would be a hard word, but the older ones also had matches and some of their words were mean, I can tell you that.

We also played geography. The school had this big globe and one team would pick out a country and the other team, standing back a bit so they couldn't read the country's name, would have to say what it was. You never picked Canada or China or big countries. That was when the British Empire was red and the whole world looked like it was the British Empire. Times have changed, ain't they?

Outside in the spring and fall we had a baseball diamond. The school board gave us one ball a year and that had to last. A bat lasted longer than that, of course, but if it broke, you could always go to the poplar bluff by the barn and whittle out another. The bat didn't matter but the ball sure did. Once it started to unravel, somebody would take it home and get their dad to fix it up.

For the little kids there were swings. Know what they were? They put up two poles and then a crossbar across the top and then they got a lot of old horsecollars, ones that were no good anymore, and they tied them with rope to the crossbar and that was the kids' swings. Pretty good too.

There was a barn. It had a poplar and mud and sod roof and some kids brought horses. Some lived more than four or five miles away and they had Indian ponies. Geldings. Usually small stock, but it would get them there and back. It was nothing to see three of one family up on a horse and jogging up the road to school.

Every year just after school was out we would have a field day. It went like this. About two days before the big day Mr. Banks or maybe his hired man would come and bring his mower and cut down any grass that had grown too tall and then he'd rake it. Then the next day the men would come, and in the barn there were several boards and stools and benches and they would set them up outside. Usually in the shade of the schoolhouse or where it was going to be shady about three in the afternoon. Somebody would mark off 50 yards—that was for the racing—and if there was any boards to be fixed up in the backstop, then they were hammered in. That was for the ballgame. That's when we got the new ball. The new ball was bought for the First of July field day and then given to the school for the rest of the year, starting some time in September.

Things started about one in the afternoon, as I recall. Everybody came. The children of the school, of course, and their families and the hired men and bachelors in the district. There always were a lot of them. But we didn't get those that weren't ours. Schools were pretty close together in those days because of the cold and children walking, so each bachelor went to his own school unless, maybe, he was sweet on the teacher. That often happened.

Things were run by the head of the school district or some important man. I mean he was the one who handed out the prizes. For the children I think a first prize in the three-legged race might be 50 cents to the winners and they'd split. Twenty-five cents to the winner of the 50-yard dash. They didn't have things like the high jump and the broad jump, as I remember. Mostly running races. There was one that was a lot of fun and everybody played it, and that was the mixed-shoe race. Down at one end everybody would take off his shoes and they'd be put together, all mumbledy-jumbledy in a pile. You had to run down and find your own shoes, put them on, and run back to the finish line. That was one race the children could play as well as the grownups. Egg and spoon race. Blindfolded race. That was funny. And just straight races, of course.

Then everybody would eat. Everybody brought pies and potato salad and cold meat and cookies, tarts, buttered buns with jam, pickles, and you just didn't eat what you'd brought. Everything was put on the table and you ate what you wanted and if you wanted more, then you went and got it. Nobody said anything.

Then there was a ballgame. Sometimes the bachelors played the married men, or sometimes a team would come from town or the next district and there would be quite a game. We had some darn fine players in those days, fellows who could throw a ball through a hole in a barn from 50 feet or slap that old ball into any part of the field they wanted to. Some, I guess, could have gone into Regina or Moose Jaw or down south and played with the big teams there, but they never seemed to. Their speed was just down on the farm.

Then there were the cows. Somebody had to milk the cows and so the party would break up about seven o'clock or so which, still even then, was getting on, and there would be a lot of cows hanging around the gate wondering what was going on. Oh well, it was just once a year.

Then we'd have three months' holiday. July, August, and September. September was for harvesting. Everybody took a hand at that, even the little ones carrying the lunch pails out to the field. As I remember, the teacher was hired for September but she'd spend that month going around to the farms getting acquainted with the children and their parents. It might help today if they did that.

Then it was back to school and the new teacher and we'd always see how far we could get with her. How much she'd let us get away with. The young ones, they might be afraid of the bigger boys, but they had to make a stand in that first week or they were pretty well finished. They usually did. They were all farm girls themselves, mostly, sometimes from the district, and they knew how the system worked. If you didn't lay down the law right quick, then you had trouble.

The little schoolhouse. About 18 by 24 feet. Built of wood and a big stove in the center. Pretty ugly, really. They all seemed to be the same. Not very good for teaching, if you're looking for pretty things to take children's minds off dull books, but they did the job. We could all read and write and do arithmetic when we came out, I must say that for them.

I Had to Be Fierce!

Oh, they told me not to take that school. They said, "You'll be eaten alive." I guess they were right because that school had already run out two teachers in the past two years. First a lady and then a man. It was the big boys that were doing it. They even beat up the man teacher. People think children today can be bad. They were bad then. Bad. If their dad couldn't lick them on the farm, they'd lick him and then they'd beat up on the teacher. Believe me, it happened.

I said I'd take the school next fall when Mr. Cassidy came to see me. He was the head of the school board. He was a nice man. He rode a big horse and when I came to the door he got off his horse and took off his big hat and talked to me. Would I take the school? I wanted to because it was near home. I wanted to, and I said I would.

He told me it was a bad school. There were some bad boys in it. I said there must be some good children too and he said yes, there were, but it was the big boys I'd have to watch for. Look at me now. I'm sort of hunched over because I'm 93, but when I was 18 I wasn't much bigger. Not much at all. I told him I wasn't scared.

The first day in school I looked the class over and I knew I had to be fierce. They wouldn't get me, no sirree. That first morning I went into the drawer and I got out the big leather strap and I took a good fierce grip on it. I said I wonder what we have here and I held it up and then I smacked it down as hard as I could on my desk. Then I smacked it down hard again and again. I was showing them that I could hit.

For the first week I walked around that room with that strap in my hand. I never smiled once. I looked fierce all the time. Fierce. I wanted them to know what was what and that I was the boss. I wasn't going to take any nonsense off of them. One big boy at the back, bigger than me, mind you and a smartie, when I went by him once he started to hum "If You Were the Only Girl in the World and I Was the Only Boy." You know the one. It was popular then. He was just making trouble. A smartie. He was about 14 and in about grade three. I stood him up and told him to hold out his hand. I whacked him and he pulled his hand away. I said it would be double then. Not six, 12. He didn't pull his hand away again. By nine or 10 he was bawling and my arm was getting weak, but I kept it up and then he ran out. I went out and he had his hand stuck in the water barrel by the door. That taught the others a lesson.

I still went around with the strap and I never smiled and they did their lessons one-two-three and their writing one-two-three and their arithmetic one-two-three. I didn't like scaring the girls and the little ones with that strap, but that's the way it had to be done. That went on for a month and there were times I didn't think I could keep that fierce look on my face any more. But it was a hard school and those children had to learn, no matter what. I had to be fierce. One let-up and, well . . .

After about a month I did let up on them and everything got better. The little children got that scared look off their faces and were learning and the big boys, they started helping out and learning too. They even started to learn. Then I'd smile a bit. I told a joke once in a while. When the inspector came around he said it was a good school and I was a good teacher. I think that surprised me. By the time of the Christmas party I think that was as good a behaved school as any in the district. But at first I had to be fierce. Not a smile. Fierce. Fierce.

How I Became a Flag-Raiser

When I was 10 years old I wanted to quit school. I was big for my age and I knew I could make four dollars a month working for my big brother Scott who'd gone farming at Minnedosa years ago, even before I was born. I figured I had had enough school and my brother offered me four dollars a month and in threshing time if I could keep up, I would get a dollar a day on the sacker, so naturally I was all set to go.

My father didn't care. My mother didn't care either. I think she was too worn out having babies. Thirteen.

I went to the teacher at Edgewood school. It disappeared years ago. I drove by there 20 years ago to look over the old home place, and there was a farm there but I could see the school. It was out by the barn, looking like it was being used as a granary.

Miss Whyte. W-h-y-t-e. She spelled it that way. She was horrified. I was her best pupil, she said. I guess I was, if I do say so. I was pretty far up on the high side when it came to education. But no, Miss Whyte, I told her, I'm going up to Minnedosa and work for my brother. I remember her saying, "Damn that Scott." She knew him, and why? Because she'd been a local girl, gone away to teach and then come back, so she knew my brother. She promised me I could have the job cleaning out the school, no matter what the trustees said. No, I said. She said if I stayed I could go into town to the high school, and I was sure to win prizes. She promised university, anything I wanted—doctor, engineer, lawyer. No, what she couldn't promise me was four dollars a month and a dollar a day in threshing time. Here is a button-nosed 10-year-old arguing his future with a grown woman, oh, 25, 24, in around there.

Then she had this idea, and she told me years later at a school picnic that it was the best idea she'd had in months, and she said, "If we had a flag-raising ceremony and I let you be the flag-raiser, would you stay?" It seems there was something in the Manitoba Schools Act that every school had to fly a flag. The Union Jack. Ours didn't. I don't think any did.

Right away, without thinking, I said yes. I mean I guess I did some flash thinking, because raising the flag would make me the number-one boy in the school. When I thought it over I knew it probably would mean a few fights with the older boys, but I figured it was worth it. Oh yes, I did have those fights too. Several of them. But I was a husky kid, big for my age, and I held my own.

We put up a flagpole, painted it white, fitted it out, and Miss Whyte even bought the flag out of her own pocket. I think she ordered the stuff from Ashdown's. And every day, every morning, the students would line up and I'd raise the flag and the teacher would blow on her little pitch pipe and we'd all sing "God Save the King." Rain or blowing snow, we had that ceremony.

Of course, nobody could take the job away from me because I let it be known if I wasn't the flag-raiser I'd quit school. A form of blackmail, I would say. I appointed a fellow named Nick Kusmack as my assistant, and he did it when I was away. That kept me in school, raising that flag. Kept me in school all day too because I had to take it down at night. For that, keeping me at the books, I've always wished Miss Whyte well and hoped she lived to a happy old age.

A Scandal in the School

One teacher we had was Miss Miles. Red-haired. Very red. You'd call her pretty. She came from somewhere in Nova Scotia. And she got pregnant. Everybody knew. Just everybody. She went and told Mr. Bran, who was the head trustee, so he knew, but soon it got out and around. Well, even the children knew.

It was an awful scandal. The school inspector came out from Regina and he and the trustees put their heads together on what to do. Here was Miss Miles, getting bigger because she was such a tiny thing and still standing there up in front by the blackboard and teaching. Somebody said we could have charged admission. Nothing like this had ever happened before. In the store everybody talked about it but nobody had a solution. One woman had taught school before she married, but she couldn't take over because she had six children. Six children in nine years. Now there was a woman who got herself in the family way as easily as the teacher.

Regina wouldn't send out a substitute, so we were stuck

with Miss Miles and she was cool as a cucumber. There was no Christmas concert that year because while she was only so much pregnant by that time, in size, she just couldn't stand up there in front of everybody, everybody knowing, and introduce the children.

But who had done it? There was a family of . . . well, I better not tell the name. But remember, in those days not everybody went to school, and this boy had gone to school for three or four years and then was off for three or four years and pretty well had to start again. So by the time he was 16 he was only about grade five. Sixteen. I doubt if Miss Miles was more than 18. Well, we figured he was the nigger in the woodpile. In fact, we were sure of it because he was the one who stayed late on Friday nights after school to give it a good cleaning. He'd get about a dollar a month for that, and there was the opportunity. Big, not a fool by any means and he must have been a fast worker. After all, school started the first of August and everybody knew what was happening by the first of December.

She had her baby all right. A boy. And this big lad married her. A nice little wedding. They went to another town and just got married and he took her away and nobody ever knew what happened to them. Except I was riding out to Vancouver on a sort of holiday about 15 years later. I am in the Calgary station and along comes this fellow. I knew him right away. No mistaking him, he's still got that big shock of hair. I stop him and we talk and I ask him what he's doing and he says he's got a section and a half up at Red Deer. He's in town seeing a lawyer to buy another quarter, and I guess there I am with my mouth hanging open. Here he was, no more than 30, and he's sitting on top of the world. The war's on and wheat is high and going higher. It's gotta go higher and it did.

Finally I get around to asking about his wife. Oh, she's fine. Just fine. And children? Fine. They've got six now. All boys. Now how do you like that? Kid of 16 leaves home without a penny and a wife and a baby and there's this cloud hanging over both of them. Now he's a big man and only 30.

Canada: a Second-Generation Land

I can see them now, barefoot in good weather, felt boots in winter, babushkas just like their mothers. Lively eyes, red cheeks, all coming to school to learn to read and write English. They had an awful good reason for learning English because they took it back to the sod shack or the shanty and taught their parents.

The railroad and the government sent people over to Poland, people who did speak Polish, and brought them back by the boatload and all they heard was Polish or Ukrainian, Russian, some dialect from the Old Country. When they landed in the immigration hall in Winnipeg they had nothing once they were out of reach of the interpreter. They knew about education. Oh, they knew that. These people weren't stupid. They may have been poor, desperately poor, and they may have been poor for a long time after they got here because, my Lord, it was a hard place to make a living, but they were not stupid. I think most of them realized it was a second-generation land. A land for their children.

That's why I was so eager to get the children moving along. I'd give them special help, in reading, writing, every way I could. In geography too. I didn't want them to think that Coulter's Road and the C.P.R. tracks were the north and south boundaries of a world they would live in forever.

And then when I'd crammed into them each day just about as much as I figured they could hold, those little tykes would toddle off down the road and, I hoped, pass on what they'd learned that day to their parents. I knew only part of it would get through but it would, I hoped, be enough that Mike or Nick or Steve or Metro would be able to take a load of potatoes to town and get a decent price for them, speaking English.

Not that their English was ever going to be perfect. That was something you could not expect. They'd still have broken English and lots of it but who are we to talk? My mother came from Scotland when she was a girl, to Ontario and to the day she died, and she was 87, she still had a burr to her words as if she'd just walked out of those Highland hills of hers. Take a lot of your Englishmen too. Why do they call them Limeys? Because 50 years in this country and they still talk Limey all the way.

So they'd take this English home and I could just see them pointing to a chair and saying "chair" in English and the parents repeating it. That is, if they had a chair in some of those places they lived in. I think the father was much more inclined to learn English than the women. I often thought of the women in terms of beasts of burden. Slaves. They certainly weren't as sharp as the men, but they didn't get a chance to get out.

But eight or ten years after a family would come across on the boat—I taught after I was married—you would see the names of these men cropping up as school trustees. They could speak good enough English and they took a hand in how things were done and it was because their daughters and sons who started school at the right time had taught them most of it. I've talked with other teachers about this and this was the way it was with them too.

It was the older boys I felt sorry for. They missed out, most of them. The bad age would be about 12 years and over. They wouldn't want to come and sit in the row with the little kids when they were big hulking lads, but the act said they had to. They'd do it for a while and then just quit. If you were smart you'd just mark them in, let it go at that, and when the inspector came around you told him they were off school that day. They were needed on the farms, like the women.

What I'm saying is that the little ones who came to school at the right time they learned fast. I believe children always will. It's just the way they are. They are quick learners and they wanted to learn. That was the main thing. Any teacher worth her salt will tell you that. I found it was a pleasure to teach those Polish children because every day, every day, mind you, you could see their minds opening up. Like flowers to the sun.

From Grade One to High School

Now this is interesting. Here were hundreds and many more, young people and many mature, and they came into Winnipeg from Central Europe, from Russia, and they didn't know any English and what were they to do with them if they wanted to work in the city and not go out to some farm far away? Just what did you do with these immigrants with no English?

The Winnipeg School Board hired a special room in the Winnipeg Jewish school and we went there. It was just one large ordinary room and our teacher was Miss Tysoe. I can see that class now and there were children, say my age upwards, 15 or so, and people in their forties. Here I was, take me for example. I had Russian, German, French, Latin, Greek, Yiddish, mathematics, geography, history of Russia, and grammar, and so, in European terms, I was very well educated for my age. But in terms of Canada, I had nothing because I didn't speak English. In Russia in those times if you could get an education, if you were in the right class to get an education, you got as good an education as it was possible to get. But in Winnipeg, what did it all mean?

This school, we entered on the first of January and then we studied until June and then finished. Then I helped in a hardware store, a cousin's store, and my friends and I we said what are we going to do? We can't waste any more time, more years in this class with these green immigrants who knew nothing and here we were with our classical educations. What were we to do?

By June, if you know what I mean, we certainly *read* English well. Very well. But our speech was terrible. Just awful. Terrible. You could cut it with a saw.

My friend Simon and I decided that we couldn't go into grade two or three next year but we had to jump right into high school. So I decided to take the bull by the horns and we went to see Dr. McIntyre, the superintendent of the school board. We would tell him we wanted to go into high school, from grade one right to high school.

We went into his office and he stood up and said, "Good

afternoon, boys, what can I do for you?" We had more or less figured out who was going to say and it was up to me because my accent was not as thick as his, although it was pretty bad. So I showed him my education diploma from Russia and that we had been through half a year at this school for foreigners. He said "Yes, what do you wish to do?" "Go to high school." He said, "High school?" and he was shocked. This just wasn't done. Going to high school and not knowing English.

Then he asked us what subjects we had in Russia and we told him and he was impressed and seemed interested. He said, "Do you really think you know enough English to go to St. John's Technical?" I said, "I think we know enough English and there we're going to learn a lot more."

And that's how we went from grade one to high school.

He took a chance on us; he said we could go to high school and we started. We passed that year and then we passed second year and that was how we got ahead in Canada.

At the end of my second year I was giving lessons in English to immigrants, and from these people I collected 15 dollars, which was just one dollar less than my 16 dollars for my room and board. So you see, with just a little help, I was able to make my own way in Canada when I was just a boy. We were always very resourceful. With the money I made helping in my cousin's hardware store out on Logan, both jobs got me through. The poor immigrant boy.

Then something happened. I'd open up the store in the mornings when I was off, and this one time it was hot in the store and cold outside and there wasn't a dog around and I fell asleep by the stove. I guess I'd been studying too hard the night before. And I had this dream. I dreamed that I saw myself many years later, still in that little hardware store, still behind the counter selling nails and stovepipe, and I vowed to myself right there that I would never do that. That such a life was not for me. Right there and then I vowed I would go to university and become a doctor. Although that came later I decided my life's work. It's a long story about how I became a doctor, but it involved a terrible lot of hard work, studying and working to make my living and many kind people who did things for me and opened doors for me so I was able to go to university and become a doctor. It was a very long hard road but I decided in that hardware stove that winter day there was no way I was going to sell nails and stovepipe for the rest of my life.

No, I was first going to become a teacher. Then I'd become a doctor. That was the second step. So the first step was teacher and that's what I became and then I became a doctor after.

Teaching Was an Adventure

Oh, things were so different then. I remember them well. I was taking teacher training in Toronto, and the principal asked some of us if we wanted to go to the West to teach in the summer. Of course we jumped at it. Why, that was adventure! Everybody had heard a lot about the West but it was just prairie to us. And a chance to earn money.

You see, there were two things. The first was that they couldn't get all that many teachers. There was a normal school in Winnipeg and one in Regina, but when you saw how those little towns were jumping up everywhere, why, you realized they could never get enough teachers. Not that we were all that qualified, not that we had our diploma framed on the wall— but at least we were better than some 17-year-old girl teaching. She'd be a local girl, usually, and like as not she might just be a year or two older than her pupils. The other thing, of course, is that because it was so cold in that part of Canada in those days, they held school wrong side about. Instead of September to June, school there would be May, early May to October. It meant you didn't get the older boys because they'd be working on the farm but you got the grade fives, fours, the little tykes.

You could work four months in a prairie school and make 160 dollars and that was your tuition back in Toronto. Besides, it was an adventure.

The first year was 1907. I went out with my cousin Bessie and the next year Bessie stayed home because she had a steady beau and another cousin came out with me. You went to Regina and then you were sent to your school. My first school was north of Melfort. Mind you, it wasn't easy. Teaching a school of 30 children and half of them would be Ukrainians and boys of 12 would be in grade one. That wasn't easy. They had only been out from the Old Country a year or two, and half the time you got the feeling their parents didn't actually want them in school. But I managed. The first school was frame, made of wood. It was a good school as far as schools went.

After all, you couldn't expect too much. Remember this was pretty well the frontier. But it did have benches and I had a desk and every child had a slate and there was a blackboard. A school trustee came every Friday afternoon and cleaned out the school, and every morning a boy who lived near brought a bucket of water for drinking. We never had to use the stove although it was big enough that I'm sure it would have warmed the place up. The people in the district used it for events during the winter. A dance. Christmas concert. It was also used as a church once a month. Lutheran in the afternoon, Presbyterian in the morning.

People were kind to me. I'd get invitations to stay at some of their houses on weekends, going home with the children and coming back Monday morn. In this way I certainly learned how some of them lived. They had hardships, you know. A lot of things went wrong and it seems to me the government was not all that concerned with their welfare. They seemed to have an awful time getting graded roads and things like that.

The countryside was filled with young bachelors. I'd say that half often would be young Englishmen. They were mostly homesteaders but if you heard the old-timers talk they, the Englishmen, didn't seem to know much about farming. Perhaps not. A girl could go walking out with these young men every evening of the week if she wanted to. But she dare not, of course. If those people demanded one thing, it was that their school marm was beyond reproach. You understand. But the bachelors were certainly starved for feminine company in those days. But everybody was.

The second year was 1908 and I was sent to a school south of Kamsack. It was filled with Old Country people and I'm not sure that I was able to jam much of the three R's into those children's heads. Half the time I could not get them to understand me. I think every European country but English was in that school. But they all managed somehow, I guess. Everybody in those days managed. But it was certainly populated by Ukrainians and Russians. Very, very poor. I was never asked to their homes. But I'd go. Homes, I said. Hovels, I guess they were. This is what they had been used to in Russia and this is what they built in the new land. Poles, mud chinking painted white, calcimined I guess, and dirt floors. It wasn't that they weren't friendly. They just weren't used to the teacher coming to visit them, and dressed, as I was, in Toronto fashions of that day. Parasol too. I don't think they had ever seen a parasol. They used to take it and look at it. But they were friendly.

That was my second year. It wasn't as good as my first year because the pay was less and, of course, my dear, dear bachelors weren't around. What bachelors there were at Kamsack would just stand and stare at me like I was some strange animal of the field.

The white people in Kamsack were nice though. Very friendly. I made friends there.

And then it was time to leave, time to go back to Toronto and finish my diploma and find the best teaching job I could get. I got a job in Hamilton that was nice and I never thought I would ever see the West again. There were things I liked about it, the prairie, the people who were friendly, and the flowers, so many flowers. So what did I up and do? In no less than three years I married a man who worked for Eaton's. Eaton's was the big store then, and still is. Mr. Wilson was transferred out to Winnipeg in 1913 and there I was, back in the West again, although it wasn't until 1962 that we got in the car and went through Saskatchewan. I tried to find the little schoolhouse at Melfort and I found the place where it had been. But a farmer nearby he said it had been bought years ago by another farmer and he'd hauled it down the road and made it into his house. Of course, by that time, it was all school buses anyway. The day of the little red schoolhouse on the prairie was as extinct as the buffalo.

Teachers Got Married Pretty Quick

There used to be a saying that a teacher didn't last too long. They'd get married pretty quick.

We always boarded the teacher in our house and I remember my mother saying once that if she didn't have such a kind heart she'd charge the teacher double because Sunday afternoon was visiting day. Every bachelor would come to visit the teacher. Sometimes there would be eight or 10 of them there and they'd stay. For supper. I think my mother used to feed the whole neighborhood on Sundays, but she didn't mind. There was always lots of food and the teacher, all she had to say was, "Come on, you fellows, who's going to help me do the dishes?" and Mother could just clear out and relax and everything would be done by the bachelors.

Some were very gay fellows and some came and hardly said a word. Just came and sat. I think they were so happy just to be in a decent house with lace curtains and a sofa and listening to people talk. There was a gramophone with a big horn and they sure used up a lot of records, the round ones, and they played cards, sang songs, and told jokes and, I guess, forgot their troubles.

I don't think we ever had a teacher more than a year. One, three months. They'd get married. Have you ever wondered how a girl makes up her mind? Well, if you were at our house you still wouldn't know. One might select the cut-up of the neighborhood and the next year, the teacher would choose the quiet one. For all I know, she might have had to do the proposing. But there would be a wedding in the church and my mother would hold the reception and then the two of them would go across the prairie to that shack he had, shiplap or sod even, and start in at housekeeping. And they'd usually stick it out. The wife would give new confidence to her husband, I suppose, and slowly, year by year, you'd see them starting to catch on. A new house, a bigger barn, another quarter, babies, that sort of thing.

A wonderful institution was the prairie school marm, let me tell you. I admired every last one of them. Not a quitter in the lot.

We Taught Them Well

Let me see. Yes, it must have depended on the school trustees but some country schools wanted only women teachers and some would take a man every time they could get them. Usually it was women though. The men, as I remember, would always try for the Winnipeg schools because they wanted the city.

Women they always figured the weak sex but when you get down to it, everything we did was just as hard as the men. We had to do exactly the same things. Keep discipline. That was the main thing. If you had a quiet room you had no mischief. No mischief, you had learning. Pupils learning, you had good students. It all worked out.

I was down at the supermarket the other day and some of us were talking waiting for the mini-bus to take us back home and one woman was saying she was a pioneer and this and that, that she'd been a teacher and she'd done this and that and I thought to myself, this woman doesn't look old enough. I said, I asked when she'd taught and she said she started in 1927 and I burst out laughing. Well, she was right in a way. She'd taught in a Ruthenian settlement in northern Saskatchewan and I imagine she had some hard times too but nothing, nothing, just nothing like we went through. We worked hard, we often had classes up to 35 and you knew you somehow had to teach everyone individually in nine classes. And the school texts weren't what we would call texts now. Not the ones I've seen. Just a few old dog-eared books and most of the work was done on the blackboard. The children had their own slates and somehow you had to get it into their heads and school, well, it depended on the board. Maybe there would be school only five or six months a year. I've heard of schools that went only July and August. Others went every month but January and February, the bitter months. There seemed to be no set time and yet there was that inspector coming around checking on you.

So, you can see the picture. A new area, and it can be open prairie and some trees and swamp and bog and good land and sandy, rocky soil but the settlers come in, one here and then another over there and then two more and so on and when about 10 or 12 families got together and their children are running around like June bugs, ignorant as tree stumps, they get together in a meeting and the first thing they do is start a school. They petition the government for a school district. They build the school. They look around for a teacher and that's when civilization starts to work and so, if you're looking around for the unsung heroines of this country, for a book, for a movie, you don't have to look any farther than the teacher. The school marm, they called her. But she was the one who brought or caused civilization to come to the prairies. Just her and her alone.

Today a girl can do what she wants. She's free as the breeze. Then we had to toe the line. That's probably why we made good teachers. We taught them well. Sometimes I think we put our duties far ahead of ourselves. And in those days we weren't dignified by the title of "profession." No sirree, we were just teachers. Doctors were the only professionals we knew. But it's all changed now. Now teachers are professionals and that's the way it should be. Shouldn't it?

15 Law, Order, and Some Chicanery

The Mounties, So Polite . . . Who Set the Wheat Field Afire? . . . Above and Beyond the Call of Duty . . . Cheating the Ukrainians . . . Booze Always Got Through . . . Settlers Were Fair Game . . . When the Chinese Wore Pigtails . . . Some Fancied They Could Fight . . . The Way Some Fellows Did Business . . . How They Really Got Their Man! . . . Guilty, They Hanged You

There was very little crime in the West. One good reason for this was that there was respect for law and order. The Mounties came in, a fledgling group but determined, and they drove out the rougher whisky-peddling elements from southern Alberta and established law and order. When the railroads came, the law was there. When the settlers began pouring in, it was there. And there it remained.

Of course there was crime, but the records show it was mostly drunkenness, saloon-brawling, bootlegging, prostitution. Hustling of settlers, feuds between railroaders and settlers and between settlers and ranchers, some thievery, mostly rustling. The bad guys were usually caught because they were often neighbors of the injured party.

Old-timers of 90 must shake their heads in wonderment today when they read the evening papers.

The Mounties, So Polite

When the police came to our place we used to know when they were coming because they came usually at the same time, on patrol.

They were fine men, usually an older one with a younger one. The older one was showing the young one how to do it and all. My sister always wore her Sunday dress for the night the mounted policemen stayed with us. They ate at our table, supper and breakfast, and gave my mother a ticket that she'd send in and get money for their room and board. They slept in the bunkhouse with my two older brothers, and you'd see the light on late at night. They were playing poker or talking.

We always found the police to be fine men. Very polite. Everything they did was quite proper, but you could tell when they were fishing. They'd ask a little question and then another little one and then another, and you knew they were looking for information. It was usually about a neighbor and usually about rustling. Somebody had stolen somebody's cow. It was things like that. Very polite, I can say that, but they seemed to know everything that was going on in the district. They should have; people would say anything those days to a policeman. They trusted them.

I remember a neighbor went haywire and smashed everything with an axe in his cabin and left, just left, and the Mounties went over and came back and soon the little questions. Finally, "Where's the flour he had?" It wasn't yet Christmas, so that meant Tom Logan's flour for winter wouldn't be half used up. But it was gone from his bust-up shack. They noticed that and they knew he had gone to town and sold his horse and left and he didn't have flour with him. Oh, of course, they found out who took it. Another neighbor. Not much you could get by those policemen. Two sacks of flour but they knew it was missing.

A lot of the policemen were from Ontario, and when their term was up they stayed, became ranchers, farmers, because they had fallen in love with the Golden West. So they stayed and prospered.

Who Set the Wheat Field Afire?

A terrible thing for any farmer was a fire in his wheat field. God-damn it but that was an awful thing. With a high wind bucking behind it, there was not a thing you could do about it. Not 10 men, not 50. You just had to plow a fireguard if you had time, which, by the way, you never did, or just hope and pray the wind would change, which it never did.

This was at Estevan. There was these two fellows. One's name was Craigie. He was a Scotchman and he was farming a section of land on shares for a man who was a millionaire in the United States. This American had several farms as I recall. Craigie had big hands but he was a little man. The other fellow was a Frenchman. A Frenchman from Quebec. His name might have been Larue. So this happened in a bar in town, about did Larue owe Craigie four days' work or three days' work. It got to be fighting and Craigie danced all around that Frenchman and beat him up real good. Finally the boys stopped it. Then Larue left. He went to the other hotel.

That night there is a good west wind blowing, blowing from the west, I remember riding home thanking my lights that it was at my back. When I went to bed I could hear that wind in the eaves. Wooooooo. Woooooo. You know how. And then I drop off and then I wake up and it's like dawn but it isn't. You know what I mean. I jump up and look out the window, and two miles away on the Scotchman's section there is the biggest goddamned fire you ever saw. I tell you it was a whopper. I know I'm safe because there's a coulee between me and the Scotchman, and in between that I've got 40 acres of summer fallow. But there's no way on God's green earth that anybody or anything is going to save that wheat. Why, the flames must have been, oh 20, 30 feet high. One thing. In those days wheat was bigger than it is now. It could stand as tall as a man's chest easily, but at the aggie schools and experimental farms they've bred a lot of that straw out of the wheat stem. So now, you see a field of good ripening late August wheat and you may ask, now how could that burn 30 feet high? Well, friend, in those days it goddamned well could.

It wasn't too long until it was all over. I'd ridden over even though that bay gelding of mine didn't like the idea one bit, riding right toward that fire. There were a few neighbors around and I asked Craigie what had happened, and he said he goddamned well didn't know, but he was going to ride into Estevan and bring out a Mountie. Right then and there. It was a long ride but he was sure mad. He kept cursing "that goddamned bead counter." He meant the Frenchman Larue, of course.

The Mountie came out about noon next day and you could see where somebody had trotted a horse down the side of Craigie's field and thrown in a piece of lighted paper every so often. There were eight places where that fire had been started, and every one of them took, what with that west wind blowing. And there went about 120 acres of some of the best wheat in that district.

Larue? Oh well, nothing. The Mountie went over there and talked to him, but what could he say? I mean what could the Mountie do? A fight in a bar didn't mean anything. Larue just said he had a few more drinks in the other hotel and rode home and went to sleep. If he wasn't going to confess there was nothing the Mountie could do. The American in Massachusetts was out his crop and Craigie was out his shares and that was all there was to it.

Above and Beyond the Call of Duty

The police in them days, they were all a good bunch of fellows. I got to know quite a few of them in my time. In big towns they always had a barracks and they'd go on patrol. Eighty miles north, then west, then south and back. Always wore scarlet. Not like they do now. They had wonderful horses, the best in the country.

There wasn't too much crime. Drinking mostly. Brawling. There was an awful lot of drinking in those days and the police, they had to put up with a lot. Not much of anything other. Not robbery or shootings. It was mostly farm community but a lot of drinking.

I was in the hotel one morning and a fellow came down and he was yelling that another fellow had stolen his coonskin coat. His coat was gone from his room and he said it was taken by a fellow he'd been drinking with the night before. Said he'd let the fellow sleep in his room and he'd taken the early-morning stage to Netherhill. That's 20 miles away. Well, the policeman checked and the fellow had gone to Netherhill, so he got on his horse and he said he'd go after him. This was in the winter, 40 below, but if the fellow was a thief he'd bring him back.

I saw him when he came back and I'll tell you what. The horse's eyes were nearly closed with ice and so were its nostrils, and we had to help the policeman out of the saddle. He went into the bar and said to the fellow, "Well, I saw the fellow and he hasn't got your coat. He says he's never seen it. Are you sure it's not in your room? Let's check again." So the policeman and the fellow and the clerk went up and the fellow went in this room. No coat. Then the clerk said, "This isn't your room. Your room is next door." They go next door and there's the coat hanging in the closet. The fellow had been so drunk the night before he'd slept in the wrong room.

Oh, there was nothing the Mountie could do. He couldn't have it out with the fellow, even though he'd had to do 40 miles on horseback in 40, 50 below.

Cheating the Ukrainians

These people hated to be cheated. They were hard-working people. They liked their fun, their dances, their big weddings. A bunch could get together with absolutely no money at all and have a grand time, and they got along well together. But the thing that made them mad was if they thought they were being cheated.

Doukhobor women worked as hard as farm animals as they strained at the breaking plow. Mounties would stop this practice whenever they saw it. (Provincial Archives of Alberta, H. Pollard Collection)

Doukhobor women would winnow grain, separating it from the chaff after it had been flailed. This sect of pacifists built up fine farms on the prairies, with affluence being the reward for back-breaking labor. (Public Archives Canada, C 8891)

Graduated like steps of a ladder, these members of a Saskatchewan family learned household and farm chores early in life. (Public Archives Canada, PA 88632)

Any farm family that had a large garden enjoyed nature's bounty, as did these youngsters in Fort Vermilion, Alberta. (Public Archives Canada, PA 46053)

Photography was a hobby with many settlers. Possibly this picture was posed, but Grandpa probably enjoyed getting into the act along with junior. (Public Archives Canada, C 42629)

Even today, getting fresh, hot milk from Bossy is still a treat for farm children. (Provincial Archives of Alberta, E. Brown Collection)

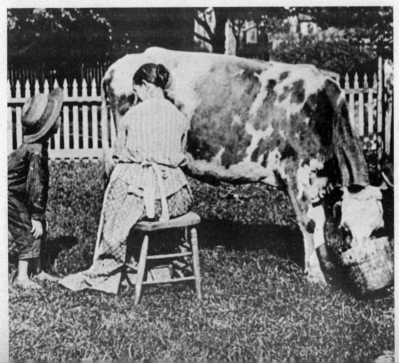

There may be only a few of these schoolhouses left on the prairies, but at one time the school was the center of the settlers' community, used for learning, for entertainment, and often as a church. Many old-timers fondly remember their schooldays and the schoolteachers who taught them the three R's. (Provincial Archives of Alberta, E. Brown Collection)

And, of course, the people who cheated them most of all in the early days? Their own people.

You didn't find one or two Polish or Galician families moving into a Scotch or English or German area, or Swedish or Finnish. No, they tended to all move into big blocks of land, so they were all together and they'd trade at one town. The closest— you could only go so far with a wagon and a pair of oxen in a day. The lawyer, the livery stable, the doctor, the storekeepers, the newspaper if they had one, well, naturally, these people were English or Jewish or German and they spoke English. The whole countryside spoke their own language, Russian or Polish or whatever it was, but you must understand that English was power. The English language was the one you did business in and to know English, if you were Ukrainian, that gave you power. And you know what power gives, don't you? Power gives you money. Not the other way around in those days. Money gives power today. In those days, English gave power gave money.

When my wife was first teaching up northwest of here, all Ukrainian. She and her friend were approached by the chief and told that they couldn't teach in his district without paying him 25 dollars. Almost a month's wages. They said no. There was a bit of a squabble, but they never paid the money and they taught. It took going to a lawyer in town though. That's the power the man had. This Ukrainian chief spoke English, you see. So he was the boss of them all.

The little boy who could speak the best English in the family, he'd go to town with his father to buy supplies and next day he'd bring the grocery list to school. He'd have you look it over. To see that the store hadn't cheated them. It was just a case of adding up the figures to see they came out right because, you know, a storekeeper can sell at whatever price he feels he can sell at. But many, many times at the bottom of the bill there would be an item of 10 percent on the bill's amount to Sivaritch for having interpreted for them. He was the chief and the storekeepers went along with his ways. You see, Sivaritch spoke English.

Now, who was responsible for this exploitation? Well, to some degree I expect the town merchants were, but you must remember that a lot of these people lived in what you might call colonies. Not actually, but. They came out in large groups and they'd all settle in one area. It was actually better that way. We used to lump them all as Galicians, but actually they were many nationalities. But when the national organization in Ottawa was arranging for them to come out, doing all the paperwork and arranging, they did have to have some person, Rumanian, Russian, Ukrainian, whatever the group was, to travel with them and see that they got settled and look after their problems and so they'd appoint a man. They'd have a word for him, the immigrants, but the foreigners would translate into the English word "chief."

I've been told by school inspectors, authorities, that this man was a great help to them. He was the go-between and a lot of trouble was avoided if the school authorities, the municipal people, even the police sometimes, if they worked with the chief. He could often be of great help and I guess he usually was. Give him credit for that. He brought the people in and set them up, something that a Canadian from Edmonton could not do.

Now it didn't happen all the time but many, many times it did, when these groupings of people came in, not knowing Canada, knowing nothing, often ignorant of even where they were until they got on their feet, they came to accept this man as their chief.

And the man, naturally, if he was that kind of a person would accept the leadership and being human, I suppose, he would get everything he could out of it and go after more.

Now I am not saying this happened all the time, but I know it happened enough among these so-called colonies that the practice of exploitation was quite common.

That's why he could demand 25 dollars from my wife to teach at a school in what he called his district and get 10 percent of the food bill for interpreting for the storekeeper.

By 1910 or 1912 I'd say this system had gone. The settlers could speak English of a sort by then, and they had title to their land and were on their way to becoming Canadians, and of course with their natural hatred of being cheated they weren't going to put up with that nonsense any longer. They probably don't want to talk about it now but it happened.

Booze Always Got Through

There always was a rule, you know, that no booze in construction camps. There always was but it was up to the bosses to find it. Like Prohibition later.

Well, we was working tearing up some of the tracks of the Canadian Northern . . . Where's that picture of the pigs? Here. This is the way they used to get the booze in. The bootleggers from Edmonton. You see, here is 10 big old hogs. Stomachs cut open and guts spilled out. Then, you see, they stuffed that gut hole with bottles of whisky. Scotch. Not rye. There was no rye in those days. Then they'd send the pigs in to the cookhouse by train and whoever was at this end, this was at one camp, well, he'd haul out all these bottles of scotch and he was in business again.

Carcasses. Full of booze. The police were always on the lookout. They'd catch some of them but a lot would get through. The bootlegger had a deal with the cook and the cook with the bootlegger and it got through. Booze always got through.

Settlers Were Fair Game

When the Barr colonists came to Saskatoon it was a place of about 100 people. I think it was less than that because they were counting the good people twice.

The colonists arrived by train and camped right out on prairie and they had nothing to take with them into the wilderness. They had no horses or oxen. A lot of the work was done by oxen in those days. They had no implements. They had to buy wagons. They had no food and they had to buy that. What they did have was money, hundreds of thousands of dollars' worth and this attracted sellers from all over. They sold them half-broken teams for 400 dollars which may have been worth 200. And so it went. Everything was high.

The sellers came from all over and some from right in the district. Some of them were poor but they sold the colonists things at high prices right off their own farms, things like animals and machinery that they actually needed to farm their own places. But it was a chance to make some money, get a few dollars. Later they'd be able to buy horses and things at the regular price, once the colonists had gone. In a couple of weeks or so.

Oh, yes, they were rooked right, left and center. What did these Englishmen know about Canada? About farming? Pioneering was to them as strange as visiting the moon. You see, very few of these Barr colonists had ever been farmers in England. An English farmer wouldn't want to leave his good English farm. He was an important man there. Why come to the wilds of Canada? The colonists were shopkeepers, professional men, clerks, postmen, factory workers, and they had no idea what they were getting into. For every one who had his wits about him, there were another nine who were simply fair game for the sharpies and swindlers and fast-talking salesmen who came along to take them. And take them they did. They were babes in the woods. Lost, completely lost and far, far from home.

When the Chinese Wore Pigtails

Those police, they were sons of gun to drink, you know. I remember once I had to deliver a parcel from the hotel to the barracks and the two of them were polishing their brass, shining things up, and I asked if the inspector was coming for an inspection. "No," says one, "no, but this damn fool got full up last week and cut off a Chinaman's pigtail."

Now that was a very serious thing. A Chinaman's pigtail was very, very important to him and he'd written to the superintendent in Regina. So the Mountie was going down to Regina for trial for cutting off the pigtail, and the other Mountie was his escort. Taking in his prisoner.

Some Fancied They Could Fight

I knew a lot of Mounties in the early days. Good fellows, mostly. But real ones for drinking. They'd go into a bar in town just like anybody else, in full uniform. Stand up to the bar.

Fights. You never saw such a town for fights. That was before the city of Edmonton put a policeman in every bar. I think there were seven hotels at that time. Before 1910. The bars were madhouses. Full of freighters and railroaders and settlers and city people, and half would be fighting and arguing and half would be in a corner crying out their misery. If a Mountie wanted to fight he had to take off his jacket and then he was a civilian. Like a soldier today. Some of them fancied they could fight.

I remember once a fellow pounded the bar and he said, "Any man who is a Mountie is a son of a bitch, and anybody who used to be a Mountie is still a son of a bitch." A fellow down the bar said, "I used to be a Mountie," and the big guy said, "Then you're a son of a bitch." Well, the fight was on. There used to be some great battles in those bars.

Once they sent two Mounties out to Entwistle to arrest a bootlegger. They got him all right, but on the way back the track just east of that ravine slipped about four feet sideways. Just slipped. So they backed the train back to Entwistle and telegraphed for a train to be sent out from Edmonton to pick up the passengers. The Mounties and the bootlegger went into the bar. Red was the bootlegger's name. Bellied up and Red ordered drinks. Then the Mounties ordered drinks. Back and forth and the train took a long time coming. When it came, the other passengers had to lead the two Mounties and Red across the trestle they were so sloppy drunk. When the train got into town the last thing people saw was the three of them reeling up the street toward the barracks and Red in the middle, holding up the two Mounties.

The Way Some Fellows Did Business

I was at a dance in Lashburn this one New Year's Eve and there was this buyer there and he asked me if I had any hogs to sell and I said yeah. I had 100 head. He said, "Are they ready to go?" I said yeah, ready to go. He said he'd drop around one of those days and I said oh no, he wouldn't, because I had run out of barley and I wasn't feeding no wheat at those prices. Wheat was a dollar a bushel. So there was a fellow from the other side of me, by town, who was coming to look at those hogs in a couple of days. Wheat was a dollar and barley was only 25 cents a bushel, so I told him the first guy that got there and gave me a fair price got those hogs. Jim McKay was the other buyer. Bud Smith was the fellow I was talking to in Lashburn.

By God, this Bud Smith came down to my farm the next day. Forty below! I figured he really wanted them hogs. He said, "What do you want for them?" That made sense, I figured. We had no scale and we had to just estimate them, figure out the total weight, and against the price at the stockyards and come up with a price. So I told him, I said for him to give me a piece of paper and he gave me half of a check from his book and I said for him to put what he figured the price was for those 100 hogs down and I'd put my price down and then we'd see. I knew hog prices was pretty low that winter. So, I wrote down 2,200 dollars and he showed me his paper and it said 2,100 dollars. In a situation like that, split the difference. So 2,150 dollars. That was a deal. Good hogs, but God, the price was that way down.

Then he said, "I'll toss you. Double or nothing." I told him to get out his coin, but he didn't have guts enough for that. I wouldn't have done it anyway but he didn't know that.

Then he saw two steers over by the haystack and he said, "Those yours?" They were in my barnyard, weren't they? Sure, I said, they're mine, and he said how much, and I said 100 dollars each. Two hundred dollars. He said to bring them along and he hadn't even looked at them close. That's the kind of fellow he was. So we'd made a deal, delivered to town.

I had a man so I sent him around to the neighbors and they came with their wagons and we loaded up and took those hogs and those two steers to the railway. Eighteen miles away, 30, maybe 40, below. This Bud had been going around the country and he had 10 cars spotted at Yucca, and there were wagons coming in from all around the country. He was buying up half the stock in the country.

So in the general store there, he wrote me a check for the whole lot. It was 2,350 dollars. That was a hell of a lot of money. He bought a carload from me and he bought nine other carloads of steers and hogs around the country, and we were all in the store there together. I was the first loaded that morning and so he wrote me the check first, and I asked, where do I cash this? I owed a binder note, last payment on a binder, and I wanted the money quick. He said, "It's in the bank at Lashburn. There's 3,000 dollars in there right now and if you're standing on the front step when that bank opens tomorrow you'll be okay." And here I saw him with my very own eyes writing checks on the counter to all them farmers. And he's telling me there's only 3,000 dollars in Lashburn.

I said to him I'd be there, 30 miles, 30 below, snow up to the horses' bellies. I had to start at midnight, but when the bank opened I was there. I was on that porch and I saw the key turn in that lock. I went in, hah, and I handed the check to the cashier and he said I had to give it to the ledger keeper and the fellow said there was no money. I said Mr. Smith told me that there was 3,000 dollars in the bank and if I was first here I'd get my check cashed and he said, "There isn't three cents."

Oh, I said. Thirty miles here, 30 miles home, snow that deep, 30 below, and then I got to come back again. No track. I even had to break my own trail. And then do it again coming back.

Well, I told him I was going to protest it. No account, okay. I was going to see McMurdo. A fellow by the name of Mc-Murdo was the lawyer. But before that I went into the room where you saw the manager and I told him to put his initials on that check so I could get my money. I said if he didn't I was going to protest that. That meant charges and Bud Smith would never do business in that country again. In fact, the best place for him was over the border in Montana. Bud was well known in that town. His game, you see, was to buy up cattle at low prices, ship them to the stockyards or sell them in the city, and then get the money and get it back to the bank before the farmers came in, then he'd have his checks covered.

He was just betting that farmers 30 or so miles from a town in 30- and 40-below weather wouldn't go hightailing into town the next day to cash checks. What he needed was a week or so of room to maneuver. Then he'd have the money in the bank and nobody would know. Once I went to McMurdo and the police came into it, then the whole jig would be up.

"You wouldn't do that to Bud, would you?" said the manager. I told him if he didn't think I wasn't going to protest that, then he didn't know me. I was going down the street to the lawyer. Right now. If he didn't do it. Initial it.

He said, "Okay, give it here," and he initialed it and I got my money. I don't know how the other farmers made out. Oh god, what a life.

A while after I see Bud Smith and he said, calm as you please, he says, "I hear you had trouble cashing my note." I says no, no real trouble, but I said he was a damn liar telling me there was money in the account. Hell, I don't even think there was an account, and I told him about going 30 miles in 40 below with snow up to my horses' bellies, and if he thought I was going to do it again, he was crazy because I would have thrown him in jail first.

He laughed about that. A cute customer. Of course, you know, eventually he was going to be good for that money when he sold the stock, but what he was doing was buying without money. Maybe 10,000 dollars just leaning against that counter in the store and writing checks and gambling that they wouldn't go through before he got the money in. Do you know what 10,000 dollars then is today? I'd say 150,000 dollars, and it isn't every day that an ordinary fellow can go out and do that time after time and come out on top. There's always somebody like me to check him up and that bank manager in Lashburn to save his bacon.

But I'll tell you another thing about Bud. He was honest. I mean it. Them two steers. When he was loading them a fellow comes along and he says, "Where did you get them steers?" Bud said, "I got them from Hennie Voss." "How much do you want for them?" Bud said, "I want $400." The fellow said, "Lead them out. I'll give you $400." Remember, Bud had bought them off me for $200. So he made 200 dollars off me without doing nothing because I'd drove them steers to the railroad for him.

But he was telling me this and he handed me 50 dollars and he said, "This is for you. Your share. Those steers was worth more than that." I said okay and I took the money and I still told him, I said, "Bud, if you ever put me in a spot like you did last time I'll still get you where the hairs is short."

He laughed. You had to laugh with that man. That's the way some fellows did business. He'd always make it right. That was just the way he operated. But he would never get by me again. No sir.

How They Really Got Their Man!

Now do you really want to know how this business came about of the Mountie always getting his man?

It's because when they went out to arrest somebody they sent out a whole pack of them, so they'd have policemen coming at the poor fellow from every point of the compass.

I remember once there was a gang of horse thieves working in the districts out east of here and the Mounties were told where they'd holed up. They had their barracks on that bluff looking over the river and this morning I see 12 Mounties, a whole string of pack horses, and a small field howitzer trailing out of town to bring in those fellows. Imagine, just imagine a small field howitzer just to arrest three or four horse thieves.

Guilty, They Hanged You

Did you ever remember Jack Kravchenko? He killed the banker, Arnold, in Plum Coulee. Boy, let me tell you, there was big doings that day. You see, it wasn't like today. There wasn't any crime, none to speak of. A bank robbery and killing, let me tell you, that was something else again.

I was away at the time and my wife was the agent and the night that happened she worked all night on the telegraph sending news to Winnipeg for the reports to the *Free Press* and *Tribune*. It was a sensation. She worked all night sending press.

This Kravchenko, he was a native of Plum Coulee. His folks lived there. Everybody in town knew him and here he tried to pull off a holdup in his own home town. Just a little place, a few hundred people. Arnold was the banker and he'd let his two men, Bill Eseau and Lloyd Wagner, go to lunch. Kravchenko was dressed up and he came into the bank and he had this gun and he got about 2,000 dollars. He had told Billy Dick, who was the liveryman, to have a rig waiting out behind the barn and he'd be along to get it in a few minutes.

He ran out of the bank and Arnold tried to follow him and Kravchenko tried to shoot him in the shoulder and shot him in the heart. Just like that. When he ran up to Billy Dick he said, "I hope I didn't kill the son of a bitch." Those were his very words. I talked to Billy Dick after. They drove almost to Winnipeg and he had a lot of experiences around there before they finally caught him and brought him back to Morden and he was sentenced to be hanged. Well, they had to bring him back to Winnipeg by train—there was cars but they decided they'd bring him back by train. He was in the baggage car handcuffed to Jack Handel and naturally the train had to go through Plum Coulee, his home town, where his folks lived, and when the train came into the station there was Jack standing in the door handcuffed and calling out to people he knew: "Hi, Barney," and "Hi Billy" and others, just as cool as could be, and then he went to Winnipeg and they hanged him there. Hanged him right in town. There was no fooling around in those days. Guilty, they hanged you.

Imagine that Kravchenko. He lived in that town. I'd seen him around. The banker knew him, he'd seen him around, and here he pulls off this job and kills the banker.

Of course, Kravchenko, I didn't think he meant to kill Arnold but something went wrong. But of course he had that gun. Oh, he always had a gun. He was mixed up in two or three things that they couldn't pin on him. Jack was a regular outlaw.

But that was a real sensation. A bank robbery and a killing right in that quiet little town. It's hard to believe, even now.

16 *Having a Darn Good Time*

You Stayed Home, You Went Visiting . . . A Wonderful Time in Calgary . . . Picnics Meant Fun and Food . . . I Got My Hands on That Fiddle . . . When the Circus Came to Town . . . They Were Just Ordinary Houses . . . We Looked Forward to a Building Bee . . . Mother Knew a Few Tricks Too . . . The Night Riders, Everybody Wanted Us . . . Debates—a Good Evening's Entertainment . . . The Winters Were Ideal for Curling . . . Baseball Was the Thing

In the West, entertainment meant box socials, building bees, tugs-of-war, and dances that lasted until dawn. Each event was a chance to get out and forget about the cares of being a farmer on the bald prairie, a chance to meet neighbors and talk about crops, new methods of farming, and, above all, district gossip.

In the towns, perhaps entertainment was a little more sophisticated. There were hockey games and curling matches, debates and fiddling contests followed by a dance. Town and country mingled at the annual fall fairs and the circuses that used to come to the main town in the district every two or three years. Movies were just the rarest of flickers then, although travelogues with lantern slides would always draw a crowd.

But dances were the main entertainment—apart from plain old-fashioned visiting back and forth—and enshrined in every museum in the West should be an old-time fiddle, for it made the music that enabled the pioneers to have a darn good time.

You Stayed Home, You Went Visiting

Everybody was hospitable. You went visiting. You went to each other's houses. You got to know everybody and it was kind of like a big happy family. Well, I shouldn't say that. There were some families that had trouble, but usually it was over money—like somebody felt they got gypped in a trade on a horse or something like that. But mostly, I'd venture to say, mostly that was very little. It wasn't like there was hatred or feuds.

You see, in town for entertainment there was nothing but the bar for men—no moving pictures, and just the occasional company would come along and put on a play in the hall. But not many people had that much money, so you stayed home. Or you went visiting. There were some awfully nice people in the town and in the farms outside it. You met them at the skating rink or the Church of England, and you invited them back to your house or you went to theirs. They wouldn't know you were coming but they would be ready. They might not have much food but there was always tea and biscuits and saskatoon or gooseberry jam, and that's all you wanted. Sometimes if you went you'd take a cake, just for visiting, or a jar of pickles or some deviled eggs. That was one of my mother's tricks, deviled eggs and my, how they went over. Sometimes there might be 20 people in that house and there would be a fiddle or a mouth organ. I don't know any of those homes that had pianos, but some had little organs they'd brought out with them from where they came. We'd sing the old songs. They weren't old songs then but they certainly are old songs now. The fun we used to have.

We used to have a man living in our town named Willy Dresden and he did monologues. I remember one he used to do called "The Story of Rip Van Winkle." He used to do another called "The Battle of Balaclava." I mean "The Charge of Bala-clava." Not the poem, you understand, but a 10-minute mono-logue and he'd have it word-perfect. There was another he'd do called "The Girl in the Cute Blue Knickers," which was supposed to be risqué but it turned out to be something quite different. Ah, Willy Dresden. He got killed in the war.

We mingled. We had card parties, you see. Whist. And there would be the occasional dance but not in a house. In a hall. Distances were so great with the horse and wagon or a cutter that one event was a big event like a dance in town. There might be two or three a year. For a charity, usually. Or for painting and coloring materials for the schoolchildren. Always for a worthy cause.

There were other kinds of parties, too, where all the people from Illinois would get together. They would be the American ones who came from the States. I often wondered later if they talked about us, the Canadians, but I don't think so. They were probably talking about how warm it was back in the States and how cold it was in our district. You know, going down to 35 below was nothing. Then the English would get together and celebrate St. George's Day. But the English they thought that just coming from England made them special. We let them think that, but when they were in trouble, who did they come to? My father. Mr. Abernathy down the road. Tom Tarduff. Those men, and all Canadians from Ontario.

Somebody was always visiting somebody. You see, there were all these horses. There were none of these motor cars and it was lovely. And wherever you went, all through that south country, whether you had just seen the person casually on the street, if you went visiting and stopped at their door, you were always welcome and asked to come in and look at the new baby and have tea and cookies. Often they'd give you the latest book that had been sent them from home.

I don't know but I think in those days it was an awful nice time for people.

A Wonderful Time in Calgary

Oh golly, girls had a darn good time here in Calgary in those early days. You see, there were very few girls and there were an awful lot of men. We had a whale of a time.

Lovely dances. There were always dances at the [police] barracks and they were fine. Mr. Hull, the butcher, was quite a prominent man in some businesses in town, and he had Hull's Opera House just over from our house—it's standing still, the opera house—and these dances were far nicer than anything you get now.

There was Hull's Opera House with balconies around each side, and you sat up there when you weren't dancing. The men, why the men in those days were wonderful. Some were ranchers, educated nice men from England. It's hard to describe how nice all those men were. Well, they were gentlemen. They came out here, many, many of them, to ranch, and they came to the dances in tails and white gloves and so on. The bank clerks, they were beaus here too. There weren't too many but they came from good homes in Canada or England and they were fine gentlemen too. And then, of course, the Mounted Police. They were fine men, the officers who came, so gentlemanly, so gentle. That was the group that made up the men at the dances, the ones us young girls cared the most about.

Mother would say, "Bring your friends, bring your friends home." I had two older sisters and our friends were Mounted Police and ranchers and bank clerks. The bank clerks at that time were like counts. I remember somebody once saying, "A bank clerk is the next thing I know of to a count." Now a bank clerk is not considered very much these days, but in those days they were right up there with the young ranchers and the dashing Mounted Police officers from the barracks.

What fun we had in those days. Loads of it. Our little house was busy and full of fun all the time. Who did I marry? I married Mr. Knight, who was a Mounted Police officer.

The dances? Oh yes, the waltz, two-step, schottische, and the lancers, always different lancers.

Then at midnight at these dances there would be a buffet, a supper, or a big sit-down supper up on the stage. They had wonderful food—some of the best food I have ever eaten was at those dances. Charlotte russe, that's what all us girls loved and there would be turkey and beef, and everything like that.

From what I can remember it was at these dances that we met the young men of the district. I can't remember much about businessmen or clerks or farmers or other people being included. No, it seemed to be police officers and ranchers and bank clerks that we were interested in.

Picnics Meant Fun and Food

I used to love the picnics. They were big events in those times. There would be about two a summer, one at our place and one over at Sangster's, which is about four miles south of Calmar.

Everybody went to those picnics for miles around, and everybody wore their very best. Everybody had pride of appearance and it didn't matter how poor you were, whether you only had a dirt floor in your house, you went to the picnics in your finery.

This is where the young girls met the young men and believe you me, a lot of marriages started at those very pictures Jim's showing you. The girls wore long white dresses and bows in their hair, and their hair was done up in the latest fashion. We had the magazines from the city, of course, and we knew the latest fashions. The boys all dressed up too.

There were games, baseball, and a lot of tennis. More houses than you would think had a tennis court laid out. Tennis was a big thing in the early 1900's. I was pretty good at hitting a tennis ball myself.

There always was a big feed. Maybe they'd just spread everything out, the sandwiches and the pies and the cookies, the lemonade and the iced tea, and everybody helped themselves. You all brought your own plates and cutlery.

Then when the picnic was over, everybody would pack up and go home. To the chores. Over those trails, over hill and dale, back to our farms. We were slaves to our horses and cows. A farmer always is.

I Got My Hands on That Fiddle

A fellow was going with my sister. He had a fiddle. He'd come over Saturday night and play that fiddle and I was just a little kid, but oh boy, I wanted a chance at that fiddle. He played and my sister accompanied him on the piano we had. I always hoped he'd leave it and by golly, one Sunday morning I came down and there's this fiddle lying on top of the piano. Boy, I grabbed that.

I'd never had a musical instrument in my hands before that. Gosh, I was only nine. But I took that fiddle and I played for a dance that Friday night. What happened? There was this big wedding on Friday and the fellow had an orchestra hired but there was no gravel roads. It was all mud and it was terrible and the town orchestra couldn't come out to play. That was the days when weddings was held at home and all the neighborhood was there. Finally everyone realized the orchestra wasn't going to come and all these young people were sitting around. I had learned three pieces. A waltz and two two-steps, and I could sing them too. I was only nine years old.

The father of the bride was a great big man, a big, big man, and he was walking around saying to himself, "I wonder what I'm going to do with all these young people?" He didn't say that but you could see what he was thinking. So I went up to him and I was just a little fellow, and I told him I thought I could help him. I said I played the violin. It was a quarter of a mile to my house and I ran all the way. I told my mother I was going to play for the dance and if the orchestra got there, I would stop. I ran all the way back.

My sister was there, of course, and they had a piano although you can't have a dance with just a piano. You have to have a fiddle. So I played this waltz and then I played it and sang it. Everybody danced and I got three encores, three times. Then I played my first two-step and I played it again, and then I played my second two-step and another encore. Then I told this big man that I couldn't do any more. That was all I knew. I'd just got this fiddle Sunday.

He said, "They don't care. Just play. Over and over. They just want music to dance to."

So I played all night.

When the party was over he went into the hall and he took down his big hat and he announced that there was nobody telling them to donate, but I had given my time free and that if they wanted to put some money in the hat, then that would be fine. Just fine. There was an awful lot of people there, so when this man handed me the hat there was more than six dollars in it. I split it with my sister. She got three and I got three and the most I'd ever had before was 25 cents. I told you I was nine, didn't I?

Years later I had my own orchestra. Five of us, and we'd go all over the country playing at dances and weddings. I've still got a set of drums out there in the garage. Anyway, for the five of us, we got five dollars and we might have to go 10, 15, 20 miles to play. That was during the Depression.

From when I was nine, I kept on playing. I've played in this district for 72 years now.

When the Circus Came to Town

Circuses used to come to town. Out beyond the cemetery it was town land but all prairie, and they'd put up their tents there right along by the tracks. Apart from the First of July it would be the big thing of the summer—most likely the year, for that matter.

They had special trains in those days and the agent would tell us when it was to come in. We knew it was coming, for sure, because these big posters were up around town. If the barber put up a poster in his window he'd get free tickets. Two. Same with the livery stables and the drugstore. They'd even tack them to the picket fences of houses on the main street.

It wouldn't always be the same circus. One year Ringling. Then maybe Sells Floto and next year the Pan American. They took turns. They all had the same things—elephants, wild animals like tigers and lions from Asia and Africa. Zebras. Ten elephants, maybe. Then there was the circus part of it with the big tent and the clowns, the trapeze artists, and all the other acts.

They'd come in early in the morning from the next big town down the line, say Brandon, and they'd set up in the morning. Everything done just so. The man you'd see making sure that the big tent went up right, that afternoon at the performance you might see him in a top hat with a whip and he was the ringmaster. Two shows. Afternoon and evening. Those show people never got much time off. Not with one day in every town, right across the West. Oh, I know, they had all winter to rest up. Yes.

The circus brought people in from all around. Towns so far down the line you never knew anybody who lived there. From across the prairie too. Wagons, democrats, gigs, everything that would carry them.

The young bucks came on their horses and they'd be ki-yi-ying up and down the main street. Not looking for trouble, just having a good time.

I've heard it said that as many as 10,000 people would be in town and that's a lot for a town of not more than 1,200. They saw the circus. Sometimes they went for both shows. Then they'd get in their wagons and head off down the roads in every direction, as far away as Baldur and Crystal City and Morris, and even across the line, and that's the last we'd see of them until next year.

The circus coming to our town was an exciting event, let me tell you.

They Were Just Ordinary Houses

As I remember they was just ordinary houses. Houses like the rest of the folks lived in. There was certainly nothing special about them, like I mean none of them had a red light hanging on the front porch or none of them had a sign. Just ordinary frame houses. Downstairs, upstairs.

The downstairs was a parlor and another room where the madam always came out of when you came in, like it was an office of hers, and then there was a kitchen. Places in Calgary or Lethbridge would have a Chinaman cooking and he'd bring you your booze too and ice if you asked. I think ice in whisky was not too popular them days, like it was just coming in and a lot of people figured it was just something fancy. The Chinaman, you called him "boy," was cook. The girls lived in the house, or most of them lived there. I guess they slept right in the bedrooms they did their business in. I know the rooms looked like it because they'd have pillows with hearts and flowers on them, and you'd see a table where they fixed themselves up and things like that. Magazines around, and some girls might have a cat for company. It was all real homey, you could say that easily.

Naw, in them days nobody thought nothing of it. There was whorehouses everywhere. Calgary had a bunch. I remember there was one in High River and as I remember, when the Mounties shut that one down there was another. There was whorehouses in Lethbridge and there must have been one in Macleod. I seem to remember one or two there. It was only after we come back from the war that there didn't seem to be any more of them or not as many as we was used to.

I don't think we called them whorehouses. Not those days. You called them brothels. If you were speaking of one special one, you'd say you were going to Mamie's or you were going to Mary's Place or you might say you were off to 123 such-and-such a street and everybody would know what you was up to.

We'd come in after three or four weeks chasing cattle and the boss would say that three of us could have three days off and the other three guys could have time off the next week. We'd usually catch the train at High River because it was closest, and we'd go into Calgary but I've seen us go to Lethbridge sometimes. Just for the hell of it, I suppose.

I'd like to remind you, mister, that we didn't go to Calgary just for the prostitutes. Mostly we went to let off a little steam. To drink. Shoot some pool. We'd just like to walk around and sleep, a decent bed for a change. Talk to other fellows. We'd talk and drink and eat. Some drinks and then we'd go and see the girls.

They was what you'd call ordinary girls. Some was pretty and some wasn't. They was just girls like you'd see shopping on the street, going into stores, and behaving themselves. That was on top. Underneath, of course, they was prostitutes. I got to know quite a few of them and they was all nice. Get them riled up and they could be mean as snakes and tough as whang leather, but just in day-by-day talk, they was just girls working at someing you could say was quite a bit different from schoolteaching or clerking in a candy store. But they was fun. When nothing was doing they'd sit around and laugh and joke.

I don't think they used their right names but what does that matter 'cause I'm not so sure all that many of us used our right names too. What? Oh, two dollars, three dollars, five dollars. I think there was houses in Calgary at five dollars but most, two dollars and three dollars. You got a girl and one drink. Usually whisky but you could get a gin if you wanted it. Sometimes a girl would try and get an extra dollar off you upstairs but that was just between you and her. For two dollars you usually got what you came for.

No, you didn't think anything of it. It was natural, like smoking a pipe, going to the bathroom. There wasn't many girls around that part of the country and they was all what you would call nice girls and here we were, a bunch of young fellows. We all had bottom, yep, we all had plenty of bottom. Ready to take on man, bear, or wildcat any time. Why, when we went to town we didn't go for ice cream. We went for whisky and poker, fun and the girls. I'm darned sorry to see the West gone. All these superhighways and high rises and such. Have you taken a good look at this town [Calgary] lately? It ain't the West anymore—not that the West was wild but it was sure a lot of fun.

An awful lot of fun. We were tough but we wasn't mean. I can say that for sure and you can ask anybody and going to a brothel wasn't nothing at all. Only the preachers screamed. Not the mayor and the police. I don't remember anybody paying all that much attention to preachers anyway.

We Looked Forward to a Building Bee

I was homesteading south of Coronation. I can remember the
bees. You had a bee to build a barn, a house, even a soddy. The
steel had gone through and the settlers were coming thick and
fast. It was quite a thing to see all those houses and barns
around you. Not that they were up to much. Most people just
put up a shack for a year or two. A log barn too. When they got a
little money put aside they'd build better. It was always the
woman who was egging on for a better house.

It was mostly good houses we'd put up. There wasn't a man in
the district that wasn't pretty handy with a hammer, a saw. Putting up those houses was duck soup and if everything was ready
a gang of men could put up a barn quick too. I've even seen a
slap of paint on a barn before the boys went home that night.

There would be a notice in the stores and at the livery barn.
Wherever people would be to read it. Tacked on to the fence
posts by the schoolhouse, and the preacher would announce it
from the pulpit. You know: "There will be a building bee at the
John Brown place on the Centre Road this Wednesday starting
at eight o'clock." That sort of thing. It was taken for granted,
naturally, that Brown would provide the liquid refreshment and
Mrs. Brown would put tables out in the yard and first come,
first served. With up to 20 or 30 men and boys they could go
through a lot of food. Roast. Maybe a ham. Potatoes, beets,
turnips, pickles, pie, cookies.

You'd see the odd one nipping from a pocket flask in the
morning, but there wasn't much drinking. The heavy work was
in the morning and after dinner, about three o'clock the hard
stuff would come out. The fellows once they seen that the house
was nearly up, which left most of the finishing to the town
carpenter, they'd start strolling over to the bar. It didn't take
them long to get going, I'll tell you that. By five and six there'd
be some pretty drunk fellows but nobody minded. They earned
their drink. There probably would be a little supper about six
but the bachelors had to go back to their little homesteads.
Cattle to feed, maybe a cow to milk. Often I've seen one buggy

going down the road with another buggy tied on behind and the fellow in the second buggy was passed out cold. His friend would be taking him home, put him to bed. But most people, they made it under their own steam. A few would hang around slapping mosquitoes until late and then the farmer would have to say, "Sorry, fellows, that's all, no more." Then everybody would hitch up or get a ride and that was our fun. We didn't mind losing a day. Heck, we weren't doing much anyway. So we looked forward to a building bee.

Mother Knew a Few Tricks Too

My mother was very musical. You could give her a piece of sheet music and she'd just look at it and then sit down and play it, and play it beautifully.

We had this organ. We were living in two granaries pulled together and fastened, but she had an organ. She'd brought it out from England, Manchester, when she came out. She'd waited four years in Manchester until my father sent for her, and we all met in Regina and then came out to two granaries. When the sleigh pulled up she said, "Well, George, if this is it, if it burns down we won't have lost anything." A wonderful sense of humor.

There were a lot of new people in the country at the time and young men would ride across the country to see her. They had sheet music with them. Their people in the Old Country would have sent it to them. I don't know what they thought Canada was, some sort of Edinburgh Festival or something. These young men would show up with the latest sheet music and Mother would sit down and play it for them, not once but maybe five times. Then she'd make tea and toast with cinnamon sprinkled on it.

Once there was one young fellow and he was very musical, although we didn't know it, and he showed up one night at one of these musicales, if you want to call them that, and he gave

Mother some sheet music. She just sat down and away she went. Well, we nearly died. What this George Cook had done was get a blank sheet music form and made up his own tune. But he'd done it by taking eight bars of this and five of that and six of this and nine of that and put them all together. So what you had, you'd have something like five bars of "Pop Goes the Weasel" and then six bars of Bach and then eight of "Here We Go Round the Mulberry Bush" and five bars of "God Save the King" and so on and so on. Well, the rest caught on pretty quickly but Mother didn't. You see, she was concentrating so hard.

When she finished we all cheered and she said, "Most unusual." She said it sounded right but it didn't sound right. So she played it again. By this time we were practically rolling around on the floor. Then she caught on. I don't know which tune made her wise to George's little game, but she laughed and laughed and said it would be one of her souvenirs. She'd keep it as that.

Then she made us tea and I made the toast and it was cinnamon toast, but she arranged the passing out of the plate so that George Cook got the last piece of toast and it wasn't cinnamon toast he got. She sprinkled his toast heavily with paprika and pepper, and nobody knew but she and George Cook—and I doubt if he knew what he was eating. He just told me later that it tasted horrible, but there was no way he could pass up her offerings. Mother was a pretty insistent little lady and she knew she had George over a barrel. So that night it was one for one. Tit for tat.

The Night Riders—Everybody Wanted Us

Everybody in our family played something. Ned played the banjo. He was a real one for it. I played the concertina, the squeeze box. My other brother, Bill, played the violin. There was an American family moved in south of us and he played the saxophone and the piano. The mouth organ too. In fact he could play anything. His name was Tom Garvey.

Ned organized us into a band. The Night Riders. I think he got it out of a penny-dreadful magazine, but we sure did a lot of night riding. There were five of us and we played for six dollars a night, all the towns around. Everybody knew us. For a July the First they'd book us the year before. The Twelfth of July was popular too. Or when some farmer was having a barn-raising bee he might hire us. In those days they had box socials and they wanted music and they'd send us a telegram saying, "Be at Wilcox at 8 p.m. October 14, dance. Signed, The Committee." We'd be there. Sometimes we rode in a wagon.

In winter, of course, it would be a cutter with a stove in it. Or we'd take the train, going up the line on the night train and coming back home next morning on the first train. Sometimes as not it would be a freight. We'd just pile into the caboose. We knew every brakeman and engineer and fireman along that line, but sometimes it would be the passenger train. We never paid. I don't think I ever paid on a passenger unless we didn't know the conductor. That didn't often happen, though.

Everybody wanted the Night Riders. We were good and we kept up on the times. There was a store in Regina and when I was in there once I saw the manager and I told him that each time a good new piece came in he was to send me the sheet music. It was always for piano but that didn't matter. We all played by ear and old Tom would only have to play it two or three times and we all had it. We used to practice in my old man's barn. I don't know if it scared the horses or not.

We'd get going about eight o'clock. A dance was a big thing in those days. We played what we called modern and we played two-step, waltz, fox trot, and a lot of square dancing. Brother Ned was the caller. Then I'd switch to violin too, so we'd have two fiddlers scraping away.

Then there would be supper and we didn't pay for that. Sandwiches and pie. Some of those halls had kitchens and you might get a hot pie like I've seen the English make. But usually it was pie and sandwiches and cookies, coffee and tea. Coffee for the Yankees. They drank it, a lot of it.

Cost would be about two bits a person to get in. Fifty cents a couple. That didn't pay for your grub. I think everybody brought their own grub and they chipped in for the coffee and tea and armored cow.

At one dance a fellow came up to Ned and he said we should get a big bass drum. He said it would sound good and you could work it with a pedal and your foot. Ned thought that would be a good idea—it would give a good beat, something we were missing. He sent away to Regina and it came back and in practice it worked just fine. Just fine. Next dance was right in town, right in our own hall, a Loyal Order of Foresters Dance, high-toned with a lot of fancy people there and a midnight supper. Some galoot nobody had ever seen before showed up. He was drunk and halfway through the evening he came running across the floor and he skidded. They polished the floor, you see, with a white borax. He said he just wanted to ask Ned to play a certain tune, but he lost his balance and skidded head-first right into that drum. End of drum. We never used the thing again. It would have been pretty darn bulky to carry around anyway, especially in the cutter. Five men and a drum in a cutter built for four people.

We had fun. Those dances were all-night affairs. If you left at three in the morning people would make cracks. As you left, you know. Like "What are you going home for?" You'd call it broad humor today, pretty mild, but then it would be pretty risqué. No, most of them dances went on until the last dog was hung. There weren't that many, you see, and it was a chance for everybody to get together. I met my wife at one of those dances.

We'd be tuckered out by six or so in the morning, but we'd always get home, back to work, to the farm, and work that day around until bed that night. We got six dollars. A dollar for each of us and a dollar for the sheet music and we didn't think we were underpaid. The price seemed right then.

Debates—a Good Evening's Entertainment

Many small towns had their debating societies. They might have called them by other names, but it was a chance to meet and discuss the topics of the day affecting Canada, or Canada and the United States, or England or the world. Or it might be a discussion on the poetry of Robert Burns or the novels of Sir Walter Scott. It was usually held in the town hall, which in those days was usually a big room over the town's restaurant or an implement shed or grain dealer, and that place would be packed. The meeting would probably start off with a young lady singing two or three sentimental songs and then the debate would go on until everybody would have their say, and then there might be coffee and cake. Then again there might not.

Tempers might get high, especially if it was politics that was being discussed or the farmers' problems or taxes, but everybody would sing "God Save the King" at the end and they'd all go home happy.

Of course, it was a chance to get social too, if you know what I mean, like to meet neighbors and friends. The young people would be eying each other up, but all in all, it was a pretty solemn thing. People took these kind of things seriously, and the men in town who were most respected were those who could discuss learnedly what a Panama Canal would do for the West or what the Kaiser was up to in Germany or, as I said, just a discussion on literature or history.

I might say it was also a chance to do a bit of politicking if a man felt so inclined. A pretty good performance on the platform before half the town was almost as good as a political meeting. People took their politics pretty seriously.

I guess you might say these meetings were kind of a way of showing off, but then we never thought of them really as such. It was a good evening's entertainment and a chance to learn something.

The Winters Were Ideal for Curling

Curling was big in the West in those days. It was a natural. Everybody could play—why, the women could play right up there alongside the men and they did too. We had a lot of enthusiastic curlers and good ones too.

We sent two rinks to the Regina Bonspiel in 1903 and the next year too and they went after the Davin Cup, which was the top award in those days. In both years they brought home the mug. In 1903 Horace Pain's rink won it and the next year it was J. J. Griffith who was skip of the winner. The whole town was proud of them and it was quite a feat, you know, having two winners in two years. We also had our town bonspiel, naturally, and a good one.

The winters, of course, were ideal for curling because you could have ice in late fall and there was curling right through to April. In fact, in some years it was such a tough winter that there was too much ice, if you know what I mean. I heard that one year they were curling on good ice in Weyburn on May 1. They didn't get the crop in that year until about May 20, as it seems to me.

The way we had our curling set up might be unique, but it showed there was plenty of ingenuity among those early pioneers. You had to have a good rink and the set-up was the council gave permission to William Townsley and William Cripps to build and operate the curling rink. On a rental deal. They went to the town's two lumber yards and rented the lumber for the rink at two dollars a 1,000 board feet. The agreement was that in the spring when they tore the rink down they would pay for any damaged lumber at the regular retail rate. This suited the lumber yards okay, for there wasn't all that much business in winter for them and they were picking up a nice bit of change for renting lumber and getting their own lumber back in the spring. Then they'd sell it to the homesteaders and town people who were raring to start building. It was all good wood.

The second thing was where to put this building, which was

two sheets of ice. Around the outside was an 18-foot rink where everybody could skate. Somebody came up with the bright idea that if it was going to be torn down every spring, why just not put it in the center of town. Fine, said everybody. So the boys built their rink in the middle of Main Street about 250 feet north of the intersection of Prairie Avenue and it worked well. Our streets were wide. There was still room for a team and wagon to pass on either side.

For four years this arrangement worked. Everybody had fine curling. The only trouble was that one year we had a terrible six-day blizzard and the weight of the snow caved in the building. Filled it with snow. Mr. Townsley just fixed it up and carried on.

Baseball Was the Thing

Everything in them days you could say was baseball. Every town would have a pasture with a chicken wire backstop, and when you was gonna have a game you'd chase the town cows off it and scrape up the cow plops and that was about it. Town teams always played town teams. Like there would be a town down the line and they'd wire us they'd be up on a Saturday afternoon. It was baseball in them days too, good ball. There was none of this spares business and four or five pitchers. Not then. If your big pitcher had a sore arm, well maybe he'd trade off with the shortstop and the shortstop would pitch that game and so it went. You could say, though, that they had pretty strong arms in them days because it was usually one pitcher, and he did all the work.

We used to take a week's holidays, the bunch of us, me, Gilbert Sedgeman, the three Warner boys, John Jackson, and a few others and we'd go baseballing. Usually we'd send letters ahead of time to the towns around, but if we didn't, it didn't matter none because it was about the first week of July we'd go and there wasn't much doing around the district, so you could always get a team up against you. For money, pass the hat. We used to get pretty good crowds. Everybody played or everybody watched. Baseball was the thing.

I remember one story—I can't remember if it happened in our district or if somebody told me about it. But it was about this engineer who pulled into this town with a mixed freight and the boys were getting set in the ball field in behind the depot and he's looking out his cab window. Then somebody yells, "Hey, can you pitch?" This engineer jumped down and said he could and he kept that train waiting there for more than two hours while he pitched for the team that was short a pitcher.

Well, back to us. We'd had a wagon fixed up with a canvas top to it and down the road we'd go. We'd come into town and the town team would usually be ready and away we'd go. If we played two games that day, an afternoon one of seven innings and a night one of seven innings, I've often seen our pitcher pitch both and not even work up too much of a sweat. Not too many night games though because the mosquitoes in most of those places were so damned awful. Besides, a lot of people had to go home and do the chores and that goes for their ball players too, you see. This was all farming country. The towns weren't awful big. This was before 1910.

When they passed the collection we might get two dollars, although I've seen it be as high as 10 dollars. That was rare. I think the only time I seen that was when a bunch of Americans looking at land, up from the States, each threw a dollar into the pot.

If things were tight we'd buy some beef and bread and butter and have a meal right out there beside the wagon after the game was over. Beef slathered with mustard and slapped on bread made a pretty wonderful sandwich after some good ball, let me tell you that. If there was a good kitty that day we'd blow it, go over to the Chink and have a good meal.

Oh, we just slept in the wagon or under the stars. If it rained, there wasn't a livery stable man in that country who wouldn't let us sleep in his hay and all he'd say was, "Okay, boys, but keep your pipes unloaded." Something like that. He didn't want any fire burning up the town and a bunch of visiting ball players with it.

We were good. I mean, I watch it on television. That is only where I watch it because there doesn't seem to be any base-ball played around here now. But we were good. Our pitchers threw hard but not as hard as today. I've never seen pitchers today with the whippy arms like some of our fellows, arms that could throw a baseball all day and all they had was the curve and the fastball and it was mostly the fastball. No, I don't think an old-time player off a farm or coming out from behind the counter of the town store could match up with them in most departments except one. That one? We had more fun. We weren't by any means making this thing our life's work. It was just fun.

There was one thing I liked about the way we played that you don't see on the television today. If it was a Saturday or Sunday and it was hot, why the ump would halt the game about the sixth inning and the players, all of us, and a bunch of spectators would walk over to the hotel for a glass or two or three of cool beer. That's something the modern game doesn't have. That was fun too. You never got drunk and in fact I think when we got back we played harder and better.

Sometimes after the game, just to give the spectators a bit more of a run for their money and burn off the energy we hadn't used up in the game, we'd challenge the other team to tug-o-war. It was nice if you had on your team a couple of 200-pounders, which was a big man then. Not so much now but a 200-pound man was big then. That's the way all these vitamins have changed us. Our hands were always good and we could hold off most other teams in tug-o-war until they were numb below their elbows. It was a test of power, all right, and you had to be tough to play and then get in one of those tug-o-wars which could go on for often maybe up to 15 minutes of sheer hard work. We were tough then and we had fun.

17 *Characters Were Everywhere*

Old Biddy Packed a Gun . . . Two Women Just Dying to Marry Him . . . Here a Plop, There a Plop . . . The Hired Man Takes a Wife . . . Horseshoe Smith, a Big Shot . . . How Many Pancakes Can an Indian Eat? . . . Dempsey and His Private Car . . . And She Said, "Whisky?" . . . Jeff, the Itinerant Blacksmith

Every new land attracts people whom others call eccentric or peculiar. These people live inside or outside the law according to their own dictates. They answer to no one but themselves.

In the West, the community or the district just accepted them. If they wanted to hang their problems or oddities out on the line for everyone to see, well, that is what they did. As long as they were not breaking the law, who was to say they were wrong?

There were characters in the old days. There still are. Plenty of them.

Old Biddy Packed a Gun

Yeah, Biddy Smith. The country was full of characters. She was one. She lived up where my brother lived, halfway to town, back on one of those little farms, and I guess, oh, every two months, she'd get on the high horse and she'd come down

340

and get the boat. You see, the boats carried a lot of passengers down the river to town. There was about five boats on the river in those days.

But anyway, old Biddy always packed a gun. A real western southerner and when she came home she'd be dead drunk and the crew would manage to get her off the boat and onto the wharf at the landing and wave goodbye to her. The minute my dad knew the boat was coming with Biddy on it back from town, he'd pull these big heavy shutters on it and close the place up and there would be Biddy coming up the road, giving a couple of whoops and firing with the old .44 of hers.

There were no policemen anywhere around, so the people in town would just stay out of her way until she'd fired off her shots and went staggering off down the road to home.

She was the kind of person that when she was alive, the kids would always remember her, and if a child was bad the mother wouldn't say she'd give the kid to the policeman to get him to behave. She'd say, "I'll give you to Biddy Smith."

In them early days there was characters wherever you looked.

Two Women Just Dying to Marry Him

I was working south of Calgary. I can't remember whose iron it was but it was a pretty fair spread. Maybe the old Stirrup brand. The boss or the company had a bunch of jolly cowboys, as the song goes.

We're lying around the bunkhouse one night and there's this one guy and he's been fretting and fussing for quite a while now and nobody knows what's wrong. Name of Carlyle and he's sure in a sweat and you know how it is in a bunkhouse, poker, cards, joshing around, clowning. Mending a saddle, making a new rope, and generally keeping busy, and all Carlyle does is sit around and mope.

Finally there's a guy named Montana Slim and he ups and

asks what the hell is the matter with him. We didn't give him the name Montana Slim. These fellows that used to drift up over the line they usually had a fancy name to hang around their necks. Anyway he gets it out of Carlyle that back in the Old Country he's got two women just dying by inches for loving him. In fact, both expect him to go back to England and marry them. He did get a lot of letters, so it must have been true. Now he doesn't want to. He hasn't got a girl in Canada but he doesn't want two girls in England, much less to be married to each of them. But he says he's a nice guy and, hell, he doesn't want to break two hearts. He just wants to be out of it.

This Slim character he just laughs. He says, "They both got the same name?" and Carlyle says no. "Okay," says Slim, "here's what you do. Write two letters. One to each girl. Make it as lovey-dovey as you can, each one, and make each think that they're the one and only. Use their names a lot in the letters. Pour it on, cowboy. Then you take Mary's letter and put it in Jane's envelope and you take Jane's letter and put it in Mary's envelope and you've got 'er beat." My God, who would have thought it would be that doggoned simple? Mary gets Jane's letter, vice versa.

In about a month Carlyle gets two letters only a few days apart. One letter says he's a cad and she never wants to see him again. The other letter says about the same thing, that he's a cad and that her brothers will dump him in the horse trough if he ever shows his face around her part of the country again. Or words to that effect. I never saw the letters but next time Carlyle went into town for the supplies he brought Slim a bottle of whisky. He did more than that. When Carlyle left our outfit to go to Calgary to work he gave Slim his horse and that was a good little horse. She'd had a quarter-horse daddy off the range, but her mother had been a brood mare with good lines and that little horse could do the quarter in 23 seconds. It was one awful good gift for just one little bit of advice.

Here a Plop, There a Plop . . .

My family were gentry but poor. Fine breeding, fine background, no money. My father had squandered it in daffy ventures of one kind or another and then didn't have the decency to stay around and console my mother. He was kicked by his horse riding to hounds. A borrowed mount I might add. No money but the desire to live high. And so he died.

There was Mother, genteel, always dressed in gray. A beautiful person. Two sisters that would have to be married off to blind men. Otherwise I'd be stuck with them for the rest of my natural days. They were that ugly.

We had a family pow-wow and it was decided I would go to Canada, buy an estate, build a home and Mother and the girls would come out. At least some cowboys might want the girls and then it would be Mother and her gentleman farmer son. It might work. We liked each other.

I came out to Canada in May of 1909. I was glad to leave England. There was no future there for me. Teach school, maybe, but I hated children and the army didn't want a man with one eye. It had been mashed quite flat by a cricket ball. I went to Lloydminster and stood at the bar in the Britannia Hotel with a lot of ranchers, farmers, bums, and listened to them tell lies to each other and then my money was nearly gone, so I found out where there was an abandoned homestead and I rode down the line to look at it. The fellow, who had built a house, had apparently run off to Chicago with the wife of one of the men in the district. It was of logs, roughly 14 feet by 16 feet and big enough for a bachelor, but putting three women into it was like trying to put another fish into a can of sardines. And, this is important, it had a sod roof. Remember that point, won't you?

My neighbor came over when he saw my first smoke coming out the chimney and he said, "Laddie, you've got no horses and anyway, it seems somebody's made off with the plow that was on the place, and that ground hasn't been worked for a year now. I'll lend you a fork and sell you some seed potatoes and you plant potatoes. If you dig a root cellar you can sell spuds all winter." I found later he was the one who had made off with the plow. Nobody ever knew what happened to the fellow's horses.

I knew nothing about farming, but I had eaten plenty of potatoes. So I put in potatoes, thousands of them, and I got the rains right and it looked like I would be doing all right. I could spend a lot of time at the bar in the Brit.

Then Mother writes. She's had the man out from town and he's appraised everything, her silver, some pictures the old man didn't pawn, some very fine furniture, and there's enough money to get her and the girls to Canada. In fact, there was no point in writing to say no because they were leaving in a week. That meant they'd be along in just a few days. And sure enough. They arrived five days later just after we've had a pouring rain for about two full days and the sun is out and the countryside looks 100 percent and this lad from town drives them out in his democrat. Trunks and luggage will arrive by the next freight.

Well, she saw the house, the stately home, and she got down and she walked up and she knocked the log side with her finger and then she walked around the house, slowly. My garbage pile just out behind. She came around in front and she said, "Pay the driver, John," and then she went into hysterics. Screaming. Laughing. Everything but tearing her hair. The two girls joined her. A regular anvil chorus. It was sickening. I knew it would be all over the country by that night and would be a front-page headline in the Saskatoon paper that week. I could see it: "Three More Crazy English Women Arrive at Marshall." The kid with the democrat was doing everything but taking notes.

I got him off and the women into the shack and built up the fire and put on tea. I thought, good old Orange Pekoe will do the trick. Make them realize they are English and used to adversity. Well, they did get calmed down but my mother kept whispering, whispering, mind you, "Oh, John, how could you do this to us?" Over and over. Jesus faint-hearted Christ, I hadn't done a thing to them. They had come out of their own free will. They were all over 21. The girls were nearly 30.

So we sat down. I mean Mother and Edith sat on my two chairs. Margaret sat on a keg I had. I stood. We ate good English biscuits, for I hadn't gone completely native and there was a store in Lloydminster that stocked them. And tea. Fine, things seemed to be going a little better but my mind was whirring. What the hell would I do about tonight? Mother in my bed, the girls sleeping in the chairs and me on the floor. That would have to be it.

Then plop. A big drop right in Mother's tea. Splash. Another plop. Plop. Here a plop, there a plop, everywhere a plop-plop. I told you about the rain. I didn't tell you about the sod roof. When a sod roof becomes saturated it won't hold any more water. Well, after that hellish rainstorm—and in those days we got some dandies—the roof had become saturated and now it was letting go its load. In minutes big drops were oozing everywhere and I knew it would rain inside for quite a while. For the night to come.

I patiently explained that to Mother. She nibbled a biscuit. Then she said, "John, you are an ungrateful son." Well, that was laying it on unfairly and I said so. She said, "John, would you get your coach ready for us. The girls and I are leaving." The old lady actually said "coach." I said I didn't even have a horse. I think that shocked her more than anything. Living in Canada and no horse to ride across the plains. If I had said that all I did was grow potatoes she'd have said, more than likely, "Just like the Irish." She hated the Irish.

So she got up and the girls got up and they put on their coats and Mother held out her hand and I shook it and stood there like a jape and she said, "Goodbye, John. We are leaving. I have a sister in Victoria, British Columbia, as you may remember, and I'm sure she will provide for us." Then out the door and up the trail they went, and when she'd gone about 50 feet she turned and called, "John, you may write us when your fortunes improve."

I went back in my shack and into the falling rain and I laughed myself sick. I thought I might wire Aunt Grace in Victoria and tell her the devil and her two attendants were about to descend on them, but I didn't.

Oh, I saw the old girl again a few years later. I got off the place, got an orchard at Kelowna and did fairly well, so I took a run down to the coast and went over to Victoria and Mother was there. She worked in a girls' school and my sisters did something in government offices and they seemed to be doing fairly well. They never married, of course.

The Hired Man Takes a Wife

My father was the doctor in town. For that matter he was also the dentist, but he was the doctor first. We lived at the edge of town where we had this big house, the biggest and best house in town, and behind it was our farm.

We had a pretty good stable out behind the house, for Dad's two horses and a place to put the buggy, and also a covered cutter, which was for long trips in winter when a woman was having a baby or something like that. There was a big room that Sam Rathwell used as his bedroom. Sam was our hired man, Dad's driver and the groom, and he helped around the farm.

There was no livestock and no work horses and every year Dad would have some neighbor put in the crop and then he'd hire an outfit in the district to take it off and somebody else to plow it and that's the way it worked. Dad being the doctor was the richest man in town, so he could do this. You could say he was kind of playing at being a real farmer although he made a little money and some years he made a fair amount.

We'd got Sam Rathwell when he just showed up at the house one afternoon. The fellow who owned the livery stable downtown had sent him because Dad had said he was looking for a new man and Sam showed up. That was about 1905, when I would have been about 10 years old. He came from around Winnipeg. That was the last place he worked. Dad always said he was good around horses. He'd certainly been around horses but where I'm not sure and Dad didn't ask questions and Sam didn't give answers. In those times if a man came along and you liked his looks and he was willing to work for the money offered, then he'd say yes or no. Quite a simple way of doing things. It's only lately that everything is so complicated. Since the last war, I dare say.

Sam wanted a wife. He told me once when I was helping him muck out the stall, he said, "I want someone to keep my feet warm at night." I had no idea what he was talking about and I told my mother this. She told me to ask my dad and he said, "Looks like old Sam is looking around for a wife," and that's all he said.

Now Sam could write but he wasn't very good at it, so one day he calls me into his room and he says, "Jeff, there's this here paper and there's men looking for wives and wives looking for men and I think I should write me up an advertisement. But you'd better help me as I can't seem to get the hang of it." Well, I didn't know either. What does a kid know about trying to get a wife? So I got the bright idea he should read the newspaper and pick out the advertisement that sounded most like him and what he wanted and put his own name on it and send it in.

He handed me the paper and said, "Here, you have a crack at it." It was the *Family Herald* and it was published in Montreal in them days and there was quite a lot of these advertisements. It made perfectly good sense. All the single women were in the East—Ontario and down that way—and all the single men were out West on farms and in small towns like ours. This was one way to get them together, so I read all the advertisements and I picked out one that sounded like my friend Sam and I wrote it out for him and addressed the letter. Just before I was going to run down to the post office with it he dug under his bunk and pulled out a magazine.

He said, "Hold yer horses, I got something else here," and it was a magazine called *Heart and Hands* or *Hands and Hearts* and what you could best call it was one of those advice to the lovelorn magazines. This wasn't just any newspaper with a couple of columns of items about who wants who and why.

This was the works, a full magazine with pictures in it and advertisements and what we'd call testimonials now which showed letters from people who'd got married through it and were happy. I read it over pretty closely and I saw that it was put out in the States, somewhere in New York or Philadelphia or some big place. In our part of the country then we'd just about had our bellyfull of the ways of some of the Americans, the sodbusters up from Kansas and Nebraska, and I told old Sam this. I said if he advertised in this book he'd be getting an American girl and she was just as likely to push him around as not. He did look kind of relieved and he said, "Damn it, Jeff, you know, I'll just bet you're right. I want a Canadian girl, don't I?" I said yes, a real good hard-working Canadian girl, that's what he wanted for the kind of country we lived in, one that knew how to work.

We sent off the letter to the *Family Herald* and in about three weeks, sure as you're shooting, there was Sam's letter right up there with all the rest of them saying things like "Hired man" and "Honest and dependable" and that he was looking for a mate, a wife. Every advert had the words "Object matrimony" and some had "No triflers, please," and when I look at those adverts in the newspapers today they still say the same words. "No triflers, please." Just like both sides wanted to get right down to business.

In about another 10 days Sam started to get letters and I'd say he got maybe five or six. This is when we had to get my father into the act because this thing sure as hell was too big for Sam and myself. Dad read every letter over and over and he'd say things like, "Good hand and she spells well; her grammar is good. That means a good education." Another he'd say, "Sounds like a sensible woman." Things like that. This was harder than picking a new coyote rifle out of the Eaton's catalogue, but finally Dad said he'd made his selection and it was one of the ones he said who sounded sensible. He told Sam he might as well write and tell her that she was the only one he'd written to as it was important for her to know that he was playing fair and square with her too. This game runs two ways, I remember my father saying, and if you get her you're with her for a long time. No sense writing all of them and then losing out and marrying one he might not have felt so highly on. Besides, that woman sent along a snap and she did look neat and sensible. Not in the flower of her youth, mind you, but less than 40 years old, we judged.

So the letter went out with a snap of Sam and we waited and soon there was a letter back and this went on all that summer, letter east, letter west, and finally Sam said she was coming out. Dad said, "To look you over?" and Sam said, "No, she's bringing her trunk. I'd say she means to stay." Dad said, "Well, well, so my bride is coming out." He called her "my bride," because after all it was my dad who had actually done the picking of her letter and not Sam at all. Sam just went along with it, figuring my dad being a doctor knew an awful lot more about women than he did. And I guess he did at that, taking everything into consideration.

Then this day comes and Sam got dressed up in his best clothes. If I said he changed from his old overalls to his new ones that wouldn't be too far from the truth, because Sam was never what you'd call a fashion plate. He hitched up the buggy and went down to the station and I wanted to go and hide around the corner of the station. I thought I'd take a couple of my cronies with me and watch the fun but my mother, she just put her foot down, and hard. There would be none of that business, not while she was around.

In about an hour the buggy comes up the lane and Sam helps this woman out. Mother and I and Dad are waiting on the porch and he brings her up and says, "This is Mary." Well, Mary was small and not quite as good-looking as her snap showed and she might never see 30 again, but she had a nice smile and she wasn't self-conscious. She knew what she was doing and I could see that Mother liked her. She didn't like most people and remember a doctor's wife in a small town was about as high as you could go, so her being nice to a serving girl was something. We all went into the house and talked a bit and then Mother said that Sam lived in the barn but Mary could stay in our spare bedroom while she and Sam got acquainted and while she decided if she wanted to stay, to see if things might work out between them.

Then she piped up and said, "Oh, that is entirely unnecessary. You see, Mr. Rathwell and I got married at the manse in town before we came up here. You see, we're man and wife now."

I heard my Dad go "Whoooosh" as he pushed a big breath out and then he laughed and jumped to his feet and shook Sam's hand and gave Mary a bit of a peck on the cheek and said, "Well, that is something, that's really something. Doesn't that really split the board right down the center?" and he laughed again. He just couldn't get over it. Mother looked a little funny and I heard her say to my father later: "I've never even seen a shotgun done so fast."

So then we had a little party, just us, some cake and a bit of sherry for the grown-ups, although Mary Rathwell didn't partake as she was temperance. Dad arranged for her to work as Mother's maid and he added 10 dollars on to Sam's salary to make up for her work with Mother. He gave them another 25 dollars to buy furniture and pots and pans and plates and blankets, and they had a bit of money anyway and that managed it. They stayed with us that winter and next spring Sam was able to take over a homestead south and quite a bit east of town and they made out. They had kids, and Sam gradually built up his place over the years and every time Dad came back from delivering another baby at the Rathwells he would say that Sam seemed to be on his feet and was building the place up.

Anyway, the point of all this is that the marriage worked. Maybe because Sam was a simple, hard-working type and maybe because Mary Rathwell was over the hill, as they say, so to speak, and that they didn't expect too much of each other and that's why the marriage worked even though it started out the way it did. Any time I'd see them in town on Saturdays they seemed happy and they seemed fond of each other. There was none of this bickering you see in some people, on the streets, not as far as I can see, and I think they did real well in the end.

Horseshoe Smith, a Big Shot

Anybody ever tell you about Horseshoe Smith? He was in the early days. He believed in doing everything big. Like he had a spread up at the Forks and that would be upstream, up the South Saskatchewan a few miles from where that town of Leader is today. Maple Creek was straight south of Smith's place.

Everything big. He had more cattle and horses and sheep than anybody, I think. His brand was a horseshoe. His real name was William but nobody called him that. He was Horseshoe or Bill. He was always on the line. If he bought 5,000 sheep in Montana for three dollars a wooly and sold them up in this country for five dollars, then the bank would take most of his profit and he'd just be left hanging on with a bit of money to pay his boys and do some more buying.

Everything big. He built a barn. If I'm not mistaken it was 600 feet long and would hold 5,000 tons of hay—but it was so darned big the air couldn't move around in it and all his hay went bad. Cutting holes in the roof wouldn't have done any good. When he died the bank took it apart and sold the lumber to settlers. When he died he didn't have nothing. Maybe he was worth in land and buildings and stock maybe a million dollars. Sure, that's possible. Oh yes. But the bank would have their hooks on 95 percent of that. Old Horseshoe didn't seem to mind. He'd come to town. Not Leader, it wasn't there then, but Medicine Hat or Maple Creek, and he'd sure make a splash. He was Horseshoe Smith with 5,000 horses and 15,000 cattle and so on. Why, he had about 100 to 150 men working for him. You could always get a job with Smith. I don't think he really wanted to be a farmer and rancher, but he wanted to be a big shot and ranching was, I guess, the way he could do it. He was Horseshoe Smith, the great Horseshoe Smith. He could sure talk to those bank men though. He didn't bother the small-town bankers. He'd get on the train and be off to Regina or maybe Calgary to do his talking.

And yet, you know. He was tight as the bark on that tree.

Once one of his cowboys came into the café and had a big meal. It was 35 cents and he walked out and didn't pay. A week later Smith comes in and I tell him he owes me 35 cents for the cowboy's meal and he got all red in the face and mad and said he wasn't paying for any cowboy's meal. I told him that maybe so but I just worked in the café and I would have to make that up out of my own pocket and that's what I did, I shamed Horseshoe Smith into paying 35 cents. Grumbling all the time.

He may have been a big man but just remember this. Who is bigger? The little fellow south of the hills with 200 cattle, 50 horses, and sharing graze and he's got 10,000 dollars in the Union Bank or old Smith with his 10,000 cows and 5,000 horses and selling horses to settlers all over the country, but at the end of the year he ends up with only 5,000 dollars in the bank and he owes half of that? I said that to the little fellow down on Ten Mile Creek and he says, "Sure, ya betcha. To me, Horseshoe Smith always was a big load of bullshit."

How Many Pancakes Can an Indian Eat?

They were great for just walking in on you. I'd be at the stove or changing the baby, doing something with my back turned, or in the other room and I'd look up and there would be one or two or three Indians sitting on the floor in the kitchen. Just like ghosts. They were always begging. "Me hungry," they'd say and point to their mouth. Always food. My husband told me to always give them something and then be firm. Send them on their way. Don't rush at them, don't yell. Just something and then off with them.

There was this old man. He was a bit of a dear, now that I think of it. I can't remember his name but it was something like Oc-mana-push-ka. You know, the names. But he was an awful beggar and sometimes he'd pester the life out of me. So anyway this day I was hanging out my clothes and when I came in there he was. All alone. "Me hungry." I figured I'd fix him and I got the stove going and we had this 50-pound bag of second-grade flour, brown, that my husband had picked up at the mill in Regina. He'd shot a coyote or his hounds had run it down, I think, and a good big fellow it was and he'd changed the pelt for the flour. The man at the mill had seen it in the wagon and offered to trade and I think it was a dollar-for-dollar deal. Except that we couldn't use it. It wouldn't make bread. The dough just would not rise.

So I got out this sack and I started making pancakes in this big skillet. Three at a time, good-sized ones, and at first I sprinkled one or two out of each pan with a bit of sugar. Indians just love sugar. People don't know that but the way to an Indian's heart is a cup of sugar. He'll just stand there with a dreamy look on his face and lick his finger, dip it in the sugar and lick his finger. I kept count. I wanted to see just how much this old glutton would eat. Ten, 20, 30, and I was getting tired but I knew he couldn't hold out. Then I stopped the sugar business and he let out a sort of "whoof," like an angry bear, but every time he reached in and took out the three. Pile them on top of each other, munch away. At 40 I knew he was slowing down and at 50 he was just about done in. When he'd eaten about 55—and these were good size, as big as a saucer—I knew he was finished. I'd fixed him good. Next time I turned around he was gone. Just disappeared. Just the way they come in, that's the way they go out. He had eaten 55 pancakes in about two hours.

I looked out the window and there he was, tottering down the pasture, just tottering. Oh, but he was in bad shape. He didn't make it out. Nearly there and he lay down. Rolled over on his back and just lay there. I thought of going out to see if he was all right but then I thought, "No, you old goat. Stew in your own gluttony."

My husband came home at noon from the field and he saw him there and he thought he was dead. When I told him what happened he laughed and laughed. It fixed him though.

Dempsey and His Private Car

We had some wonderful characters on the railroad. Never see the like of them again. Dempsey. An Irishman. When they hooked up the railroad into Prince George, the Grand Trunk Pacific, they made Dempsey superintendent from Prince George to Smithers. They gave him his own car, his own private railway car.

Mind you, this was before the thing hadn't dropped out of sight yet, the Grand Trunk Pacific bubble. Things were still going fine, it was a working railroad, but there was big lawsuits going on, the railroad, the government, other people, about land up there. They were having this big trial in Winnipeg and everything was going to be settled at this.

So they wired Dempsey to come down to Winnipeg. They wanted him to give evidence in this lawsuit. Okay, he'd go. So Demps hooks his car to the tail end of the train and he starts out for Winnipeg and you know what he done? Now here is a big important man on the railroad. He picked up a couple of girls out of a house in Prince George, he went to Winnipeg and he hooked his car to the Duluth, Winnipeg and Pacific and went down to Minneapolis and had a great time there and all the time they're waiting for him in Winnipeg to give evidence. A couple of sporting girls from Prince George, him and his private car and traveling all over the country. What a ball! What a man!

Oh, he came back. Yes, he came back but when he did they fired him.

And She Said, "Whisky?"

One day I was sitting on the stoop of this old shack doing my hair and I see a dot coming across the prairie. By the time my hair had dried and I'd put on a bonnet because of the sun I could see it was a woman. An Indian. She turned off the trail and came up and I called hello and Mother came to the door and said, "Good Lord, what does she want?" and shut the door. The old woman saw it but didn't let on.

Indians are direct, you know. They see something, they want it, and they ask for it. If they don't get it, well, that is that. Maybe some would come back in the night and take it, but that was their nature. She stopped and said, "Me thirst." I went in the house and got a cup of milk from the jar and took it to her. She looked at it and giggled. I might have known Indians don't get that thirsty. She said, "Me whisky." Oh no, I said, we don't have whisky. Not in this house. If she'd read English I could have brought out the pledge my father had signed in England saying he'd never allow liquor, spirits, to cross his lips again. It was called The Pledge. They did things like that in those days. Temperance. Rallies. And men would actually go up on the platform and sign, with a pen, pledging that they'd be temperance the rest of their lives. So I went in and got a dipperful of water and she drank that.

She sat down. She wore a skirt and an old sweater. I think they stopped wearing their native clothes as soon as they saw the white man's clothes. On her feet she wore wool socks and moccasins and over the moccasins she had rubbers. It was hot and her feet must have been sweltering.

On the prairie, bones, big ones, and they were buffalo bones. Dad to make things neater had laid these white bones end to end for a few feet out from the door. It made a little path. She touched one and said, "Him gone." She meant the buffalo. There had been thousands and thousands, but when they migrated to the States like they did every year the Americans had killed them. It took years, of course. You'd see the rotting skulls out on the prairie if you walked far enough off the trail to where there were no more homesteaders.

The old woman . . . now how old would she be? You could say she was 50, which to me would be old, but maybe she was 70. With those people, some of them, you can't tell. They get old and they just keep the same oldness.

If I'd only had some paper and pencil with me because that old woman told me about the buffalo. She could speak some English but mostly she used gestures. Very good at it. She'd stick her little old wrinkled head out and sniff, nose going like this, squinch, and you could see a bull on guard smelling for a wolf or maybe a white man or maybe an Indian. She would put out her hands so far and stroke the air and do something with her hands and even I could see she was describing a rifle, stroking the butt and working the bolt. She crept through the grass. She'd aim. She'd run forward and cut, cut, cut. That was the women cutting up the buffalo that the men had killed. She'd thrust in. That was cutting the jugular vein of a wounded animal. She would move her arms out wide, from horizon to horizon and say, "Many." She'd say that several times.

Indians had horses, of course, and were wonderful riders and she'd give little yips and prance up and down and that was the riders coming in to the camp. She'd rub her tummy and that meant, I'm sure, that they'd have a big feast and she showed me how they dried the meat. We'd call it jerky today. They made pemmican of it, dried meat, ground up, berries and lots of grease. It kept well. She went through all this, a few English words, some muttering in her own tongue, Cree, I guess. And there was the whole story of her life and the sighting of the buffalo down by the river and the young men riding off, yipping, with their rifles. "Bang, bang, bang," she'd say. They'd caught up to the herd.

She was simply the most marvelous mimic you've ever seen and not only with her face but with her body. This went on for at least an hour, a whole education for a white child to tell her what the Indian life was like and how it was the Indians' life to hunt and kill the buffalo. She was telling me what it was like for her long before the first settlers came, long before the half-breeds came up the river from Red River. I can see me now, sitting on the stoop fascinated and this old woman putting on this simply marvelous show. A wonderful theater.

Then she sat down in the grass again and I clapped my hands, clapped and clapped, and then you know what that old lady did. Guess what?

She looked at me, grinned. No teeth. Just gums. She grinned at me and held out her hand and she said, "Whisky?"

Jeff, the Itinerant Blacksmith

One man I used to like to see come to our place was the black-smith. He was an itinerant, come and go, this way and that way. If he wanted to turn left at a crossroads he'd do it but if he didn't he might just keep straight ahead. But after a time he came to every farm. His name was Jeff but I think his real name was Jeffries. His last name. I heard people call him, like, "You seen Old Man Jeffries around?" When they'd want some work done. There's always blacksmithing to be done around a farm and if it wasn't a real quick job that had to be taken into the blacksmith at Vulcan, like as not it would wait for Jeffries. He'd show up.

He was what he was: a traveling blacksmith shop, all on his wagon, with the back part the shop and the front part a little tent. He slept in there. One time he came with a mule. That was the first time any of us knew what a mule was. My father knew. He said, "That's a mule, a funny critter." This Jeff was a real character. He called the mule Patrick Murphy. Why? I don't know, I just know he did. That was for only one year and next time he came back my brother asked him where Mr. Murphy was and he said, "I sentenced him to pull a bread wagon in town."

Another time he came in in a car. I'll never forget that. That was when you didn't see any cars except unless you went into town. This was a White Steamer. I don't mean it was white, colored white, but White Steamer was its name. It was like a little train with its own steam, and when it came down the lane Dad said, "Don't say anything about that darn thing. Don't even think like you see it there." So we just acted that Jeff was not in anything more than his old horse and wagon and, boy, did that ever make him mad. You could see it. The next time he came back with a horse and Dad and I were in the barn, standing in the door, and he said, "See where Jeff has got some sense back," and he went over and shook his hand. Jeff, he laughed and said, "Thing was always breaking down," and that's all he said.

Dad always said he was a good blacksmith. He could gentle down almost any horse and he was fast. He could mend mowers and binders, just about anything, and if he couldn't he'd tell you. Everybody liked him, I figure, except Mother didn't like the way he drank his soup straight out of the bowl at dinner. Just up and down it would go and if it was vegetable soup then down everything would go anyway. After dinner he'd sit on the porch and tell stories. He'd tell what was happening in Calgary because that was where he spent the winter, and he'd talk about things what were happening at High River and towns to the north of us. He'd even tell us about things that were going on in our own district, in Vulcan, that we didn't know about. Stands to natural, don't it? He was always talking to farmers and people in the towns and it was like Jeff, if he met somebody on the road, then they'd pull over and have a talk. Time didn't mean much to him. I don't think he needed much money. He always slept at farms or in his little tent on his wagon and he ate most of his meals at farms. I mean he made enough to get by and I guess that's all he wanted.

One year he brought a helper with him. A Chinaman. There he was sitting up on the wagon seat with old Jeff and he just said the Chinaman was his helper. I think that Jeff must have come to the farm twice that year, going and coming, and I never heard the Chinaman say one word. Mother wouldn't let him in the house to eat. He ate out on the grass by the porch off a plate Mother gave us kids to give to him. No rice or any of that business. Canadian meat and potatoes and bread. What he did I don't know. When Jeff was working on the horses the Chinaman didn't do anything. He didn't even work the bellows or pass things to Jeff. He just stood by.

This got my dad's goat, and one day, next year when he didn't have the Chinaman with him, Dad said, "Jeff, what in tarnation did you have that Chink fellow with you last year for?" and Jeff said, "Oh, companionship. I got tired of talking to nothing but a fool horse." That was Jeff. When he talked he liked to talk.

One year he came around with a boy. He said he was his helper but you could see he was simple. Anybody with half an eye could see the lad wasn't all there. He was better than the Chinaman though. He helped Jeff, kept the forge going, held the horse's head. Even the wildest he seemed to have a gentle way with them. Some people have the knack and I believe simpletons have it best. Animals seem to know. There was the affair with the pig. We had this old sow and we'd had her for years but she was too mean even to have a name. She was just Pig. Dad kept her around because she gave good, big litters and she was in this big pen made of boards. The boards wouldn't have kept her in, not with that snout of hers, if she wanted to get out but she didn't. This boy sees her and he hops over the fence. Now a big sow, she can take a chunk out of your leg like nothing you ever saw, but he just walked up to her, jumped on, and kicked her in the rump and away she ran. Around and around and around and we're all staring there like we were seeing men from the moon. Around and around. Then he yanks back on her ears and jumps off and climbs over the fence and there he is, laughing to himself like nothing had happened. Why, if you or I had tried that, goodbye leg.

Next year Jeff was alone again. I can see him now. He was short but he was wide and he wore a Stetson with the front flared up like a cavalry hat. I think it was called a Fort Worth Flare. That's the style. He wore plain ordinary boots and I can see him as plain as day now, he wore blue levis like a lot of men around, my father did, and he wore what was called a smock and that was a short jacket. A lot of cowboys wore smocks. He was bald. Not bald bald but partly bald, and that was something you didn't see too much those days. I don't know why. Not too many men were bald. Certainly, certainly, oh definitely not as many as today. It must have something to do with what men to-day eat or how they live, but Jeff was partly bald. He had big strong hands and he was broad through the chest. Now that I think of it, he was a funny-looking man but I've no doubt that he was all man. He was strong and he was a hard worker.

There are a lot of other things I can remember about him, now that I'm talking about him. I don't think he could read. I know he couldn't write but that was no sin. In those days a lot of people couldn't read or write. If your dad wanted you on the farm, then you worked on the farm and didn't go to school. That was it and you didn't complain about it. He told us once he was an American, from Kansas. He said he started his blacksmithing trade when he was 12. He had been a cowboy too and worked on a ferry on the Columbia River because he used to tell us about the Indians he met there. He came up to Canada after that lawyer did him out of his land claim, and the only thing he seemed to remember about that was he had to give up his pistol to the Mounties at the border or at Lethbridge or Macleod or wherever they first found he had it. He said it was no good anyway, that nobody could hit anything over 20 yards with it and he just carried one because everybody else did.

But he didn't do everything like everybody else did. He was the only traveling blacksmith we ever saw, before and after, and he was pretty independent. He was like a lot of people in the West in those days. He came out for his own reasons and he was his own man. He went his own way. That's a lot, I think, to say for any man.

18 *But Life Went on...*

A Death in the Family ... Frozen in the Snow ... It
Happened Every Winter ... The Country Was Too
Much for Him ... A Regular Horse Plague ...
'07—a Terrible Winter ... Dear Brother and Sister
... Always Sad Things Happening ... Two Little
Caskets, One Lonely Grave ... A Strange Story but
True ... A Suicide in the District ... The Frank
Slide Disaster

*It was a lonely land, and when people are far from friends,
isolated from neighbors, tragedy seems so much sharper, so
much more intense. That's the way it was in the West.*

*It could be a small thing to the community, but big to one
family. It usually meant death—from accident, disease, a
deliberate act born out of frustration, or it could be from nature
on the rampage.*

*But when tragedy occurred, people converged to help as the
"moccasin telegraph" of the prairies went into operation. The
police came to give authority to the scene, and when it was
over, the damage repaired, the crisis resolved, the brown earth
smoothed over the grave, life went on as before.*

A Death in the Family

My aunt and her family had moved out to a homestead four miles from us. Then a brother of my mother's arrived with his family. They had four little girls. The three families, we were a small community of our own out there on the prairie.

One morning my uncle rode on his horse into our yard to tell my mother that one of the little girls was very ill. We all had had measles that spring after we arrived at the homesteads and were ill and weak, and it took some time before we could be up and about. But this wasn't measles. My father and mother immediately went in their democrat across the prairie where this little girl was sick and they were gone all day. I was left to look after little Roy and I had Don to help me.

When my parents returned their faces were very saddened. The little girl Bernice had died of pneumonia. My father had ridden his horse to town 30 miles and brought back Dr. Lord, but when he got to the shack he was too late.

She was buried a few rods north of the house. It was a pitiful service. There were so few neighbors to attend and a young student minister, a Protestant, came out from the town to read the service. My aunt was Catholic but there was no priest in that new and strange country, so my aunt had to get what comfort she could from the alien religion and land.

Little Bernice was our first funeral in our home on the prairie.

Frozen in the Snow

About the middle of October I'd get out a long piece of wire I had and I'd string it between the house and the barn because when one of those blizzards came up, you could easily get lost between the house and the barn. You couldn't see a foot or two in front of you. And if you got lost, you would perish.

Many, many people perished in those days. They'd find them

after the storm, you know, see a lump in the snow and dig under, and there would be the body. Or they'd find them two miles away next spring when the snow went. They'd just wandered, trying to get back to the house or the barn, and walk until they fell and once you went down, that was it.

Gilbert Perry's sister's husband perished that way. He couldn't see, and he got to the gate and it appeared that for some reason he was trying to open the gate and she found him the next morning. The storm had abated and there he was, standing up, sort of leaning against the gate and frozen stiff. Frozen solid.

What a thing for a wife to find!

It Happened Every Winter

I used to get magazines and I'd save them and then I'd swap them with a policeman we had named Pat Aitken. He was another good policeman. I went down to the barracks and I saw a farm wagon outside the door, full of settler's effects, his goods, and I went in and I asked Pat if he had any magazines to exchange. "Sure," he said, "go in the back. There's a pile right by the door."

I went in the back and there's a stiff. A man, frozen stiff, lying on the floor of the storage room.

I grab the magazines and I come out and ask and Pat says, "Oh, another one of those. They live alone out there, nobody to help them and the fire goes out and they freeze to death in their bed. Neighbor doesn't see smoke for a couple of days and finds him and they call us. Happens every winter."

He said if cold didn't get the poor buggers, then they suffocated to death from coal oil fumes.

What the Mountie would do was go out and load up everything the poor fellow had, hitch up his team to the wagon, and throw him on top and bring the whole thing in. They'd have an auction and get enough to bury him. If there was anything left over it would go to somebody, kinfolk somewhere.

The Country Was Too Much for Him

We had a suicide in our district. The Hanna district. This Englishman came out, bought this farm and you could see he didn't know anything about farming. When he went to town the first time you wondered how his horses could pull the wagon because he had everything wrong. Collar wrong, harness. People laughed at him right in the street.

He tried. Oh, he tried hard and he did learn, but he had bought into a bad deal. Somebody had really skinned him. After a while we saw how hard he worked and how little he got for it, just how little he got for all his work and people in the neighborhood took sorry for him. Some Sundays I used to send the boy over on the mare and ask him for Sunday dinner and he'd eat and eat and you could see he was well bred. I mean, he'd have a second and he could eat some more and there was more on the platters, pork, chicken, beef, potatoes, beets, gravy, but he was too polite to ask for a third because by that time the rest of us had finished eating.

He'd stay as long as he could because he didn't want to go back to that shack out there in the dark, and Mother, my wife, would always give him a loaf of bread. Cut up, you see, and buttered, and a jar of pickled beets and onions. Other neighbors did the same thing so he got one good meal a week.

One Sunday I sent the boy over on the mare to ask Jack for dinner and he came back saying there was nobody around. Place deserted. I said he's probably in town. The boy said if he was he'd walked because his team was in the corral. Did he look in the shack? I asked him. No. Why not? Didn't think it right. Well, Mother gave me a look and I got on the mare and took off over there and, yep, there he was. In bed. Clothes on. Boots on. Straight razor in his hand. Nobody used anything but in those days. He'd just taken that blade and stroked it right across his neck, straight and firm and deep right across his neck. Then he laid his arm down by his side and waited. That's the way I figured it out.

There was no note. I know he had folks because they used to

send him English newspapers, and he'd pass them on to us. He told me once he'd come from Devon and he missed the larks in springtime. I had said that he'd have to get along with a good old Canadian meadowlark and he said it wasn't the same thing. What he meant was that Canada wasn't Devon. I've been there and it is a lovely place.

The Mountie found an address and notified his folks. What he had wasn't worth anything, a team, some equipment, but nothing really. The land went back to the company. I don't even think there was an auction.

We went to his funeral. Oh yes, there was a proper funeral, but nobody showed up. Just the minister, my wife, me and the grave digger. It was a terrible thing in those days to commit suicide. It meant your soul was going straight to hell. Grave digger and the undertaker's driver and myself had an awful time getting that old box into the hole. We finally had to ask the minister to help us and we got it in okay. The country was just too much for him. He should have gone home.

A Regular Horse Plague

The first two years my father didn't have any crops. Nothing broken, you see. He had horses. He had invested in horses. Very beautiful horses, and they all got swamp fever and died. Except four scrubs that he'd bought when he got here. But all the beautiful horses died. We landed here in what everybody said was the first year of a seven-year rainy cycle. It rained for seven years. It was dry, dry country the year before, and the next year it just rained and rained and rained, and the sloughs just overflowed and the water got bad, and all the horses in the country died of swamp fever. All the wonderful horses the settlers brought in. Only the scrubs born and raised in this country could drink that polluted swamp water and live.

My father and the other farmers around did everything they

could to save those horses. Percherons. But they didn't live. That was the start of my father's life in Alberta, or the Territories as it was called then. Wiped out. The swamp fever was some kind of bug and my father had been a veterinarian too, but he couldn't eliminate it from the horses.

The draft horses, the bigger horses that the settlers were bringing in, a tremendous lot of them died. Not all but a tremendous number. Yes, it was a regular horse plague and it hit a lot of settlers hard. Just a bit of history you never hear about.

'07—a Terrible Winter

In '06 and '07, them were the worst two years ever. Right through November and December of them two years and it was blizzards all the time and no chinooks. Nothing that never really looked like a chinook, and the cattle just drifted away and the ranchers, there was nothing they could do about it. And 30, 40 below all the time. Sometimes 50.

When spring come the superintendent said, "You fellows go out and look over the whole country. I want to know how bad it was." So we went. Patrols all through that country and you know what we found? More than 40,000 dead cattle. Piled up everywhere. In cutbanks, against drift fences. Everywhere you'd expect to find dead cattle they was there. The final tally when we was finished was 41,000 cattle. A terrible winter. There was nothing like it before and nothing been like it since.

Dear Brother and Sister . . .

When my grandfather left Ontario, he and his sister Katey, his brother Hugh, and their father went to Winnipeg and then traveled to Edmonton. They were farming west of there when the smallpox hit them. This is the letter he wrote home:

Dear Brother and Sister:

I now sit down to write you these few lines to let you know how we are getting along. We have written to you some time ago but I got no answer, so I will write to you to let you know who is dead and who is living.

In the first place I have to inform you that Katey who has been taken sick and when she got a little better Hughey took them and he was sick for 11 days and died on Thursday, the 21st at 9 o'clock P.M. And Father took sick a few days after Hughey did and died on Thursday, the 21st. That is, the same day.

Duncan McDonald, blacksmith, and Hector buried them as no one else will go near them.

Duncan lost two of his family by that dreadful disease.

And you may judge how Katey is, as she is home all alone and nobody dare go to see her nor she to see anyone else except Mc-Donald's family. She dare not come out for some time, until all danger of spreading the disease is past.

She has cows and calves that cannot even be given away and she can make no use of them. Besides a great many other things as well.

As luck happened I was away on the river when this awful disease broke out and I did not go home at all nor it is not likely that I shall go home now. Roger and Margaret have kept clear of it. They are living on a farm about five miles from what used to be my home. They are all well.

Always Sad Things Happening

There were always sad things happening on the prairies, and neighbors had to stick together and help each other out because the towns were so far apart. It took hours and hours to get a doctor to help and sometimes there just wasn't any doctor at all.

I remember one winter when we were all alone far from anywhere and my father was very ill with pneumonia. One night Mom was crying and two neighbors had come over to help with the stock and I heard them saying to themselves that my father, he could die that night.

I was only a child but I believe this was the first time I had ever prayed and meant it, my first real prayer, and next morning my father had taken a turn for the better. My little prayer had been answered. Mother, with God's help, had nursed him through pneumonia.

In the spring he was too weak to put in the crop and my eldest sister who was under 12, she put in the crop herself. How she did it I'll never know. We all worked all summer, picking rocks, burning weeds, and milking the cows and hoping for a crop, but when the fall came there was no crop. There had been no rain.

I remember well the evening they came after Mother and Dad. A neighbor's boy, Dick, had been accidentally shot in the stomach. There were no telephones anywhere in those days and the train ran once a week from Foremost to Lethbridge. So they carried him from the field to Mrs. Ully's home, which was closest, and Mother stayed there and nursed him for a week until the train could take him to Lethbridge, to a doctor and a hospital. Dick now lives in Seattle.

My mother knew what to do in almost every case of sickness or accident, and she had many a cut finger to bandage.

Mr. and Mrs. Lum Sheet's twin son Luther was cleaning out his well and it caved in on him and they worked, neighbors coming from near and far, neighbors, they worked in shifts but when they reached him it was too late. He left a young wife and little son.

Another close neighbor while threshing stepped on wood on top of the cylinder on top of the threshing machine and it broke and his foot was badly mangled. Gangrene set in, ending his life. He left his wife a widow.

Dave Grabowski, who was also a neighbor, he grew very ill and died. He left his wife and three little girls, and she was a frail woman. But she worked like a man and ran the farm herself and suppported her three little ones.

Some women lost their husbands in the war too, gone, leaving them to carry on as best they could.

These are just a few of the accidents and deaths I remember in our one little district, just a small district, but in those days accidents happened a lot. There were midwives, of course, in every district and they helped and people like my mother who had some training in medical help. But if a person was seriously injured it was a serious matter. People in those days died of diseases that they never die of now, or are never even heard of anymore. There also were farming accidents, men killed in runaways and many other ways.

It was a hard life but you could always count on your neighbors in trouble. There were neighbors who bore your great sorrow along with their own hardship and never complained. Everybody in troubled times prayed for strength that only could come from the Lord.

Two Little Caskets, One Lonely Grave

Oh, it was a very sad sight, seeing that yellow card hanging on the farm gate or the door. I think it was yellow for diphtheria and red for scarlet fever. It always seemed to get the children.

Nobody ever knew how it came. I mean there would be 15 children in the school and only two would get it. Diphtheria. The others wouldn't. It was mystifying and the poor little tykes, it didn't seem as if they ever got better from it either.

With the card on the gate that meant the house was quarantined. Nobody but the doctor could go in that house, and sometimes I guess there weren't even doctors. Two or three children in one family would be wiped out and it came quick and it didn't take long before the poor little creatures had gone to heaven.

I remember a neighbor named Isbister coming over to our house one day and asking my father if he'd come with him to the cemetery to help him. The day before, they had lost their two kiddies, a little boy of five and his sister seven, and my mother got her coat and said she'd go along with them to their gate and get off and go in and sit with Mrs. Isbister. "No," said Mr. Isbister, "I'm afraid you can't do that. Nobody can go in that house," so that poor woman was left in that house alone with the bodies of her only children. The men went off to the cemetery and dug just one grave and that would do for both of them, you see. Next morning I was looking out the school window and I saw this wagon coming and on the spring seat sat Mr. Isbister and Mrs. Isbister and behind rode the minister from town on his horse and in the wagon were the two little caskets that Mr. Isbister had made. It was an awful sight. No mourners. Just those two people and the only family they had, both dead, going to bury them.

They left Shoal Lake after that and went back to Ontario where they had come from. They just wanted to never see that country again.

A Strange Story but True

I'm going to tell you a story you might find hard to believe, but it is true as I stand here. It is about the death of a hired man and something which is more than strange, and it is all true.

There was a Mr. Camil A. Coupal who ran a combination horse ranch and farm on Wascana Creek. He broke wild horses to work his land and he had a shack and a stable on the northeast corner of Section 22 in our township. His hired man was a man named Victor Malfugeon from France who I remember quite well. He was a man of medium build and he had a full beard and at this time he was 45 years old.

This day he was using five of these broncs, half broke, plowing with a single-bottom riding plow. Though everything I guess was going quite well, when you've got five broncs abreast with no steady ones among them, all in a line across, that is real dynamite at any time. They were halter tied in pairs with bits tied to halters, and they drank, ate, and slept with harness left on, and ate with their bits in their mouths. That was the situation. They were learning fast.

Then on the 15th day of August something went wrong. Nobody knows. But those horses bolted, jerking that plow about in short, twisted jumps—you could tell that from the tracks they left. That night the hired man didn't come in, which wasn't unusual because he was sleeping in another place. But anyway, as there had been a very heavy storm that night, the next day Mr. Coupal rode over and all he found was the plow. He searched around and found his man in a straw pile.

The way the police put together what happened was that when the horses bolted, for whatever reason they bolted, the man was thrown forward and hooked by the point of the share. Because he knew no help would come, he had crawled a quarter of a mile to this straw pile and stuffed straw into the big hole in his stomach, into the wound in his lower abdomen, to keep his bowels in place. He was a pipe smoker and so he carried matches and you could see where he had lighted matches and tried to set the straw pile on fire so there would be a lot of smoke and somebody would come and investigate. But for some reason the darn straw wouldn't burn and he used up the last of his matches. You could imagine what his thoughts must have been, dying on a farm in Canada far from his native France. Then that night the big storm came, heavy rain, much thunder, forked lightning. He must have died sometime during that wild night.

You can look back on it and see that Frenchman on his hands and knees with his guts coming out, dragging himself a quarter of a mile in one last effort to attract someone to help him. But nobody came.

But that's not the end of the story. Where were the broncs, the five of them? We wondered how many miles had they traveled, and no one knows, but they were finally found behind some low hills about a mile and a quarter from where they had bolted, on their last wild run, I guess. Remember that when they had broke loose from the plow they were still harnessed together, so they ran together. They ran headlong over the rim of a four-foot cut-bank of a pothole in Mud Creek, and that's where we found them. I can see them now.

You've got to get the picture. There they were, five horses, tied together, standing together, upright on their feet, perfectly spaced, and all of them were having an unusually deep drink. Their eyes were about three inches above the water and their noses rested on the mud. There was about five inches of water in the pothole. The waterline, which you could see, was eight inches below their backs. This is what happened. They were running that night when the storm brought a flash flood down and they hit the creek and drowned. Right where they were. They didn't get away or didn't have enough sense in their heads to save themselves. It hit them so fast that they just died as they stood. It was an amazing thing to see, five horses standing dead just as if they were alive.

A Suicide in the District

This was in December of 1909. One morning as Mother and Anna the hired girl were busy with breakfast in the kitchen, the door suddenly burst open and Mrs. Hutten ran in and almost collapsed in Mother's arms. The Huttens lived on the old Court place, half a mile south.

The Huttens had a hired man, an Englishman out from England by the name of Farr, and Mr. Hutten was away from the farm for a day. When Mrs. Hutten had breakfast ready she stepped out the door and shouted to him. To Farr. He didn't answer or come and she called him two times more and there was no response, nothing, so she walked over to the barn and opened the door. Well, she didn't call him again. She saw a man lying on his back in the middle of the barn floor with the back of his head toward the door. She slammed the door shut and ran up that snowed-in trail the half-mile to our place and she was a badly scared woman. Poor woman.

I got on a horse and rode over there right away and strange to say, as I rode up something told me that I wouldn't find the man alive. That I'd find him dead. He was.

What he'd done was this. He'd stepped up into the loft behind a big team of horses and the hole where you shoved down the hay was about 30 inches square. He'd taken a new ball of twine and fashioned a noose using three strands just long enough to tie to the cross stringer boom that supported the loft floor, just over the rump of that big team, and he'd made a common slip knot and put the noose around his neck. Then he just stepped down off the ladder that was there. There was no drop, not like in a hanging. He'd just strangled himself. The three strands of the rope he'd made had broken off about an inch above the slip noose, but of course the slip noose had held and it never let go of him, so he just strangled.

Somebody went to get the Mounted Police and Tom Rooney, an Irishman who worked around, and myself, we stayed at the Hutten farm and we did the chores, but we didn't touch the body. We just stepped over it or walked around it as we did the chores.

I can still see that tall Mountie sergeant when he came that night. In the lamplight he looked down at the body and he looked for what must have been a full minute and then he said, "The poor devil." A sermon could not have said more. Now what would make a man hang himself, and like that? Was it the country, such a hard place to make a living, and no future but just as a hired man, or was it something else, something within him? It was a hard country.

Because I was the person who had found the body I signed the statement for the Mountie, and that night, out there in an empty granary, Tom Rooney and me shaved the man and fixed him up and laid him out in a nice new coffin we'd built, just as an undertaker would have done. Dad had already got in touch with Smedley and the people had dug a grave in their new cemetery, one mile west and two miles south of the town. Before we headed for town with the coffin we opened it up for his wife, Mrs. Farr, to have a last look at her poor husband, and his color had come back up from that welt on his neck and he was the most natural-looking man I have ever seen at that time in life.

We started for the cemetery and met the little English minister in his horse and cutter rig and at the grave was Tom Rooney, Jack Hutten, the minister, Mrs. Farr, and myself. We took the lines from the harness to lower the casket into the grave, and as we started to lower it the minister seemed to slip his grip on his end of the line and lost his balance. I was across from him at that end so I grabbed his line too and stopped the casket, which hung at an alarming angle. We got it righted and lowered it steadily enough.

When the little Englishman conducted the service his hands shook so he could hardly read his Bible. Then we filled the grave and put the lines back into the harness. Then we stood there for a few minutes at the grave in that new cemetery, just four men and a woman, Tom Rooney, myself, Mr. Hutten, and the minister and Mrs. Farr. We shook hands with the minister and that was a grim day, burying a man who had hanged himself a long way from his native land.

The Frank Slide Disaster

I had a brother Charlie doing some subcontracting in the coal mine at Frank in Alberta, so I figured I'd ride out and see him. I arrived on a Sunday, 10.30 A.M., and on Monday afternoon I went to work in the mine at three dollars for eight hours.

Well, Frank was quite a town then. I guess there were about

800 to 1,000 men working there. I arrived there on the April 19. In 10 days, on the 29th of April, at five minutes after four in the morning, Turtle Mountain took a notion to tumble down and bury the valley. It was one of the worst disasters up to that time in Canadian history, let me tell you, and don't just believe the newspapers. Listen to me, I was there. Eighty-seven people killed and about 50 injured.

Well, my brother and I was sleeping in the Union Hotel, just across the street from the Crowsnest Pass main line. Well, just about that time a freight train used to go through, and I used to wake up. This time I thought to myself that that was an awful long and loud freight train. So I woke up Charlie, who was sleeping with me, and he said, "Hell, that ain't no freight train."

And just then the building began to shake and the roar got louder and I said, "I guess it's an earthquake." But a blacksmith with a nice name, Dick Slugg, came running down the hall yelling, "Everybody out, the mine has blown, the mine has blown up." I threw up the window curtain and there was half an inch of frost on the window, just like there is in cold wintertime, and when we got outside all the puddles that had been wet and muddy the night before was suddenly frozen hard. We couldn't figure it out, but it had something to do with Temple Mountain coming down into the valley and forcing all the warm air out, the cold air from way up in the mountains pouring in in an instant and freezing everything. At least that's the theory: the change of air from 3,500 feet up coming down.

We groped our way around in the dark and went down the street, and there was this huge company bunkhouse, maybe 100 men sleeping in it and just beyond it, not 30 feet away, was this huge wall of rock of dark limestone and that building, so close, and not even one pane of glass broken. It took quite a bit of time for us to get it through our heads that everything and everybody beyond that point, where the wall of rock began, was dead. Was blank.

Oh, I could tell you much more, but what did we do? We went over to where some miners' cottages had been hit by a small slide coming off the big slide, and we found dead people in some of the cottages, but we rescued some. This is where the legend of the Frank Slide Baby began, that out of that whole town there was just one survivor and that was a baby. I still see it in newspapers, in articles in magazines and books about the Frank Slide, and they all say that there was only one survivor, a baby. I know about the baby. It was the baby belonging to a Mr. and Mrs. Frank Leech and it was saved. But remember, Frank was a fairly big town and there were hundreds of miners, and only those at one end of the town, the fringe, 87 people were killed. But to this day, to this very day, people are still writing about the Frank Slide and the only survivor, a baby, which was the Leech baby, which was rescued when I was there. In fact, it wasn't rescued. Its mother put it on a bale of hay that had rolled down from the livery barn and when we come along, all us rescuers, there was the baby outside, in its blanket, safe and sound. Its mother went back in the house and was killed by some more rock and mud. Its father, Frank Leech, died too and two boys did, but two girls, teen-agers, in that house, we got them out. They went to hospital and was okay after a while. So there were hundreds safe in the town and not just one baby. That was in 1903 and 73 years later they're still talking about that one baby.

Eighteen men were trapped in the mine. The night shift, and when the slide came it blocked the river and a lake began to form. But the railroad construction crews knew powder and they got to work and blew out a path and the water began to go down after it had crept up to the knees, the thighs, and then the waists of the 18 men trapped in the mine. They got themselves out by digging a raise 45 feet and coming out higher up the mountain. The first one out was a little fellow named Shorty Dawson, who wiggled through the hole they'd made further up and yelled "Help" to us who were working in gangs trying to get in to them from below. We got all 18 out then and the only one who was injured a fellow named Warrington, who'd hurt his leg. It was after five o'clock in the afternoon when we took them up through town to the hospital and it was like a parade, miners and townspeople carrying these miners who had dug themselves out. Yes, it was like a parade.

That's a very short telling of how it actually was. It would take a whole book to tell of how they were trapped in there, how the explosions blew in the doors and the air shut off and the water coming up. But they got out because they kept their heads and figured out what was to be done and did it. There were some very experienced miners on that night shift and they led them out, out through that raise, but they was lucky too.

The people killed, all but a few of the 87, are still under all that rock in the valley. That was their graveyard. Whole families, single men, townspeople, Canadians, Welshmen.

But there's one story I want to tell you. Thirty-one days after the Frank Slide disaster, the first men went back into that mine to look at the damage. My brother was one of them. In there with safety lamps, half a candle flame, and they don't know what they'll find and they're groping their way in and they hear chains rattling. Well, chains can only mean ghosts and spirits. There is nothing alive in that mine. Remember, it's 31 days. So, grown men that they were, they turned turtle and got out of there. But then they stopped and said, "We can't do this. This sort of thing isn't done. We've got a job to do." So they went back in again past where they'd been, and they saw two round eyes reflecting in their lamps and they found this horse, they called him Big Charlie. One of the miners on the night shift had taken him in the night of the slide to do some particular work. This horse was still alive, lying with his head toward the ditch where he could lap the mine water.

Well, sir, they hugged him, they cried over him, they sent out for a veterinary, and they did everything to comfort that animal. And the mine manager offered a reward of 1,000 dollars if the vet could save him. Well, they tried but next morning he died because his stomach was so full of wood which he had gnawed off the wooden side of the mine cars, gnawed the wood off the sides of those cars in that mine in pitch darkness trying to keep alive. Thirty-one days.

Well, that's the story of Big Charlie. He was the last casualty of the Frank Slide Disaster, as they call it now.

19 *Those Were the Days...*

Pancakes Made a Man of Him . . . All That London Finery . . . We Always Needed Firewood . . . Mosquitoes Were the Worst . . . Six Days to Build a Barn . . . We Didn't Have the Money to Go Home . . . How People Dress, That's Important . . . I Delivered the Baby Myself . . . Bless That Iron Pot . . . I Ran the House. I Had to . . . We Papered the Walls with Stories . . . Miles from Anywhere— and Pregnant . . . I Was a Little Tyke . . . The Hired Man Remembered Me . . . How I Became an Anglican . . . Please Come Home. Bring Douglas . . . A Bowler Hat on the Prairies . . . Ranching in the Early Days . . . The Whole Country Was Ours

This chapter is not an epilogue, although I suppose I would be entitled to one if I planned to draw conclusions about The Pioneer Years. *I like every story in this book, but maybe I like this small group a little more, and so I have saved them for the end.*

Each of them makes its point about the early days. Each of them shares a special memory of what it was like to be a settler in western Canada. As one of them says, so eloquently: "We were the first white people ever to go to that piece of land . . . No one before us. The whole country was ours."

Pancakes Made a Man of Him

I can remember my mother's pancake griddle. She'd brought it out from the East with her, and and it was so big it sat over three holes on the Home Comfort stove and it made three huge pancakes. Three of her pancakes inside a man allowed him to battle the elements for several hours, I can tell you, and you had to. Those winters at Crossfield were something we'd never been used to before, I'll tell you.

In 1902, we arrived in May and while the men put up a house we lived in a shack which was on a neighbor's homestead. We set up our home in it. Not long after we arrived there was a raging blizzard. A really bad one. Yes, in May. Then above the howling of the blizzard our family heard the bawling of cattle and the yelling of cowboys and the thin walls of this shack, they began to go in and out. The cattle were being driven right through our place and the shack was in danger. In those days there was no herd law, so the cattle were everywhere. The ranchers were kings.

Near, the cowboys found a place to put their cattle out of the blizzard and then my dad brought them in to thaw out. The herders, their chaps were covered with snow and chunks of snow hanging from them. Their dogs were just as bad. They all crowded around the stove dripping everywhere and my mother stood there, the big pancake pan on the stove, and she cooked pancakes for them, more and more and more. They were very hungry. Even the dogs got their share. When the blizzard got less they went on their way.

Years later my husband and I were at a dance and a man came up and said, "Do you remember Pancake Ranch?" I said yes. That was what they called our ranch after that. This man said, "When we came in out of the storm your mother's pancakes made a man out of me. But I vowed after that night that I never wanted to see another cow again."

All That London Finery

When we came out from the Old Country my parents brought trunks and trunks of finery. The finest clothes, suitable for the London season. Silks, satins, shoes by the dozen. Coats and hats, bonnets. Enough to stock a women's store, a millinery store, a men's haberdashery store, a boot shop. We were going to certainly put on a grand parade for the natives in the new land.

Then we found out what Canada was really like. We arrived in Winnipeg in mid-March and found the good hotels filled, so Father said that instead of us staying in Winnipeg while he found our new land we'd all go with him. Winnipeg was a neat, tidy little city, I think, but Father said we might as well stick together and, my dear, stick together we surely did until we were all stuck together in a shack on a ranch a man had near Westwood. The trunks went into a shed and when we moved to our own place, eventually, at long last, they went into another shed. And finally when Father scraped enough together to build a house, the trunks went into the attic and there they stayed.

Not once, to my recollection, did anyone open a trunk. Mother wouldn't hear of it, even when my sisters and all of us were almost in rags and those clothes could have been cut down and made into warm garments. Never, she said, never. I guess she was waiting for that fancy-dress ball that never came to the prairies.

Dance, oh sure, but if you wore anything a bit fancy you were looked on as high-faluting, a fancy, and you'd never hear the last of it, believe you me. So those trunks just sat up there, all those beautiful clothes. Why, the way fashions are, they must have gone in and out of style two or three times.

I don't know what ever happened to those trunks. They may have been sold sight unseen at the auction. I never got to it, being in B.C. at the time Dad passed on, but I expect that's what happened to all that London finery.

We Always Needed Firewood

The first thing I remember as well as I remember my own grandchildren was that there were no trees where we first took up our homestead and you could look as far as the eye could see, every direction, and not a tree could you see.

We needed firewood. Coal was too expensive for us. We needed something that was free and of course there still were buffalo chips around which we could use. You know what buffalo chips are. Well, we were actually after a time using cow chips but we still called them buffalo chips. I never thought they made a real fire, not hot enough for a lot of baking like I used to do.

There *were* trees, plenty of them, but Dad had to go about 20 miles for them over to the river and he'd bring back a load of poles and we'd cut them up and they were used during the worst kind of winter. It was hard work and it took about two days to make a trip there and back and it was winter work, mostly, and cold, but Dad used to do it about once a week all that first winter. The wood was green but once you got it going it kept going a long time, like good coal although it didn't throw off much heat. We used to get pretty close to that old stove at night, I can tell you, and we went to bed pretty early too. There was no sense staying up and freezing when you can half-freeze in bed, Dad used to say.

We'd moved onto the place in the spring and put up a tent while we were building a house. Just a shack, really, which we added onto later. But we always needed firewood and Dad said next year he'd buy coal because it was cheaper now that the railroad was in and that was fine with me. I said I'd get along somehow.

He always used to make a joke, saying I had my own trees. By my own trees he meant my lilacs. I had brought a lot of lilac startings out from England and I had a green thumb and I got them going. They were just a few inches high but the lilac, I don't think there is a lovelier shrub alive. Especially when it's blooming, all pink and lavender and white, but even when it is just green. If they are trimmed right, they look so round and smooth and cool, like a rich lady going to a ball. I guess most of the lilacs in that country came from my cuttings. I know just about every old-time place has a few in the yard.

But it was the cold that always got to me, into my bones and it was because of the firewood. The green fir, some poplar and it never got a chance to dry out. We were always cold. Cold just thinking of it.

Mosquitoes Were the Worst

Oh my goodness. The first year we homesteaded it was a dry year, but in the second year, in the spring we had a lot of water and they were just . . . well, we had a jam pot full of wet grass smoldering, these jam pots sitting outside every window just to keep the mosquitoes from getting into the house.

You breathed them in. You couldn't help it. When you went outside they were around your face by the thousands. Yes, you actually ate them. Mosquito netting didn't do all that good because the smaller ones could still get through. It seemed their only purpose in life was to attack you.

And the poor cattle. You'd go out and set fire to a big manure pile with some straw, and it would burn for days and the cattle learned to stand in the smoke. When the wind shifted and the smoke moved around, they'd move around too.

Everything tasted and smelled of smoke. I can understand why the Indians smell like they do. Of smoke. We almost smelled like the Indians too.

But as time went on and the land got broken up and the sloughs dried up or they drained them, then the mosquitoes got less bad. It was just those first few years when they were so bad that they made your life miserable. Some people actually left. They were the very worst thing about pioneering in the early days.

Six Days to Build a Barn

I remember the time I built a barn on a homestead away from our own place and I was staying on it working it for my Dad and this day, October 30, 1903, a neighbor came by my place and he had a letter for me.

It was from my Dad and in it there was enough money for me to build a barn and he laid out the dimensions. It was to be 26 feet wide by 60 feet long and eight feet high with a board roof. You can see that that was quite a healthy size. I sat up almost all night with a square and figured out the rafter cut and all the details. This was to be a 10-inch lap siding.

I had to haul the lumber from Balogonie, which was south of Regina, and I knew time was going to be short because the weather had that bleak look and you could tell that winter was coming on.

I was up early. I drove one team and trailed the other and I was north of the St. Peter's Colony even before the sun was up. I loaded those two loads of lumber, about 1,350 feet each, and started back after I had given my two teams a good feed. That was 25 miles each way, 50 for the full trip, and I got back about 10 o'clock that night. I got me something to eat and then unloaded those two loads of lumber where the barn was going to be. Then I went to sleep and got two hours.

Next day I was on the trail with two fresh teams before any sign of light. I got to Balogonie, loaded up, ate, and got back this time about 11 o'clock.

Next morning I started in on that barn and I worked. How I worked. Just think, a barn 26 feet by 60 feet by eight feet high and I finished that barn in just six days. And I was all by myself. Nobody else around. Just me. We knew how to work in those days. We sure knew how to work.

We Didn't Have the Money to Go Home

Oh yes, I know, you can read all you want about how romantic it was out on the prairie, what a good life it was and all that, but it wasn't. It was a terrible life and it never seemed to get any better. I don't think it was because my husband was too proud to take us back. As I look back on it now, it was that we didn't have the money. That quarter section and that little shack in the bluff was all we had.

That first winter it must have been 30 to 40 below for weeks at a time and we had come from Devon. Devon, mind you, where you might see a bit of snow once in a long while, and here we had snow for five months and deep snow at that. And I was alone with the kiddies because my husband worked that winter in Regina. He had to; we couldn't have lived elsewise. Every two weeks he'd come out with a load of groceries, kerosene, things that we needed, and this went on and on and of course, there was no school for the two eldest. I gave them what lessons I could. Taught them out of the Bible and all the time the wind blew around the house and there was nowhere to go, nothing to see. Not even a neighbor to visit. That was the romance of living on the prairies that the land company filled my husband's head with, made him give up a good living as a stone mason and pack up everything into trunks and away out to Saskatchewan.

I wasn't alone. The countryside was filled with people like us, from the Old Country who had come to the West to have their own farm. But nobody told us how cold it was and how long the winter lasted. I suppose if we'd gone into the library and looked up Canada in the books it would have told us, but I guess we just believed what was in the pamphlets. I can't think even to this day of people cheating other people that way, saying it was a land of milk and honey when actually it was a frozen dungeon.

A lot of people did quit though, you know. Some of our neighbors just packed everything up and got a dray from town, loaded it up and left. Some went home but what was there? Nothing, it had all been sold. Some went to British Columbia, it was only about two days by train. I know of some who settled in the Okanagan Valley and they liked it there, fruit trees and sunshine, or some went on to the coast, which was a lot like home, and they built their lives there.

But no, my man stuck it out and every time spring came around and the first crows would come back he would say to me that it looked like it was going to be a good year. He must have said that a dozen times. He didn't count the mosquitoes, which were unbelievable and never seemed to get any better. The man didn't talk about the early frosts or the late frosts or the cost . . . I mean the value of a bushel of wheat, which never seemed to work out for us. It always seemed to be going down when we were selling. I used to think that as soon as he headed out the gate and down the lane with a box of wheat, that made some little lever click in Winnipeg and the stock exchange would go down or start down.

Half of our cows got into some larkspur once and that was the end of them. Six cows. That was a dark day I'll always remember. He never thought of the dust storms that used to come up and there could be storms of grasshoppers blowing around his head and he'd think it was a fine day. That man was a fool, a fool of an optimist.

He used to come in from duck shooting in the fall and he'd have a bag of ducks and he'd say, "Isn't this the most wonderful country in God's creation?" Yet who had to clean those ducks? Ever cleaned ducks? I'd rather clean skunks. And by the time we'd eaten five of them he wouldn't eat them, saying he was sick and tired of duck. He'd ask if we had any pork. He was like that.

And then it would be fall again and ice on the pond and I'd get the children's woolies out of the trunks and he'd be off to Regina looking for winter work. Who would be left behind, doing all the things that had to be done, things that a man should have been doing? Me and my two eldest doing the chores. Milking cows. One load of cream into town on Saturday and one rack of hay from the stack down on the big field once a week. Up at six in the morning, home by lantern light and little Billy doing it all himself and why, the boy was only 10 years old and there was his father working in town and probably having a grand old time every night. He must have, for all the money he brought home to us.

It wasn't a romantic life. Frankly, even if I do say so, it was a hell of a life, but I suppose it sounded all right in the story books. I see they are still writing the same kind of twaddle and on television there's a series about life on a pioneer farm. Everybody loving each other and singing around the fire at night and eating popcorn and having a wonderful time. That's what the power of imagination will do for you. Turn you into a blame fool. That's what it will do. A blame fool.

How People Dress, That's Important

There's one thing I'd like to say. It's about dress. I mean nowadays. People go to weddings and parties, to things at the church and the hall, and they look like they were living off the Salvation Army. Awful. Just awful.

When I was a girl, when my husband was a boy, when I was a young woman, my husband a young man, we dressed. Everybody dressed. If you went visiting you wore your best dress and a bonnet or at least a nice white ribbon. Same with the boys, the men. Suits, shirts, ties, shoes nicely shone.

It didn't matter how rich or poor you were, you dressed well —at a picnic, a party at somebody's house, at the hall, the school. Every event was an occasion, a party, and if you went to a house, you honored your host and hostess by dressing in your very best. Poor people had good clothes. It wasn't a matter of money as compared to today. My husband then could buy a suit, Scottish tweed, measured, for 25 dollars. What would it cost you today, measured? I'd say 250 dollars and I wouldn't be far wrong. So prices were about the same. But rich, medium-fair, or poor, you dressed well. There was none of this jeans and sloppy sweaters and bare feet, the boys looking like the girls or the girls looking like the boys.

When we were young, we took our cue from our elders and dressed clean and neat and proper. We didn't wear jeans when the bishop came around or at the Christmas concert.

I Delivered the Baby Myself

We was out on the homestead far from everybody and my wife was pregnant. We was having our third child and we'd been to town and seen the doctor and he said it would be about so-and-so. Well, it wasn't about so-and-so and it came along one night and my wife said, "We're going to have the baby."

I sent my oldest girl, six, over to the neighbor bachelor and he rode into town, and I delivered the baby myself. I didn't know the first thing about what to do but she helped me, and when the neighbor got back from town I met the doctor at the door and I said good morning to him, and then I said I'd send the baby out to help him unhitch his buggy. He laughed and I laughed and that was how our third eldest was born.

Bless That Iron Pot

I always remember our iron pot. I don't think you could buy one now, but this one was so so big, all black. I believe it was made of cast iron, and it had three stubby legs just so high so it would keep it just about this high. If you were putting it on the stove and didn't want it on the stove itself but on the open fire, then you'd just take off the lid and set it in. It was a wonderful pot.

You could boil clothes in it. I've seen my mother make lye in it for soap. If you wanted hot water, if you were going to a dance or a wedding, that was the way you got it. In the morning our porridge was made in it, and there were 11 in our family so it was a big potful. Porridge and a bit of syrup poured over it and then some milk. Stews. You made stews in the pot. Throw everything in. Greens, scraps of meat, leftover porridge, salt, what else? Cook or simmer it all day and it made good food. A real meal.

If you wanted to boil a pig's head, in it went. We loved this time. The eyes were out of the pig and the bones and the hair was off and it was boiled, or maybe simmered, all day and then Mother used to put it through the grinder and she'd put in spices. This, that, every spice she had and then it was kind of a bit like jelly, like it was loose but it would set by itself. I think she did something else to it that I forget and it was delicious. I can taste it now. It was like a kind of paté. We would sit around after coming home from school and spread this jelly on our bread. Homemade bread turns just slightly sour after a couple of days, you know that, and the sour smell and smell of the head cheese used to come right up in our nostrils. Oh, it was a lovely smell. I could eat a ton of it right now, old as I am. It is something I remember from my childhood—that head cheese. Bless that iron pot.

I Ran the House. I Had to

I was only 10, 11, just a little girl, but I was my dad's girl. I helped him in everything. My mother was no good at anything and she'd say, "Ada, you do it." And I did.

We'd been living in one room, a cabin with dirt floor, and he decided to build a bigger house and I helped him get the logs up. I don't know to this day how I did it, but I did. My father and I built this log house with a big kitchen, three bedrooms, and he managed to get hold of some shingles and I laid all the shingles and he nailed them. Together that summer we got that house finished.

Once he cut his knee terribly, but I managed the tourniquet with him telling me how to do it and then bandaging it. Then when it was all over I remember I was terribly sick.

I helped him lay out his fields too. Just a little girl of 10, but he'd put me at the corner marker and he'd say, "Now I'm going up there and I want you to stay here and I want you to sight in and tell me exactly where to put the stakes in line.

Then came the job of stringing wire. We had a team of oxen and I had to drive the oxen down the line and stop them and get them to pull the wire tight to the post my father had put in, all the posts. It got so I could do it pretty good. I'd get them so they'd just move up to past each pole and stop. Stop right where they had to.

The house, the first house? Not any bigger than this room, I don't think it was. Wait a minute. That rug is nine by 12, so our first house on the prairie was about 12 by 14. For all our family. Six people, And, as I say, it had a sod roof. The house logs were fitted in, saddled in the end so they'd fit in nicely, and then we drove in bits of wood between the logs where there were big gaps and then we plastered everything over. Mud from the slough mixed with hay, and it hardened hard and it was quite warm.

It wasn't all that warm at night, but if you wanted it warm you'd have to sit up all night. I'd get up in the middle of the night and put some more wood on, or Dad would, and in the morning I'd get up again. I had to do these things because I was the eldest in the family. Yes, I was 10 years old.

The roof was peaked. What Dad did, and I helped him and this was when I was nine, we got a ridge pole up and then we put picket poles up to the peak and then, let's see, we put straw from a neighbor's farm on it, and then laid down sod from the prairie and it was okay. It never used to leak.

There's a joke. They used to say that in a two-day rain, during those two days, your house is dry inside, but the next two days it's wet because all that accumulated rain leaks through. That never happened in the first house Dad and I made.

We made a nice warm house. We had just one window in the house, just one door. No floor. There was no problem. We all lived in that little room.

Furniture? My dad made a bed of poles for he and my mother. He made the table of poles and the top of lumber, so big and so wide. Kids slept on the table. We got boxes that food came in and those were our chairs. The stove we had then, it was an old-fashioned cast-iron stove with a door that opened each side, you know. A ledge out the front. It heated the place nicely. In winter you could keep the fire going part of the night if you got up, but a bowl of water over by the window would be frozen solid in the morning. That's the way it was. And still is, I guess.

Another thing that fell to me was to get the water. My mother would say, "Ada, you get the water." This was in the winter. In the summer there was water in our own well, but in the winter I had to drive the two oxen and the cow and her calf half a mile down the gulley to the river. Chop the ice open to get at the water. I remember one day I went down there and it was 60 below on our thermometer and a neighbor said his thermometer read 70 below. I went down there and watered that stock and mind you, I seldom wore a coat. I wore a sweater. In 50-60 below. I don't understand it today. We didn't feel the cold. We didn't even have shoes or overshoes. We used to make moccasins. I had a jacket on that day though, and a cap on my head, but I took the stock down there and chopped a hole through the ice. Watered the stock. The reason . . .? Oh yes, I forgot. The reason we didn't use the well in winter was because it was so low that if we used it to water the stock, then if there was a blizzard there would be no water and the stock would die. That's the way we figured it. That's why we went to the river.

We were alone on the prairie, my mother and us, those years. My father couldn't make a living on the farm, so he'd go to towns, to Regina, to anywhere, working at whatever he could get, carpentering, digging, just to get a few dollars to keep us going the winter and the rest of the year. He told me once that in Regina he worked in construction and you could buy a meal ticket at the Chinese restaurant and it gave you seven meals for a dollar, and you couldn't eat all they piled on your plate. At home it was different.

When I was a little girl living on a homestead and nobody

there to help me, there was so much to do to keep the place going, the house and the barn and the cattle and all through the winter, six months of winter, you know, and people say to me now, and I'm 83, they say, "How and where did you learn to do all these things you can do?" I say, "Well, by golly, in those years when I was a little girl on the prairie, if you didn't know how to do a lot of things, then you did without." That's the way it was.

My mother was no help to me. She was an English lady and useless. She considered Canada a godforsaken land. She wanted adventure but she didn't want to work at it. My brothers and sisters were much younger, so I ran the house. I had to. I always seemed to keep going. I washed and kept the house and the other children clean.

There was not much to eat. We would have a couple of sacks of flour. One of potatoes. We had grease. Grease on bread and tea for breakfast. We'd have some soup for lunch. Just a bit of meat and a lot of vegetables and some sugar. I used to love rolled oats and tea for supper. Yes, potatoes and turnips and soup, sugar, rolled oats and tea. Certainly. Of course, today it would be considered a poverty diet. Look at it. Where's the protein, and other things? Where does protein start, or does it end somewhere? You're right. We were on a poverty diet, impoverished all that time. I agree. But we did okay. I'm sure we did.

We Papered the Walls with Stories

My dad, and then my husband and I, we used to take our grain to the old grist mill across the tracks here. It's burned down now. We'd take in a load of grain and we'd get flour, shorts, bran, cream of wheat, things that you could use.

The miller took one bushel out of six or seven, quite fair, I must say, and you'd also get the seconds. Whatever you wanted to use it for. Wallpaper, if you wanted. It made good paste.

Everybody, or most people, used to wallpaper their houses with paper. Not so much newspaper but the graphic newspapers we got from England. It was hard and glossy and it made good insulation. Besides, it was interesting. You can still see the living room papered that way in my old log house down on the farm.

Not Canadian papers. Old Country papers. The shiny ones. If you had a visitor for dinner or someone new came into the house, you'd often see them walking slowly around the room looking at the stories. Reading them. They had long, long articles in those days about many interesting subjects. It might have been 10 years old but they'd stand there reading it. Sometimes when I had nothing to do I'd read too. I can remember some of those stories today. All about Africa, places like that.

These pages also had great big pictures of something or other. I can remember one old chap, he was driving around, school inspector I think he was, and he was sitting there eating his dinner and he said to me: "My goodness but hasn't that lady got a lot of dry goods on her." What he meant was this woman in the picture was all dressed up fit to kill in a fancy dress and so on. A wedding dress, I think.

Those were the days. There was always somebody coming around who had a sense of humor.

Miles from Anywhere—and Pregnant

I remember my husband was coming back from town and he met this woman walking over the prairie. Miles from anywhere, he thought. It was 27 miles to our post office, or town if you want to call it that. In those days a two-bit general store and a wee hotel was a town. So my husband stops his buggy and he sees the woman is crying. In fact, he says she's hysterical. He doesn't know what to do but he can take her back to town and leave her at the store and the construction train can take her to the end of steel and the doctor is there. Then he sees a man running across the prairie toward him. Yelling and waving his arms. It's the husband, of course. Oh, I forgot to say. This woman was obviously pregnant.

They get her in the buggy and then my husband heads off over the prairie. Not a stick of a tree, nothing, but he's following the way the man is pointing and over a rise and down a dip and there's two oxen, a wagon, and what my husband says is the start of a sod shack. A shack, maybe, but the first big wind and it'll go over or cave in, he figures.

They go into the house and . . . no, the man has put up a tent and they're living in that and my husband gets it out little by little what it is all about. Of course, he knows. He'd have to have no eyes in his face not to see what had happened.

First of all, there was a Persian rug on the floor of the tent. There was the finest of china and crystal stacked around. Beautiful clothes, trunks of things, and not a single thing that would be practical for homestead living.

What was the story? I'll tell you. The man was a printer. He'd inherited his father's small business just outside London and in this depression I told you about he went broke. He couldn't collect on his debts and others were taking him to court, and when he got out of it all he just had a few hundred pounds, I guess. Then he saw this advertisement, these promoting concerts for Canada put on by this land company. I'll say this for Englishmen, they weren't afraid to take a chance and try a new land. But he was a printer and not a farmer and Canada was not a land of milk and honey. It could be if you worked awfully long and awfully hard. Yes, it could be. It did well for us. But we were different, as I said.

My husband came home quickly and I forget what I was doing, washing, baking bread, something, and he said to get in the wagon and away we went over to this tent. I met the woman. Mrs. Metcalfe, Mrs. Charles Metcalfe. Grace Metcalfe and when she saw me she started to cry. Here, a baby coming and a sod shack that he'd never finish in a thousand years and all this finery around, this rug on the floor of the tent and barrels of all sorts of nice I-don't-know-whats in the wagon still—and there they were.

Another thing, it was late August. You know what that means.

There could be snow any time. I've seen snow on August 17. Wheat frozen black on August 14. Different years, of course.

My husband explained all this to the husband, how it went down to 50 below and nobody stayed in that country in the winter. We left and my husband worked wherever we could. I went back to Minnesota. I was usually pregnant anyway. He said the country was a desert in the winter, except for a few bachelors and coyotes. Didn't anybody tell him these things? No, nothing. Just the shiny pictures and the nice words, all the nice things about green fields and streams. I don't think there was anything but a springtime coulee within 15 miles of us.

There's nothing like a Minnesota Swede for being practical. They say they only make good stonepickers and track layers, but not my Ingemar. No sir. He told that fellow, he asked, "How much money have you got left?" I think he had 500 dollars. Something like that. My husband was saying that he had to get out of the country, go to Winnipeg, get a job in a printer's place and work and maybe next year. Ever read that book, *Next Year*? It's a good one. The West is next-year country. I'd brought over a loaf of bread and some butter and eggs with me and I was cooking us up a nice omelet and I caught the drift of what was going on and I started telling Mrs. Metcalfe that they just couldn't stay. Not with no house. Certainly not with a baby coming. I guess I scared her. I meant to. Put the fear of God and the prairies and the winter into her.

Together before lunch was finished Mr. Metcalfe was saying he'd take her back to Winnipeg or Toronto and she was laughing, her regular happy little self. I don't think she had too many parts of the gray matter but she was a happy little person and she was happy about her baby coming and happier to be getting away. Do you know, she told me she was even fearful of the little gophers that used to run around? So, there you had it.

Next day we came over and helped them load up and my husband, oh, he had nothing much to do, so he went into Rollscar with the Metcalfes, just to see that they got there, and they did. Left everything on the prairie, tent, a big tub for washing and a scrub board when there was no water. Food, nails, the little stove, axes, and a walking plow. They took the wagon and oxen and the barrels of nice things and that rug

I'd have given my eye teeth for, and away they went. That was the last I saw of them. We took the other things over to our place.

My husband came back next day and he was shaking his head and he said, "Do you know?" And I said no, and he said, "They were there for days and he didn't unharness the oxen because if he did he knew he'd never be able to do it again." You know, I've lived a long time. I've heard that story, I've heard it about oxen and horses and I've heard about them putting the harness on backward and I guess even upside down, but this is what I'm telling you. That is not just a joke they made up about greenhorns in those days. It happened to those Metcalfes.

I Was a Little Tyke

When my mother and I left Saskatoon we joined up with a family called Hixon, and it was these people we traveled with because they had a wagon pulled by three horses. To pay for the privilege of sleeping with the Hixon family, my mother volunteered to drive their cow to Lloydminster, but she very quickly tired of these things, so driving the cow was turned over to myself. One of the claims to fame I have is that I drove a cow from Saskatoon to Lloydminster and that is about 200 miles, I think. And I was a little tyke barely able to see above the tall grass of the prairie.

The Hired Man Remembered Me

We came from England in the latter part of March of 1903 and I was going on eight. Eight in June. My father was a scientific instrument maker and worked on inventions and he knew nothing about farming. He had a very bad cold for a long time and the doctor said he was in the incipient stage of t.b. [tuberculosis], so when the doctor left he got out of bed and told us, "Well, if I'm going to die I'm going to die outside where there is lots of fresh air." This was how he made up his mind to come to Canada.

We got as far as Saskatoon where the railway ended and that day, I can see it now, there was still snow, a bit of snow on the ground, or anyway the ground was still frozen hard, and we had to camp on this land. Our tents had no floors and none of us had anything but blankets. I remember a man riding through on a big horse where our tents were and he looked at us and shook his head. When he got to his farm he told his hired man to load a hay rack with hay and take it into Saskatoon and give it to these poor colonists who had to sleep on the frozen ground. And the man did. He delivered the hay, he brought it in and the result was, the hay was spread around and people put it inside their tents and that's how we passed those few days, sleeping on hay.

Now we go ahead to 1939 when I decided I'd move to the coast. My father was worn out by this time so I took him along with me. He had worked on the bridge and building gang of the C.P.R. all his life, and in 1939 they let him go three months before he was to retire with a pension. This was the way the railroad treated its old-timers. So I took him with me to Vancouver.

I wanted a bit of land outside of Vancouver where we could do things, so we went to Cloverdale and I drove into the main street and there was a real estate man in an office there. I went to talk to him about land and we got chatting away and then he asked if I was from England and I said, "Well, I once was."

He said, "From Yorkshire?" and I said yes and he said, "Were you ever in Saskatoon?" I said I was when I was younger and he said, "Barr colonist?" Yes, I said. He said, "Do you remember the hired man who brought a load of hay so you people could use it?" I said, "Yes, as a mattress. I remember it well." He said, "I was the hired man."

Now, mind you, this is a true story. I was a little girl of eight and he was a grown man and it was a long, long time ago but he remembered me. I've always thought that was a very remarkable story.

How I Became an Anglican

Do you want to hear how I became an Anglican? Oh, this is a fine story.

Well, when the war came along I told my wife I was going to join up and she said that would be okay, not to worry about her. So I went down to the recruiting station to attest, to take the king's shilling as it were.

You know when you join up, you're standing there stark naked in front of an officer and there's a sergeant there and they ask you where you're from, your age, occupation, and all like that and then he got down to the other things and he said, "What religion?" and I said I didn't have one. Well, we couldn't have that. When a man joins up to fight he's got to have some God, you know. It was that way in '14 and it's still the same way, 65 years later. He said, "You mean to tell me you're going to France to kill Germans without a religion?" I said sure. So he looks at the sergeant and he says, "What are we going to do about this? How many Catholics have we made this morning?" And the sergeant says, "Oh, three." "And how many Presbyterians?" "Seventeen, sir," says the sergeant. So the captain says, "Fine, make this silly bugger an Anglican."

And that's how I became an Anglican.

Please Come Home. Bring Douglas

I went to work for this farmer in Portage La Prairie. He was a big man. With his two sons I guess he had about 1,500 acres then and that was an awful lot of land. He owned land on both sides of the river and he had his own scow to get the equipment across. He hired me two minutes after I stepped off the train. He looked me over and said, "Aye, you're a brawny lad. Now where do you come from?" I said Inverness and he said, "I'll give you 20 dollars a month and teach you how to farm." I told him he'd have to give me 30 dollars a month because I already could farm. He looked me over again and saw my size and he said, "Aye, 30 then. If I don't you'll be off to join the police force in Winnipeg. You're big enough."

I should say that in those days all the Winnipeg police force were Scottish. You had to be six feet and the weight to go with it, and in winter when they wore those buffalo coats they looked bigger than the buffalo themselves.

This farmer had a daughter and I was sweet on her and she was sweet on me in a short time. I'd sleep in the bunkhouse and when she was doing the eggs or some other chores she'd always manage to slip a note under my pillow. This went on for some weeks. You know, for every lad there's a lass, but my prospects were dim. Finally I said I'd just go and see the old man.

He said, "I've been expecting it. The calf eyes she's been making at you and you looking like a moon-struck lout. The answer is no. Get off the farm. Take your duds and you'll walk in to town." I told him he'd driven me to the farm, he'd drive me back. His two sons were out on the verandah and he called them in, Sandy and Will, and he told them what was up. That I wanted to marry Annie. Will, I'll give him credit, he said, "Well, what's wrong with that?" That shook up old man Duncan and he said I was no damn good, had no prospects, no money, I was just a drifter off the boat, and there was going to be no marriage to a drifter.

Mrs. Duncan chimed in and said, "The man's no drifter, Jock, and our Annie's daft about him." No, the old man wasn't having anything to do with it. Then Annie came into the kitchen and she had a little satchel and she said, "Get your clothes, Douglas, and, Father, pay him the money he has coming to him. We're leaving to get married." That did me in. I didn't know our sparking had gone that far. The old man told Sandy to lay me out and I said if he did it would be the last punch he ever threw at anyone. I wasn't mad at Sandy. Will was on my side and so was the missus, and if I had wanted to I could have separated Sandy's head from his neck with one stiff one.

So he paid me and we hiked to town. Nine miles and Annie crying every foot of the way. She wanted to leave but she didn't, and a dozen times I told her I'd take her back and she'd go boo-hoo-hoo and say, "Douglas, if you do I'll never speak to you again. I swear it on my mother's grave and the first child we're going to have." Women. I'll never understand them.

The Presbyterian minister in town wouldn't marry us. He said her father was against it. You see, the old bastard must have seen all this coming. If I paid him five dollars I guess her father had promised him double. That's the way I figured it. So she said, "Well, Douglas, it's Winnipeg for us." We went across to the C.P.R. and there was a train about two and we got on it and we got in about five o'clock. Only 60 miles but you've got to remember, the trains in those days didn't go as fast as they do now.

Annie had a friend on Colony Street and I took her there and I think I went to the Empire. Next morning we went to City Hall and the clerk married us. Now I'm going to say this to show you just what it was like in those days. When we got to the Clarendon, and that was a grand hotel in those days, as good as any in the city, and here's me putting my bride up in the Clarendon when the Lord knew I only had about 15 dollars in my pocket, it was then that I kissed her. I hadn't kissed her on the farm. Our courtship was the letters we used to write back and forth and hide under my pillow in the bunkhouse. You'd never see that again. Two people married and in the hotel room for their first night, or day for that matter, and they hadn't even kissed. No, I don't mind telling you. I suppose it happened that way to a lot more than us. After all, I was just a farm hand.

What did we do? Oh, I got a job. Not with the police force. They had places where they advertised for jobs in them days. An office and signs in the window, telling what jobs, and I walked in and the man said, "Two dollars and you're hired." I gave him his fee and walked out of there and over to the brewery, the big one in town, and they put me on the wagons delivering beer. That was a good job. Then in about a month when we were living on Furby Street my wife got a letter from her mother. "Please come home. Bring Douglas. All is forgiven."

So we went. There's something about the farm life. Since I retired I've missed every single day I haven't been at it.

A Bowler Hat on the Prairies

This is a picture in my mother's house. It shows my father standing beside the iron post of his quarter at Veteran, Alberta. That is a little tent behind him. He's a bachelor. This was in 1908. My mother was still in Hamilton at the time. I think the end of steel at the time was Stettler and my father was way ahead of the track looking for a good homestead. He had come across with a wagon, two horses, and he found his land. But this picture. They took darn good pictures in those days, sharp and clear. But what still gets me, what I marvel at, was that my father, after all those days on the trail, was still wearing the business suit, the boots, the clothes he wore in the bank in Hamilton. And on his head, believe it or not, a bowler hat. A bowler hat! That's what got me. Out on the prairies, a bowler hat.

Ranching in the Early Days

In the early days when I first went ranching, you can't imagine the grass on the prairies. I got my first ranch in '07. Yes, '07, the year my boy was a baby. You just can't imagine the lushness of that grass.

There was nobody there. Oh yes, people along the railroad between Calgary and Edmonton, oh yes, and along the line between Saskatoon and Edmonton where the railroad and the trails ran. But if you went south of there, from where the big ranchers moved in, you could go from my place to Calgary and there wasn't a mark in the grass, not a road. Old buffalo trails, the old trails, but nothing else. The whole West was open.

It was all prairie wool. That's a heavy grass, very nutritious, very heavy and it would grow high, high in places as a horse's belly, if it wasn't taken out by prairie fire. And you must understand, man, that there were always fires burning on the prairie, but the stuff would grow up again the next spring. But if the fires missed one section, an area, one year it would have grown high and then been blown over or been forced down by the weight of the snow, and next year another crop would come up and it would be forced over until it was all tangled up. It's difficult to describe, I tell you, but it was even more difficult to walk through. You sort of had to take big plunging steps it was so heavy and rich.

And then around the edges of every copse, every slough, where saskatoons grew, there would be thick patches of pea vine and vetch. But mostly pea vine. That's pure pea. Some of the richest cattle food in the world and we wouldn't even put up any hay unless it was pure pea vine. My, how those cattle thrived on that. Our horses and cattle went crazy on that.

You can see what it would do. The mares would foal, the cows would have calves, and the young ones would suck the milk made from this pea vine and that prairie wool, well, I don't think you could make richer feed if you had a huge laboratory and a dozen assistants. The animals would go crazy on it. When it was stacked and had cured right, the vitamins in it. My God.

And there was nobody in the country. Everybody wanted to be along the railroad, everybody wanted to raise wheat, everybody wanted to live just a few miles from town, but if you wanted to go out further, there was all the land you could ever want. I could best put it this way. There was my cattle on this land, and except by accident those animals never grazed in the same place twice. There was so much land, so much feed. Grazing land, hills like this, gentle, and in every hollow was a little slough with good water and in every valley there was a little lake. The ranch was about as big as the Fraser Valley today, I'd guess.

People think of Saskatchewan as it is today, they think it only has ranching down around the Cypress Hills and Maple Creek, down there where a cow needs 80 acres to keep going. What they don't know is that all through the central part of that country at the turn of the century was some of the finest grazing lands in the world.

The only problem a cow had in those days was the mosquitoes. Other than that, they just had to lie down and eat and get up once in a while and have a drink of water. They were so big and so fat that when I wanted to move them—if a prairie fire was coming or I wanted to take some out to sell or to the corral to brand—those animals couldn't walk more than half a mile without playing out. They were that fat. The calves just the same. Half a mile and they were played out carrying all that weight. Herefords. Each one just like a square block. Huge. There was no cattle in the country like those. Nobody ever had cattle like them.

The Whole Country Was Ours

There was a filing office at the place, this Lloydminster to be, and Dad got on one of our horses and he rode away to the north. He'd taken about a dozen potatoes, two bannock, and some bacon and a frying pan and he was gone. Off to look for our land. He said he'd be gone a day or two and we were to sit tight. All around us people were in tents and talking and wondering what in the name of heaven had got them out of London and on to this prairie. They talked so much of London I swear you could almost taste the fog. Homesick, that's what it was.

Once, one day because Father didn't come back in two days, we were sitting there and Mother was fussing with this little tin stove we had, trying to cook us something, and she was crying to herself. She did a lot of crying. She was that kind of woman. Along comes this man, a great big man, and he had a voice like a shout and I can remember to this day him stopping his horse and saying, "What's the tears for, missus? You've got all you'll ever want. Land, wood, and water. Send the little girl out and pick some wild flowers. They'll do your heart good. A regular tonic."

I never knew who he was. Just some kind man trying to cheer folks up.

The third day, that evening, Dad came back. He'd found our land and he had located the posts and the number and next morning early away we went. I was in the back of the wagon sitting on some sacks of flour and our potatoes, and after a while you could look back and see nothing of the tents of the place we'd been, nothing but sloughs here and there and bunches of trees and the track of our horses and wagon out behind us through the grass like a trail. We were the first white people ever to go to that piece of land and I suppose it was like Columbus felt when he discovered America. No one before us. The whole country was ours.